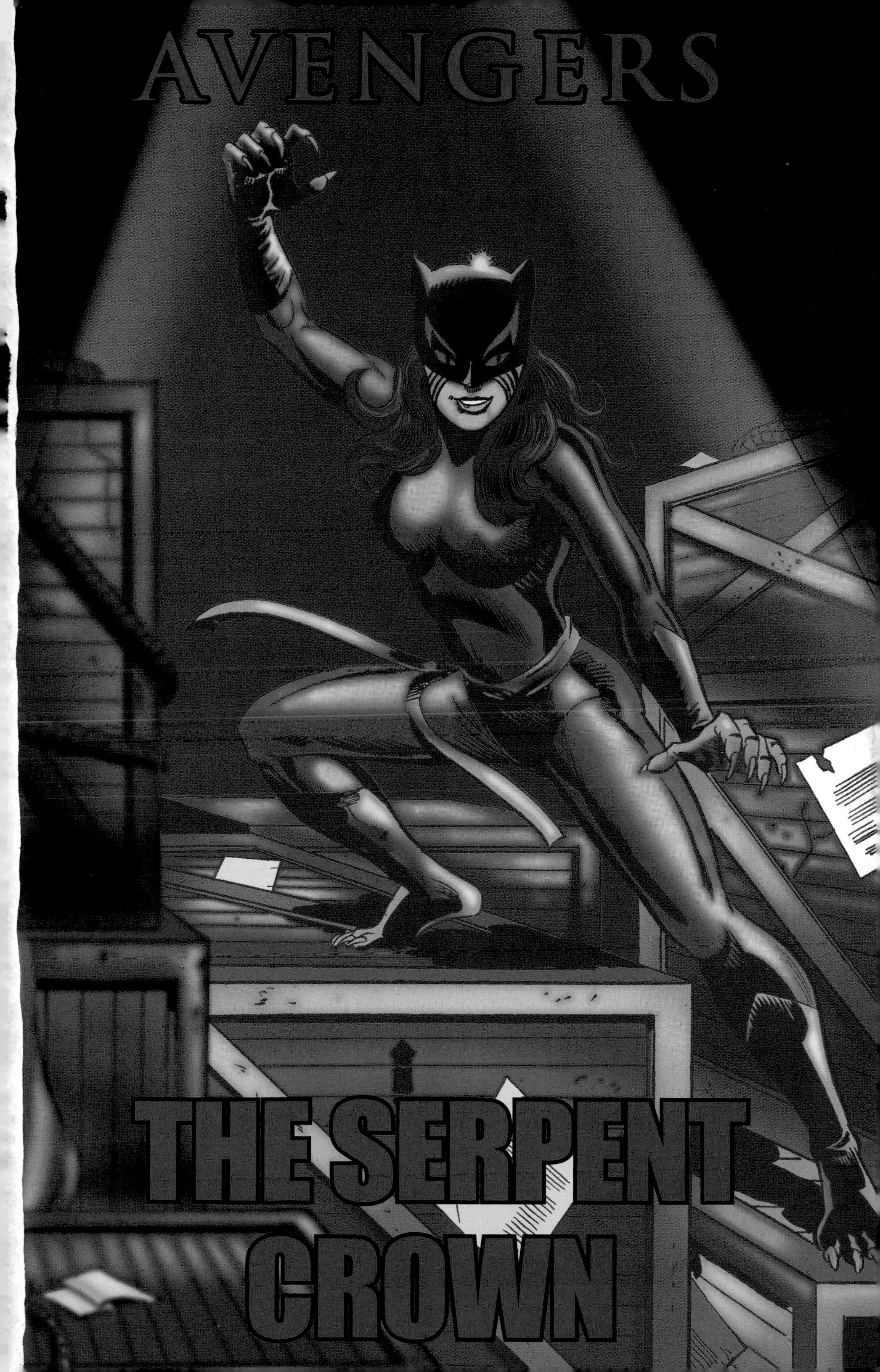
AVENGERS
THE SERPENT CROWN

AVENGERS

WRITER
STEVE ENGLEHART

PENCILER
GEORGE PÉREZ

INKERS
VINCE COLLETTA, SAM GRAINGER & MIKE ESPOSITO

COLORISTS
JANICE COHEN, GEORGE ROUSSOS, PETRA GOLDBERG & HUGH PALEY

LETTERERS
TOM ORZECHOWSKI & DENISE WOHL

EDITOR
MARV WOLFMAN

FRONT COVER ARTISTS
GIL KANE & FRANK GIACOIA

FRONT COVER COLORIST
TOM SMITH

BACK COVER ARTISTS
GIL KANE & JOHN ROMITA

BACK COVER COLORIST
CHRIS SOTOMAYOR

COLLECTION EDITOR
NELSON RIBEIRO

ASSISTANT EDITOR
ALEX STARBUCK

EDITORS, SPECIAL PROJECTS
MARK D. BEAZLEY & JENNIFER GRÜNWALD

SENIOR EDITOR, SPECIAL PROJECTS
JEFF YOUNGQUIST

PRODUCTION
JERRON QUALITY COLOR

SENIOR VICE PRESIDENT OF SALES
DAVID GABRIEL

SVP OF BRAND PLANNING &
COMMUNICATIONS
MICHAEL PASCIULLO

EDITOR IN CHIEF
AXEL ALONSO

CHIEF CREATIVE OFFICER
JOE QUESADA

PUBLISHER
DAN BUCKLEY

EXECUTIVE PRODUCER
ALAN FINE

THE SERPENT CROWN

AVENGERS: THE SERPENT CROWN. Contains material originally published in magazine form as AVENGERS #141-144 and #147-149. First printing 2012. ISBN# 978-0-7851-5751-9. Published by MARVEL WORLDWIDE, INC., a subsidiary of MARVEL ENTERTAINMENT, LLC. OFFICE OF PUBLICATION: 135 West 50th Street, New York, NY 10020. Copyright © 1975, 1976 and 2012 Marvel Characters, Inc. All rights reserved. $24.99 per copy in the U.S. and $27.99 in Canada (GST #R127032852); Canadian Agreement #40668537. All characters featured in this issue and the distinctive names and likenesses thereof, and all related indicia are trademarks of Marvel Characters, Inc. No similarity between any of the names, characters, persons, and/or institutions in this magazine with those of any living or dead person or institution is intended, and any such similarity which may exist is purely coincidental. **Printed in China.** ALAN FINE, EVP - Office of the President, Marvel Worldwide, Inc. and EVP & CMO Marvel Characters B.V.; DAN BUCKLEY, Publisher & President - Print, Animation & Digital Divisions; JOE QUESADA, Chief Creative Officer; DAVID BOGART, SVP of Business Affairs & Talent Management; TOM BREVOORT, SVP of Publishing; C.B. CEBULSKI, SVP of Creator & Content Development; DAVID GABRIEL, SVP of Publishing Sales & Circulation; MICHAEL PASCIULLO, SVP of Brand Planning & Communications; JIM O'KEEFE, VP of Operations & Logistics; DAN CARR, Executive Director of Publishing Technology; SUSAN CRESPI, Editorial Operations Manager; ALEX MORALES, Publishing Operations Manager; STAN LEE, Chairman Emeritus. For information regarding advertising in Marvel Comics or on Marvel.com, please contact John Dokes, SVP Integrated Sales and Marketing, at jdokes@marvel.com. For Marvel subscription inquiries, please call 800-217-9158. **Manufactured between 1/2/2012 and 2/13/2012 by R.R. DONNELLEY ASIA PRINTING SOLUTIONS, DONGGUAN, GUANGDONG, CHINA.**

10 9 8 7 6 5 4 3 2 1

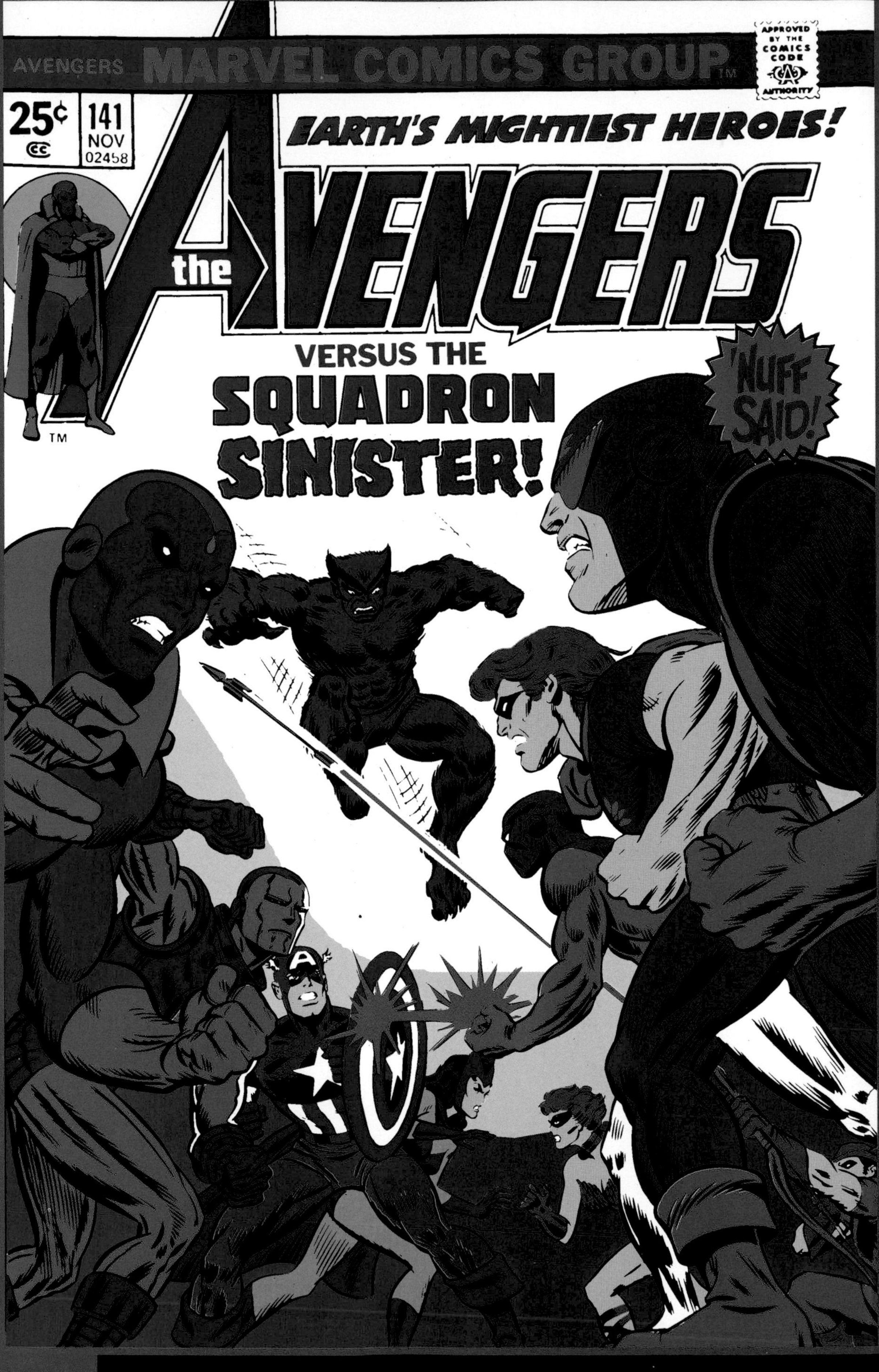
AVENGERS
MARVEL COMICS GROUP
APPROVED BY THE COMICS CODE AUTHORITY
25¢
141
NOV
02458
EARTH'S MIGHTIEST HEROES!
the AVENGERS
VERSUS THE
SQUADRON
SINISTER!
'NUFF SAID!

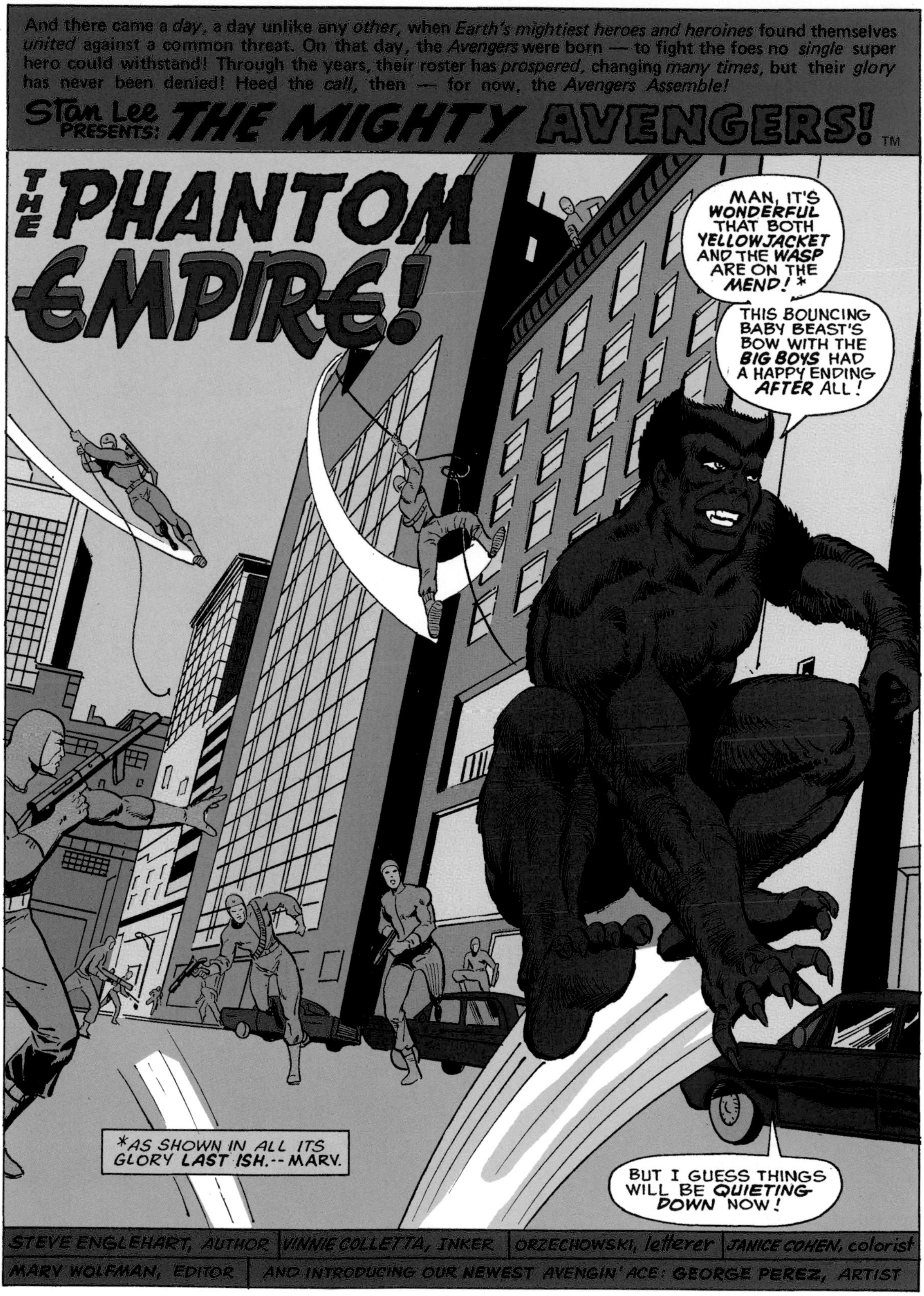
And there came a day, a day unlike any other, when Earth's mightiest heroes and heroines found themselves united against a common threat. On that day, the Avengers were born — to fight the foes no single super hero could withstand! Through the years, their roster has prospered, changing many times, but their glory has never been denied! Heed the call, then — for now, the Avengers Assemble!
Stan Lee PRESENTS: THE MIGHTY AVENGERS! TM
THE PHANTOM EMPIRE!
MAN, IT'S WONDERFUL THAT BOTH YELLOWJACKET AND THE WASP ARE ON THE MEND! *
THIS BOUNCING BABY BEAST'S BOW WITH THE BIG BOYS HAD A HAPPY ENDING AFTER ALL!
*AS SHOWN IN ALL ITS GLORY LAST ISH.-- MARV.
BUT I GUESS THINGS WILL BE QUIETING DOWN NOW!
STEVE ENGLEHART, AUTHOR
VINNIE COLLETTA, INKER
ORZECHOWSKI, letterer
JANICE COHEN, colorist
MARY WOLFMAN, EDITOR
AND INTRODUCING OUR NEWEST AVENGIN' ACE: GEORGE PEREZ, ARTIST

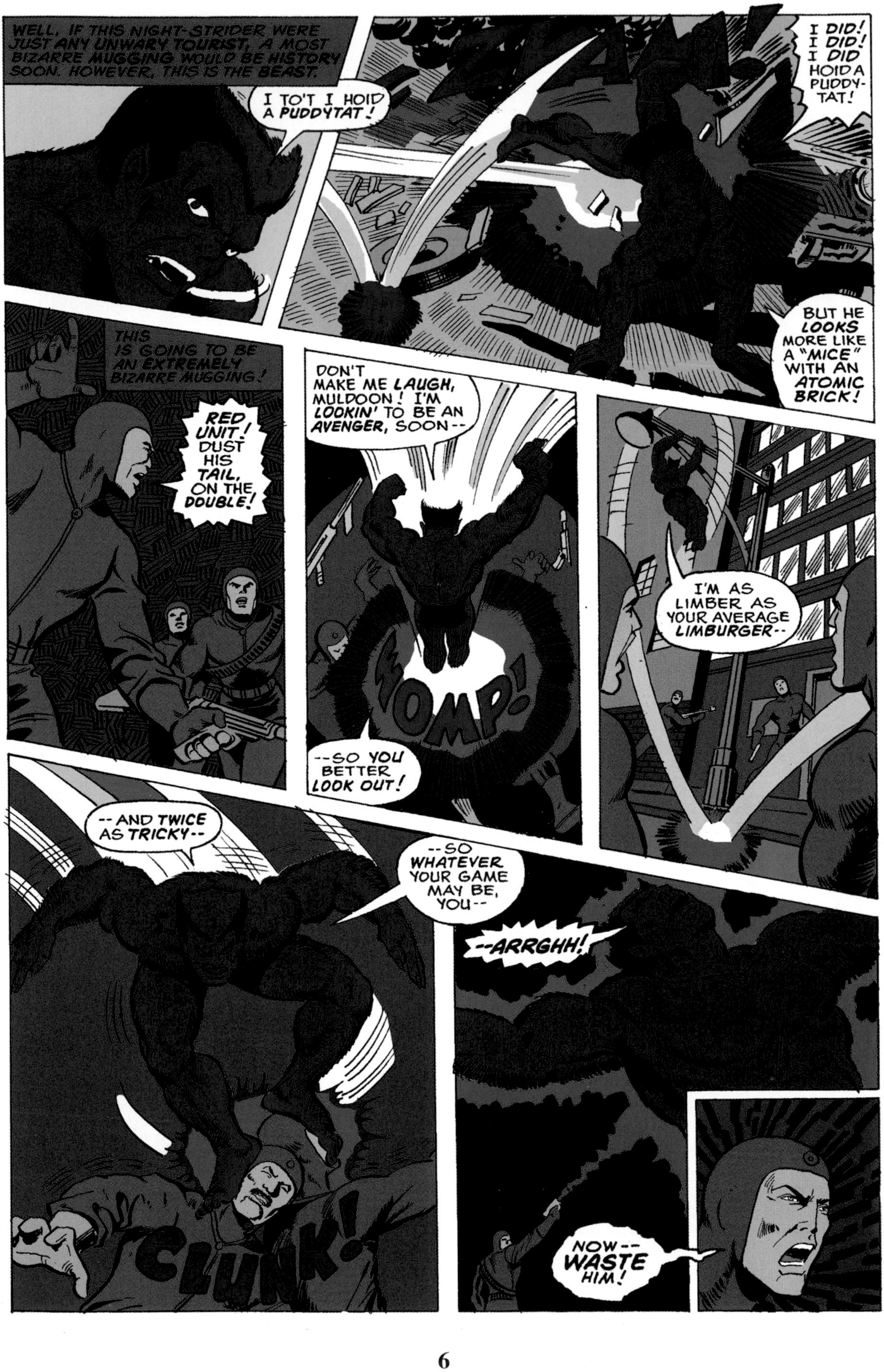
WELL, IF THIS NIGHT-STRIDER WERE JUST ANY UNWARY TOURIST, A MOST BIZARRE MUGGING WOULD BE HISTORY SOON. HOWEVER, THIS IS THE BEAST.
I TO'T I HOID A PUDDYTAT!
I DID! I DID! I DID HOID A PUDDY-TAT!
BUT HE LOOKS MORE LIKE A "MICE" WITH AN ATOMIC BRICK!
THIS IS GOING TO BE AN EXTREMELY BIZARRE MUGGING!
RED UNIT! DUST HIS TAIL, ON THE DOUBLE!
DON'T MAKE ME LAUGH, MULDOON! I'M LOOKIN' TO BE AN AVENGER, SOON--
WOMP!
--SO YOU BETTER LOOK OUT!
I'M AS LIMBER AS YOUR AVERAGE LIMBURGER--
--AND TWICE AS TRICKY--
--SO WHATEVER YOUR GAME MAY BE, YOU--
--ARRGHH!
CLUNK!
NOW-- WASTE HIM!

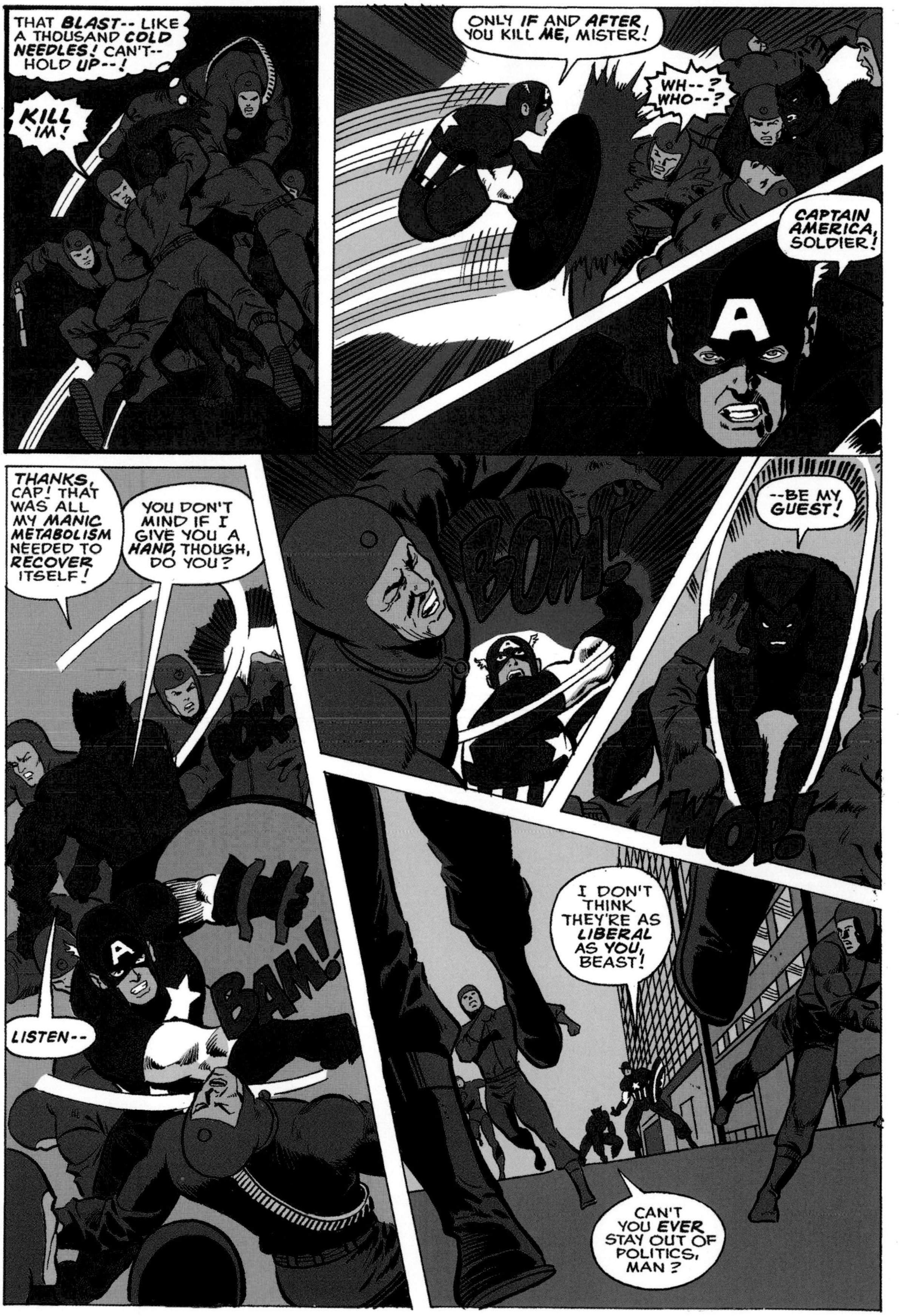
THAT BLAST-- LIKE A THOUSAND COLD NEEDLES! CAN'T-- HOLD UP--!
KILL 'IM!
ONLY IF AND AFTER YOU KILL ME, MISTER!
WH--? WHO--?
CAPTAIN AMERICA, SOLDIER!
THANKS, CAP! THAT WAS ALL MY MANIC METABOLISM NEEDED TO RECOVER ITSELF!
YOU DON'T MIND IF I GIVE YOU A HAND, THOUGH, DO YOU?
BOM!
--BE MY GUEST!
WOP!
BAM!
LISTEN--
I DON'T THINK THEY'RE AS LIBERAL AS YOU, BEAST!
CAN'T YOU EVER STAY OUT OF POLITICS, MAN?

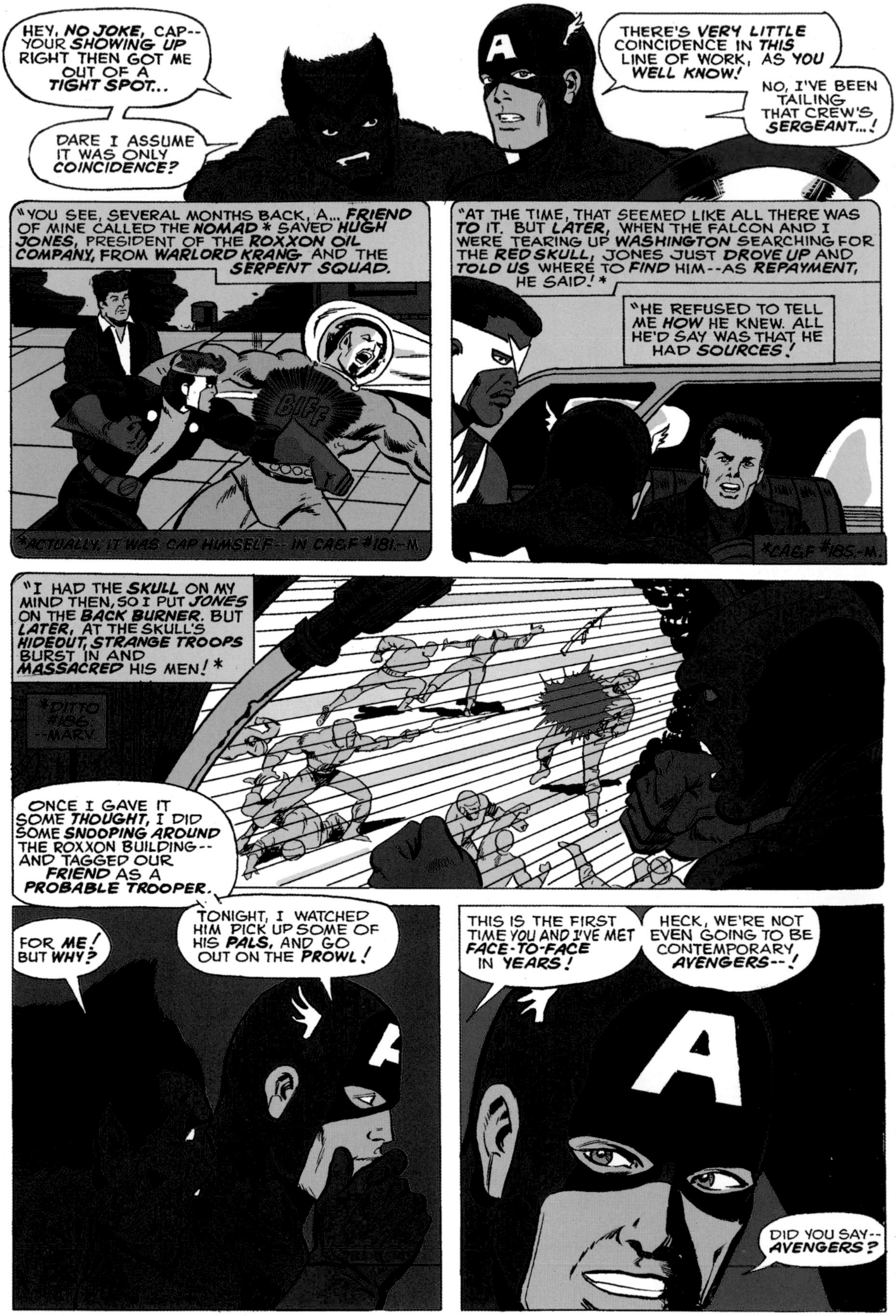
HEY, NO JOKE, CAP-- YOUR SHOWING UP RIGHT THEN GOT ME OUT OF A TIGHT SPOT...
DARE I ASSUME IT WAS ONLY COINCIDENCE?
THERE'S VERY LITTLE COINCIDENCE IN THIS LINE OF WORK, AS YOU WELL KNOW!
NO, I'VE BEEN TAILING THAT CREW'S SERGEANT...!
"YOU SEE, SEVERAL MONTHS BACK, A... FRIEND OF MINE CALLED THE NOMAD * SAVED HUGH JONES, PRESIDENT OF THE ROXXON OIL COMPANY, FROM WARLORD KRANG AND THE SERPENT SQUAD.
BIFF
*ACTUALLY, IT WAS CAP HIMSELF-- IN CA&F #181.-M.
"AT THE TIME, THAT SEEMED LIKE ALL THERE WAS TO IT. BUT LATER, WHEN THE FALCON AND I WERE TEARING UP WASHINGTON SEARCHING FOR THE RED SKULL, JONES JUST DROVE UP AND TOLD US WHERE TO FIND HIM--AS REPAYMENT, HE SAID! *
"HE REFUSED TO TELL ME HOW HE KNEW. ALL HE'D SAY WAS THAT HE HAD SOURCES!
*CA&F #185.-M.
"I HAD THE SKULL ON MY MIND THEN, SO I PUT JONES ON THE BACK BURNER. BUT LATER, AT THE SKULL'S HIDEOUT, STRANGE TROOPS BURST IN AND MASSACRED HIS MEN! *
*DITTO #186. --MARV.
ONCE I GAVE IT SOME THOUGHT, I DID SOME SNOOPING AROUND THE ROXXON BUILDING-- AND TAGGED OUR FRIEND AS A PROBABLE TROOPER.
TONIGHT, I WATCHED HIM PICK UP SOME OF HIS PALS, AND GO OUT ON THE PROWL!
FOR ME! BUT WHY?
THIS IS THE FIRST TIME YOU AND I'VE MET FACE-TO-FACE IN YEARS!
HECK, WE'RE NOT EVEN GOING TO BE CONTEMPORARY AVENGERS--!
DID YOU SAY-- AVENGERS?

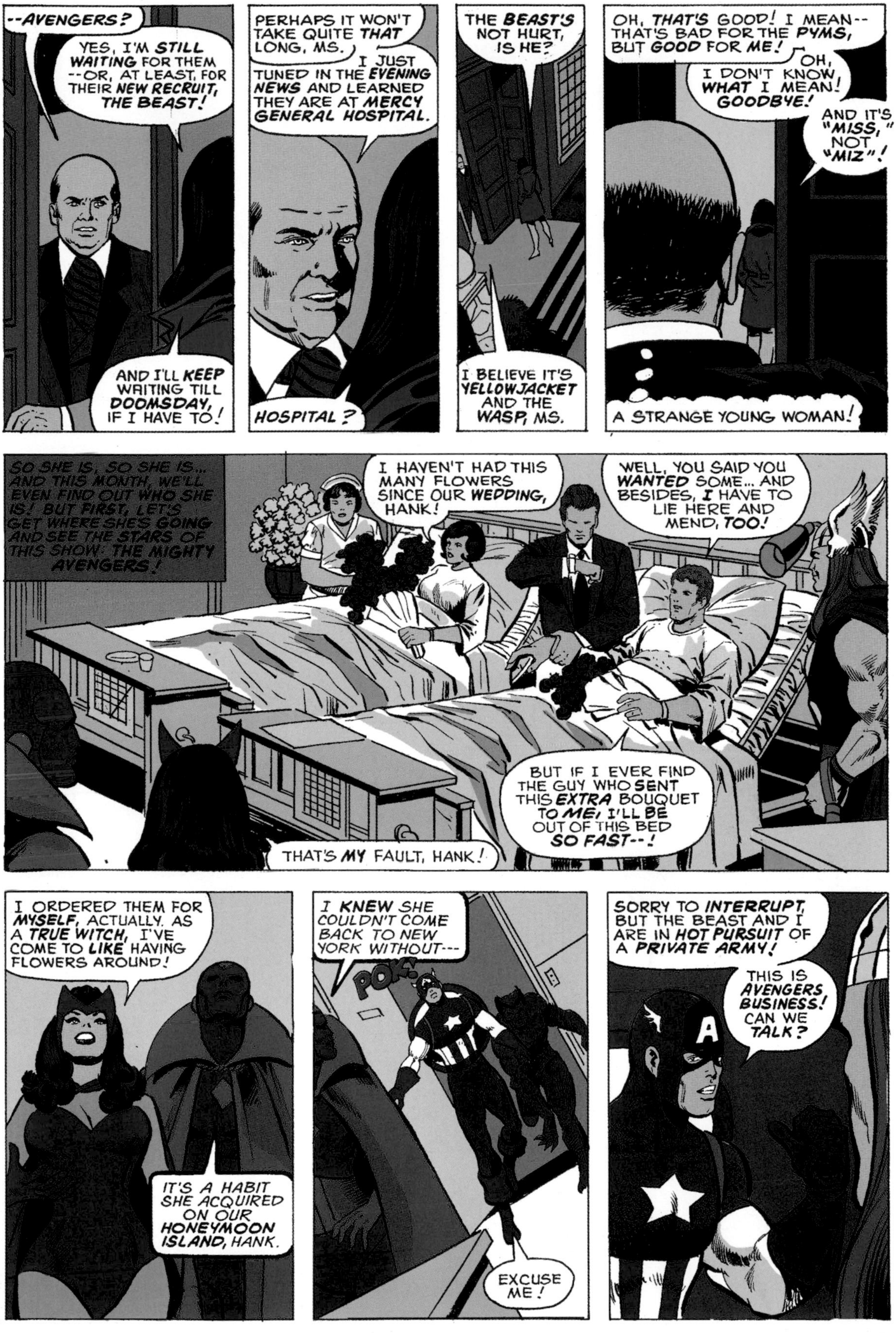
--AVENGERS?
YES, I'M STILL WAITING FOR THEM --OR, AT LEAST, FOR THEIR NEW RECRUIT, THE BEAST!
AND I'LL KEEP WAITING TILL DOOMSDAY, IF I HAVE TO!
PERHAPS IT WON'T TAKE QUITE THAT LONG, MS.
I JUST TUNED IN THE EVENING NEWS AND LEARNED THEY ARE AT MERCY GENERAL HOSPITAL.
HOSPITAL?
THE BEAST'S NOT HURT, IS HE?
I BELIEVE IT'S YELLOWJACKET AND THE WASP, MS.
OH, THAT'S GOOD! I MEAN-- THAT'S BAD FOR THE PYMS, BUT GOOD FOR ME!
OH, I DON'T KNOW WHAT I MEAN! GOODBYE!
AND IT'S "MISS," NOT "MIZ"!
A STRANGE YOUNG WOMAN!
SO SHE IS, SO SHE IS... AND THIS MONTH, WE'LL EVEN FIND OUT WHO SHE IS! BUT FIRST, LET'S GET WHERE SHE'S GOING AND SEE THE STARS OF THIS SHOW: THE MIGHTY AVENGERS!
I HAVEN'T HAD THIS MANY FLOWERS SINCE OUR WEDDING, HANK!
WELL, YOU SAID YOU WANTED SOME... AND BESIDES, I HAVE TO LIE HERE AND MEND, TOO!
BUT IF I EVER FIND THE GUY WHO SENT THIS EXTRA BOUQUET TO ME, I'LL BE OUT OF THIS BED SO FAST--!
THAT'S MY FAULT, HANK!
I ORDERED THEM FOR MYSELF, ACTUALLY. AS A TRUE WITCH, I'VE COME TO LIKE HAVING FLOWERS AROUND!
IT'S A HABIT SHE ACQUIRED ON OUR HONEYMOON ISLAND, HANK.
I KNEW SHE COULDN'T COME BACK TO NEW YORK WITHOUT---
POK!
EXCUSE ME!
SORRY TO INTERRUPT, BUT THE BEAST AND I ARE IN HOT PURSUIT OF A PRIVATE ARMY!
THIS IS AVENGERS BUSINESS! CAN WE TALK?

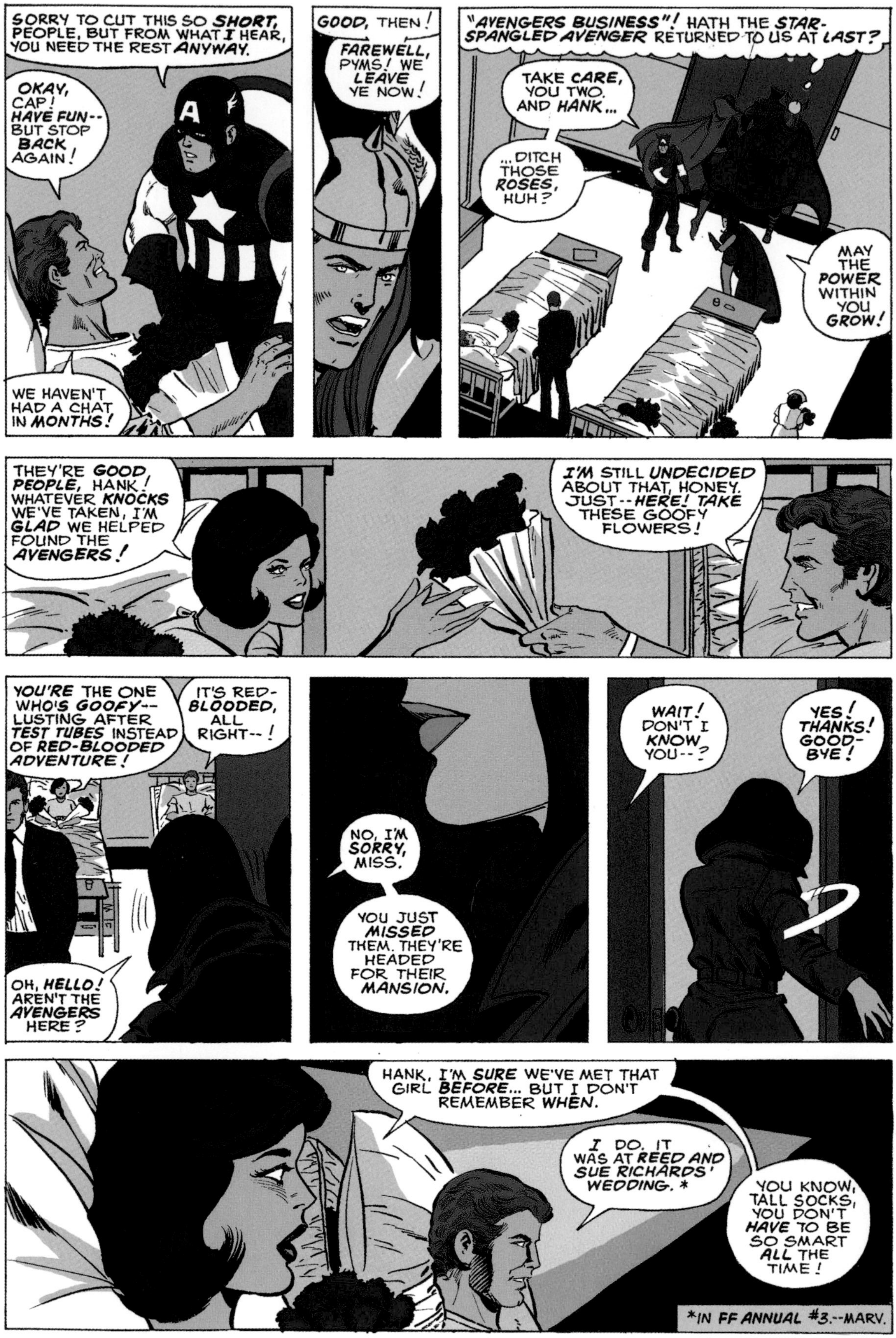
SORRY TO CUT THIS SO SHORT, PEOPLE, BUT FROM WHAT I HEAR, YOU NEED THE REST ANYWAY.
OKAY, CAP! HAVE FUN-- BUT STOP BACK AGAIN!
WE HAVEN'T HAD A CHAT IN MONTHS!
GOOD, THEN!
FAREWELL, PYMS! WE LEAVE YE NOW!
"AVENGERS BUSINESS"! HATH THE STAR-SPANGLED AVENGER RETURNED TO US AT LAST?
TAKE CARE, YOU TWO. AND HANK...
...DITCH THOSE ROSES, HUH?
MAY THE POWER WITHIN YOU GROW!
THEY'RE GOOD PEOPLE, HANK! WHATEVER KNOCKS WE'VE TAKEN, I'M GLAD WE HELPED FOUND THE AVENGERS!
I'M STILL UNDECIDED ABOUT THAT, HONEY. JUST--HERE! TAKE THESE GOOFY FLOWERS!
YOU'RE THE ONE WHO'S GOOFY-- LUSTING AFTER TEST TUBES INSTEAD OF RED-BLOODED ADVENTURE!
IT'S RED-BLOODED, ALL RIGHT-- !
OH, HELLO! AREN'T THE AVENGERS HERE?
NO, I'M SORRY, MISS.
YOU JUST MISSED THEM. THEY'RE HEADED FOR THEIR MANSION.
WAIT! DON'T I KNOW YOU--?
YES! THANKS! GOOD-BYE!
HANK, I'M SURE WE'VE MET THAT GIRL BEFORE... BUT I DON'T REMEMBER WHEN.
I DO. IT WAS AT REED AND SUE RICHARDS' WEDDING. *
YOU KNOW, TALL SOCKS, YOU DON'T HAVE TO BE SO SMART ALL THE TIME!
*IN FF ANNUAL #3.--MARV.

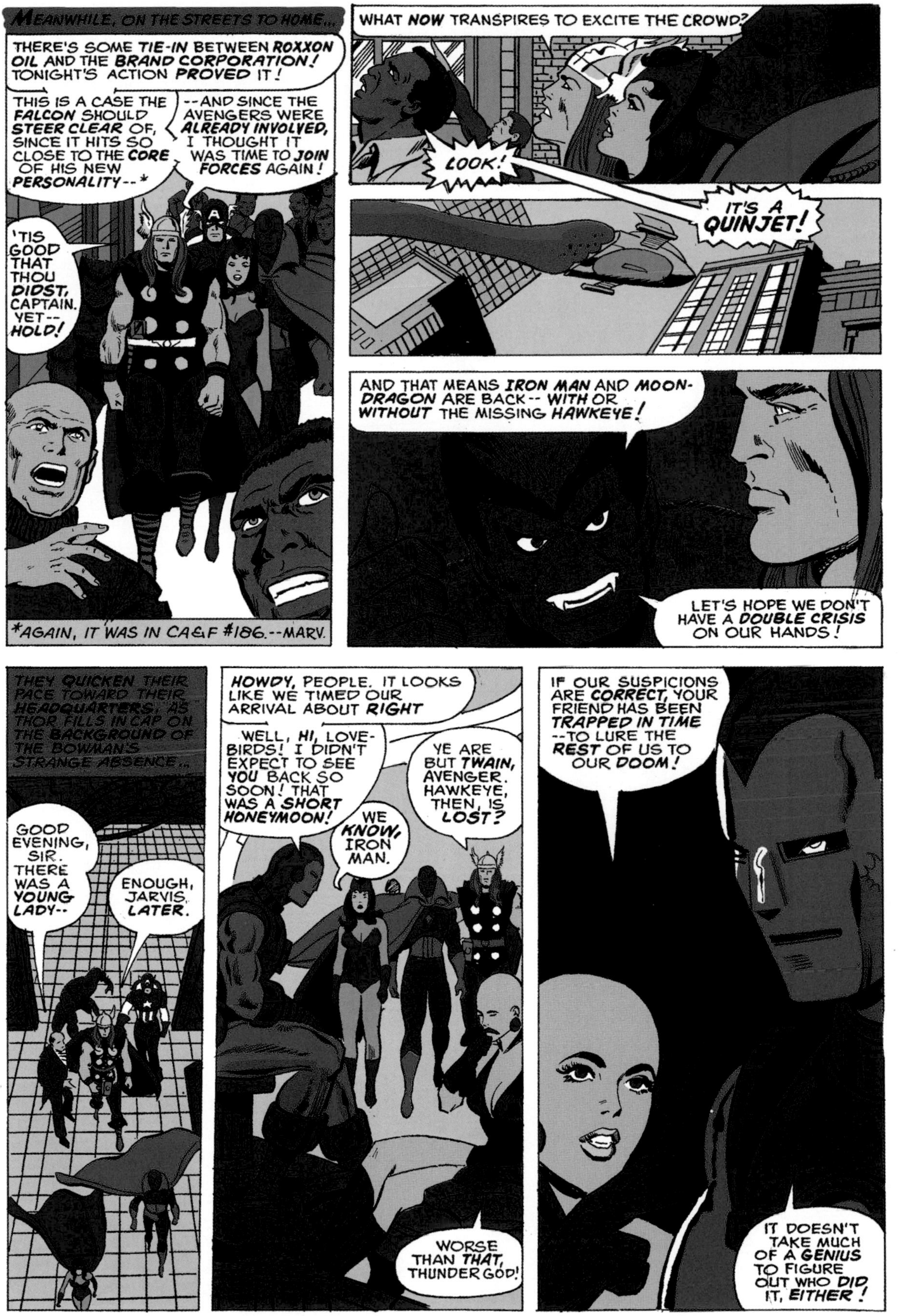
MEANWHILE, ON THE STREETS TO HOME...
THERE'S SOME TIE-IN BETWEEN ROXXON OIL AND THE BRAND CORPORATION! TONIGHT'S ACTION PROVED IT!
THIS IS A CASE THE FALCON SHOULD STEER CLEAR OF, SINCE IT HITS SO CLOSE TO THE CORE OF HIS NEW PERSONALITY--*
--AND SINCE THE AVENGERS WERE ALREADY INVOLVED, I THOUGHT IT WAS TIME TO JOIN FORCES AGAIN!
'TIS GOOD THAT THOU DIDST, CAPTAIN. YET--HOLD!
*AGAIN, IT WAS IN CA&F #186.--MARV.
WHAT NOW TRANSPIRES TO EXCITE THE CROWD?
LOOK!
IT'S A QUINJET!
AND THAT MEANS IRON MAN AND MOON-DRAGON ARE BACK--WITH OR WITHOUT THE MISSING HAWKEYE!
LET'S HOPE WE DON'T HAVE A DOUBLE CRISIS ON OUR HANDS!
THEY QUICKEN THEIR PACE TOWARD THEIR HEADQUARTERS, AS THOR FILLS IN CAP ON THE BACKGROUND OF THE BOWMAN'S STRANGE ABSENCE...
GOOD EVENING, SIR. THERE WAS A YOUNG LADY--
ENOUGH, JARVIS. LATER.
HOWDY, PEOPLE. IT LOOKS LIKE WE TIMED OUR ARRIVAL ABOUT RIGHT
WELL, HI, LOVE-BIRDS! I DIDN'T EXPECT TO SEE YOU BACK SO SOON! THAT WAS A SHORT HONEYMOON!
YE ARE BUT TWAIN, AVENGER. HAWKEYE, THEN, IS LOST?
WE KNOW, IRON MAN.
WORSE THAN THAT, THUNDER GOD!
IF OUR SUSPICIONS ARE CORRECT, YOUR FRIEND HAS BEEN TRAPPED IN TIME --TO LURE THE REST OF US TO OUR DOOM!
IT DOESN'T TAKE MUCH OF A GENIUS TO FIGURE OUT WHO DID IT, EITHER!

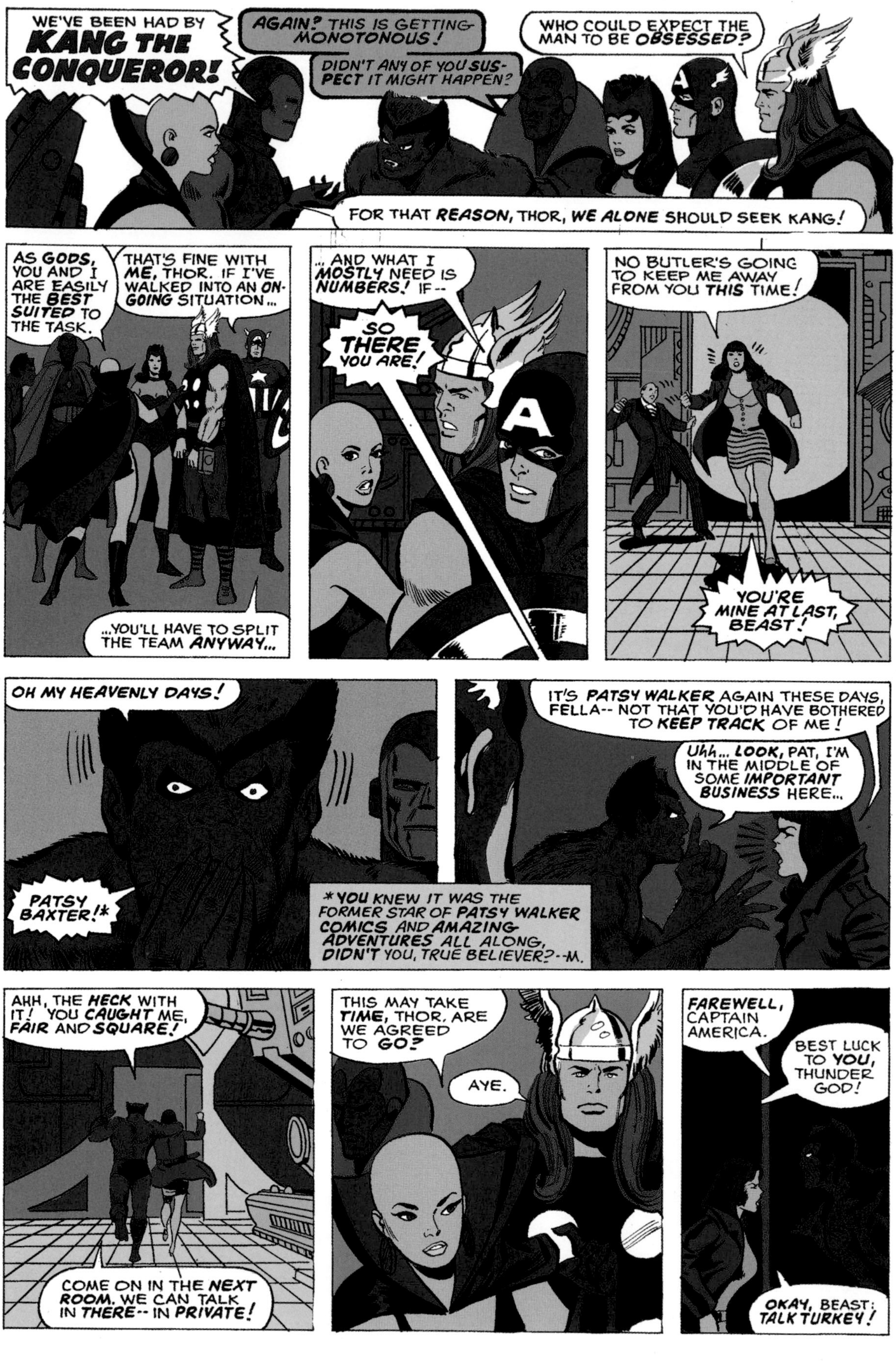

WE'VE BEEN HAD BY KANG THE CONQUEROR!
AGAIN? THIS IS GETTING MONOTONOUS!
DIDN'T ANY OF YOU SUSPECT IT MIGHT HAPPEN?
WHO COULD EXPECT THE MAN TO BE OBSESSED?
FOR THAT REASON, THOR, WE ALONE SHOULD SEEK KANG!
AS GODS, YOU AND I ARE EASILY THE BEST SUITED TO THE TASK.
THAT'S FINE WITH ME, THOR. IF I'VE WALKED INTO AN ON-GOING SITUATION...
...YOU'LL HAVE TO SPLIT THE TEAM ANYWAY...
...AND WHAT I MOSTLY NEED IS NUMBERS! IF--
SO THERE YOU ARE!
NO BUTLER'S GOING TO KEEP ME AWAY FROM YOU THIS TIME!
YOU'RE MINE AT LAST, BEAST!
OH MY HEAVENLY DAYS!
PATSY BAXTER!*
IT'S PATSY WALKER AGAIN THESE DAYS, FELLA-- NOT THAT YOU'D HAVE BOTHERED TO KEEP TRACK OF ME!
Uhh... LOOK, PAT, I'M IN THE MIDDLE OF SOME IMPORTANT BUSINESS HERE...
*YOU KNEW IT WAS THE FORMER STAR OF PATSY WALKER COMICS AND AMAZING ADVENTURES ALL ALONG, DIDN'T YOU, TRUE BELIEVER? --M.
AHH, THE HECK WITH IT! YOU CAUGHT ME, FAIR AND SQUARE!
COME ON IN THE NEXT ROOM. WE CAN TALK IN THERE-- IN PRIVATE!
THIS MAY TAKE TIME, THOR. ARE WE AGREED TO GO?
AYE.
FAREWELL, CAPTAIN AMERICA.
BEST LUCK TO YOU, THUNDER GOD!
OKAY, BEAST: TALK TURKEY!

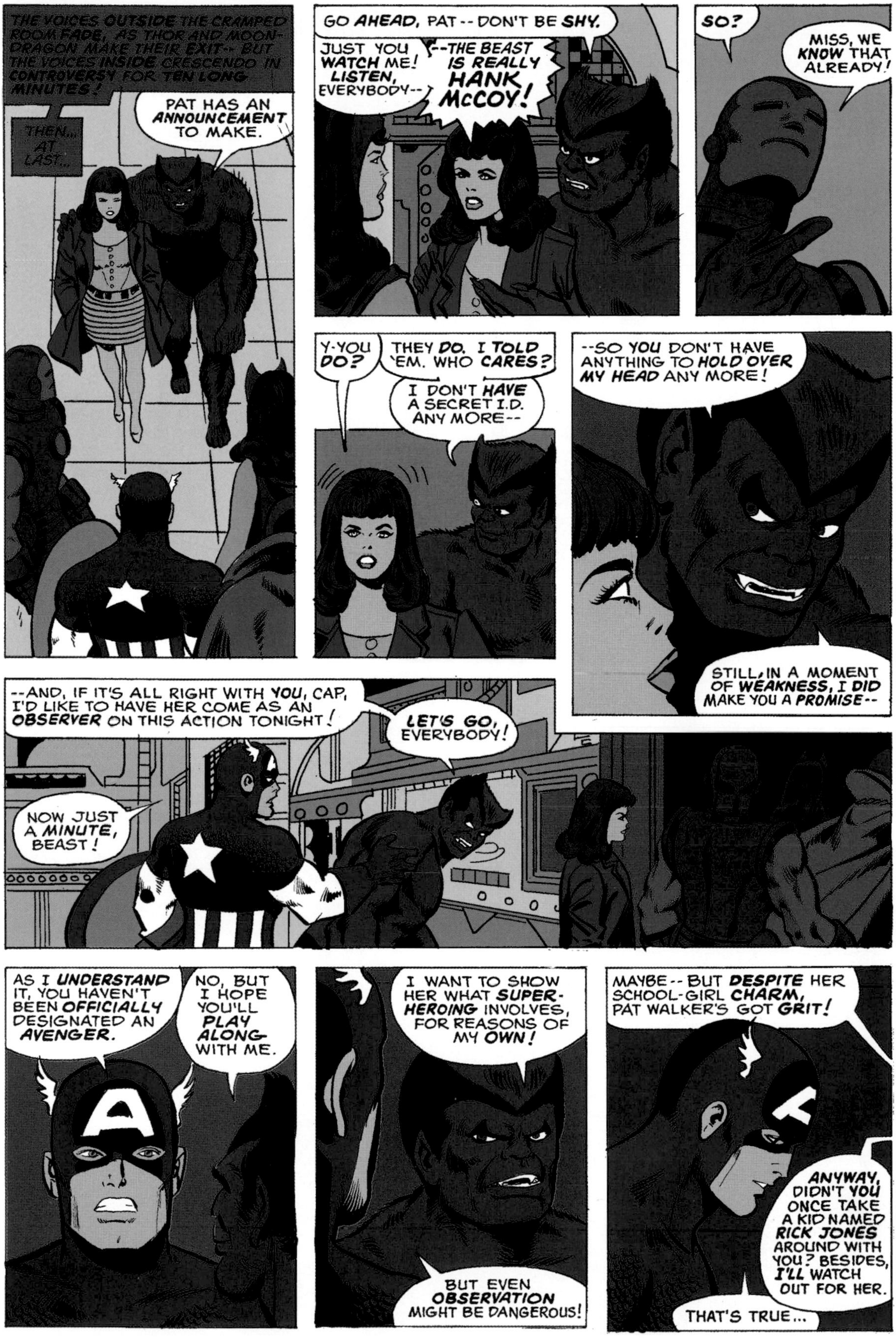
THE VOICES OUTSIDE THE CRAMPED ROOM FADE, AS THOR AND MOONDRAGON MAKE THEIR EXIT-- BUT THE VOICES INSIDE CRESCENDO IN CONTROVERSY FOR TEN LONG MINUTES!
THEN... AT LAST...
PAT HAS AN ANNOUNCEMENT TO MAKE.
GO AHEAD, PAT -- DON'T BE SHY.
JUST YOU WATCH ME! LISTEN, EVERYBODY--
--THE BEAST IS REALLY HANK McCOY!
SO?
MISS, WE KNOW THAT ALREADY!
Y-YOU DO?
THEY DO. I TOLD 'EM. WHO CARES?
I DON'T HAVE A SECRET I.D. ANY MORE--
--SO YOU DON'T HAVE ANYTHING TO HOLD OVER MY HEAD ANY MORE!
STILL, IN A MOMENT OF WEAKNESS, I DID MAKE YOU A PROMISE--
--AND, IF IT'S ALL RIGHT WITH YOU, CAP, I'D LIKE TO HAVE HER COME AS AN OBSERVER ON THIS ACTION TONIGHT!
LET'S GO, EVERYBODY!
NOW JUST A MINUTE, BEAST!
AS I UNDERSTAND IT, YOU HAVEN'T BEEN OFFICIALLY DESIGNATED AN AVENGER.
NO, BUT I HOPE YOU'LL PLAY ALONG WITH ME.
I WANT TO SHOW HER WHAT SUPER-HEROING INVOLVES, FOR REASONS OF MY OWN!
BUT EVEN OBSERVATION MIGHT BE DANGEROUS!
MAYBE -- BUT DESPITE HER SCHOOL-GIRL CHARM, PAT WALKER'S GOT GRIT!
ANYWAY, DIDN'T YOU ONCE TAKE A KID NAMED RICK JONES AROUND WITH YOU? BESIDES, I'LL WATCH OUT FOR HER.
THAT'S TRUE...

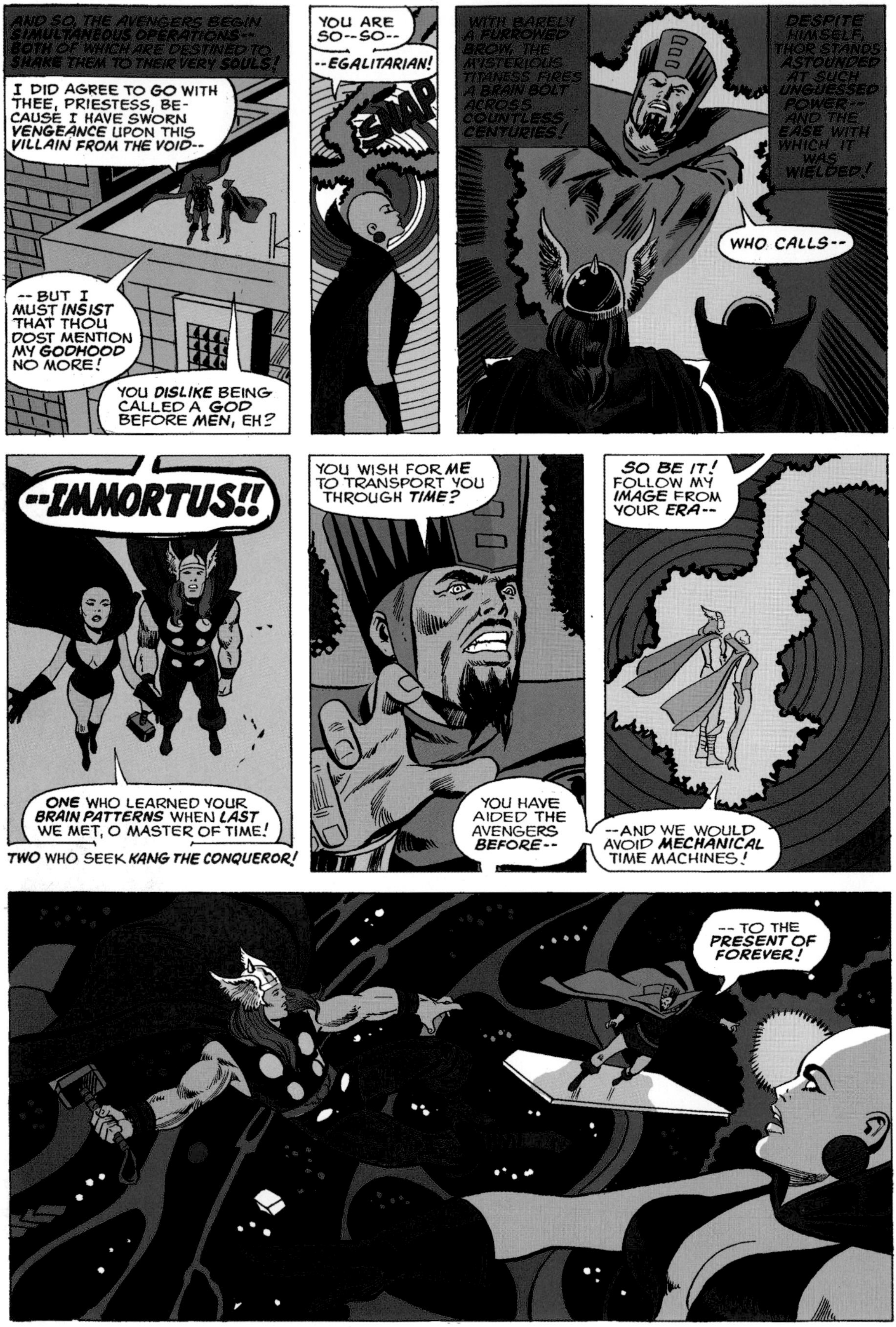
AND SO, THE AVENGERS BEGIN SIMULTANEOUS OPERATIONS-- BOTH OF WHICH ARE DESTINED TO SHAKE THEM TO THEIR VERY SOULS!
I DID AGREE TO GO WITH THEE, PRIESTESS, BECAUSE I HAVE SWORN VENGEANCE UPON THIS VILLAIN FROM THE VOID--
--BUT I MUST INSIST THAT THOU DOST MENTION MY GODHOOD NO MORE!
YOU DISLIKE BEING CALLED A GOD BEFORE MEN, EH?
YOU ARE SO--SO--
--EGALITARIAN!
SNAP
WITH BARELY A FURROWED BROW, THE MYSTERIOUS TITANESS FIRES A BRAIN BOLT ACROSS COUNTLESS CENTURIES!
DESPITE HIMSELF, THOR STANDS ASTOUNDED AT SUCH UNGUESSED POWER-- AND THE EASE WITH WHICH IT WAS WIELDED!
WHO CALLS--
--IMMORTUS!!
ONE WHO LEARNED YOUR BRAIN PATTERNS WHEN LAST WE MET, O MASTER OF TIME!
TWO WHO SEEK KANG THE CONQUEROR!
YOU WISH FOR ME TO TRANSPORT YOU THROUGH TIME?
YOU HAVE AIDED THE AVENGERS BEFORE--
--AND WE WOULD AVOID MECHANICAL TIME MACHINES!
SO BE IT! FOLLOW MY IMAGE FROM YOUR ERA--
-- TO THE PRESENT OF FOREVER!

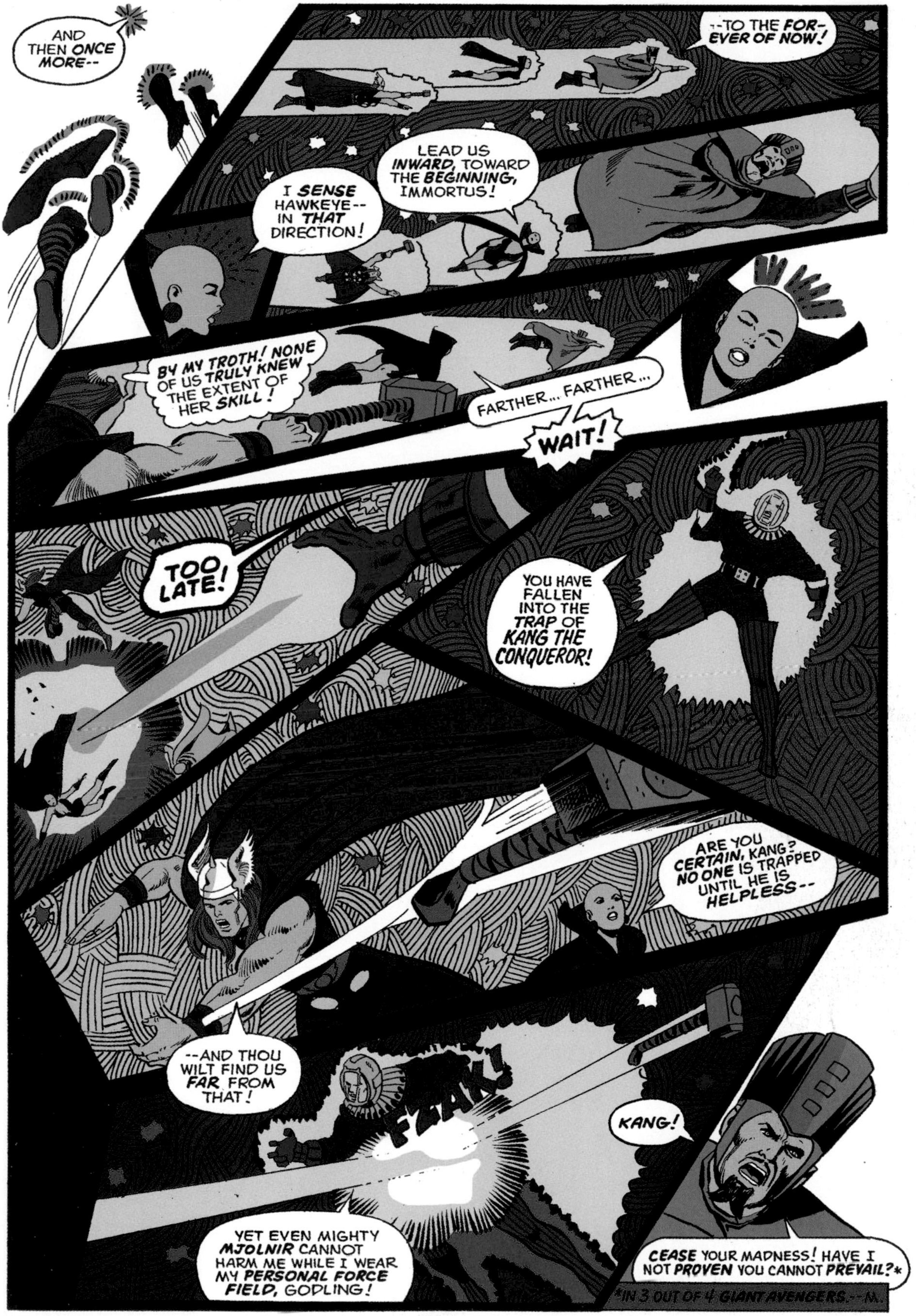
AND THEN ONCE MORE--
--TO THE FOREVER OF NOW!
LEAD US INWARD, TOWARD THE BEGINNING, IMMORTUS!
I SENSE HAWKEYE-- IN THAT DIRECTION!
BY MY TROTH! NONE OF US TRULY KNEW THE EXTENT OF HER SKILL!
FARTHER... FARTHER...
WAIT!
TOO LATE!
YOU HAVE FALLEN INTO THE TRAP OF KANG THE CONQUEROR!
ARE YOU CERTAIN, KANG? NO ONE IS TRAPPED UNTIL HE IS HELPLESS--
--AND THOU WILT FIND US FAR FROM THAT!
FZAK!
KANG!
YET EVEN MIGHTY MJOLNIR CANNOT HARM ME WHILE I WEAR MY PERSONAL FORCE FIELD, GODLING!
CEASE YOUR MADNESS! HAVE I NOT PROVEN YOU CANNOT PREVAIL?*
*IN 3 OUT OF 4 GIANT AVENGERS.--M.

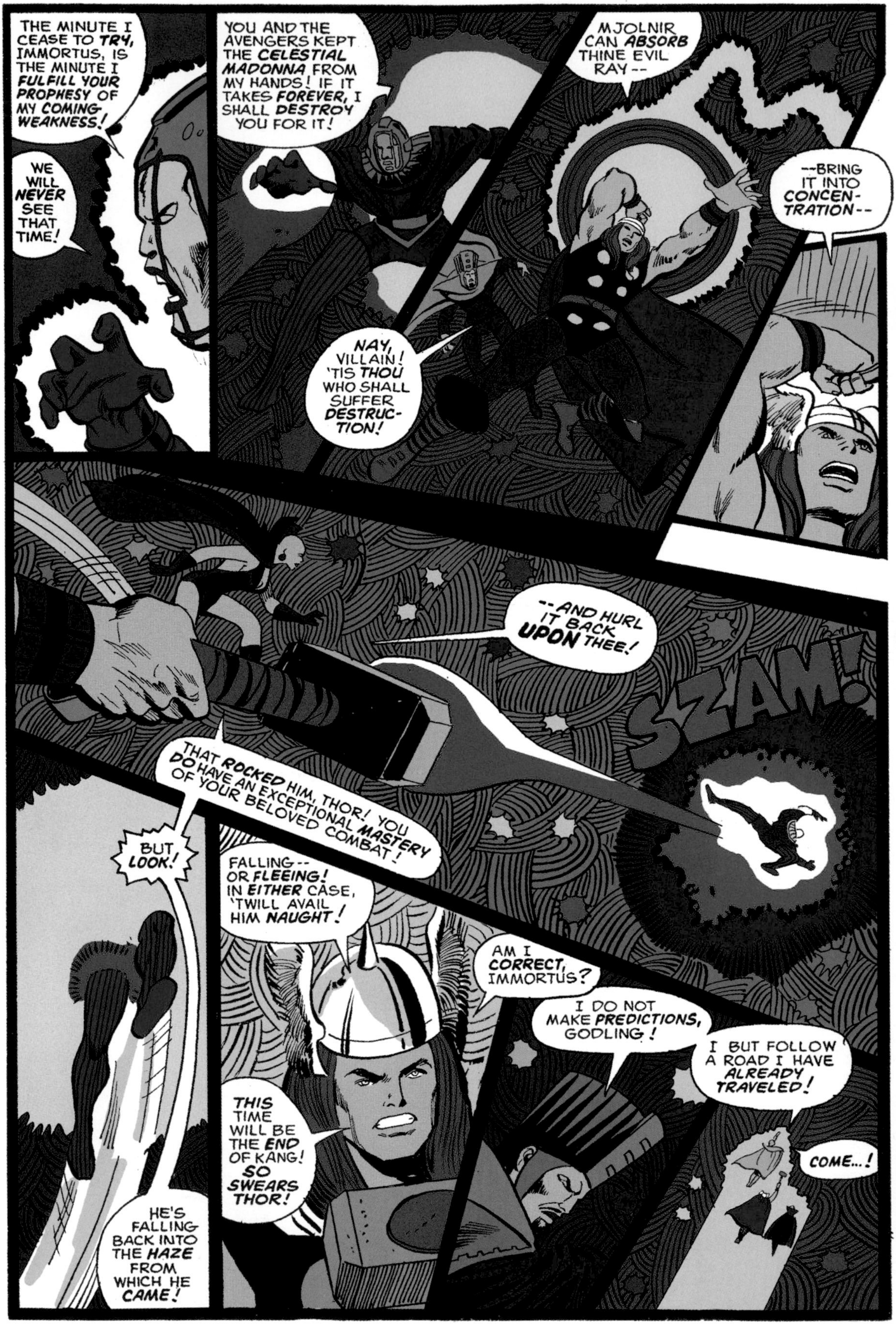
THE MINUTE I CEASE TO TRY, IMMORTUS, IS THE MINUTE I FULFILL YOUR PROPHESY OF MY COMING WEAKNESS!
WE WILL NEVER SEE THAT TIME!
YOU AND THE AVENGERS KEPT THE CELESTIAL MADONNA FROM MY HANDS! IF IT TAKES FOREVER, I SHALL DESTROY YOU FOR IT!
NAY, VILLAIN! 'TIS THOU WHO SHALL SUFFER DESTRUCTION!
MJOLNIR CAN ABSORB THINE EVIL RAY --
--BRING IT INTO CONCENTRATION--
--AND HURL IT BACK UPON THEE!
SZAM!
THAT ROCKED HIM, THOR! YOU DO HAVE AN EXCEPTIONAL MASTERY OF YOUR BELOVED COMBAT!
BUT LOOK!
HE'S FALLING BACK INTO THE HAZE FROM WHICH HE CAME!
FALLING -- OR FLEEING! IN EITHER CASE, 'TWILL AVAIL HIM NAUGHT!
THIS TIME WILL BE THE END OF KANG! SO SWEARS THOR!
AM I CORRECT, IMMORTUS?
I DO NOT MAKE PREDICTIONS, GODLING!
I BUT FOLLOW A ROAD I HAVE ALREADY TRAVELED!
COME...!

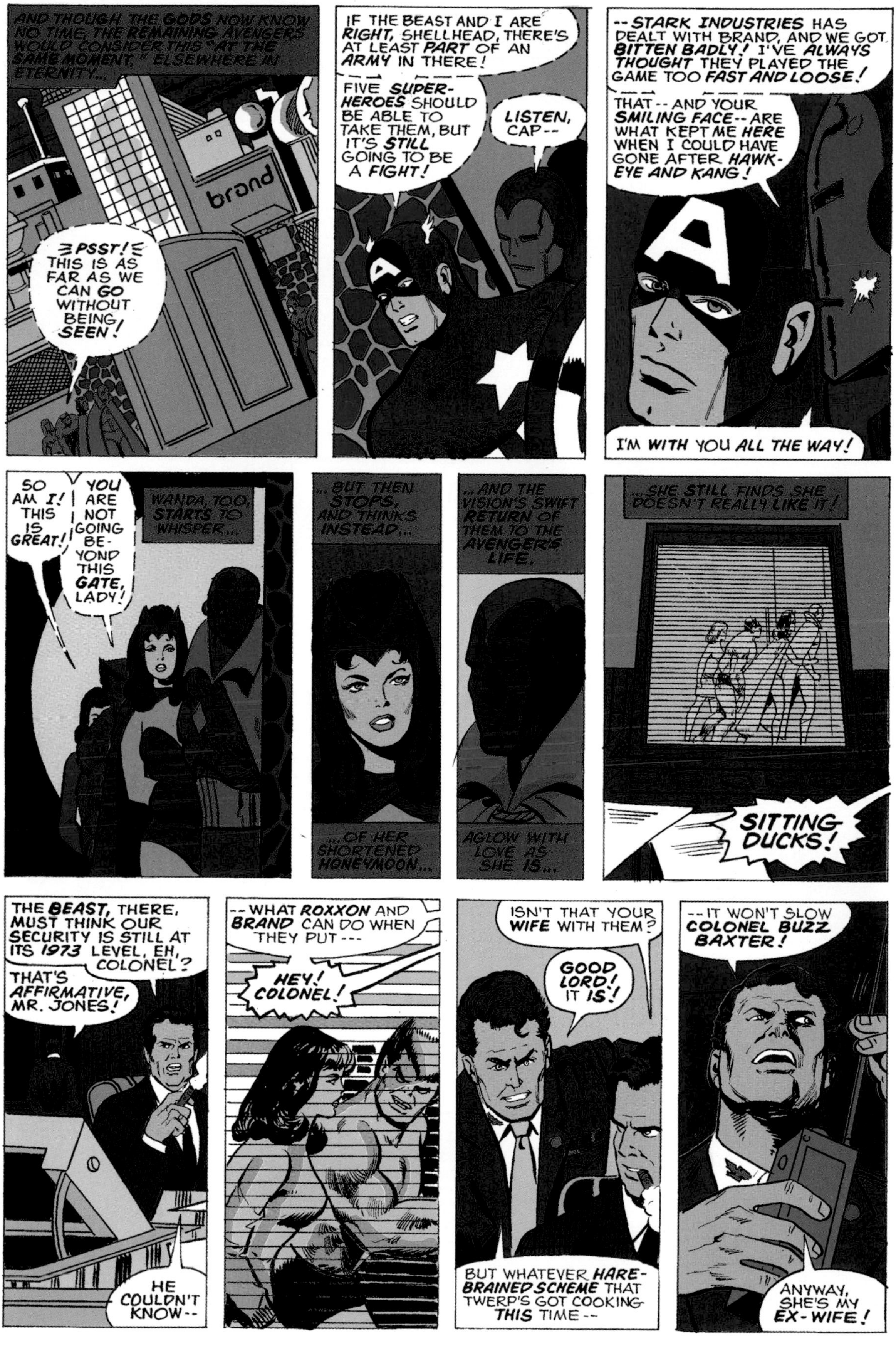
AND THOUGH THE GODS NOW KNOW NO TIME, THE REMAINING AVENGERS WOULD CONSIDER THIS "AT THE SAME MOMENT," ELSEWHERE IN ETERNITY...
brand
PSST! THIS IS AS FAR AS WE CAN GO WITHOUT BEING SEEN!
IF THE BEAST AND I ARE RIGHT, SHELLHEAD, THERE'S AT LEAST PART OF AN ARMY IN THERE!
FIVE SUPER-HEROES SHOULD BE ABLE TO TAKE THEM, BUT IT'S STILL GOING TO BE A FIGHT!
LISTEN, CAP--
--STARK INDUSTRIES HAS DEALT WITH BRAND, AND WE GOT BITTEN BADLY! I'VE ALWAYS THOUGHT THEY PLAYED THE GAME TOO FAST AND LOOSE!
THAT--AND YOUR SMILING FACE--ARE WHAT KEPT ME HERE WHEN I COULD HAVE GONE AFTER HAWK-EYE AND KANG!
I'M WITH YOU ALL THE WAY!
SO AM I! THIS IS GREAT!
YOU ARE NOT GOING BE-YOND THIS GATE, LADY!
WANDA, TOO, STARTS TO WHISPER...
...BUT THEN STOPS, AND THINKS INSTEAD...
...OF HER SHORTENED HONEYMOON...
...AND THE VISION'S SWIFT RETURN OF THEM TO THE AVENGER'S LIFE.
AGLOW WITH LOVE AS SHE IS...
...SHE STILL FINDS SHE DOESN'T REALLY LIKE IT!
SITTING DUCKS!
THE BEAST, THERE, MUST THINK OUR SECURITY IS STILL AT ITS 1973 LEVEL, EH, COLONEL?
THAT'S AFFIRMATIVE, MR. JONES!
HE COULDN'T KNOW--
--WHAT ROXXON AND BRAND CAN DO WHEN THEY PUT---
HEY! COLONEL!
ISN'T THAT YOUR WIFE WITH THEM?
GOOD LORD! IT IS!
BUT WHATEVER HARE-BRAINED SCHEME THAT TWERP'S GOT COOKING THIS TIME--
--IT WON'T SLOW COLONEL BUZZ BAXTER!
ANYWAY, SHE'S MY EX-WIFE!

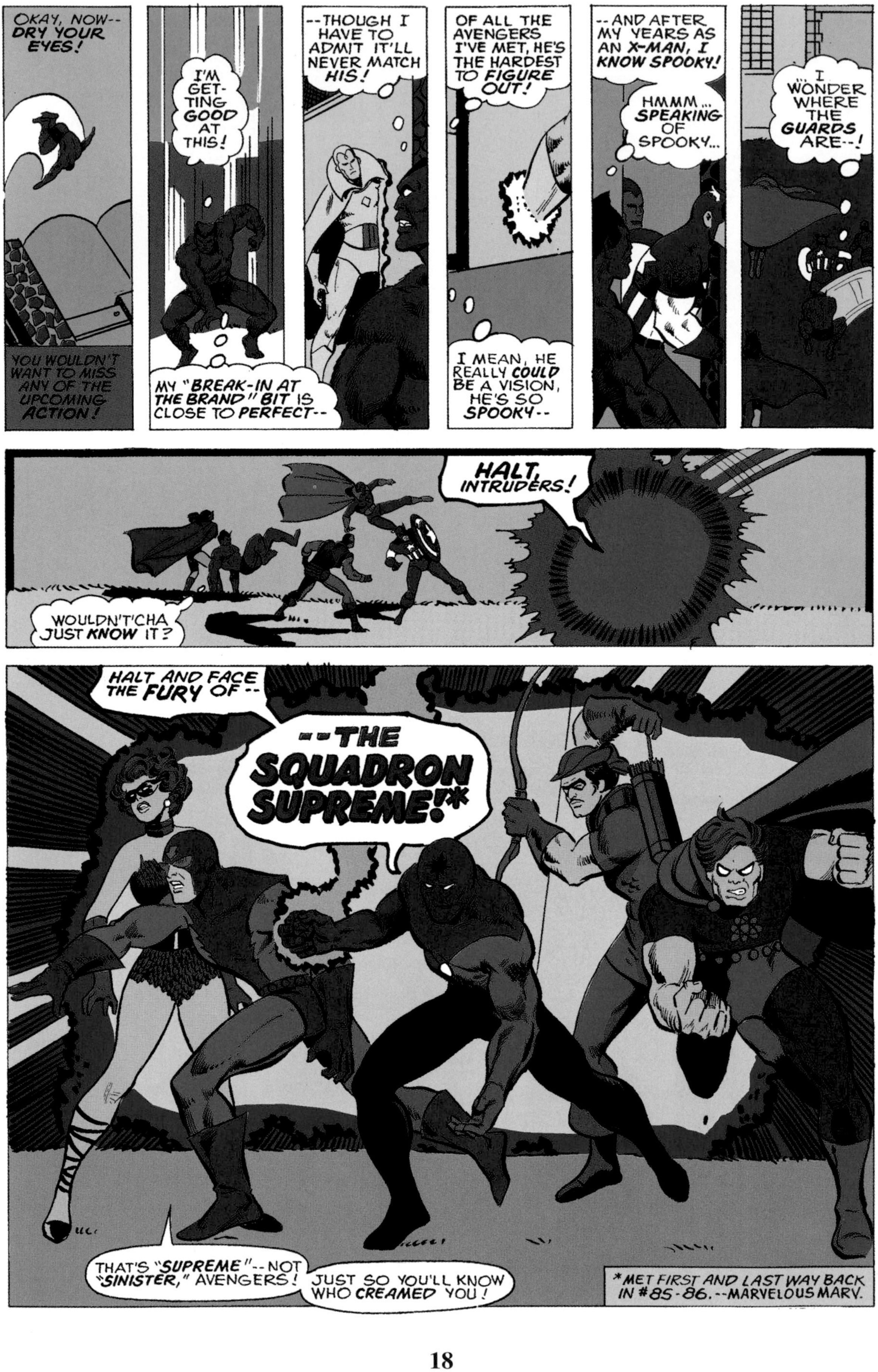
OKAY, NOW-- DRY YOUR EYES!
YOU WOULDN'T WANT TO MISS ANY OF THE UPCOMING ACTION!
I'M GETTING GOOD AT THIS!
MY "BREAK-IN AT THE BRAND" BIT IS CLOSE TO PERFECT--
--THOUGH I HAVE TO ADMIT IT'LL NEVER MATCH HIS!
OF ALL THE AVENGERS I'VE MET, HE'S THE HARDEST TO FIGURE OUT!
I MEAN, HE REALLY COULD BE A VISION, HE'S SO SPOOKY--
--AND AFTER MY YEARS AS AN X-MAN, I KNOW SPOOKY!
HMMM... SPEAKING OF SPOOKY...
...I WONDER WHERE THE GUARDS ARE--!
HALT, INTRUDERS!
WOULDN'T'CHA JUST KNOW IT?
HALT AND FACE THE FURY OF--
--THE SQUADRON SUPREME!*
THAT'S "SUPREME"--NOT "SINISTER," AVENGERS!
JUST SO YOU'LL KNOW WHO CREAMED YOU!
*MET FIRST AND LAST WAY BACK IN #85-86. --MARVELOUS MARV.

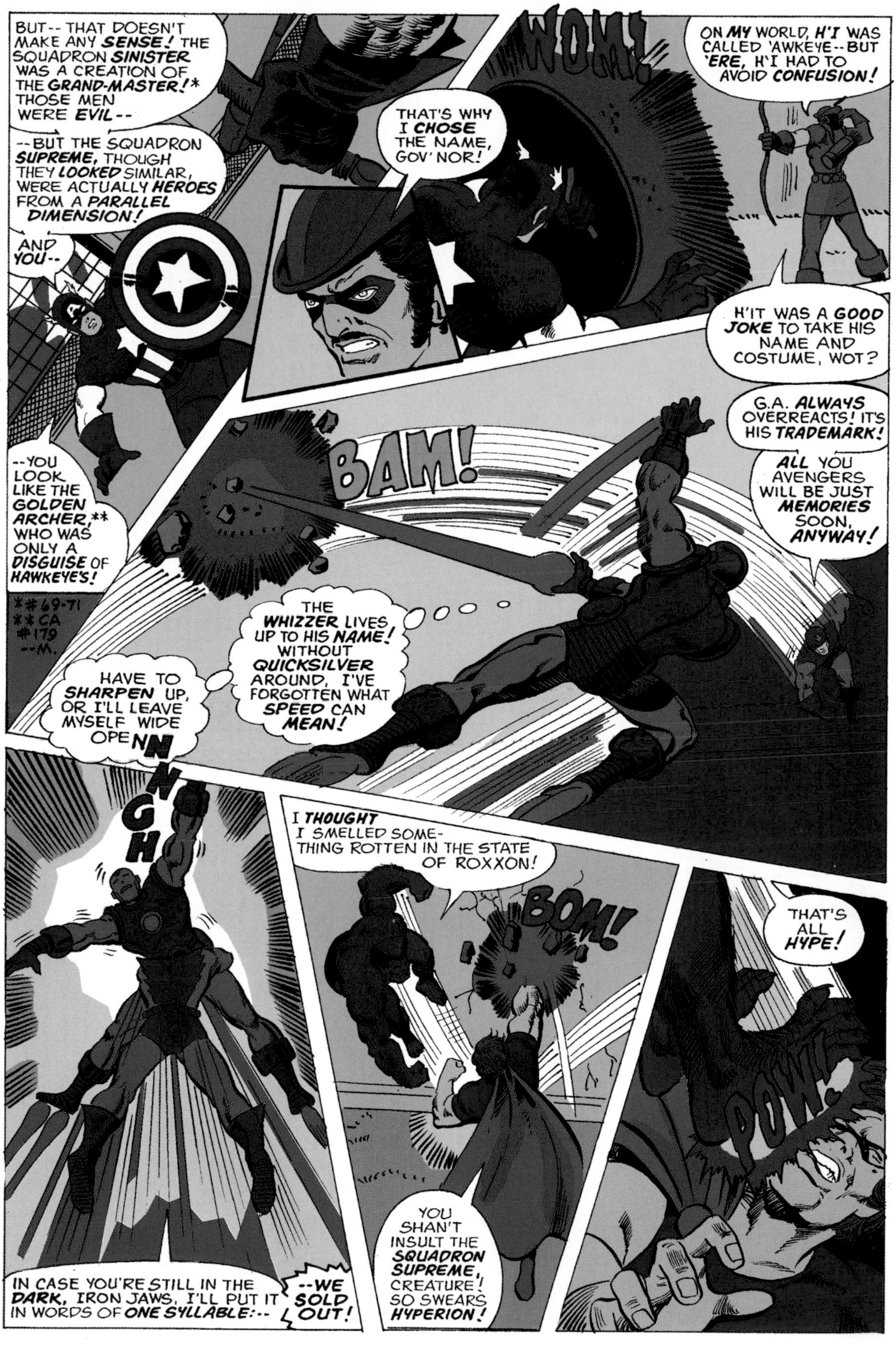
BUT-- THAT DOESN'T MAKE ANY SENSE! THE SQUADRON SINISTER WAS A CREATION OF THE GRAND-MASTER!* THOSE MEN WERE EVIL--
--BUT THE SQUADRON SUPREME, THOUGH THEY LOOKED SIMILAR, WERE ACTUALLY HEROES FROM A PARALLEL DIMENSION!
AND YOU--
WOM!
THAT'S WHY I CHOSE THE NAME, GOV'NOR!
ON MY WORLD, H'I WAS CALLED 'AWKEYE--BUT 'ERE, H'I HAD TO AVOID CONFUSION!
H'IT WAS A GOOD JOKE TO TAKE HIS NAME AND COSTUME, WOT?
--YOU LOOK LIKE THE GOLDEN ARCHER,** WHO WAS ONLY A DISGUISE OF HAWKEYE'S!
*#69-71 **CA #179 --M.
BAM!
G.A. ALWAYS OVERREACTS! IT'S HIS TRADEMARK!
ALL YOU AVENGERS WILL BE JUST MEMORIES SOON, ANYWAY!
HAVE TO SHARPEN UP, OR I'LL LEAVE MYSELF WIDE OPENNN
THE WHIZZER LIVES UP TO HIS NAME! WITHOUT QUICKSILVER AROUND, I'VE FORGOTTEN WHAT SPEED CAN MEAN!
NNGH!
IN CASE YOU'RE STILL IN THE DARK, IRON JAWS, I'LL PUT IT IN WORDS OF ONE SYLLABLE:--
--WE SOLD OUT!
I THOUGHT I SMELLED SOMETHING ROTTEN IN THE STATE OF ROXXON!
BOM!
YOU SHAN'T INSULT THE SQUADRON SUPREME, CREATURE! SO SWEARS HYPERION!
THAT'S ALL HYPE!
POW!

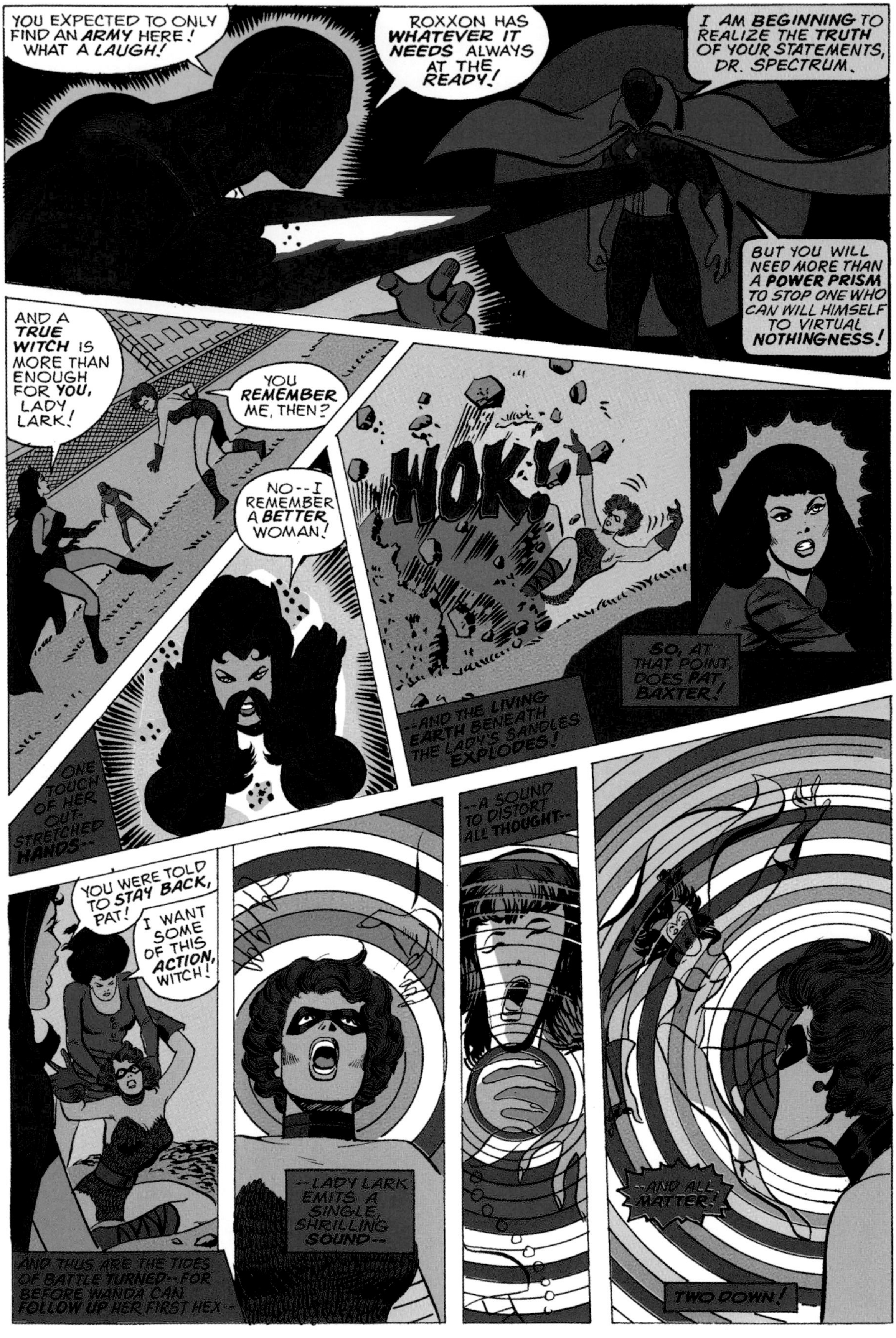
YOU EXPECTED TO ONLY FIND AN ARMY HERE! WHAT A LAUGH!
ROXXON HAS WHATEVER IT NEEDS ALWAYS AT THE READY!
I AM BEGINNING TO REALIZE THE TRUTH OF YOUR STATEMENTS, DR. SPECTRUM.
BUT YOU WILL NEED MORE THAN A POWER PRISM TO STOP ONE WHO CAN WILL HIMSELF TO VIRTUAL NOTHINGNESS!
AND A TRUE WITCH IS MORE THAN ENOUGH FOR YOU, LADY LARK!
YOU REMEMBER ME, THEN?
NO--I REMEMBER A BETTER WOMAN!
ONE TOUCH OF HER OUT-STRETCHED HANDS--
WOK!
--AND THE LIVING EARTH BENEATH THE LADY'S SANDLES EXPLODES!
SO, AT THAT POINT, DOES PAT BAXTER!
YOU WERE TOLD TO STAY BACK, PAT!
I WANT SOME OF THIS ACTION, WITCH!
AND THUS ARE THE TIDES OF BATTLE TURNED--FOR BEFORE WANDA CAN FOLLOW UP HER FIRST HEX--
--LADY LARK EMITS A SINGLE, SHRILLING SOUND--
--A SOUND TO DISTORT ALL THOUGHT--
--AND ALL MATTER!
TWO DOWN!

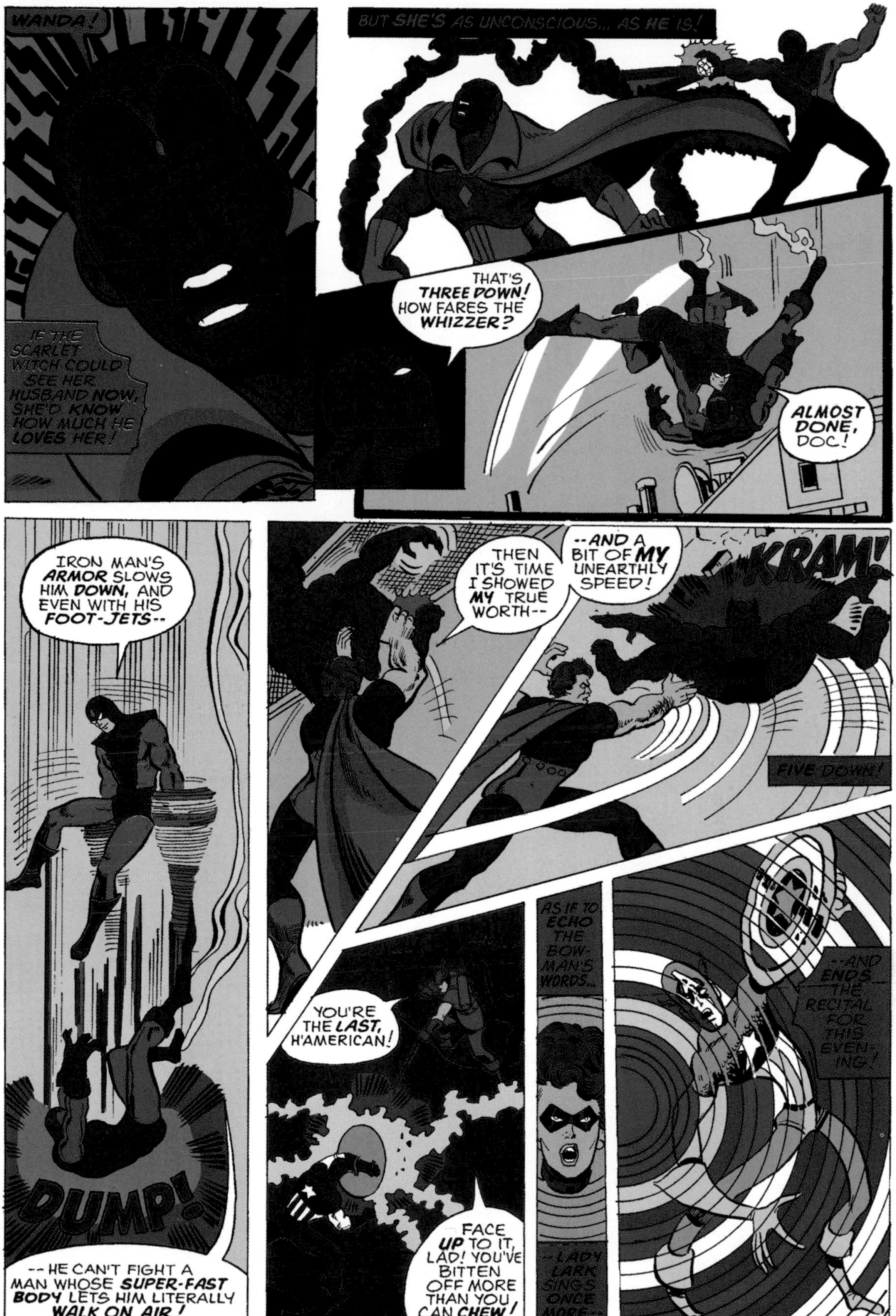
WANDA!
BUT SHE'S AS UNCONSCIOUS... AS HE IS!
IF THE SCARLET WITCH COULD SEE HER HUSBAND NOW, SHE'D KNOW HOW MUCH HE LOVES HER!
THAT'S THREE DOWN! HOW FARES THE WHIZZER?
ALMOST DONE, DOC!
IRON MAN'S ARMOR SLOWS HIM DOWN, AND EVEN WITH HIS FOOT-JETS--
DUMP!
--HE CAN'T FIGHT A MAN WHOSE SUPER-FAST BODY LETS HIM LITERALLY WALK ON AIR!
THEN IT'S TIME I SHOWED MY TRUE WORTH--
--AND A BIT OF MY UNEARTHLY SPEED!
KRAM!
FIVE DOWN!
YOU'RE THE LAST, H'AMERICAN!
FACE UP TO IT, LAD! YOU'VE BITTEN OFF MORE THAN YOU CAN CHEW!
AS IF TO ECHO THE BOW-MAN'S WORDS...
--LADY LARK SINGS ONCE MORE--
--AND ENDS THE RECITAL FOR THIS EVEN-ING!

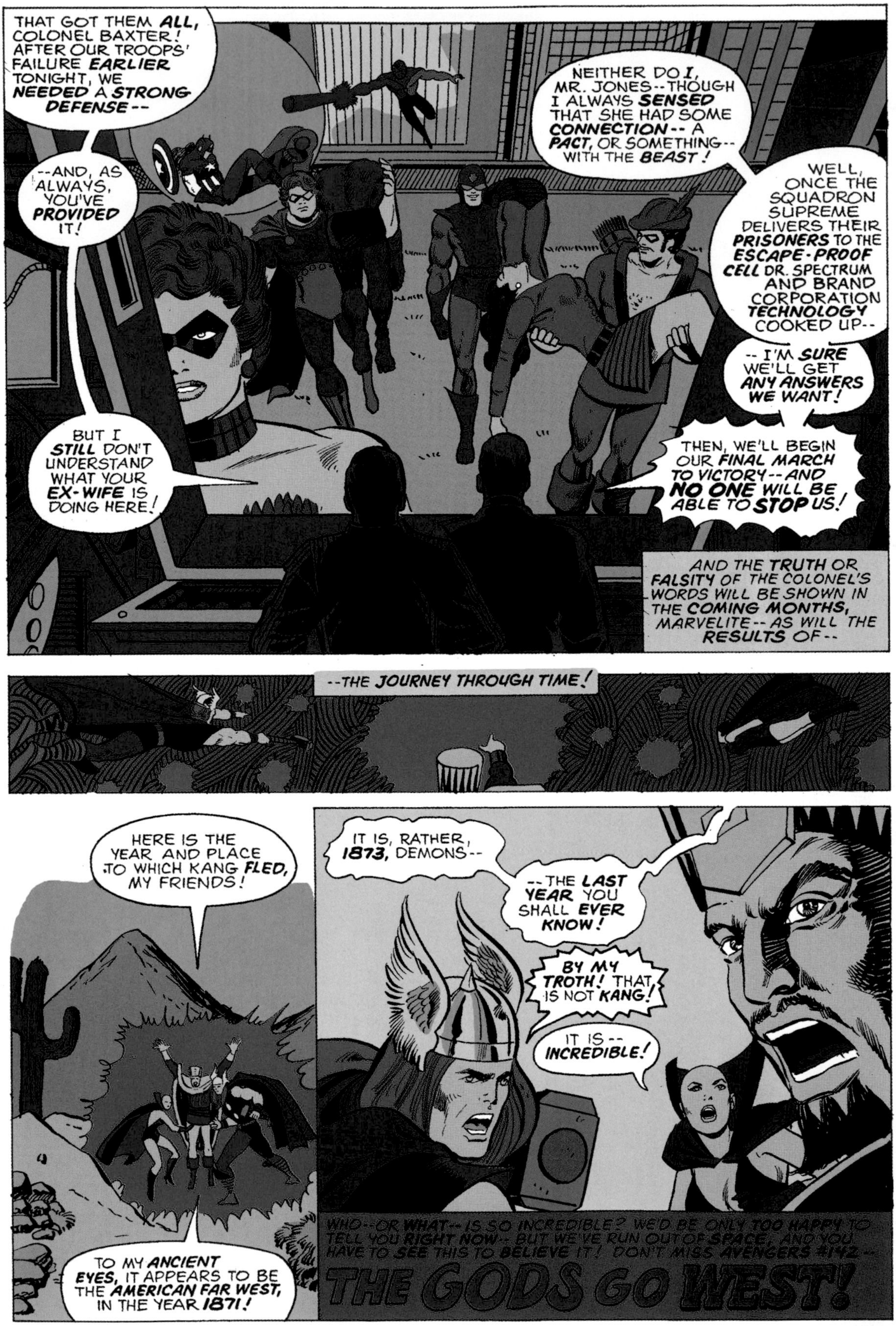
THAT GOT THEM ALL, COLONEL BAXTER! AFTER OUR TROOPS' FAILURE EARLIER TONIGHT, WE NEEDED A STRONG DEFENSE--
--AND, AS ALWAYS, YOU'VE PROVIDED IT!
BUT I STILL DON'T UNDERSTAND WHAT YOUR EX-WIFE IS DOING HERE!
NEITHER DO I, MR. JONES--THOUGH I ALWAYS SENSED THAT SHE HAD SOME CONNECTION-- A PACT, OR SOMETHING-- WITH THE BEAST!
WELL, ONCE THE SQUADRON SUPREME DELIVERS THEIR PRISONERS TO THE ESCAPE-PROOF CELL DR. SPECTRUM AND BRAND CORPORATION TECHNOLOGY COOKED UP--
-- I'M SURE WE'LL GET ANY ANSWERS WE WANT!
THEN, WE'LL BEGIN OUR FINAL MARCH TO VICTORY--AND NO ONE WILL BE ABLE TO STOP US!
AND THE TRUTH OR FALSITY OF THE COLONEL'S WORDS WILL BE SHOWN IN THE COMING MONTHS, MARVELITE-- AS WILL THE RESULTS OF--
--THE JOURNEY THROUGH TIME!
HERE IS THE YEAR AND PLACE TO WHICH KANG FLED, MY FRIENDS!
TO MY ANCIENT EYES, IT APPEARS TO BE THE AMERICAN FAR WEST, IN THE YEAR 1871!
IT IS, RATHER, 1873, DEMONS--
--THE LAST YEAR YOU SHALL EVER KNOW!
BY MY TROTH! THAT IS NOT KANG!
IT IS -- INCREDIBLE!
WHO--OR WHAT--IS SO INCREDIBLE? WE'D BE ONLY TOO HAPPY TO TELL YOU RIGHT NOW--BUT WE'VE RUN OUT OF SPACE, AND YOU HAVE TO SEE THIS TO BELIEVE IT! DON'T MISS AVENGERS #142--
THE GODS GO WEST!

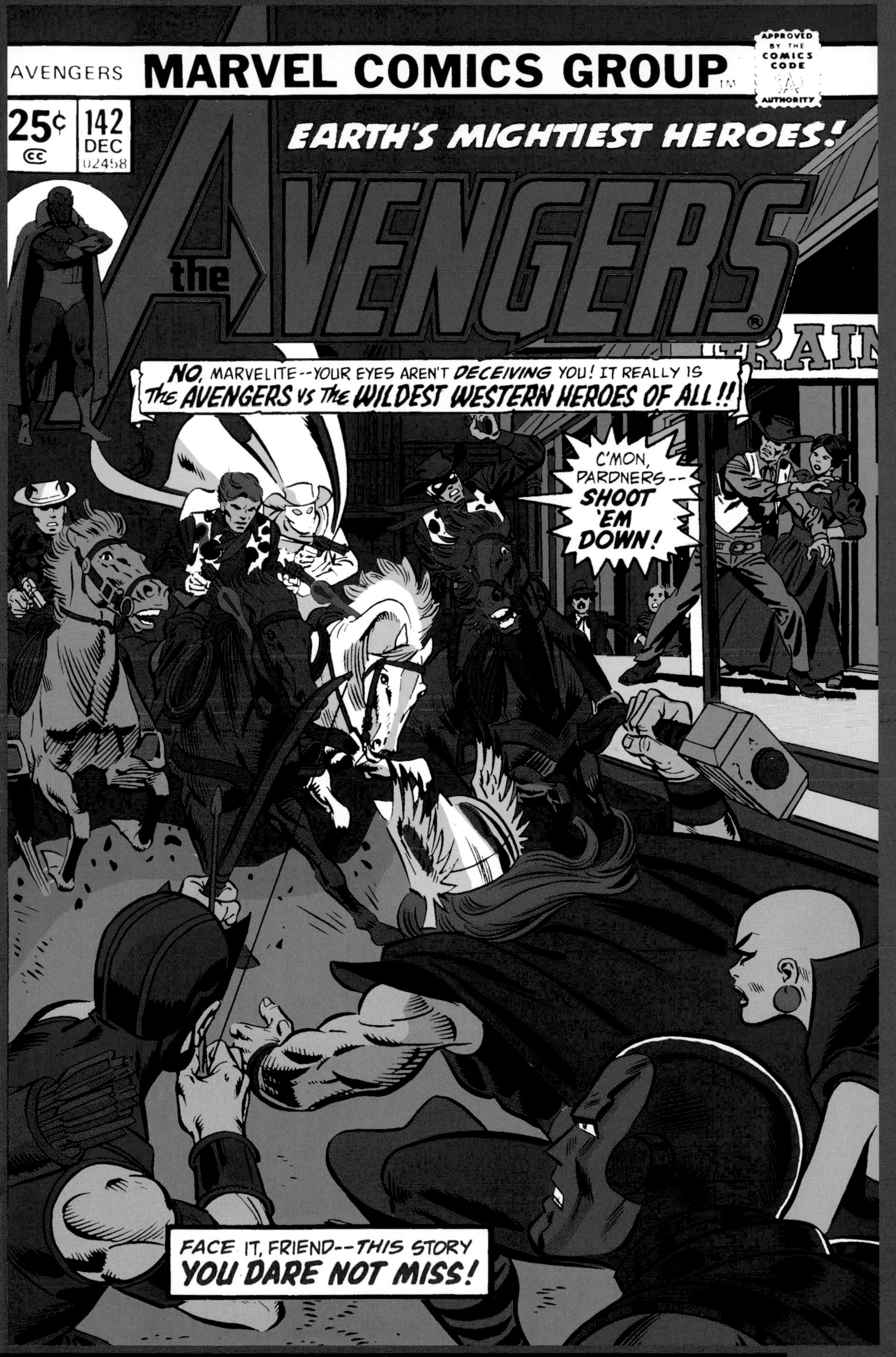
AVENGERS
MARVEL COMICS GROUP
APPROVED BY THE COMICS CODE AUTHORITY
25¢
142
DEC
02458
EARTH'S MIGHTIEST HEROES!
the AVENGERS
NO, MARVELITE--YOUR EYES AREN'T DECEIVING YOU! IT REALLY IS The AVENGERS vs The WILDEST WESTERN HEROES OF ALL!!
C'MON, PARDNERS--SHOOT 'EM DOWN!
FACE IT, FRIEND--THIS STORY YOU DARE NOT MISS!

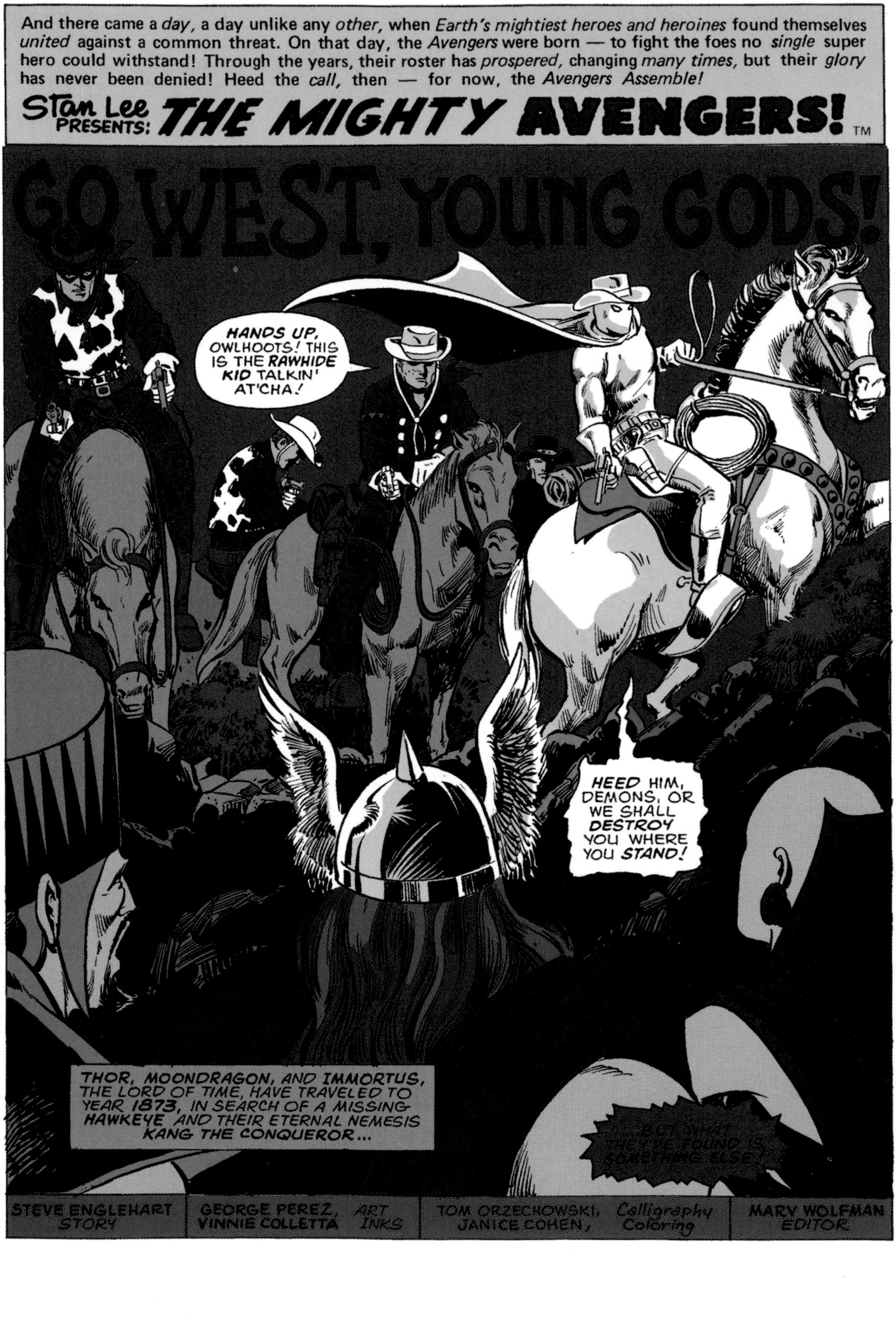
And there came a *day*, a day unlike any *other*, when *Earth's mightiest heroes and heroines* found themselves *united* against a common threat. On that day, the *Avengers* were born — to fight the foes no *single* super hero could withstand! Through the years, their roster has *prospered*, changing *many times*, but their *glory* has never been denied! Heed the *call*, then — for now, the *Avengers Assemble!*
Stan Lee PRESENTS: THE MIGHTY AVENGERS! TM
GO WEST, YOUNG GODS!
HANDS UP, OWLHOOTS! THIS IS THE RAWHIDE KID TALKIN' AT'CHA!
HEED HIM, DEMONS, OR WE SHALL DESTROY YOU WHERE YOU STAND!
THOR, MOONDRAGON, AND IMMORTUS, THE LORD OF TIME, HAVE TRAVELED TO YEAR 1873, IN SEARCH OF A MISSING HAWKEYE AND THEIR ETERNAL NEMESIS KANG THE CONQUEROR...
...BUT WHAT THEY'VE FOUND IS SOMETHING ELSE!
STEVE ENGLEHART STORY
GEORGE PEREZ, ART
VINNIE COLLETTA INKS
TOM ORZECHOWSKI, Calligraphy
JANICE COHEN, Coloring
MARY WOLFMAN EDITOR

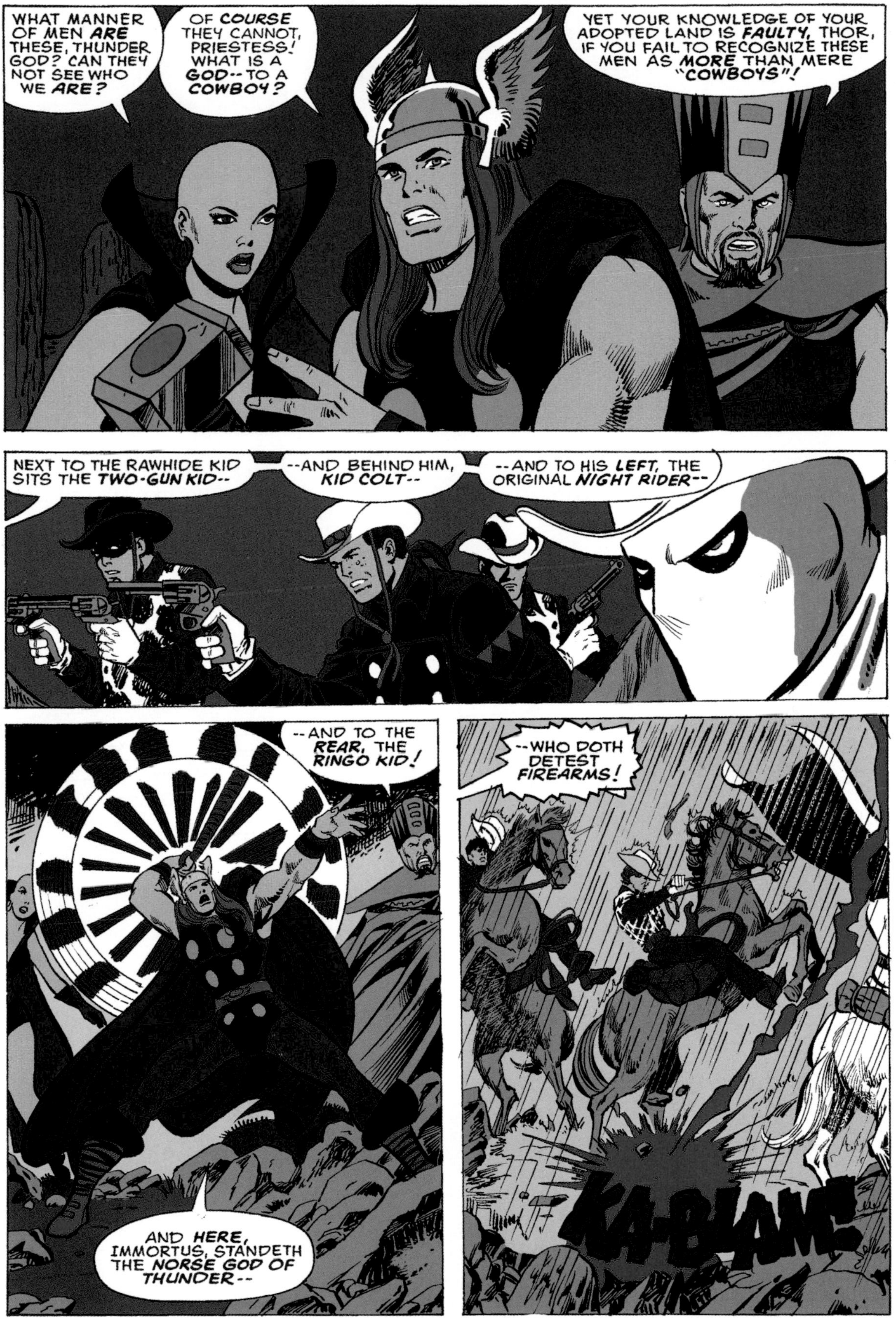
WHAT MANNER OF MEN ARE THESE, THUNDER GOD? CAN THEY NOT SEE WHO WE ARE?
OF COURSE THEY CANNOT, PRIESTESS! WHAT IS A GOD--TO A COWBOY?
YET YOUR KNOWLEDGE OF YOUR ADOPTED LAND IS FAULTY, THOR, IF YOU FAIL TO RECOGNIZE THESE MEN AS MORE THAN MERE "COWBOYS"!
NEXT TO THE RAWHIDE KID SITS THE TWO-GUN KID--
--AND BEHIND HIM, KID COLT--
--AND TO HIS LEFT, THE ORIGINAL NIGHT RIDER--
--AND TO THE REAR, THE RINGO KID!
AND HERE, IMMORTUS, STANDETH THE NORSE GOD OF THUNDER--
--WHO DOTH DETEST FIREARMS!
KA-BLAM!

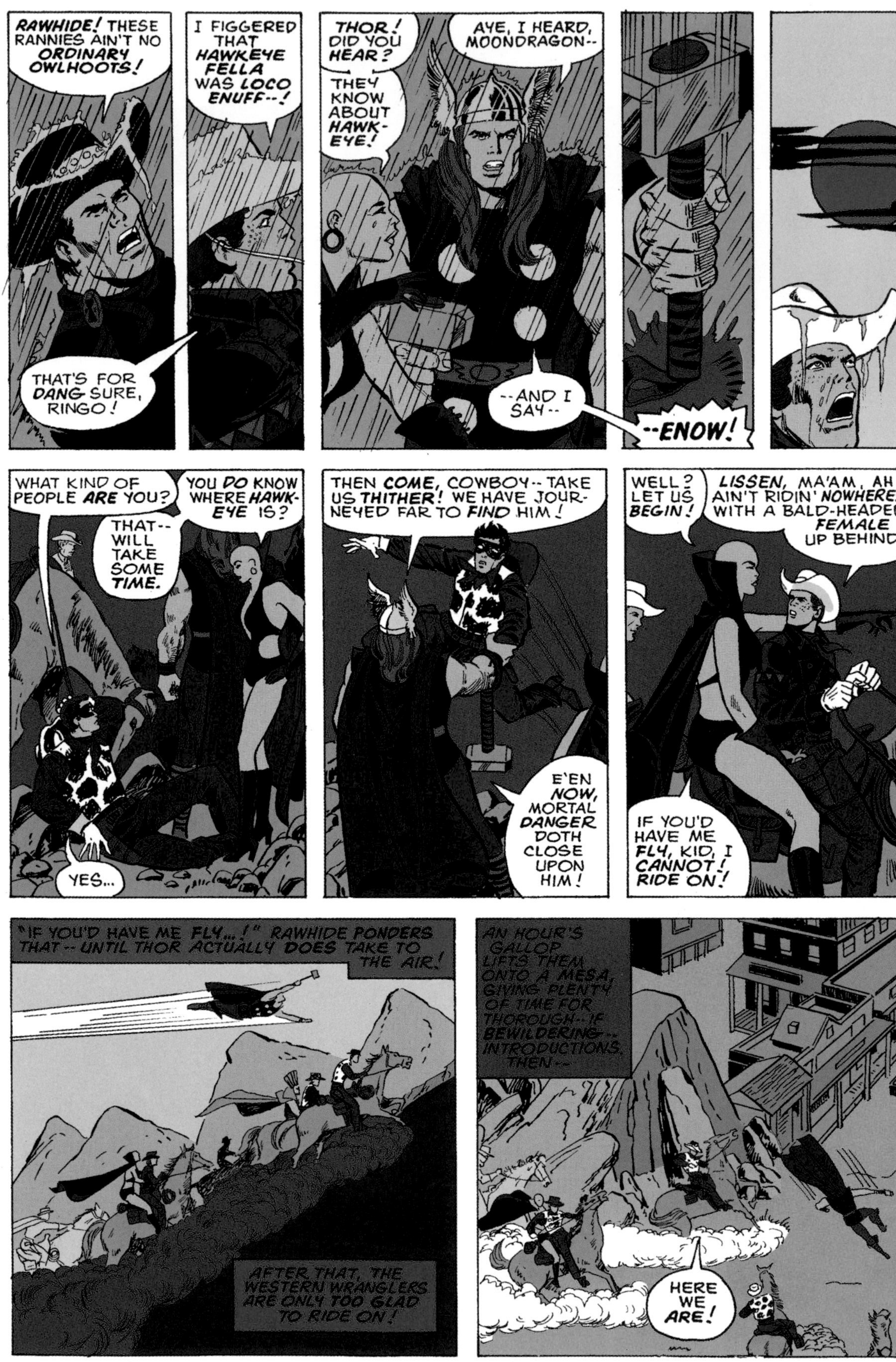
RAWHIDE! THESE RANNIES AIN'T NO ORDINARY OWLHOOTS!
I FIGGERED THAT HAWKEYE FELLA WAS LOCO ENUFF--!
THAT'S FOR DANG SURE, RINGO!
THOR! DID YOU HEAR?
THEY KNOW ABOUT HAWK-EYE!
AYE, I HEARD, MOONDRAGON--
--AND I SAY--
--ENOW!
WHAT KIND OF PEOPLE ARE YOU?
YOU DO KNOW WHERE HAWK-EYE IS?
THAT--WILL TAKE SOME TIME.
YES...
THEN COME, COWBOY--TAKE US THITHER! WE HAVE JOURNEYED FAR TO FIND HIM!
E'EN NOW, MORTAL DANGER DOTH CLOSE UPON HIM!
WELL? LET US BEGIN!
LISSEN, MA'AM, AH AIN'T RIDIN' NOWHERES WITH A BALD-HEADED FEMALE UP BEHIND!
IF YOU'D HAVE ME FLY, KID, I CANNOT! RIDE ON!
"IF YOU'D HAVE ME FLY...!" RAWHIDE PONDERS THAT--UNTIL THOR ACTUALLY DOES TAKE TO THE AIR!
AFTER THAT, THE WESTERN WRANGLERS ARE ONLY TOO GLAD TO RIDE ON!
AN HOUR'S GALLOP LIFTS THEM ONTO A MESA, GIVING PLENTY OF TIME FOR THOROUGH--IF BEWILDERING--INTRODUCTIONS. THEN--
HERE WE ARE!

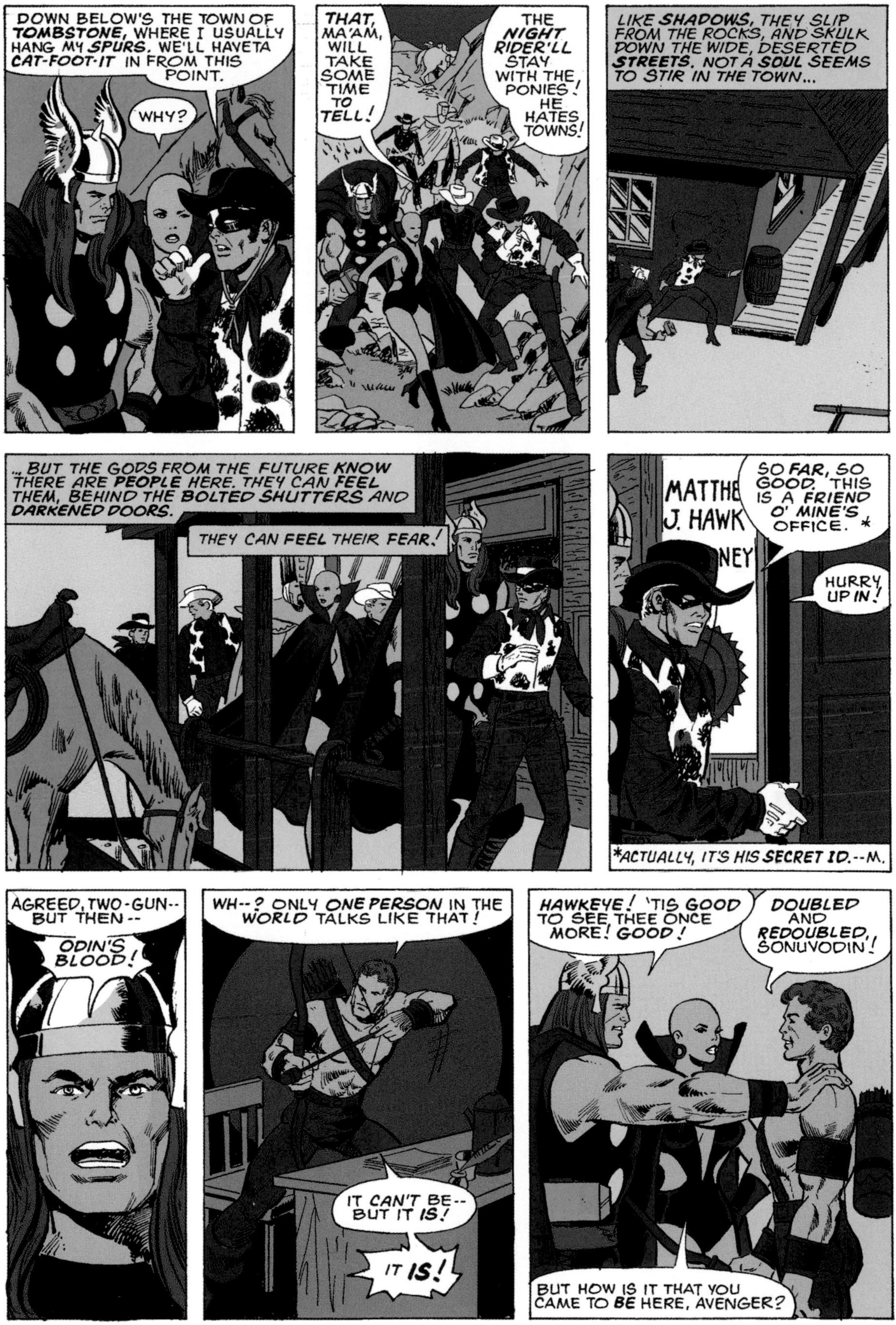
DOWN BELOW'S THE TOWN OF **TOMBSTONE**, WHERE I USUALLY HANG MY **SPURS**. WE'LL HAVETA **CAT-FOOT-IT** IN FROM THIS POINT.
WHY?
THAT, MA'AM, WILL TAKE SOME TIME TO **TELL**!
THE **NIGHT RIDER'LL** STAY WITH THE PONIES! HE HATES TOWNS!
LIKE **SHADOWS**, THEY SLIP FROM THE ROCKS, AND SKULK DOWN THE WIDE, DESERTED **STREETS**. NOT A **SOUL SEEMS** TO **STIR** IN THE TOWN...
... BUT THE GODS FROM THE FUTURE **KNOW** THERE ARE **PEOPLE** HERE. THEY CAN **FEEL** THEM, BEHIND THE **BOLTED SHUTTERS** AND **DARKENED DOORS**.
THEY CAN **FEEL** THEIR **FEAR**!
MATTHE
J. HAWK
NEY
SO **FAR**, SO GOOD. THIS IS A **FRIEND** O' MINE'S OFFICE. *
HURRY **UP IN**!
*ACTUALLY, IT'S HIS **SECRET ID**.--M.
AGREED, TWO-GUN-- BUT THEN --
ODIN'S BLOOD!
WH--? ONLY **ONE PERSON** IN THE **WORLD** TALKS LIKE THAT!
IT **CAN'T** BE-- BUT IT **IS**!
IT **IS**!
HAWKEYE! 'TIS **GOOD** TO SEE THEE ONCE MORE! **GOOD**!
DOUBLED AND **REDOUBLED**, SONUVODIN!
BUT HOW IS IT THAT YOU CAME TO **BE** HERE, AVENGER?

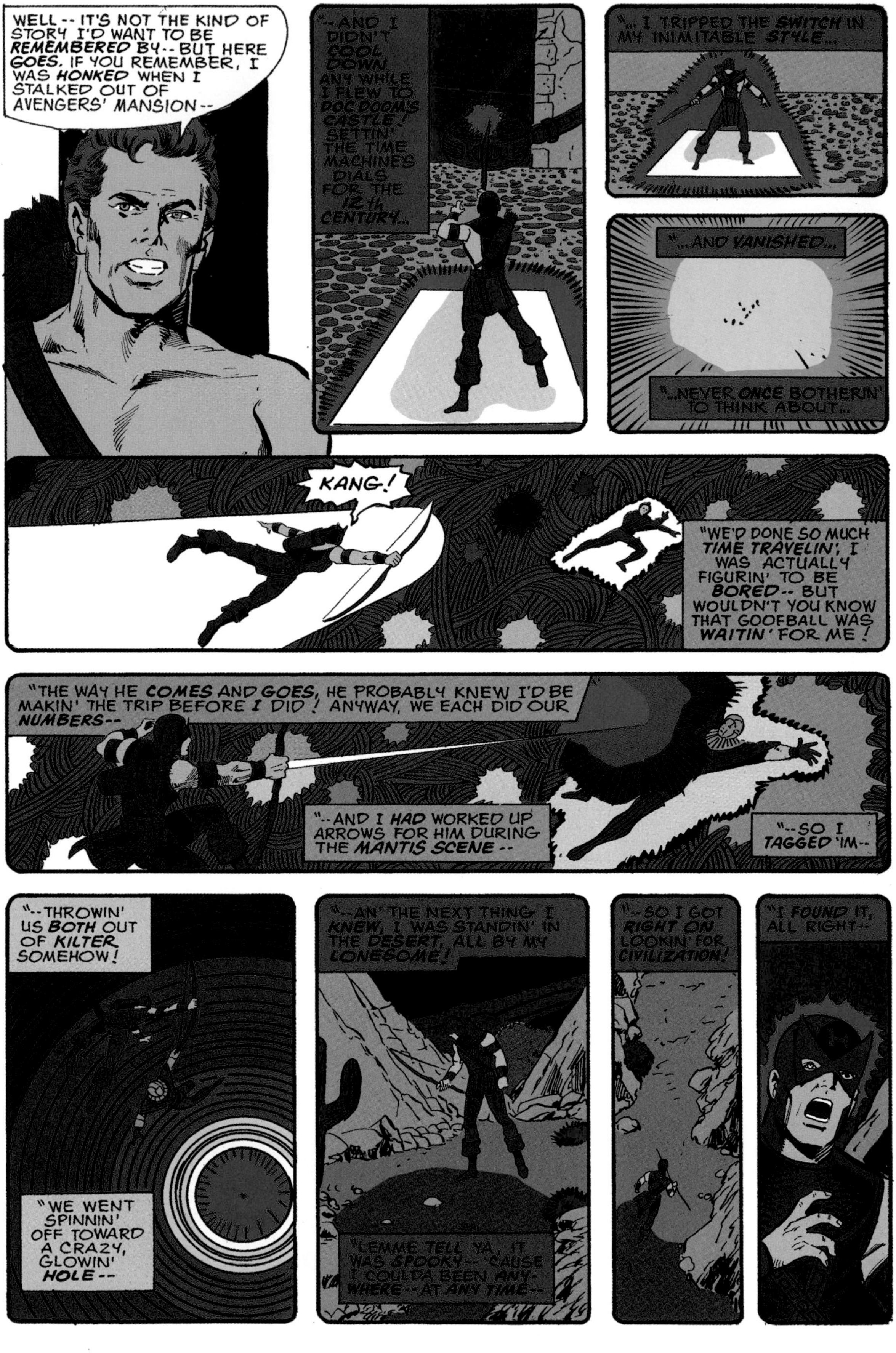

WELL -- IT'S NOT THE KIND OF STORY I'D WANT TO BE REMEMBERED BY -- BUT HERE GOES. IF YOU REMEMBER, I WAS HONKED WHEN I STALKED OUT OF AVENGERS' MANSION --
"-- AND I DIDN'T COOL DOWN ANY WHILE I FLEW TO DOC DOOM'S CASTLE! SETTIN' THE TIME MACHINE'S DIALS FOR THE 12th CENTURY...
"... I TRIPPED THE SWITCH IN MY INIMITABLE STYLE...
"...AND VANISHED...
"...NEVER ONCE BOTHERIN' TO THINK ABOUT...
KANG!
"WE'D DONE SO MUCH TIME TRAVELIN', I WAS ACTUALLY FIGURIN' TO BE BORED -- BUT WOULDN'T YOU KNOW THAT GOOFBALL WAS WAITIN' FOR ME!
"THE WAY HE COMES AND GOES, HE PROBABLY KNEW I'D BE MAKIN' THE TRIP BEFORE I DID! ANYWAY, WE EACH DID OUR NUMBERS --
"-- AND I HAD WORKED UP ARROWS FOR HIM DURING THE MANTIS SCENE --
"-- SO I TAGGED 'IM --
"-- THROWIN' US BOTH OUT OF KILTER SOMEHOW!
"WE WENT SPINNIN' OFF TOWARD A CRAZY, GLOWIN' HOLE --
"-- AN' THE NEXT THING I KNEW, I WAS STANDIN' IN THE DESERT, ALL BY MY LONESOME!
"LEMME TELL YA, IT WAS SPOOKY -- 'CAUSE I COULDA BEEN ANYWHERE -- AT ANY TIME --
"-- SO I GOT RIGHT ON LOOKIN' FOR CIVILIZATION!
"I FOUND IT, ALL RIGHT --

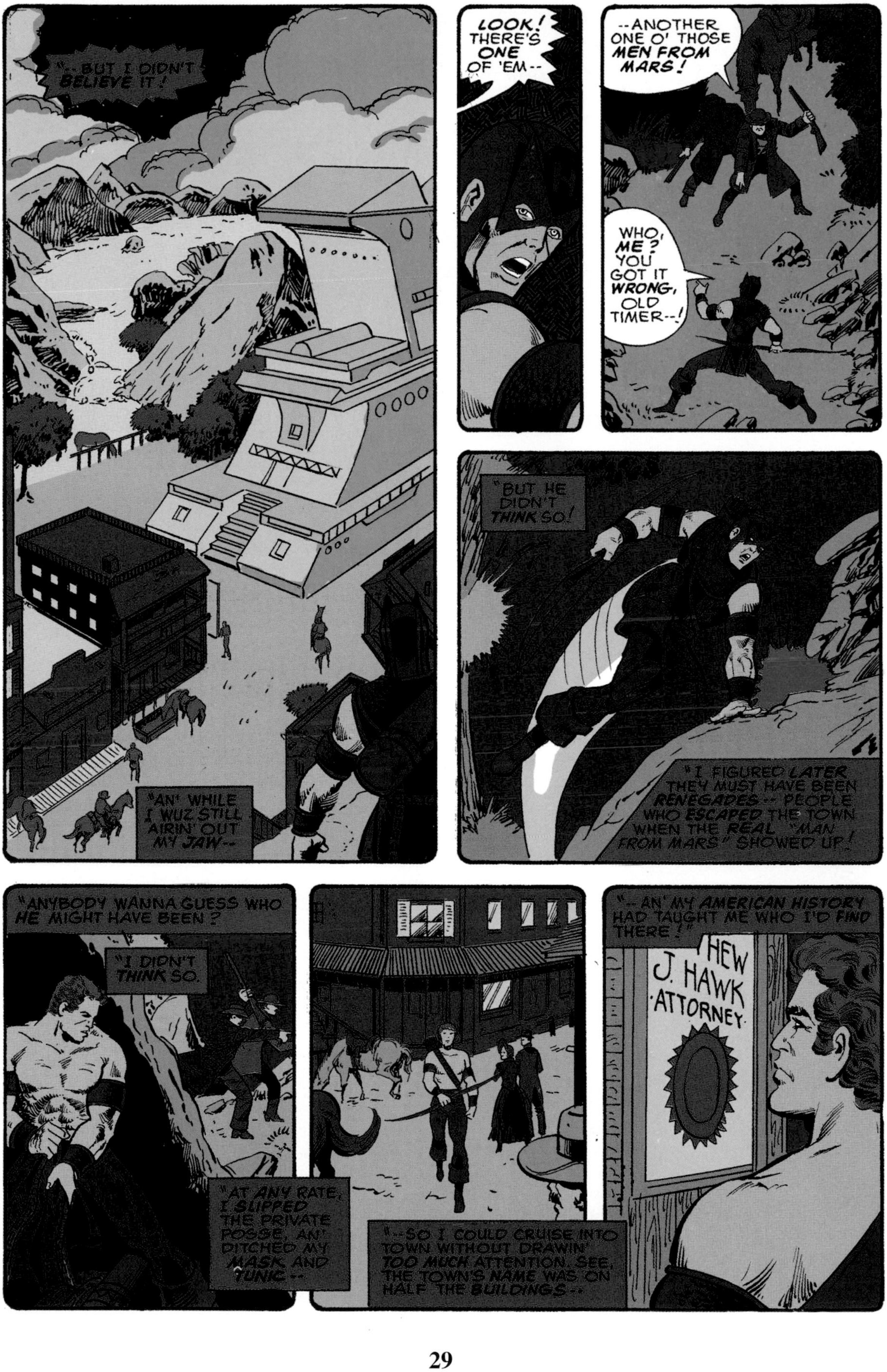
"--BUT I DIDN'T BELIEVE IT!
"AN' WHILE I WUZ STILL AIRIN' OUT MY JAW--
LOOK! THERE'S ONE OF 'EM--
--ANOTHER ONE O' THOSE MEN FROM MARS!
WHO, ME? YOU GOT IT WRONG, OLD TIMER--!
"BUT HE DIDN'T THINK SO!
"I FIGURED LATER THEY MUST HAVE BEEN RENEGADES--PEOPLE WHO ESCAPED THE TOWN WHEN THE REAL "MAN FROM MARS" SHOWED UP!
"ANYBODY WANNA GUESS WHO HE MIGHT HAVE BEEN?
"I DIDN'T THINK SO.
"AT ANY RATE, I SLIPPED THE PRIVATE POSSE, AN' DITCHED MY MASK AND TUNIC--
"--SO I COULD CRUISE INTO TOWN WITHOUT DRAWIN' TOO MUCH ATTENTION. SEE, THE TOWN'S NAME WAS ON HALF THE BUILDINGS--
"--AN' MY AMERICAN HISTORY HAD TAUGHT ME WHO I'D FIND THERE!"
HEW
J. HAWK
ATTORNEY

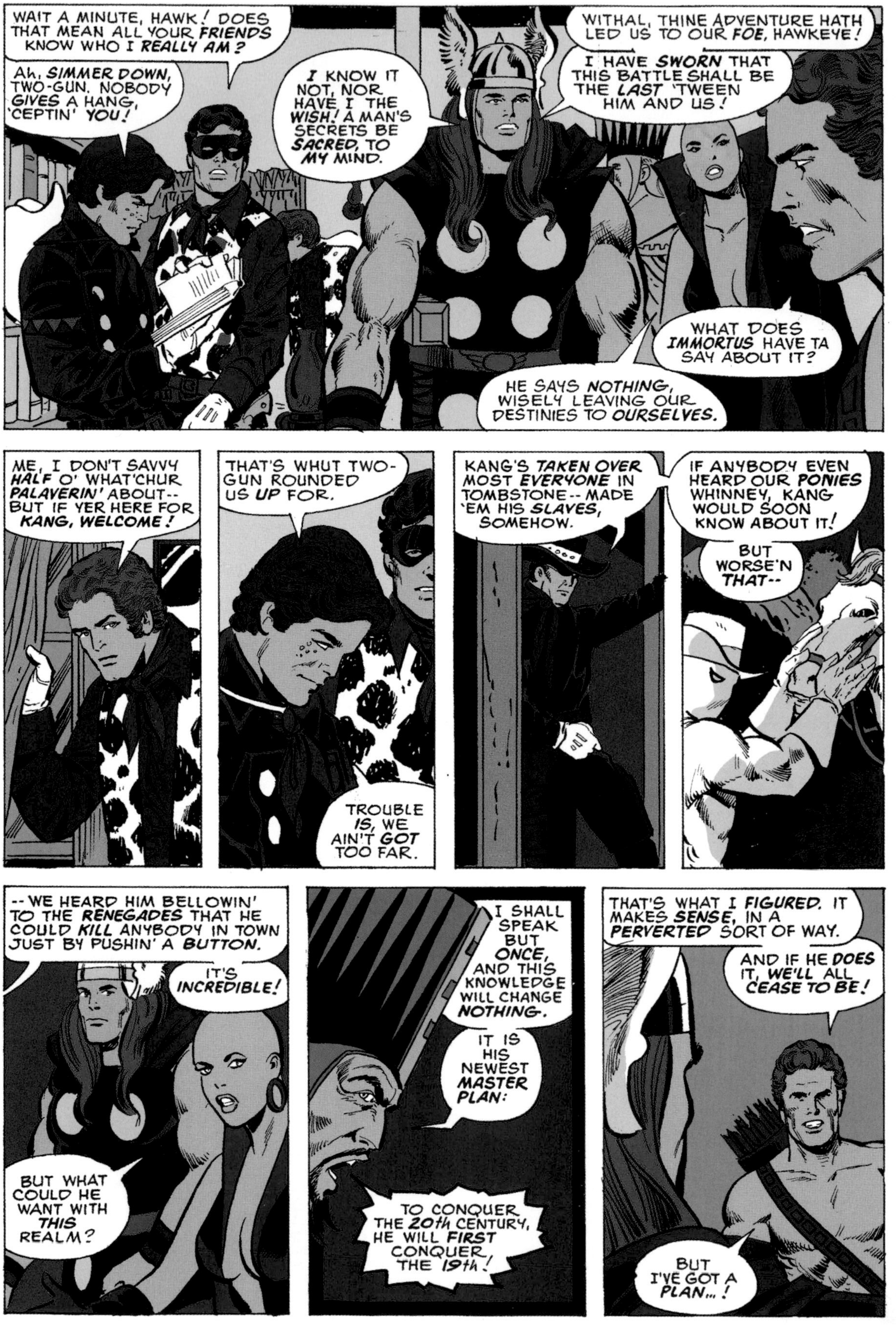
WAIT A MINUTE, HAWK! DOES THAT MEAN ALL YOUR FRIENDS KNOW WHO I REALLY AM?
AH, SIMMER DOWN, TWO-GUN. NOBODY GIVES A HANG, 'CEPTIN' YOU!
I KNOW IT NOT, NOR HAVE I THE WISH! A MAN'S SECRETS BE SACRED, TO MY MIND.
WITHAL, THINE ADVENTURE HATH LED US TO OUR FOE, HAWKEYE!
I HAVE SWORN THAT THIS BATTLE SHALL BE THE LAST 'TWEEN HIM AND US!
WHAT DOES IMMORTUS HAVE TA SAY ABOUT IT?
HE SAYS NOTHING, WISELY LEAVING OUR DESTINIES TO OURSELVES.
ME, I DON'T SAVVY HALF O' WHAT'CHUR PALAVERIN' ABOUT-- BUT IF YER HERE FOR KANG, WELCOME!
THAT'S WHUT TWO-GUN ROUNDED US UP FOR.
TROUBLE IS, WE AIN'T GOT TOO FAR.
KANG'S TAKEN OVER MOST EVERYONE IN TOMBSTONE-- MADE 'EM HIS SLAVES, SOMEHOW.
IF ANYBODY EVEN HEARD OUR PONIES WHINNEY, KANG WOULD SOON KNOW ABOUT IT!
BUT WORSE'N THAT--
--WE HEARD HIM BELLOWIN' TO THE RENEGADES THAT HE COULD KILL ANYBODY IN TOWN JUST BY PUSHIN' A BUTTON.
IT'S INCREDIBLE!
BUT WHAT COULD HE WANT WITH THIS REALM?
I SHALL SPEAK BUT ONCE, AND THIS KNOWLEDGE WILL CHANGE NOTHING.
IT IS HIS NEWEST MASTER PLAN:
TO CONQUER THE 20th CENTURY, HE WILL FIRST CONQUER THE 19th!
THAT'S WHAT I FIGURED. IT MAKES SENSE, IN A PERVERTED SORT OF WAY.
AND IF HE DOES IT, WE'LL ALL CEASE TO BE!
BUT I'VE GOT A PLAN...!

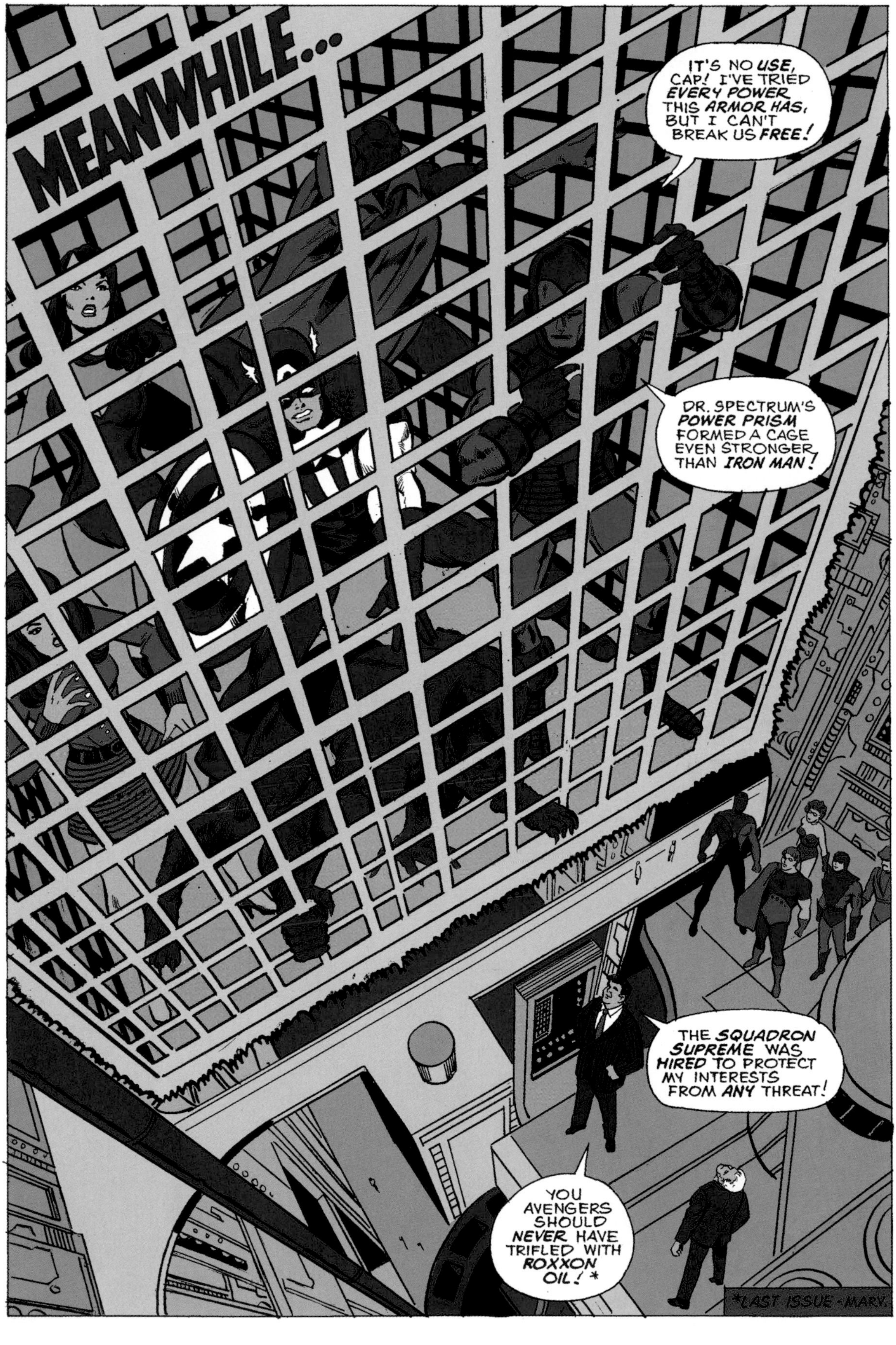
MEANWHILE...
IT'S NO USE, CAP! I'VE TRIED EVERY POWER THIS ARMOR HAS, BUT I CAN'T BREAK US FREE!
DR. SPECTRUM'S POWER PRISM FORMED A CAGE EVEN STRONGER THAN IRON MAN!
THE SQUADRON SUPREME WAS HIRED TO PROTECT MY INTERESTS FROM ANY THREAT!
YOU AVENGERS SHOULD NEVER HAVE TRIFLED WITH ROXXON OIL! *
*LAST ISSUE -MARV.

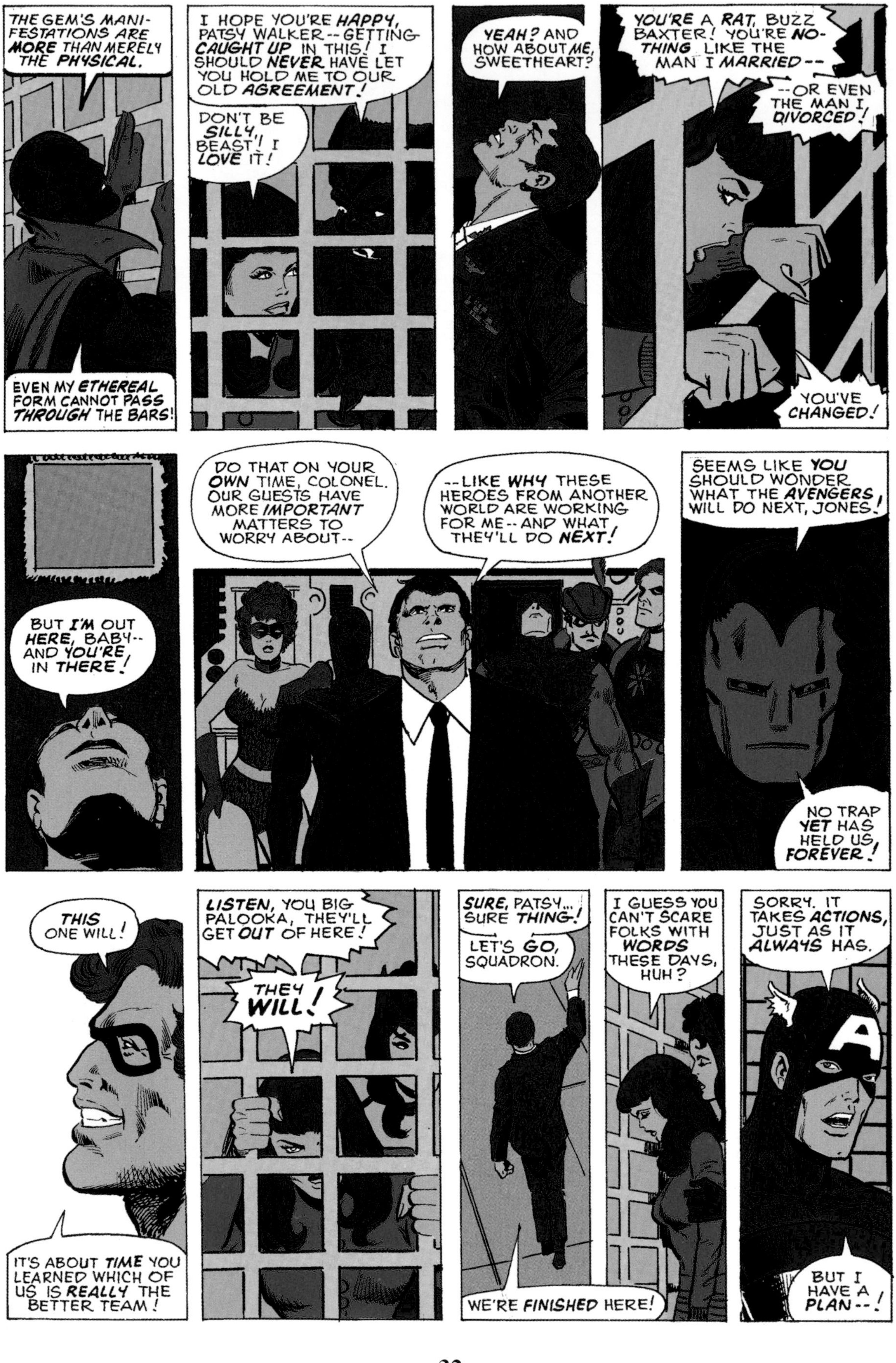
THE GEM'S MANI-FESTATIONS ARE MORE THAN MERELY THE PHYSICAL.
EVEN MY ETHEREAL FORM CANNOT PASS THROUGH THE BARS!
I HOPE YOU'RE HAPPY, PATSY WALKER -- GETTING CAUGHT UP IN THIS! I SHOULD NEVER HAVE LET YOU HOLD ME TO OUR OLD AGREEMENT!
DON'T BE SILLY, BEAST! I LOVE IT!
YEAH? AND HOW ABOUT ME, SWEETHEART?
YOU'RE A RAT, BUZZ BAXTER! YOU'RE NO-THING LIKE THE MAN I MARRIED --
--OR EVEN THE MAN I DIVORCED!
YOU'VE CHANGED!
BUT I'M OUT HERE, BABY-- AND YOU'RE IN THERE!
DO THAT ON YOUR OWN TIME, COLONEL. OUR GUESTS HAVE MORE IMPORTANT MATTERS TO WORRY ABOUT--
--LIKE WHY THESE HEROES FROM ANOTHER WORLD ARE WORKING FOR ME -- AND WHAT THEY'LL DO NEXT!
SEEMS LIKE YOU SHOULD WONDER WHAT THE AVENGERS WILL DO NEXT, JONES!
NO TRAP YET HAS HELD US, FOREVER!
THIS ONE WILL!
IT'S ABOUT TIME YOU LEARNED WHICH OF US IS REALLY THE BETTER TEAM!
LISTEN, YOU BIG PALOOKA, THEY'LL GET OUT OF HERE!
THEY WILL!
SURE, PATSY... SURE THING!
LET'S GO, SQUADRON.
WE'RE FINISHED HERE!
I GUESS YOU CAN'T SCARE FOLKS WITH WORDS THESE DAYS, HUH?
SORRY. IT TAKES ACTIONS, JUST AS IT ALWAYS HAS.
BUT I HAVE A PLAN--!

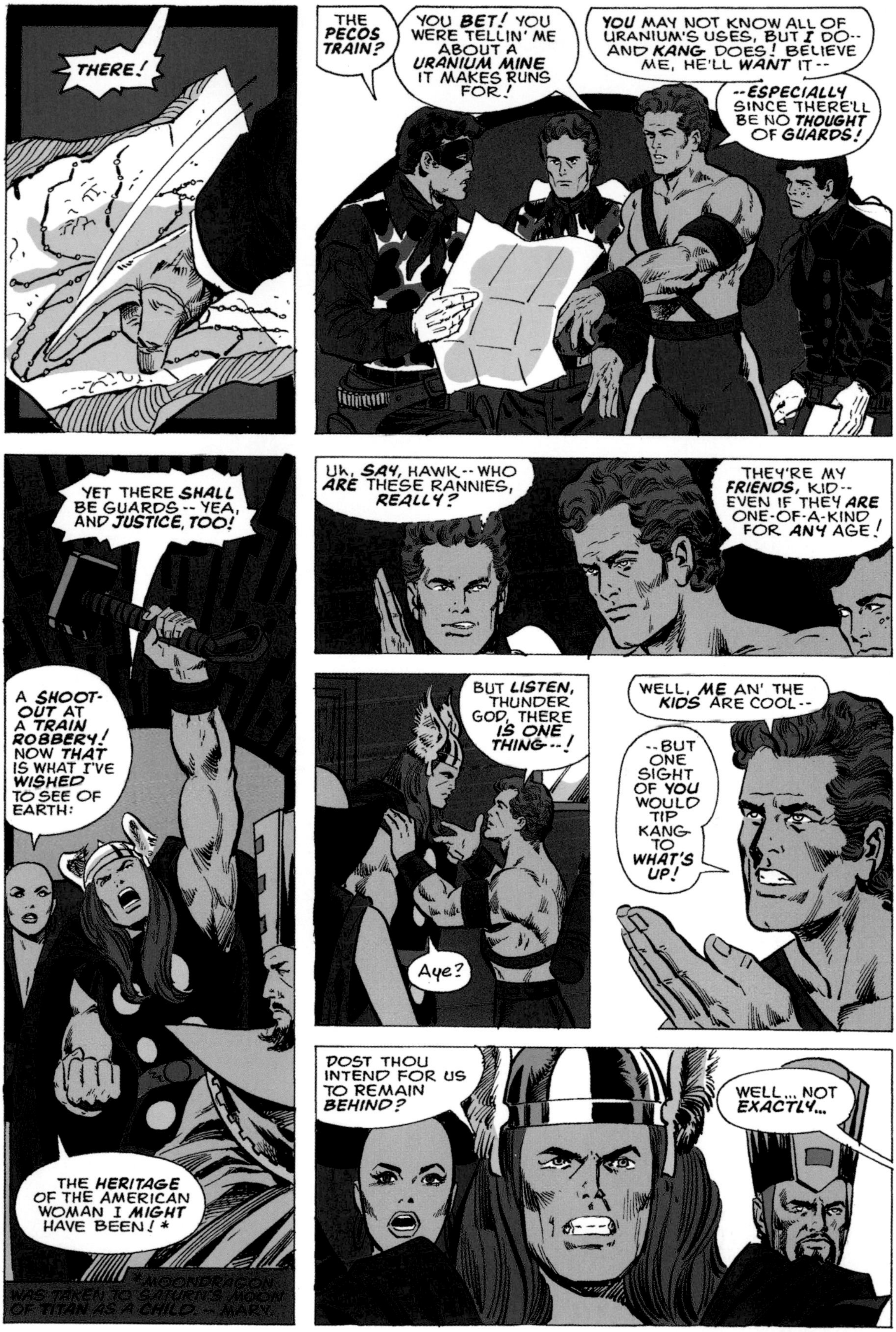
THERE!
THE PECOS TRAIN?
YOU BET! YOU WERE TELLIN' ME ABOUT A URANIUM MINE IT MAKES RUNS FOR!
YOU MAY NOT KNOW ALL OF URANIUM'S USES, BUT I DO-- AND KANG DOES! BELIEVE ME, HE'LL WANT IT--
--ESPECIALLY SINCE THERE'LL BE NO THOUGHT OF GUARDS!
YET THERE SHALL BE GUARDS -- YEA, AND JUSTICE, TOO!
A SHOOT-OUT AT A TRAIN ROBBERY! NOW THAT IS WHAT I'VE WISHED TO SEE OF EARTH:
THE HERITAGE OF THE AMERICAN WOMAN I MIGHT HAVE BEEN! *
*MOONDRAGON WAS TAKEN TO SATURN'S MOON OF TITAN AS A CHILD. -- MARY.
UH, SAY, HAWK -- WHO ARE THESE RANNIES, REALLY?
THEY'RE MY FRIENDS, KID -- EVEN IF THEY ARE ONE-OF-A-KIND FOR ANY AGE!
BUT LISTEN, THUNDER GOD, THERE IS ONE THING--!
Aye?
WELL, ME AN' THE KIDS ARE COOL--
--BUT ONE SIGHT OF YOU WOULD TIP KANG TO WHAT'S UP!
DOST THOU INTEND FOR US TO REMAIN BEHIND?
WELL... NOT EXACTLY...

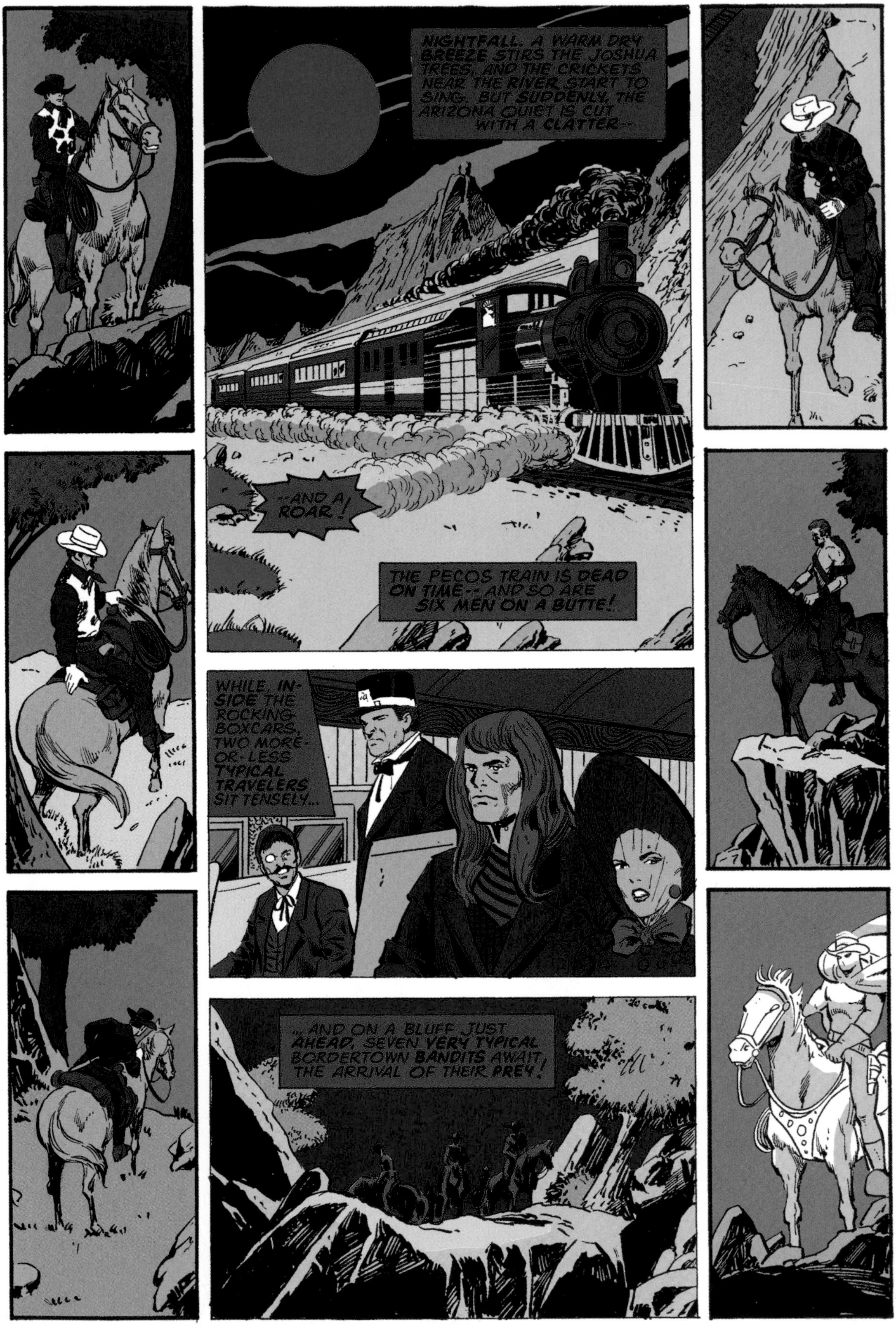
NIGHTFALL. A WARM DRY BREEZE STIRS THE JOSHUA TREES, AND THE CRICKETS NEAR THE RIVER START TO SING. BUT SUDDENLY, THE ARIZONA QUIET IS CUT WITH A CLATTER--
--AND A ROAR!
THE PECOS TRAIN IS DEAD ON TIME-- AND SO ARE SIX MEN ON A BUTTE!
WHILE, INSIDE THE ROCKING BOXCARS, TWO MORE-OR-LESS TYPICAL TRAVELERS SIT TENSELY...
...AND ON A BLUFF JUST AHEAD, SEVEN VERY TYPICAL BORDERTOWN BANDITS AWAIT THE ARRIVAL OF THEIR PREY!

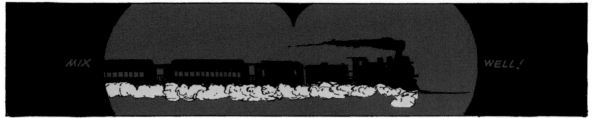

MIX

WELL!

LET'S *TAKE* 'ER, BOYS!

SHE'S AS RIPE FOR *MILKIN'* AS A SOW A WEEK *STRAYED!*

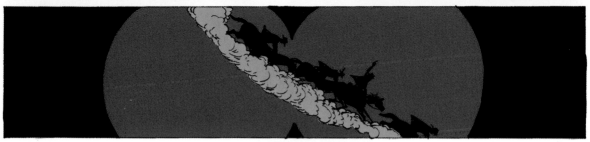

THERE GO THE SLICKERS WE'VE BEEN *WAITIN'* FOR. DON'T SEE *KANG* WITH 'EM, THOUGH.

WELL, WE DON'T REALLY *NEED* 'IM! WE'LL GET WHAT WE WANT JUST THE *SAME*, OR MY NAME'S NOT --

-- THE *HAWKEYE* KID!

THE *SIGNAL!*

TIME TO RIDE INTO ACTION! BUT WHO WOULD HAVE THOUGHT--

-- THAT WHEN I CHOSE TO MAINTAIN A *SECRET IDENTITY,* SUCH PEOPLE AS "*THE AVENGERS*" WOULD *FOLLOW!*

GODS!

I'VE MET *GODS!*

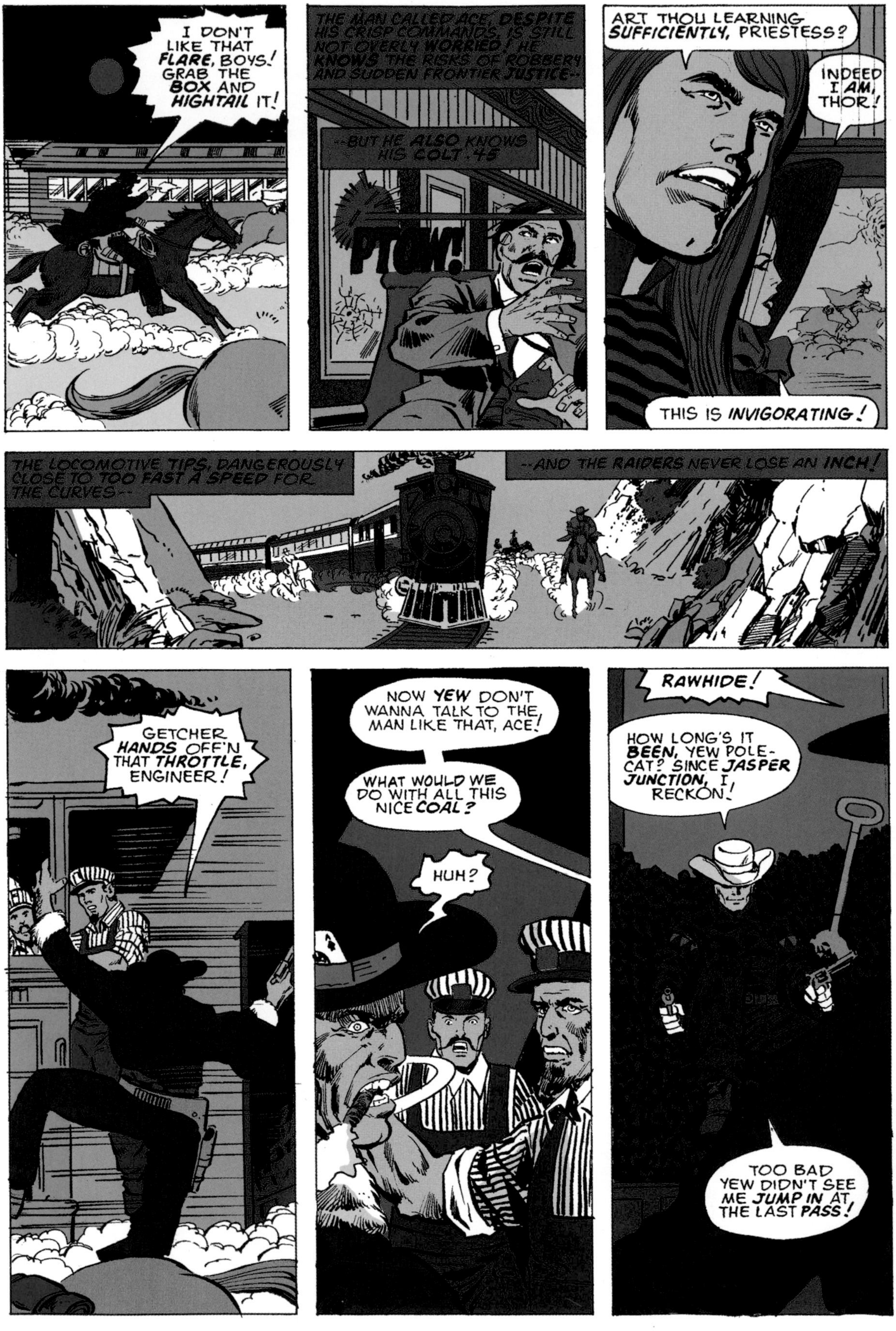
I DON'T LIKE THAT FLARE, BOYS! GRAB THE BOX AND HIGHTAIL IT!
THE MAN CALLED ACE, DESPITE HIS CRISP COMMANDS, IS STILL NOT OVERLY WORRIED! HE KNOWS THE RISKS OF ROBBERY AND SUDDEN FRONTIER JUSTICE--
--BUT HE ALSO KNOWS HIS COLT .45
PTOW!
ART THOU LEARNING SUFFICIENTLY, PRIESTESS?
INDEED I AM, THOR!
THIS IS INVIGORATING!
THE LOCOMOTIVE TIPS, DANGEROUSLY CLOSE TO TOO FAST A SPEED FOR THE CURVES--
--AND THE RAIDERS NEVER LOSE AN INCH!
GETCHER HANDS OFF'N THAT THROTTLE, ENGINEER!
NOW YEW DON'T WANNA TALK TO THE MAN LIKE THAT, ACE!
WHAT WOULD WE DO WITH ALL THIS NICE COAL?
HUH?
RAWHIDE!
HOW LONG'S IT BEEN, YEW POLE-CAT? SINCE JASPER JUNCTION, I RECKON!
TOO BAD YEW DIDN'T SEE ME JUMP IN AT THE LAST PASS!

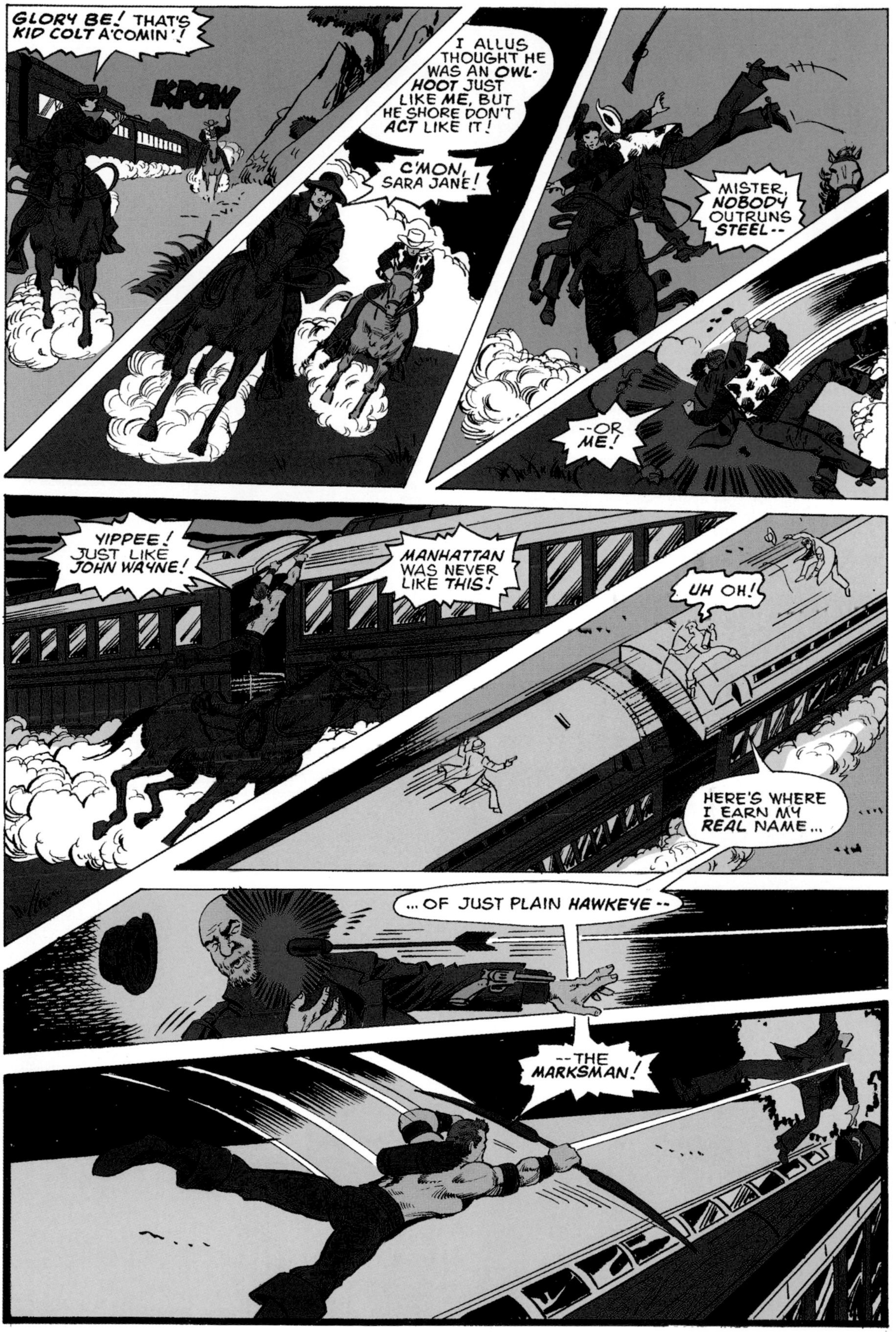
GLORY BE! THAT'S KID COLT A'COMIN'!
KPOW
I ALLUS THOUGHT HE WAS AN OWL-HOOT JUST LIKE ME, BUT HE SHORE DON'T ACT LIKE IT!
C'MON, SARA JANE!
MISTER, NOBODY OUTRUNS STEEL--
--OR ME!
YIPPEE! JUST LIKE JOHN WAYNE!
MANHATTAN WAS NEVER LIKE THIS!
UH OH!
HERE'S WHERE I EARN MY REAL NAME...
...OF JUST PLAIN HAWKEYE--
--THE MARKSMAN!

PARDNER, I *SEEN* WHAT YOUR BOSS DID TO THE FOLKS IN *TOMBSTONE* --

WOP!

-- AN' I DIDN'T *LIKE* IT ONE *BIT!*

ANY MAN THAT'D HIRE HIS GUN TO THAT *KANG* RANNY AIN'T EVEN WORTH THE PRICE OF A *BULLET!*

POW!

MY *FISTS* ARE ALL --

AW SHUCKS!

HE AIN'T *LISTENIN'!*

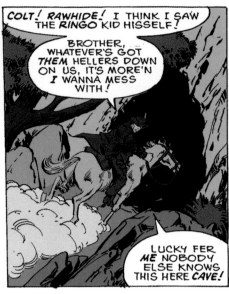

COLT! RAWHIDE! I THINK I SAW THE *RINGO* KID HISSELF!

BROTHER, WHATEVER'S GOT *THEM* HELLERS DOWN ON US, IT'S MORE'N *I* WANNA MESS WITH!

LUCKY FER *ME* NOBODY ELSE KNOWS THIS HERE *CAVE!*

WRONG, MORTAL: THE SON OF THE SPIRITS KNOWS *ALL!*

OH MUH GAWD! THE N-NIGHT RIDER!

THIS IS *TOO MUCH!* THERE AIN'T *NOTHIN'* ANY WORSE --

WUMP!

ALL *RIGHT,* INJUN-MAN -- YUH GOT MUH *SIDE-KICKS* --

-- BUT AH'M RIGHT *BEHIND* 'EM --

-- AN' SINCE I *ALREADY* GOT MY GUN POINTED AT YER *LIVER*..

-- YER GONNA *PAY!*

G'WAN! WHY DON'TCHA TRY SOMETHIN' FANCY...?

38

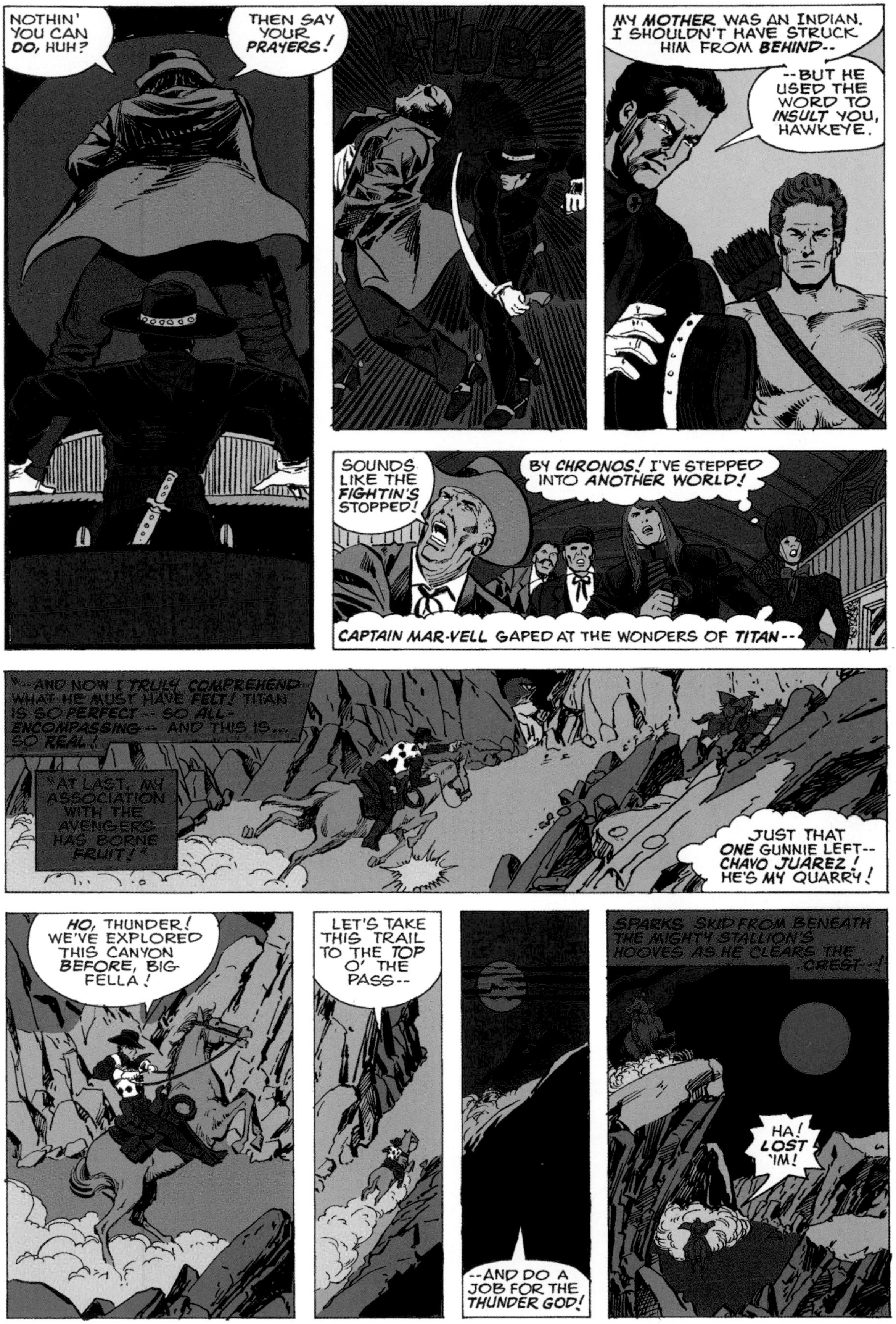
NOTHIN' YOU CAN DO, HUH?
THEN SAY YOUR PRAYERS!
MY MOTHER WAS AN INDIAN. I SHOULDN'T HAVE STRUCK HIM FROM BEHIND--
--BUT HE USED THE WORD TO INSULT YOU, HAWKEYE.
SOUNDS LIKE THE FIGHTIN'S STOPPED!
BY CHRONOS! I'VE STEPPED INTO ANOTHER WORLD!
CAPTAIN MAR-VELL GAPED AT THE WONDERS OF TITAN--
"--AND NOW I TRULY COMPREHEND WHAT HE MUST HAVE FELT! TITAN IS SO PERFECT -- SO ALL-ENCOMPASSING -- AND THIS IS... SO REAL!
"AT LAST, MY ASSOCIATION WITH THE AVENGERS HAS BORNE FRUIT!"
JUST THAT ONE GUNNIE LEFT-- CHAVO JUAREZ! HE'S MY QUARRY!
HO, THUNDER! WE'VE EXPLORED THIS CANYON BEFORE, BIG FELLA!
LET'S TAKE THIS TRAIL TO THE TOP O' THE PASS--
--AND DO A JOB FOR THE THUNDER GOD!
SPARKS SKID FROM BENEATH THE MIGHTY STALLION'S HOOVES AS HE CLEARS THE CREST--!
HA! LOST 'IM!

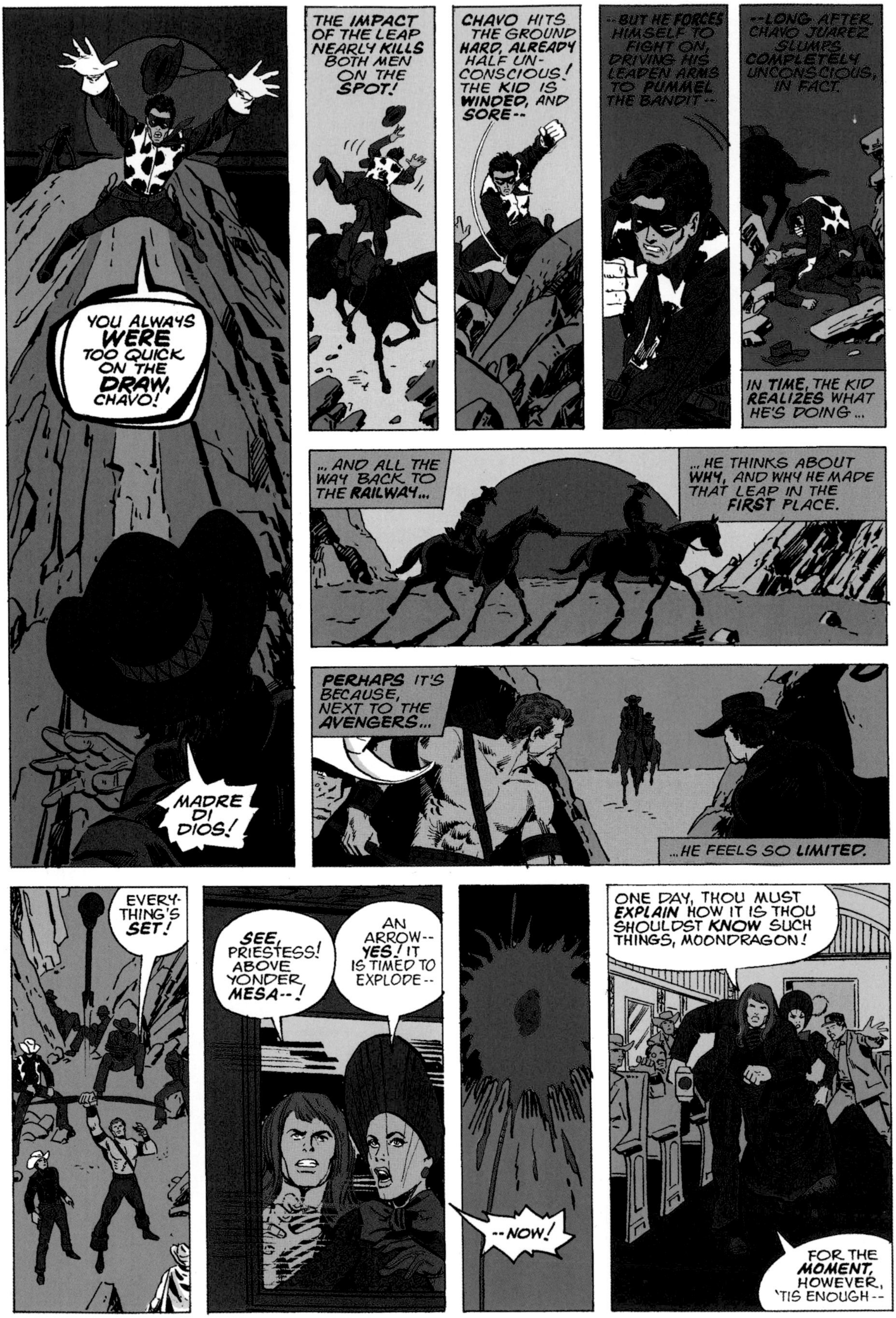
YOU ALWAYS WERE TOO QUICK ON THE DRAW, CHAVO!
MADRE DI DIOS!
THE IMPACT OF THE LEAP NEARLY KILLS BOTH MEN ON THE SPOT!
CHAVO HITS THE GROUND HARD, ALREADY HALF UN-CONSCIOUS! THE KID IS WINDED, AND SORE--
--BUT HE FORCES HIMSELF TO FIGHT ON, DRIVING HIS LEADEN ARMS TO PUMMEL THE BANDIT--
--LONG AFTER CHAVO JUAREZ SLUMPS COMPLETELY UNCONSCIOUS, IN FACT.
IN TIME, THE KID REALIZES WHAT HE'S DOING...
...AND ALL THE WAY BACK TO THE RAILWAY...
...HE THINKS ABOUT WHY, AND WHY HE MADE THAT LEAP IN THE FIRST PLACE.
PERHAPS IT'S BECAUSE, NEXT TO THE AVENGERS...
...HE FEELS SO LIMITED.
EVERY-THING'S SET!
SEE, PRIESTESS! ABOVE YONDER MESA--!
AN ARROW--YES! IT IS TIMED TO EXPLODE--
--NOW!
ONE DAY, THOU MUST EXPLAIN HOW IT IS THOU SHOULDST KNOW SUCH THINGS, MOONDRAGON!
FOR THE MOMENT, HOWEVER, 'TIS ENOUGH--

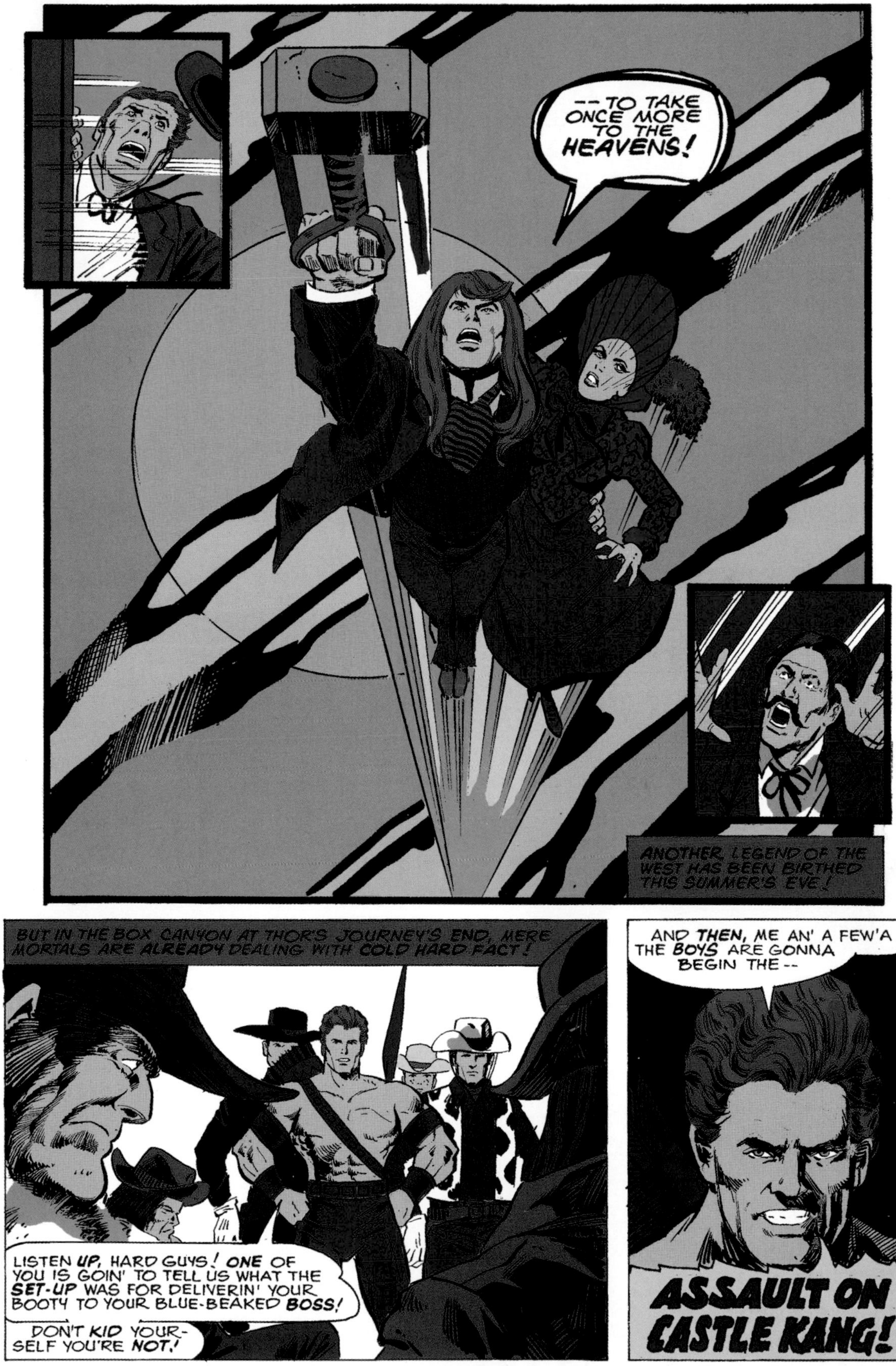
-- TO TAKE ONCE MORE TO THE HEAVENS!
ANOTHER LEGEND OF THE WEST HAS BEEN BIRTHED THIS SUMMER'S EVE!
BUT IN THE BOX CANYON AT THOR'S JOURNEY'S END, MERE MORTALS ARE ALREADY DEALING WITH COLD HARD FACT!
LISTEN UP, HARD GUYS! ONE OF YOU IS GOIN' TO TELL US WHAT THE SET-UP WAS FOR DELIVERIN' YOUR BOOTY TO YOUR BLUE-BEAKED BOSS!
DON'T KID YOURSELF YOU'RE NOT!
AND THEN, ME AN' A FEW'A THE BOYS ARE GONNA BEGIN THE --
ASSAULT ON CASTLE KANG!

MARVEL COMICS GROUP
APPROVED BY THE COMICS CODE AUTHORITY
25¢
143
JAN
02458
EARTH'S MIGHTIEST HEROES!
the AVENGERS
AVENGERS ASSEMBLE!!
AT LAST!! THE FINAL BATTLE AGAINST THE POWER OF KANG!
THE AVENGERS BREAK LOOSE!

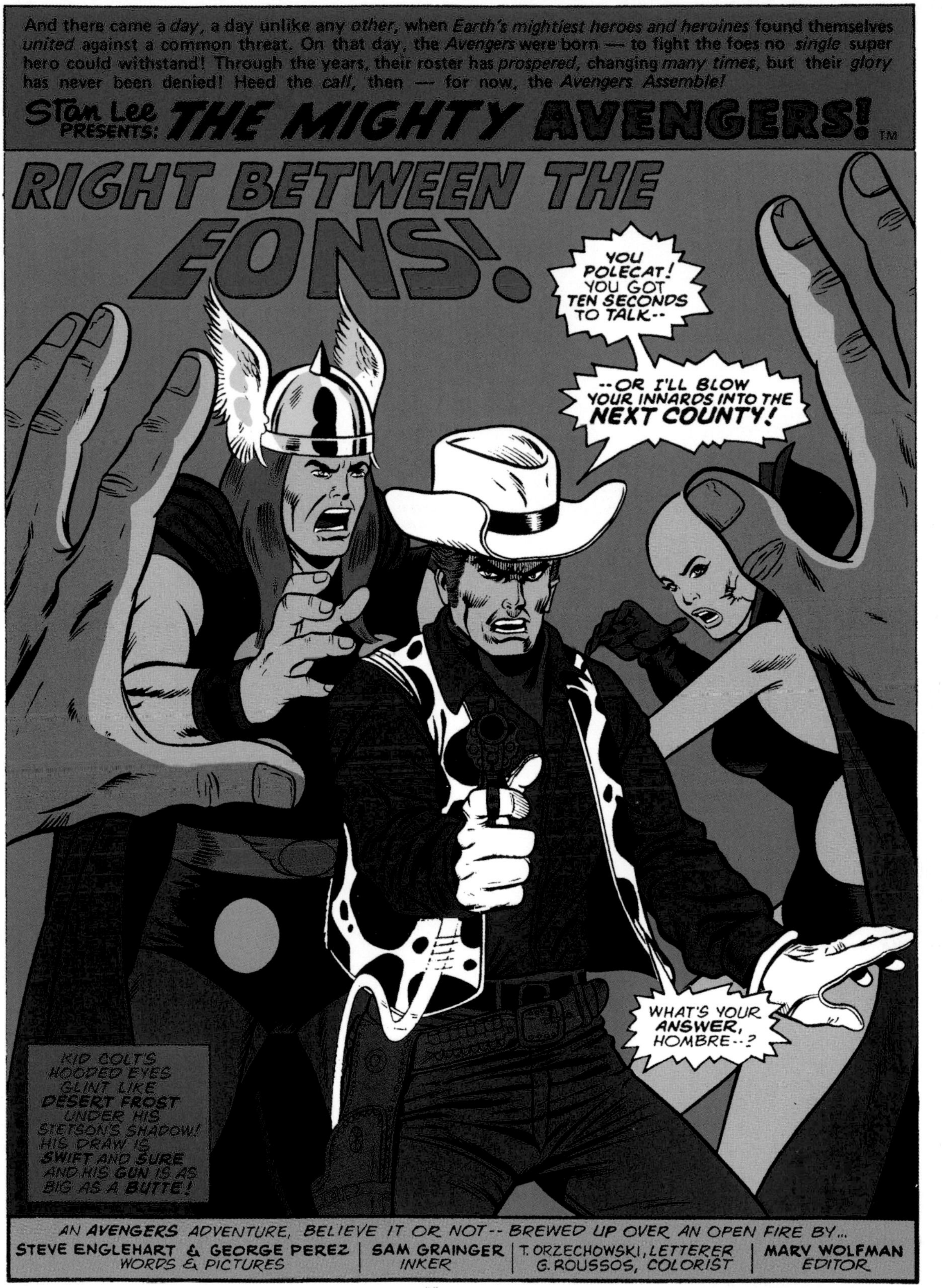
And there came a *day*, a day unlike any *other*, when *Earth's mightiest heroes and heroines* found themselves *united* against a common threat. On that day, the *Avengers* were born — to fight the foes no *single* super hero could withstand! Through the years, their roster has *prospered*, changing *many times*, but their *glory* has never been denied! Heed the *call*, then — for now, the *Avengers Assemble!*
Stan Lee PRESENTS: THE MIGHTY AVENGERS! TM
RIGHT BETWEEN THE EONS!
YOU POLECAT! YOU GOT TEN SECONDS TO TALK--
--OR I'LL BLOW YOUR INNARDS INTO THE NEXT COUNTY!
WHAT'S YOUR ANSWER, HOMBRE--?
KID COLT'S HOODED EYES GLINT LIKE DESERT FROST UNDER HIS STETSON'S SHADOW! HIS DRAW IS SWIFT AND SURE AND HIS GUN IS AS BIG AS A BUTTE!
AN AVENGERS ADVENTURE, BELIEVE IT OR NOT-- BREWED UP OVER AN OPEN FIRE BY...
STEVE ENGLEHART & GEORGE PEREZ WORDS & PICTURES | SAM GRAINGER INKER | T. ORZECHOWSKI, LETTERER G. ROUSSOS, COLORIST | MARV WOLFMAN EDITOR

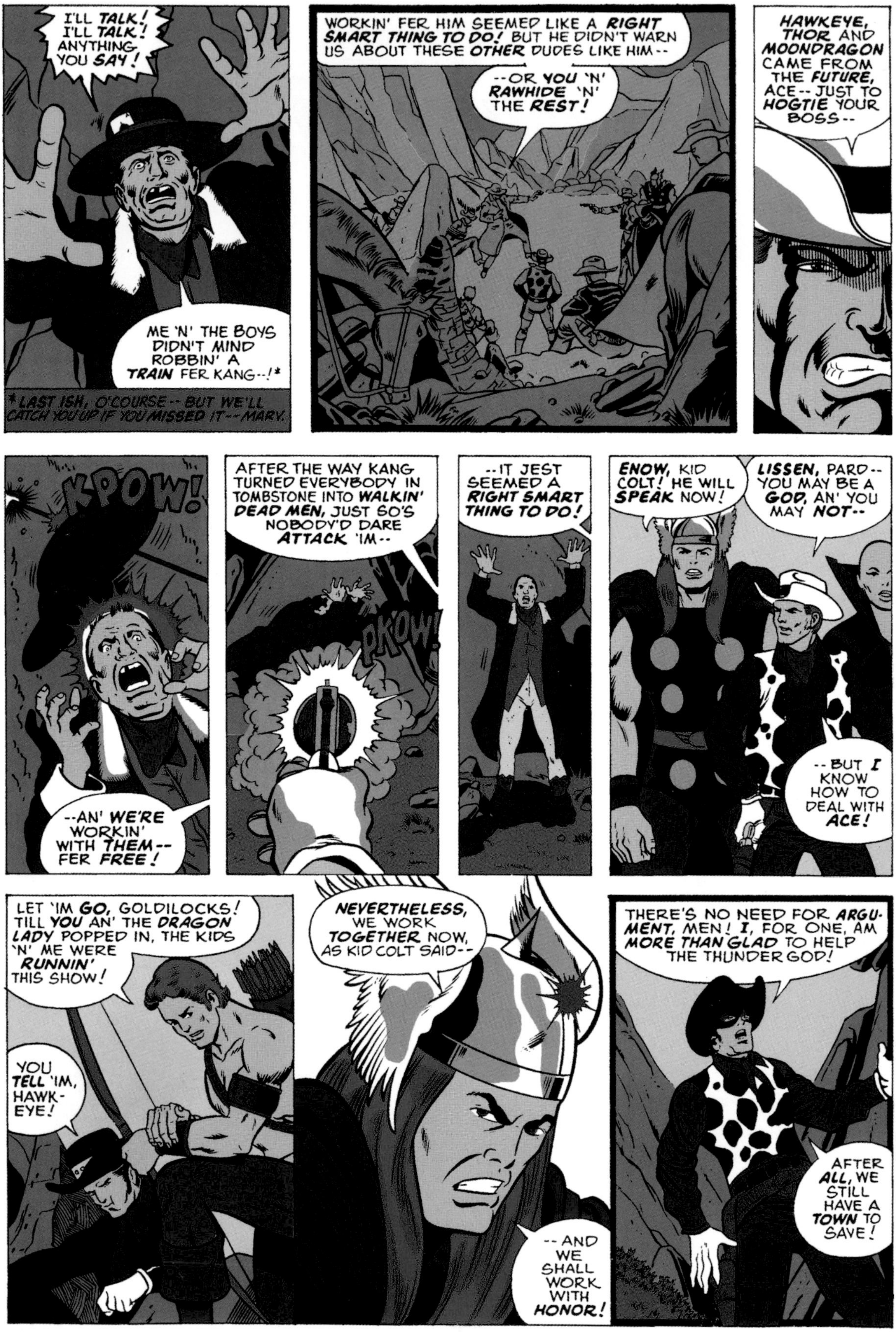
I'LL TALK! I'LL TALK! ANYTHING YOU SAY!
ME 'N' THE BOYS DIDN'T MIND ROBBIN' A TRAIN FER KANG--!*
* LAST ISH, O'COURSE -- BUT WE'LL CATCH YOU UP IF YOU MISSED IT -- MARV.
WORKIN' FER HIM SEEMED LIKE A RIGHT SMART THING TO DO! BUT HE DIDN'T WARN US ABOUT THESE OTHER DUDES LIKE HIM --
--OR YOU 'N' RAWHIDE 'N' THE REST!
HAWKEYE, THOR AND MOONDRAGON CAME FROM THE FUTURE, ACE -- JUST TO HOGTIE YOUR BOSS --
KPOW!
--AN' WE'RE WORKIN' WITH THEM -- FER FREE!
AFTER THE WAY KANG TURNED EVERYBODY IN TOMBSTONE INTO WALKIN' DEAD MEN, JUST SO'S NOBODY'D DARE ATTACK 'IM --
PKOW!
--IT JEST SEEMED A RIGHT SMART THING TO DO!
ENOW, KID COLT! HE WILL SPEAK NOW!
LISSEN, PARD -- YOU MAY BE A GOD, AN' YOU MAY NOT --
-- BUT I KNOW HOW TO DEAL WITH ACE!
LET 'IM GO, GOLDILOCKS! TILL YOU AN' THE DRAGON LADY POPPED IN, THE KIDS 'N' ME WERE RUNNIN' THIS SHOW!
YOU TELL 'IM, HAWKEYE!
NEVERTHELESS, WE WORK TOGETHER NOW, AS KID COLT SAID --
-- AND WE SHALL WORK WITH HONOR!
THERE'S NO NEED FOR ARGUMENT, MEN! I, FOR ONE, AM MORE THAN GLAD TO HELP THE THUNDER GOD!
AFTER ALL, WE STILL HAVE A TOWN TO SAVE!

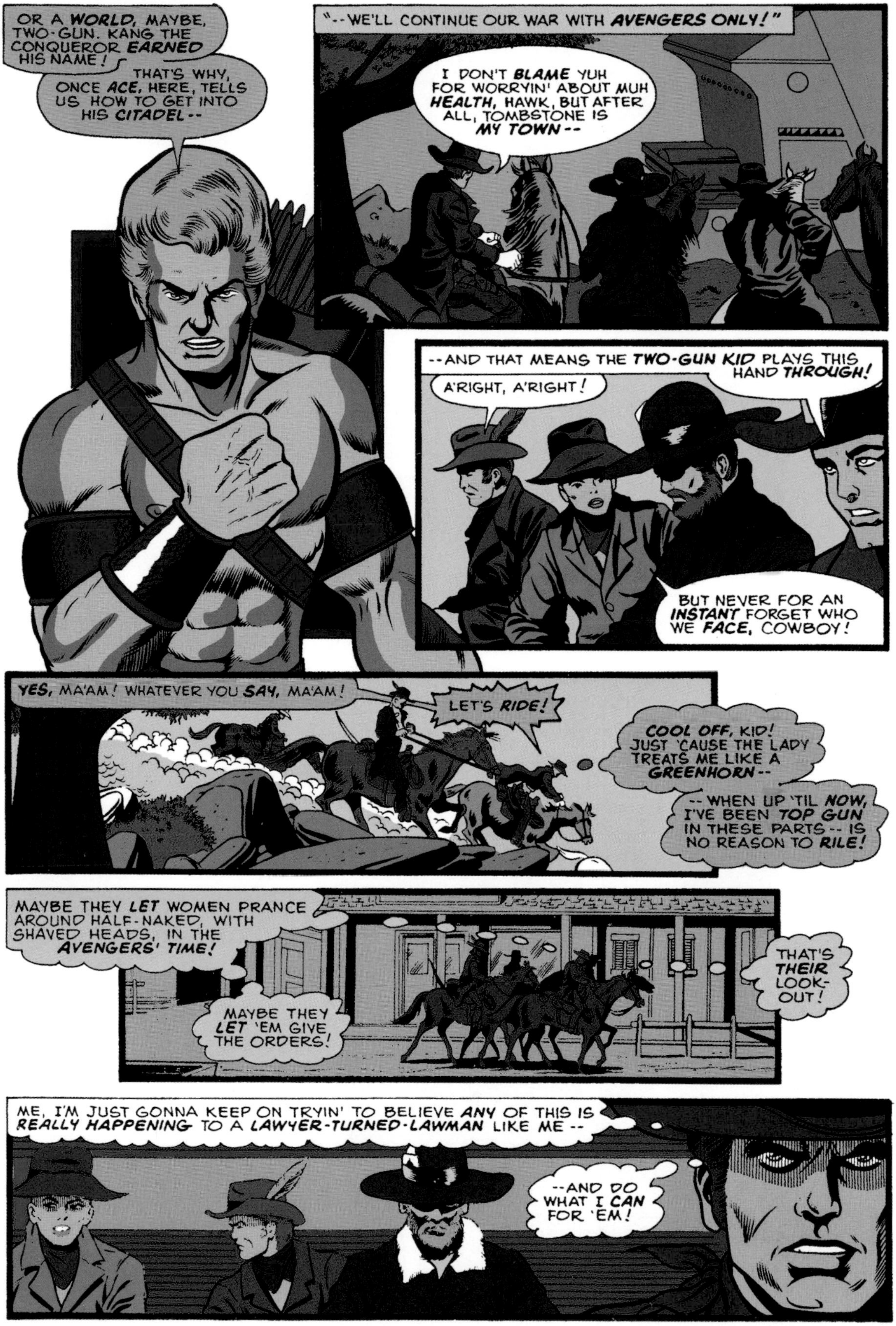

OR A WORLD, MAYBE, TWO-GUN. KANG THE CONQUEROR EARNED HIS NAME!
THAT'S WHY, ONCE ACE, HERE, TELLS US HOW TO GET INTO HIS CITADEL --
"-- WE'LL CONTINUE OUR WAR WITH AVENGERS ONLY!"
I DON'T BLAME YUH FOR WORRYIN' ABOUT MUH HEALTH, HAWK, BUT AFTER ALL, TOMBSTONE IS MY TOWN --
-- AND THAT MEANS THE TWO-GUN KID PLAYS THIS HAND THROUGH!
A'RIGHT, A'RIGHT!
BUT NEVER FOR AN INSTANT FORGET WHO WE FACE, COWBOY!
YES, MA'AM! WHATEVER YOU SAY, MA'AM!
LET'S RIDE!
COOL OFF, KID! JUST 'CAUSE THE LADY TREATS ME LIKE A GREENHORN --
-- WHEN UP 'TIL NOW, I'VE BEEN TOP GUN IN THESE PARTS -- IS NO REASON TO RILE!
MAYBE THEY LET WOMEN PRANCE AROUND HALF-NAKED, WITH SHAVED HEADS, IN THE AVENGERS' TIME!
MAYBE THEY LET 'EM GIVE THE ORDERS!
THAT'S THEIR LOOK-OUT!
ME, I'M JUST GONNA KEEP ON TRYIN' TO BELIEVE ANY OF THIS IS REALLY HAPPENING TO A LAWYER-TURNED-LAWMAN LIKE ME --
-- AND DO WHAT I CAN FOR 'EM!

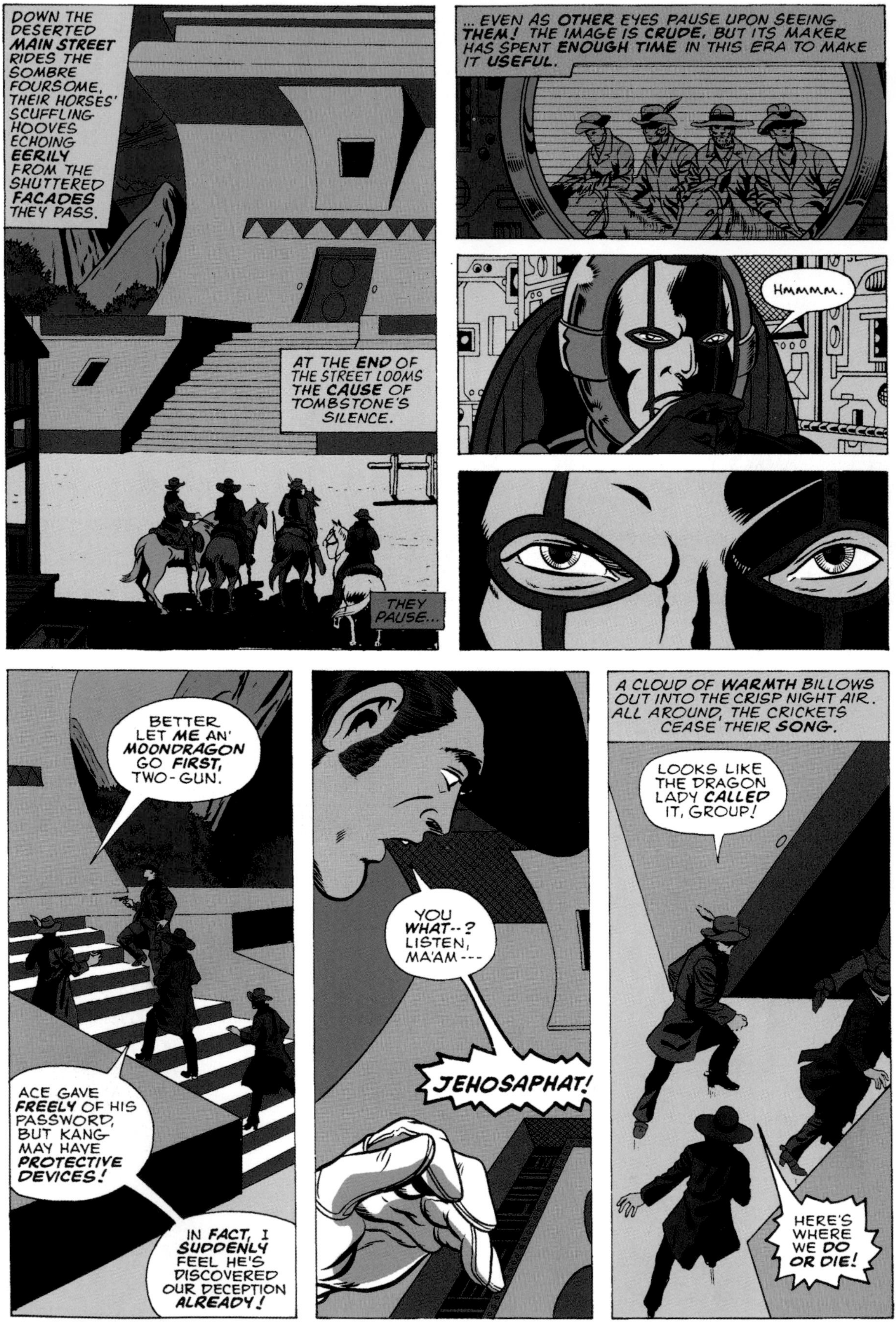
DOWN THE DESERTED MAIN STREET RIDES THE SOMBRE FOURSOME, THEIR HORSES' SCUFFLING HOOVES ECHOING EERILY FROM THE SHUTTERED FACADES THEY PASS.
AT THE END OF THE STREET LOOMS THE CAUSE OF TOMBSTONE'S SILENCE.
THEY PAUSE...
... EVEN AS OTHER EYES PAUSE UPON SEEING THEM! THE IMAGE IS CRUDE, BUT ITS MAKER HAS SPENT ENOUGH TIME IN THIS ERA TO MAKE IT USEFUL.
HMMMM.
BETTER LET ME AN' MOONDRAGON GO FIRST, TWO-GUN.
ACE GAVE FREELY OF HIS PASSWORD, BUT KANG MAY HAVE PROTECTIVE DEVICES!
IN FACT, I SUDDENLY FEEL HE'S DISCOVERED OUR DECEPTION ALREADY!
YOU WHAT--? LISTEN, MA'AM---
JEHOSAPHAT!
A CLOUD OF WARMTH BILLOWS OUT INTO THE CRISP NIGHT AIR. ALL AROUND, THE CRICKETS CEASE THEIR SONG.
LOOKS LIKE THE DRAGON LADY CALLED IT, GROUP!
HERE'S WHERE WE DO OR DIE!

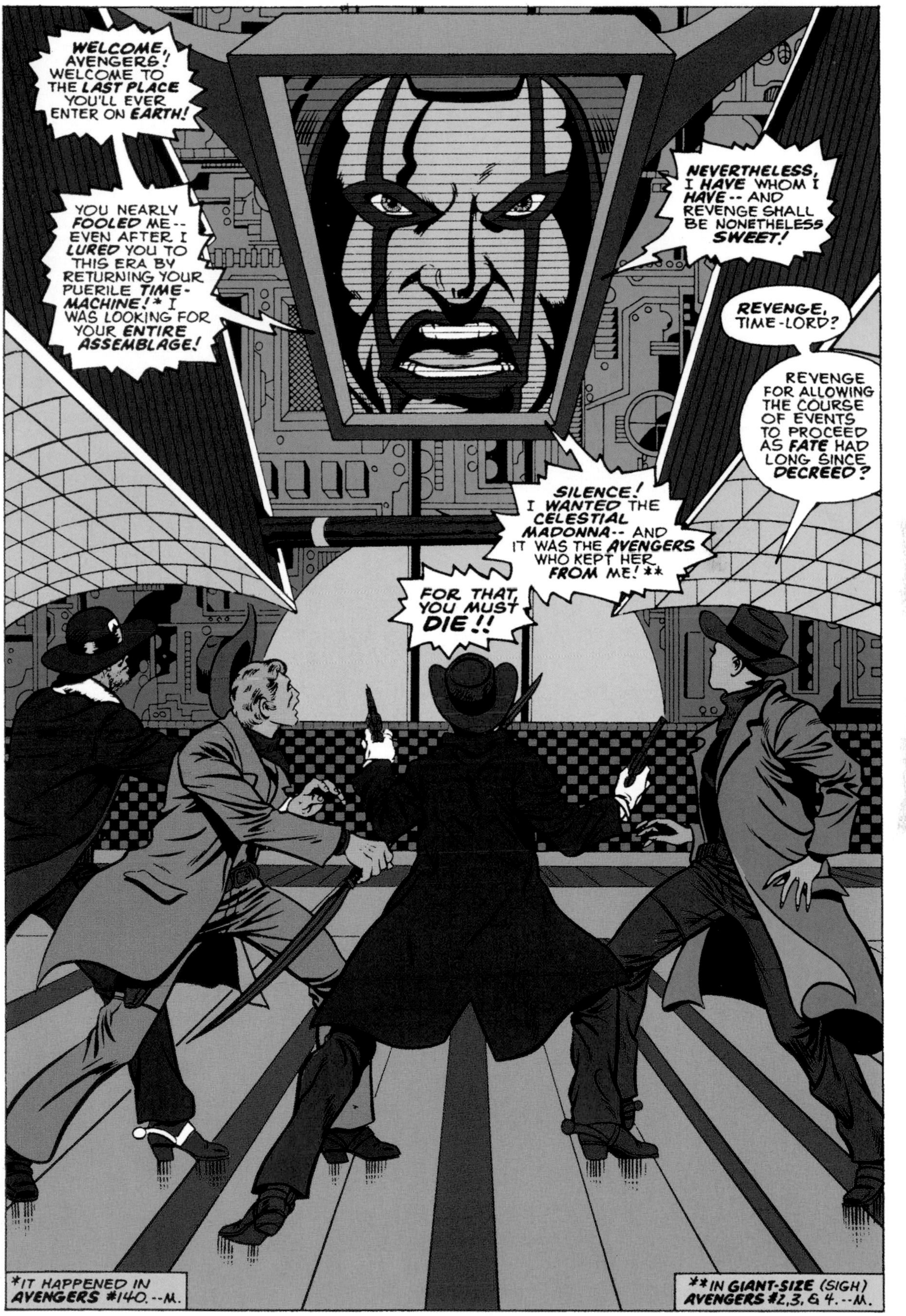
WELCOME, AVENGERS! WELCOME TO THE LAST PLACE YOU'LL EVER ENTER ON EARTH!
YOU NEARLY FOOLED ME -- EVEN AFTER I LURED YOU TO THIS ERA BY RETURNING YOUR PUERILE TIME-MACHINE!* I WAS LOOKING FOR YOUR ENTIRE ASSEMBLAGE!
NEVERTHELESS, I HAVE WHOM I HAVE -- AND REVENGE SHALL BE NONETHELESS SWEET!
REVENGE, TIME-LORD?
REVENGE FOR ALLOWING THE COURSE OF EVENTS TO PROCEED AS FATE HAD LONG SINCE DECREED?
SILENCE! I WANTED THE CELESTIAL MADONNA-- AND IT WAS THE AVENGERS WHO KEPT HER FROM ME!**
FOR THAT, YOU MUST DIE!!
*IT HAPPENED IN AVENGERS #140.--M.
**IN GIANT-SIZE (SIGH) AVENGERS #2,3, & 4.--M.

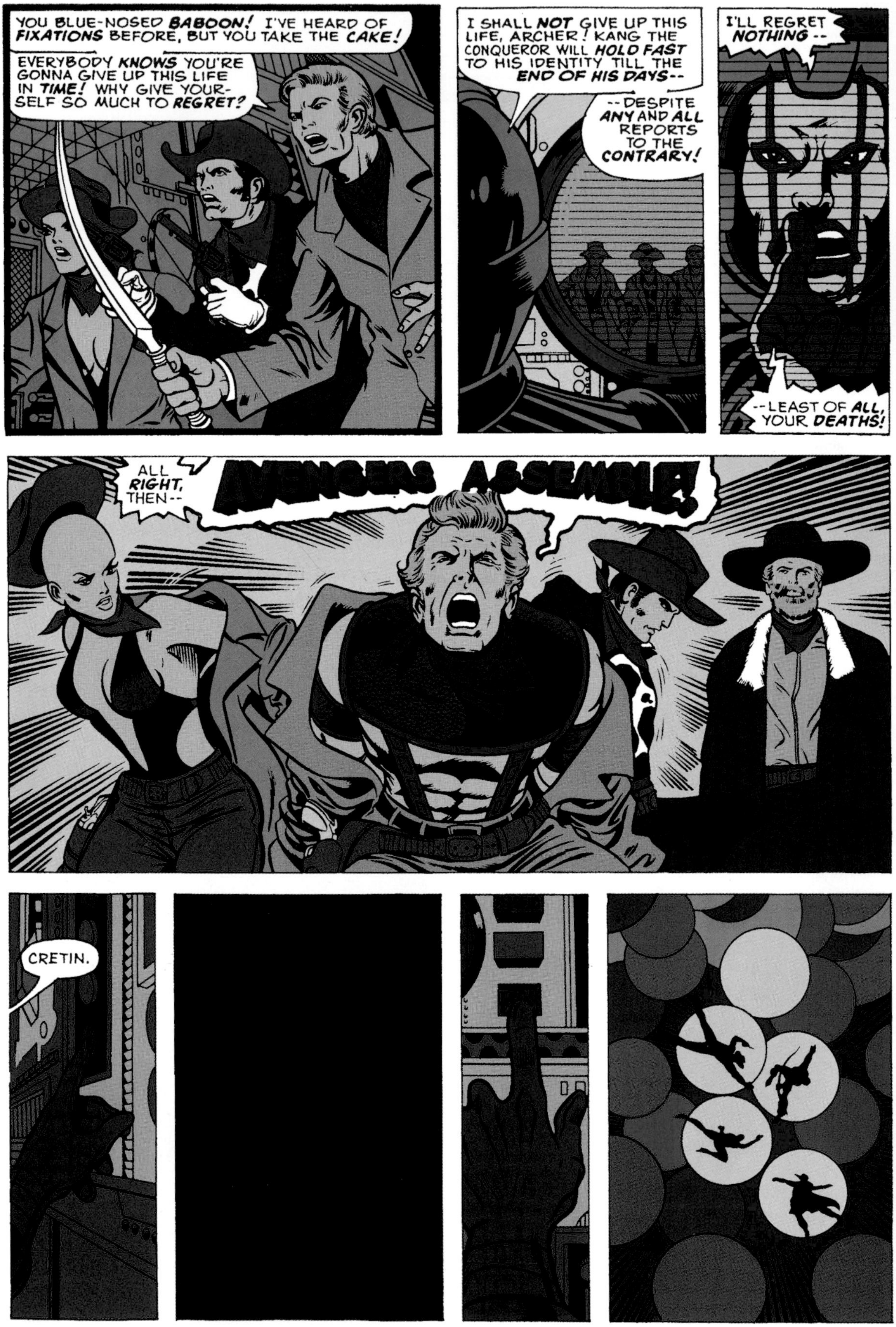
YOU BLUE-NOSED BABOON! I'VE HEARD OF FIXATIONS BEFORE, BUT YOU TAKE THE CAKE!
EVERYBODY KNOWS YOU'RE GONNA GIVE UP THIS LIFE IN TIME! WHY GIVE YOURSELF SO MUCH TO REGRET?
I SHALL NOT GIVE UP THIS LIFE, ARCHER! KANG THE CONQUEROR WILL HOLD FAST TO HIS IDENTITY TILL THE END OF HIS DAYS--
--DESPITE ANY AND ALL REPORTS TO THE CONTRARY!
I'LL REGRET NOTHING --
--LEAST OF ALL, YOUR DEATHS!
ALL RIGHT, THEN--
AVENGERS ASSEMBLE!
CRETIN.

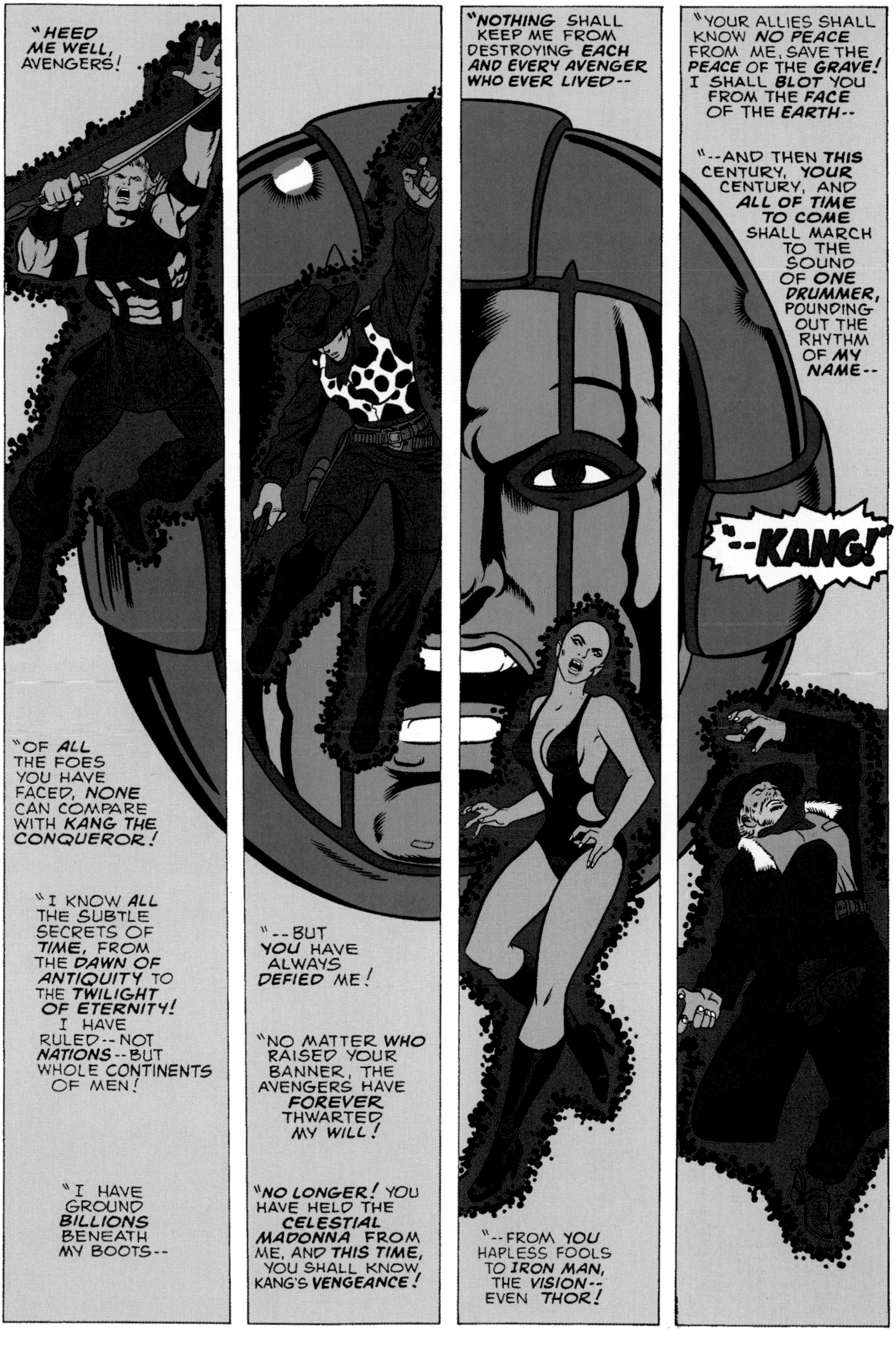
"HEED ME WELL, AVENGERS!
"OF ALL THE FOES YOU HAVE FACED, NONE CAN COMPARE WITH KANG THE CONQUEROR!
"I KNOW ALL THE SUBTLE SECRETS OF TIME, FROM THE DAWN OF ANTIQUITY TO THE TWILIGHT OF ETERNITY! I HAVE RULED--NOT NATIONS--BUT WHOLE CONTINENTS OF MEN!
"I HAVE GROUND BILLIONS BENEATH MY BOOTS--
"--BUT YOU HAVE ALWAYS DEFIED ME!
"NO MATTER WHO RAISED YOUR BANNER, THE AVENGERS HAVE FOREVER THWARTED MY WILL!
"NO LONGER! YOU HAVE HELD THE CELESTIAL MADONNA FROM ME, AND THIS TIME, YOU SHALL KNOW KANG'S VENGEANCE!
"NOTHING SHALL KEEP ME FROM DESTROYING EACH AND EVERY AVENGER WHO EVER LIVED--
"--FROM YOU HAPLESS FOOLS TO IRON MAN, THE VISION--EVEN THOR!
"YOUR ALLIES SHALL KNOW NO PEACE FROM ME, SAVE THE PEACE OF THE GRAVE! I SHALL BLOT YOU FROM THE FACE OF THE EARTH--
"--AND THEN THIS CENTURY, YOUR CENTURY, AND ALL OF TIME TO COME SHALL MARCH TO THE SOUND OF ONE DRUMMER, POUNDING OUT THE RHYTHM OF MY NAME--
"--KANG!"

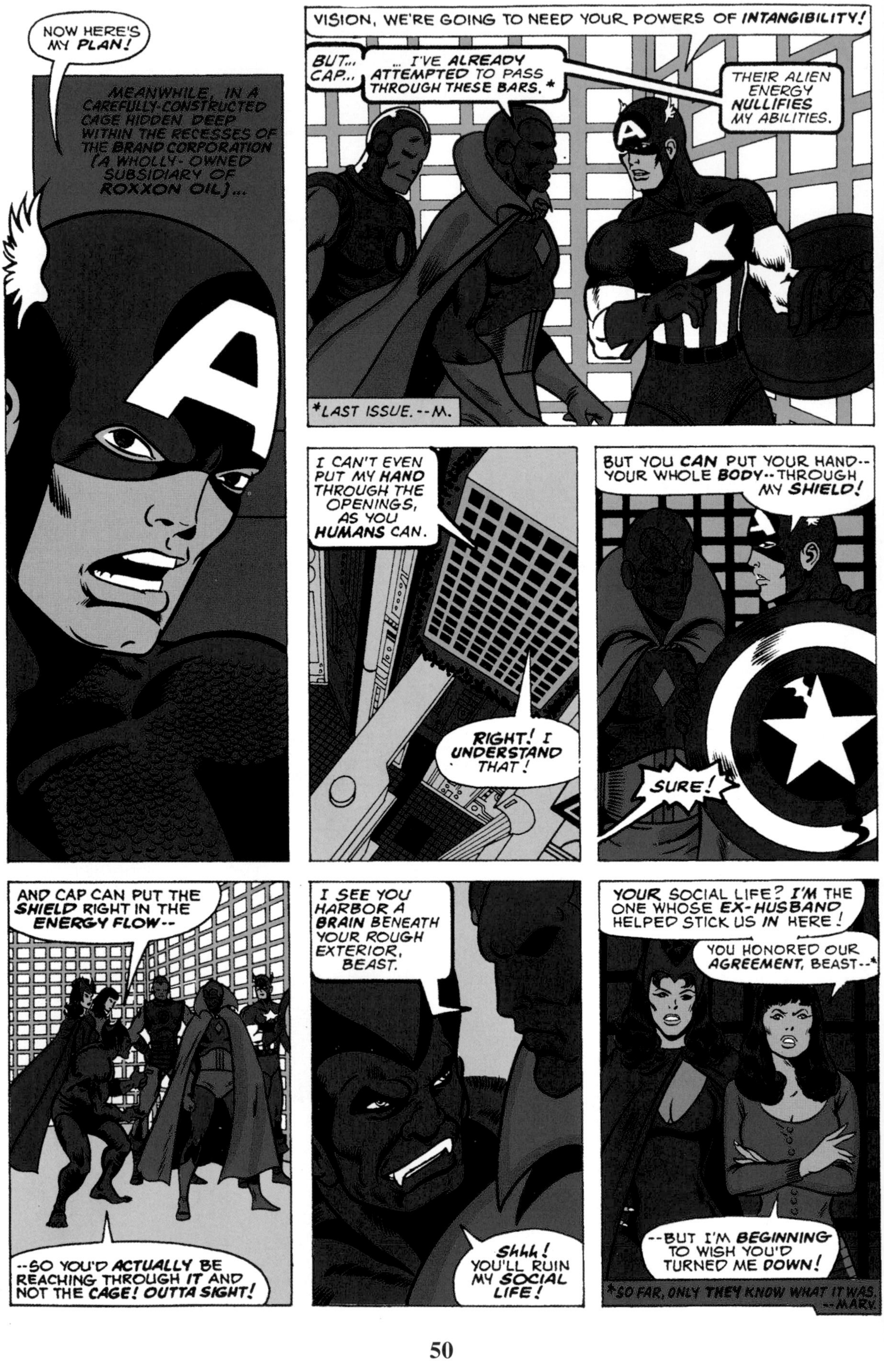
NOW HERE'S MY PLAN!
MEANWHILE, IN A CAREFULLY-CONSTRUCTED CAGE HIDDEN DEEP WITHIN THE RECESSES OF THE BRAND CORPORATION (A WHOLLY-OWNED SUBSIDIARY OF ROXXON OIL)...
VISION, WE'RE GOING TO NEED YOUR POWERS OF INTANGIBILITY!
BUT... CAP...
... I'VE ALREADY ATTEMPTED TO PASS THROUGH THESE BARS.*
THEIR ALIEN ENERGY NULLIFIES MY ABILITIES.
*LAST ISSUE. --M.
I CAN'T EVEN PUT MY HAND THROUGH THE OPENINGS, AS YOU HUMANS CAN.
RIGHT! I UNDERSTAND THAT!
BUT YOU CAN PUT YOUR HAND-- YOUR WHOLE BODY--THROUGH MY SHIELD!
SURE!
AND CAP CAN PUT THE SHIELD RIGHT IN THE ENERGY FLOW--
--SO YOU'D ACTUALLY BE REACHING THROUGH IT AND NOT THE CAGE! OUTTA SIGHT!
I SEE YOU HARBOR A BRAIN BENEATH YOUR ROUGH EXTERIOR, BEAST.
Shhh! YOU'LL RUIN MY SOCIAL LIFE!
YOUR SOCIAL LIFE? I'M THE ONE WHOSE EX-HUSBAND HELPED STICK US IN HERE!
YOU HONORED OUR AGREEMENT, BEAST--*
--BUT I'M BEGINNING TO WISH YOU'D TURNED ME DOWN!
*SO FAR, ONLY THEY KNOW WHAT IT WAS. --MARV.

WE CAN WORRY ABOUT THAT *LATER*, MISS BAXTER. I DIDN'T RETURN TO THE AVENGERS TO *STAY* COOPED UP!

READY, VISION?

HE'S *THROUGH!*

WELL DONE! I *TOLD* THE SQUADRON SUPREME NOT TO UNDERESTIMATE US!

INCREDIBLE! MY MAN IS *INCREDIBLE!*

HE *NEVER* TAKES *BOWS*, BUT HIS POWERS PUT *EVERYONE* ELSE TO SHAME!

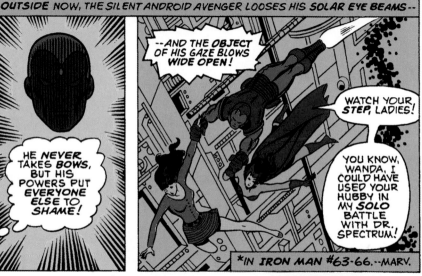

OUTSIDE NOW, THE SILENT ANDROID AVENGER LOOSES HIS SOLAR EYE BEAMS--

--AND THE OBJECT OF HIS GAZE BLOWS WIDE OPEN!

WATCH YOUR *STEP*, LADIES!

YOU KNOW, WANDA, I COULD HAVE USED YOUR *HUBBY* IN MY *SOLO* BATTLE WITH DR. SPECTRUM!

*IN IRON MAN #63-66.--MARV.

EVERY DAY, I SEE MORE *WISDOM* IN HAVING HELPED *FOUND* THIS TEAM!

NUTS, I.M.! SPECTRUM AND HIS PALS WERE *LOST* FROM THE *START!*

YOU KNOW WHAT THEY *SAY*--

--"*FOUR* WALLS DO NOT A *PRISM* MAKE!"

YOU'RE *REALLY* CONSIDERING THIS GUY FOR *MEMBERSHIP*, HUH?

COME ON, HEROES-- --WE HAVE SOME *PEOPLE* TO SEE!

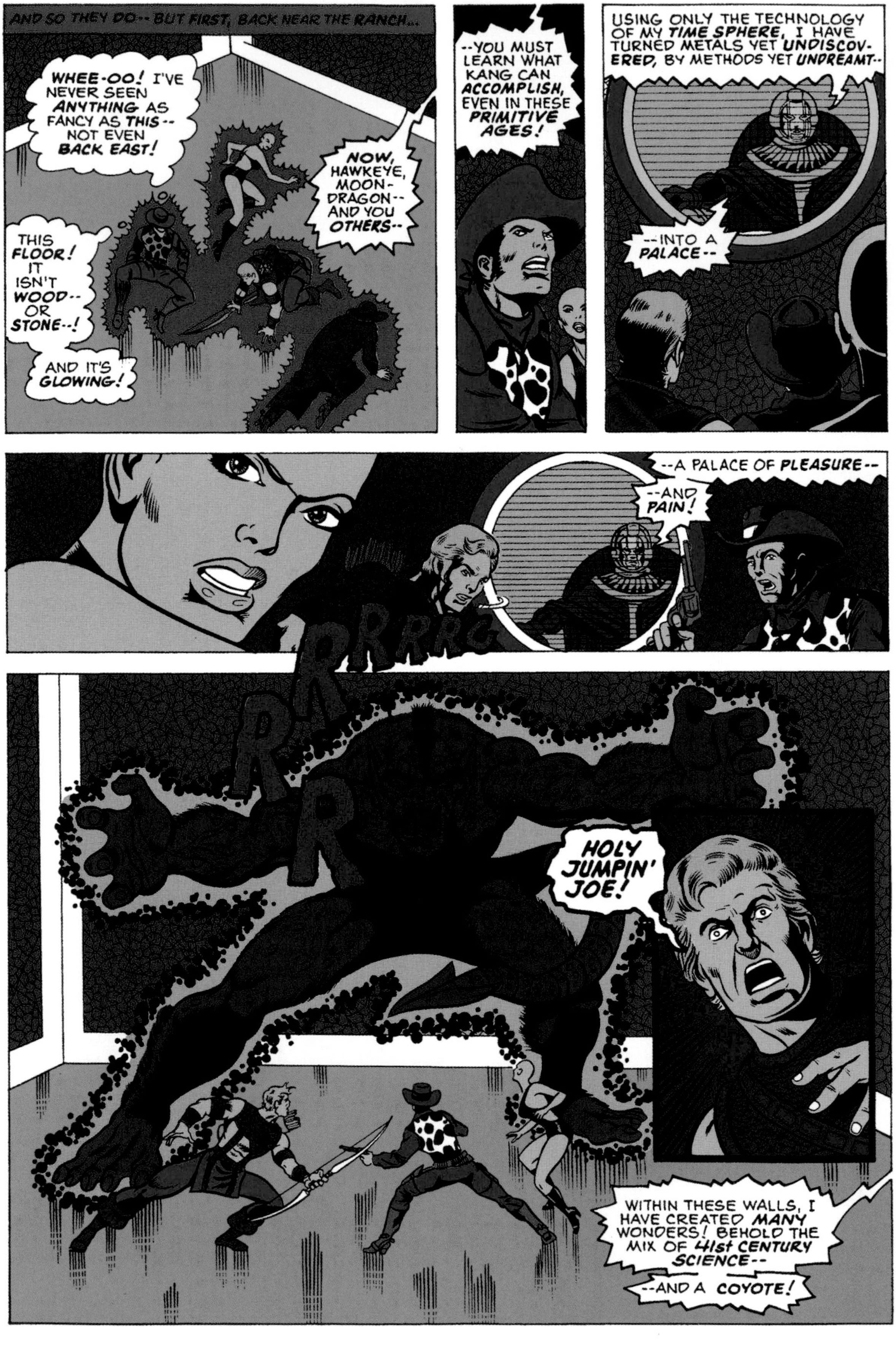
AND SO THEY DO-- BUT FIRST, BACK NEAR THE RANCH...
WHEE-OO! I'VE NEVER SEEN ANYTHING AS FANCY AS THIS-- NOT EVEN BACK EAST!
THIS FLOOR! IT ISN'T WOOD-- OR STONE--!
AND IT'S GLOWING!
NOW, HAWKEYE, MOONDRAGON-- AND YOU OTHERS--
--YOU MUST LEARN WHAT KANG CAN ACCOMPLISH, EVEN IN THESE PRIMITIVE AGES!
USING ONLY THE TECHNOLOGY OF MY TIME SPHERE, I HAVE TURNED METALS YET UNDISCOVERED, BY METHODS YET UNDREAMT--
--INTO A PALACE--
--A PALACE OF PLEASURE--
--AND PAIN!
RRRRG
RRR
HOLY JUMPIN' JOE!
WITHIN THESE WALLS, I HAVE CREATED MANY WONDERS! BEHOLD THE MIX OF 41st CENTURY SCIENCE--
--AND A COYOTE!

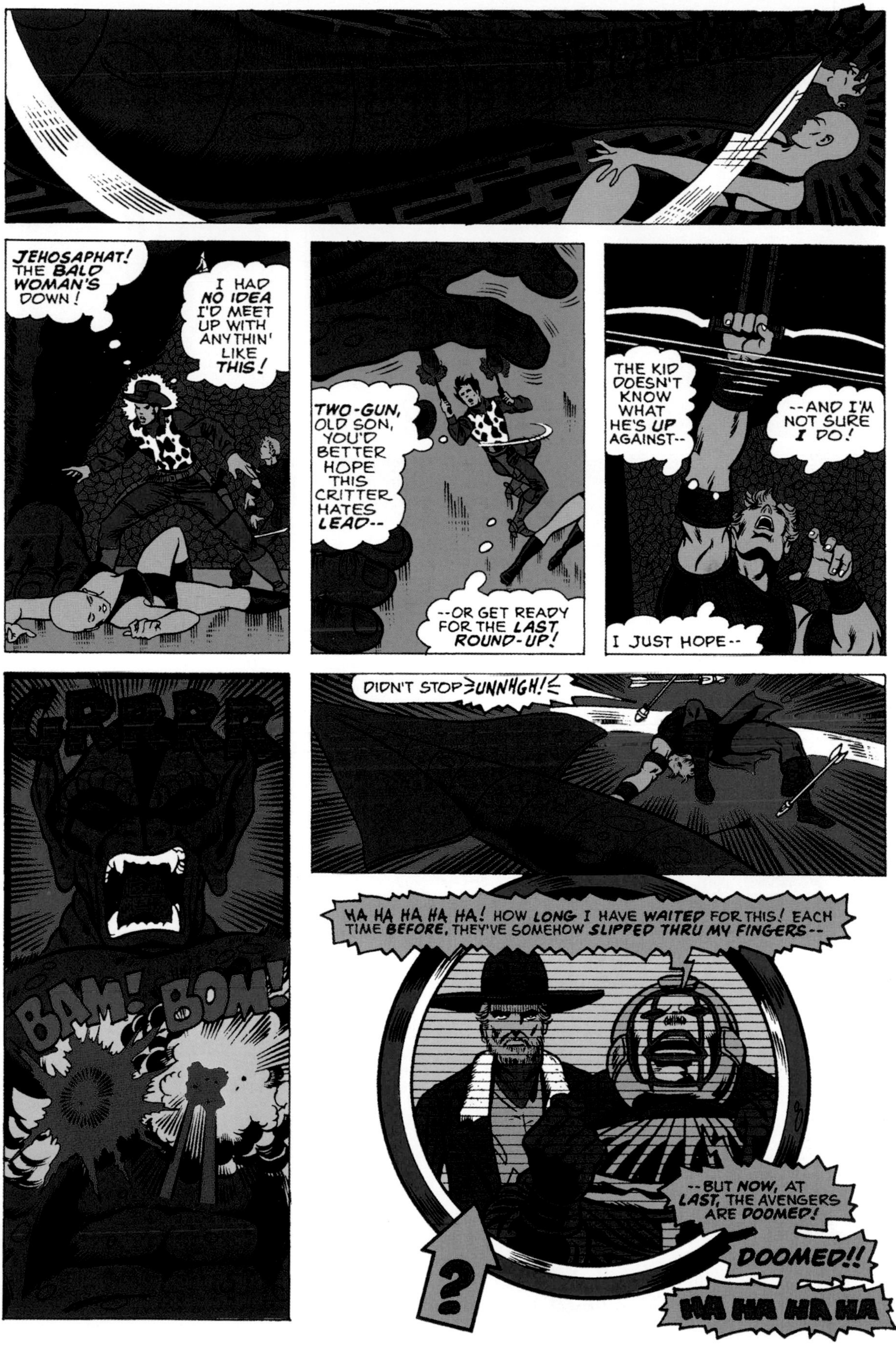
JEHOSAPHAT! THE BALD WOMAN'S DOWN!
I HAD NO IDEA I'D MEET UP WITH ANYTHIN' LIKE THIS!
TWO-GUN, OLD SON, YOU'D BETTER HOPE THIS CRITTER HATES LEAD--
--OR GET READY FOR THE LAST ROUND-UP!
THE KID DOESN'T KNOW WHAT HE'S UP AGAINST--
--AND I'M NOT SURE I DO!
I JUST HOPE--
DIDN'T STOP UNNHGH!
BAM! BOM!
HA HA HA HA HA! HOW LONG I HAVE WAITED FOR THIS! EACH TIME BEFORE, THEY'VE SOMEHOW SLIPPED THRU MY FINGERS--
--BUT NOW, AT LAST, THE AVENGERS ARE DOOMED!
DOOMED!!
HA HA HA HA
?

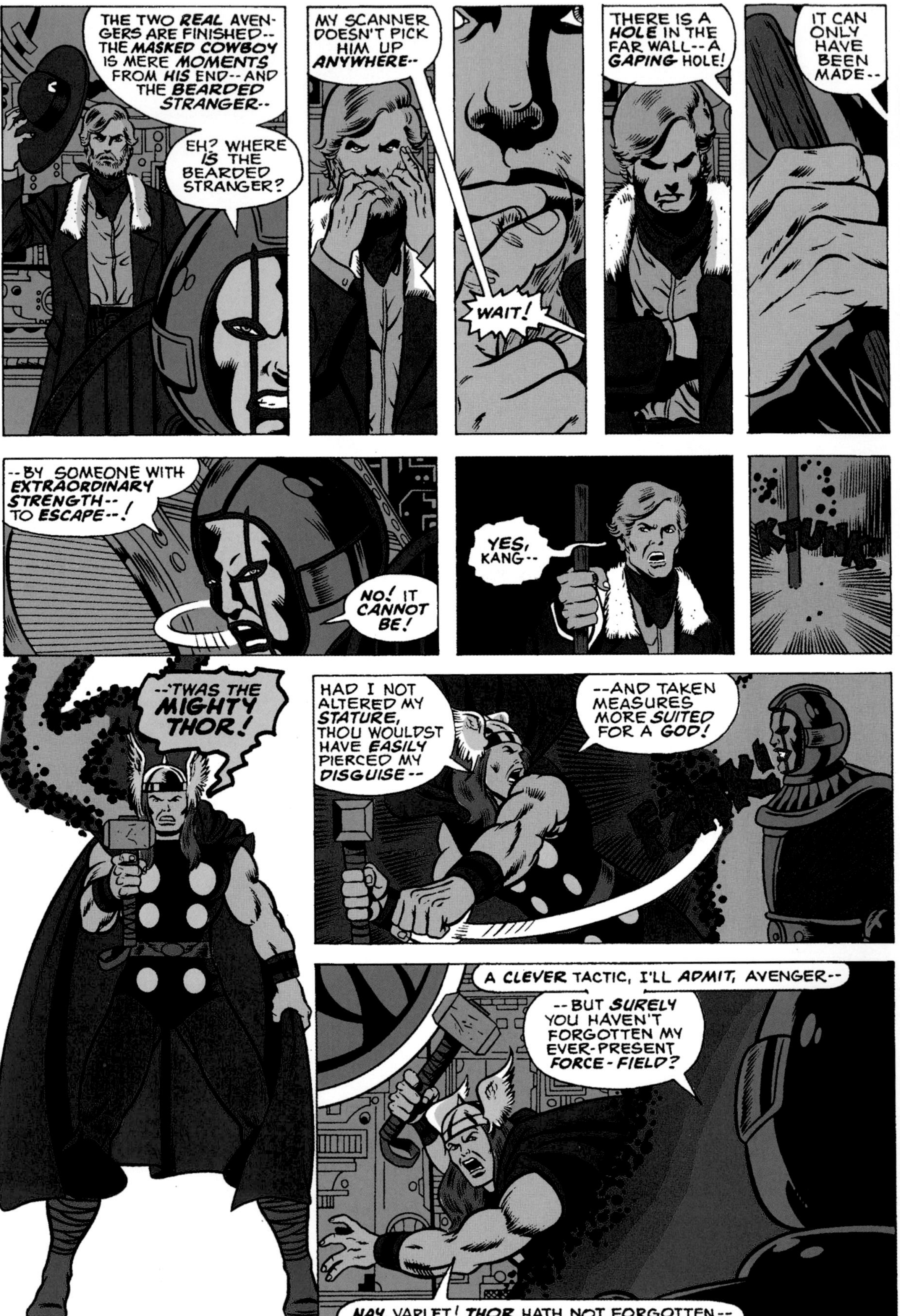
THE TWO REAL AVENGERS ARE FINISHED-- THE MASKED COWBOY IS MERE MOMENTS FROM HIS END-- AND THE BEARDED STRANGER--
EH? WHERE IS THE BEARDED STRANGER?
MY SCANNER DOESN'T PICK HIM UP ANYWHERE--
WAIT!
THERE IS A HOLE IN THE FAR WALL-- A GAPING HOLE!
IT CAN ONLY HAVE BEEN MADE--
--BY SOMEONE WITH EXTRAORDINARY STRENGTH-- TO ESCAPE--!
NO! IT CANNOT BE!
YES, KANG--
KTUNK!
--'TWAS THE MIGHTY THOR!
HAD I NOT ALTERED MY STATURE, THOU WOULDST HAVE EASILY PIERCED MY DISGUISE--
--AND TAKEN MEASURES MORE SUITED FOR A GOD!
A CLEVER TACTIC, I'LL ADMIT, AVENGER--
--BUT SURELY YOU HAVEN'T FORGOTTEN MY EVER-PRESENT FORCE-FIELD?
NAY, VARLET! THOR HATH NOT FORGOTTEN--

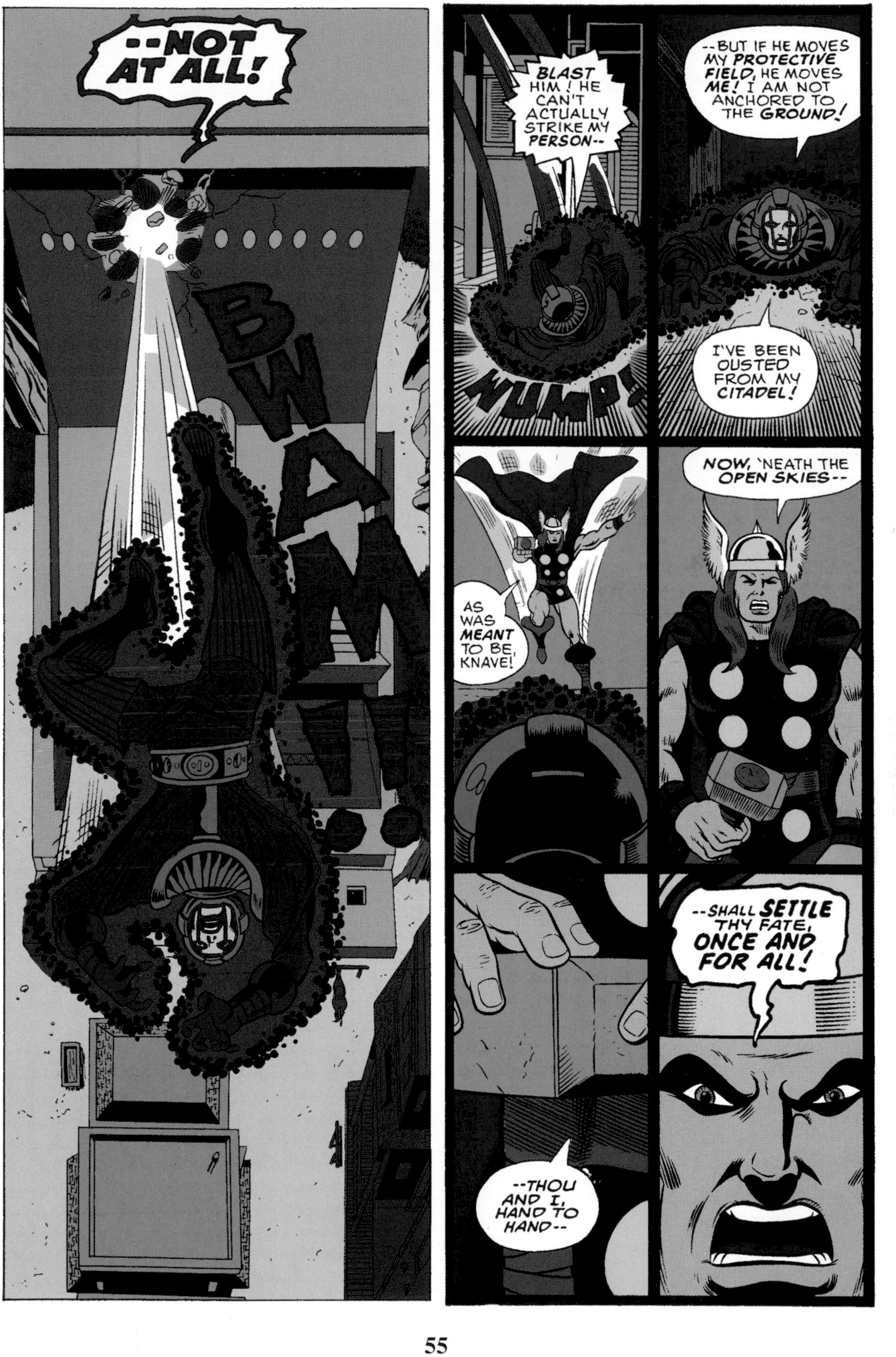
--NOT AT ALL!
BWAM!
BLAST HIM! HE CAN'T ACTUALLY STRIKE MY PERSON--
--BUT IF HE MOVES MY PROTECTIVE FIELD, HE MOVES ME! I AM NOT ANCHORED TO THE GROUND!
WUMP!
I'VE BEEN OUSTED FROM MY CITADEL!
AS WAS MEANT TO BE, KNAVE!
NOW, 'NEATH THE OPEN SKIES--
--THOU AND I, HAND TO HAND--
--SHALL SETTLE THY FATE, ONCE AND FOR ALL!

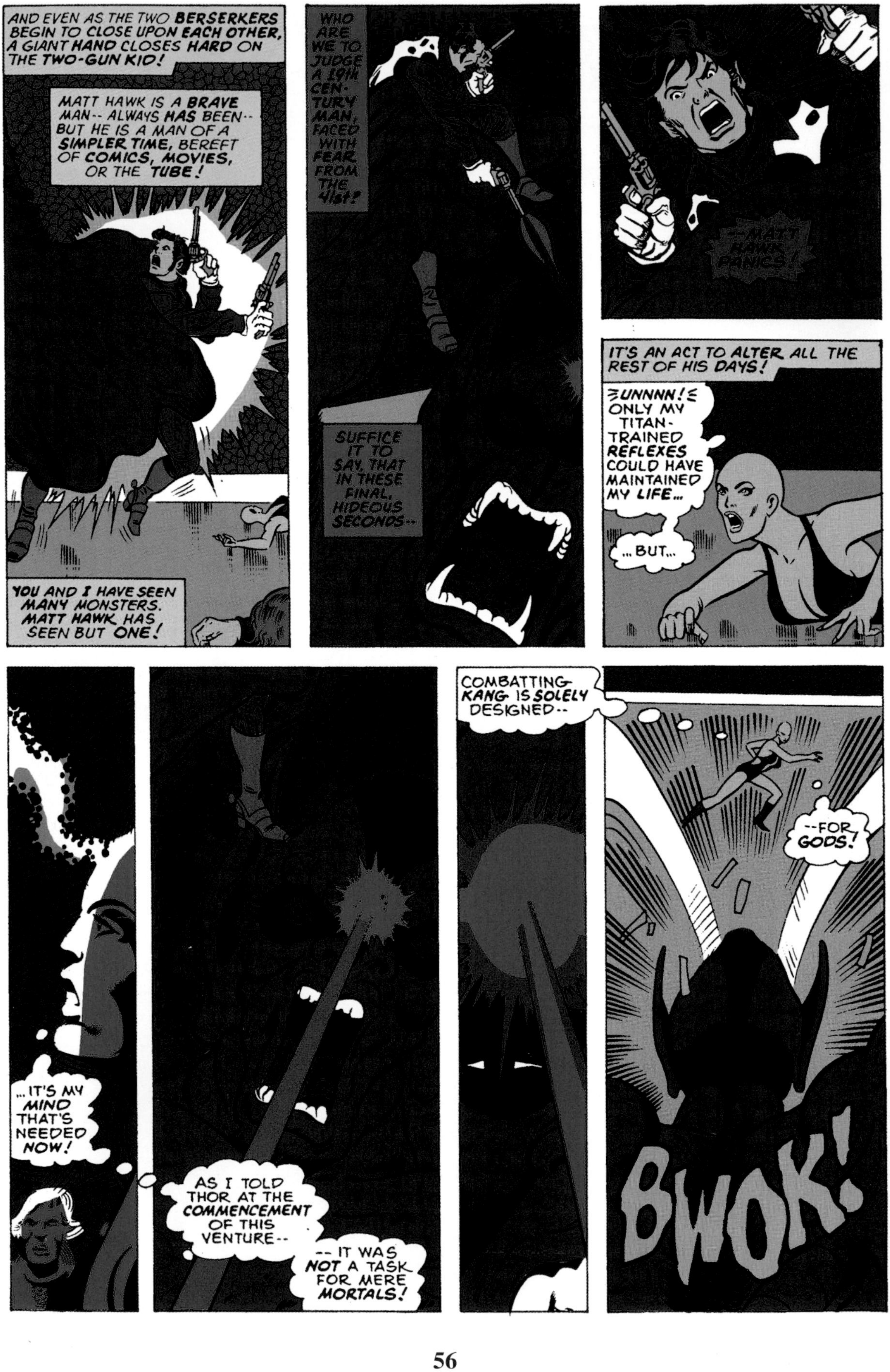
AND EVEN AS THE TWO BERSERKERS BEGIN TO CLOSE UPON EACH OTHER, A GIANT HAND CLOSES HARD ON THE TWO-GUN KID!
MATT HAWK IS A BRAVE MAN-- ALWAYS HAS BEEN-- BUT HE IS A MAN OF A SIMPLER TIME, BEREFT OF COMICS, MOVIES, OR THE TUBE!
YOU AND I HAVE SEEN MANY MONSTERS. MATT HAWK HAS SEEN BUT ONE!
WHO ARE WE TO JUDGE A 19TH CENTURY MAN, FACED WITH FEAR FROM THE 41ST?
SUFFICE IT TO SAY, THAT IN THESE FINAL, HIDEOUS SECONDS--
--MATT HAWK PANICS!
IT'S AN ACT TO ALTER ALL THE REST OF HIS DAYS!
UNNNN! ONLY MY TITAN-TRAINED REFLEXES COULD HAVE MAINTAINED MY LIFE...
...BUT...
...IT'S MY MIND THAT'S NEEDED NOW!
AS I TOLD THOR AT THE COMMENCEMENT OF THIS VENTURE--
--IT WAS NOT A TASK FOR MERE MORTALS!
COMBATTING KANG IS SOLELY DESIGNED--
--FOR GODS!
BWOK!

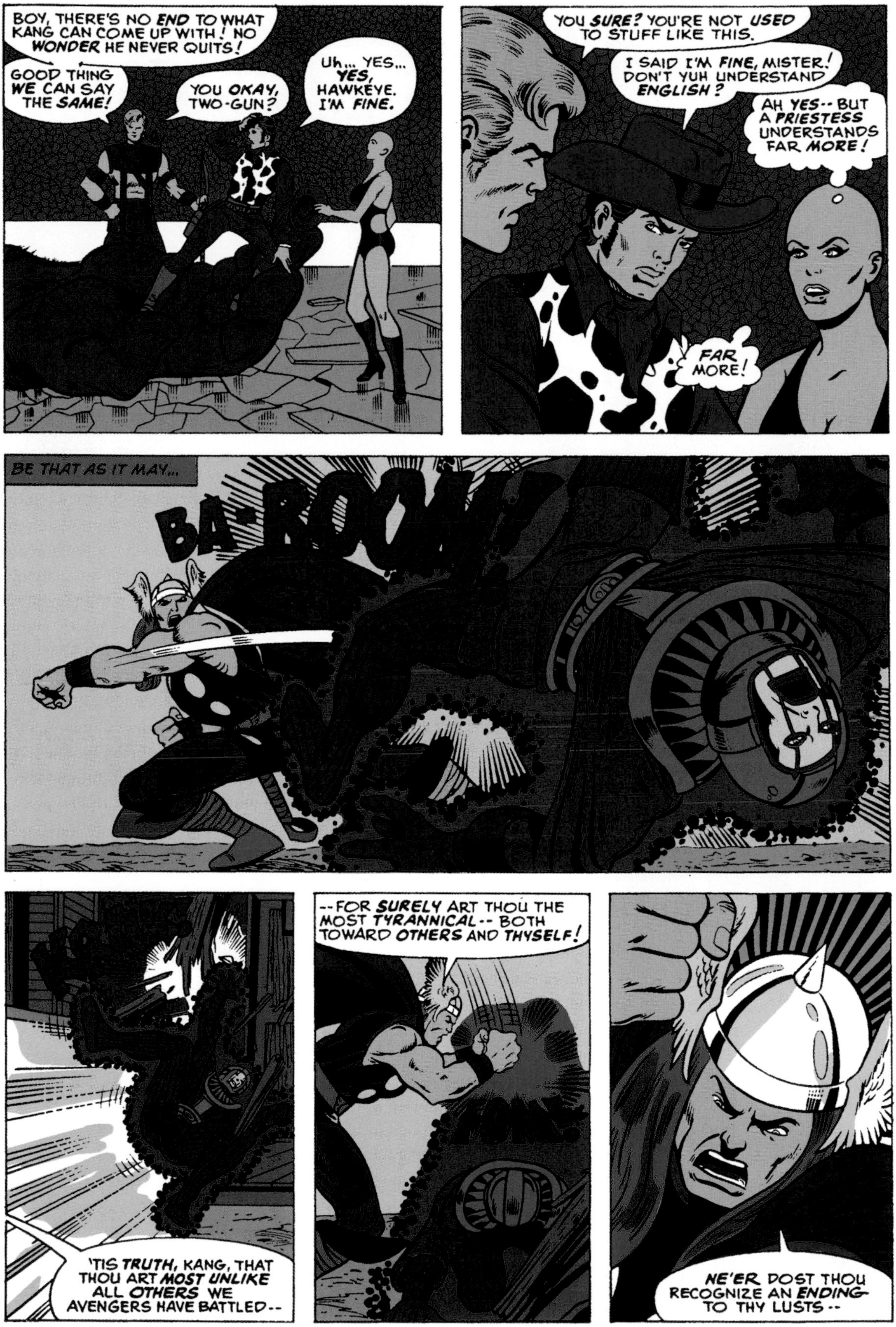
BOY, THERE'S NO END TO WHAT KANG CAN COME UP WITH! NO WONDER HE NEVER QUITS!
GOOD THING WE CAN SAY THE SAME!
YOU OKAY, TWO-GUN?
Uh... YES... YES, HAWKEYE. I'M FINE.
YOU SURE? YOU'RE NOT USED TO STUFF LIKE THIS.
I SAID I'M FINE, MISTER! DON'T YUH UNDERSTAND ENGLISH?
AH YES-- BUT A PRIESTESS UNDERSTANDS FAR MORE!
FAR MORE!
BE THAT AS IT MAY...
BA-ROOM
'TIS TRUTH, KANG, THAT THOU ART MOST UNLIKE ALL OTHERS WE AVENGERS HAVE BATTLED--
--FOR SURELY ART THOU THE MOST TYRANNICAL-- BOTH TOWARD OTHERS AND THYSELF!
NE'ER DOST THOU RECOGNIZE AN ENDING TO THY LUSTS--

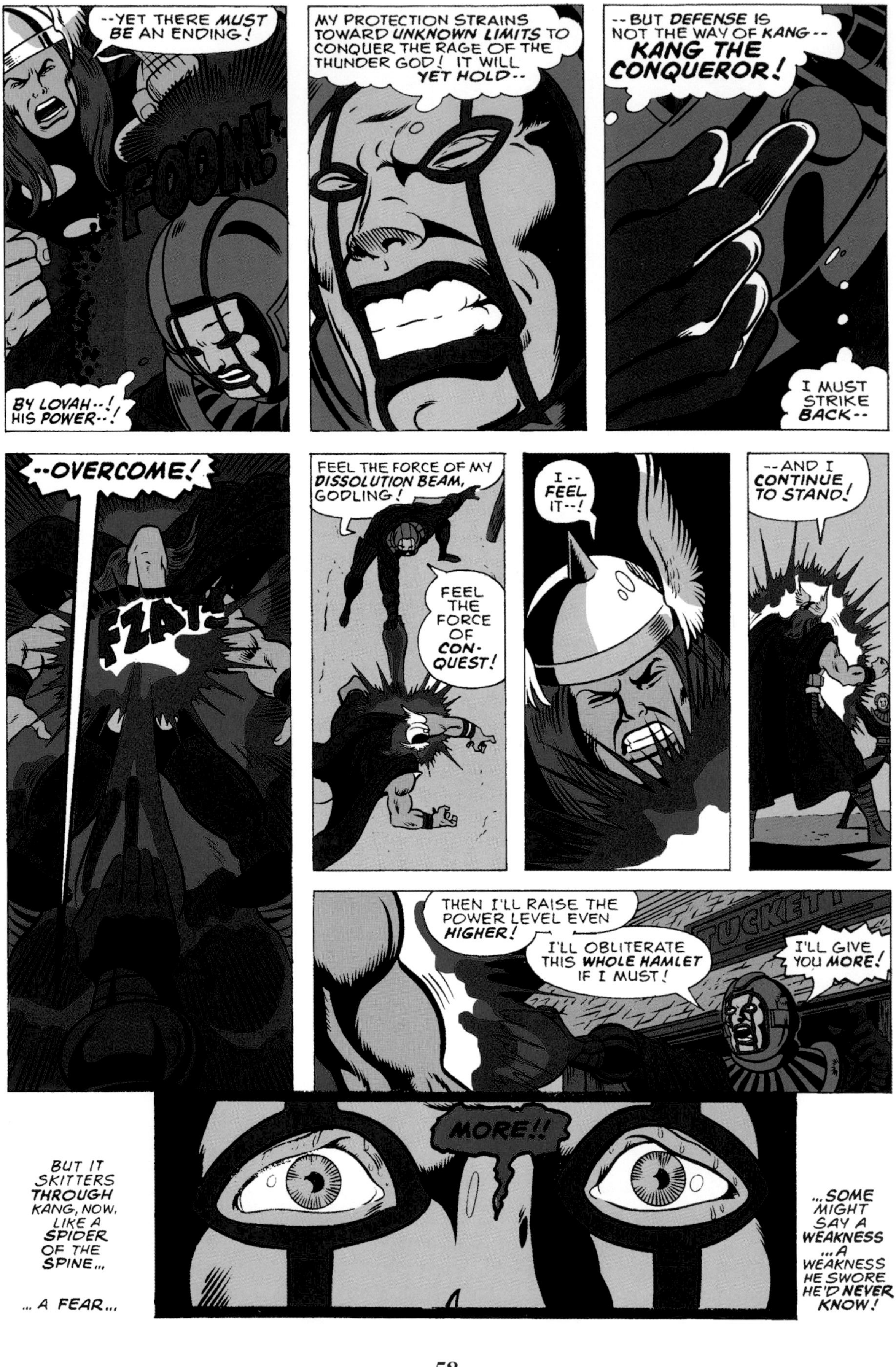
--YET THERE *MUST* BE AN ENDING!
FOOM!
BY *LOVAH*--! HIS *POWER*--!
MY PROTECTION STRAINS TOWARD *UNKNOWN LIMITS* TO CONQUER THE RAGE OF THE THUNDER GOD! IT WILL *YET HOLD*--
--BUT *DEFENSE* IS NOT THE WAY OF *KANG*--
KANG THE CONQUEROR!
I MUST STRIKE *BACK*--
--*OVERCOME!*
FZAT!
FEEL THE FORCE OF MY *DISSOLUTION BEAM*, GODLING!
FEEL THE FORCE OF *CON-QUEST!*
I-- *FEEL* IT--!
--AND I *CONTINUE TO STAND!*
THEN I'LL RAISE THE POWER LEVEL EVEN *HIGHER!*
I'LL OBLITERATE THIS *WHOLE HAMLET* IF I MUST!
I'LL GIVE YOU *MORE!*
MORE!!

BUT IT SKITTERS **THROUGH** *KANG, NOW, LIKE A* **SPIDER** *OF THE* **SPINE**...

... A **FEAR**...

... **SOME** *MIGHT SAY A* **WEAKNESS** *... A WEAKNESS HE SWORE HE'D* **NEVER** *KNOW!*

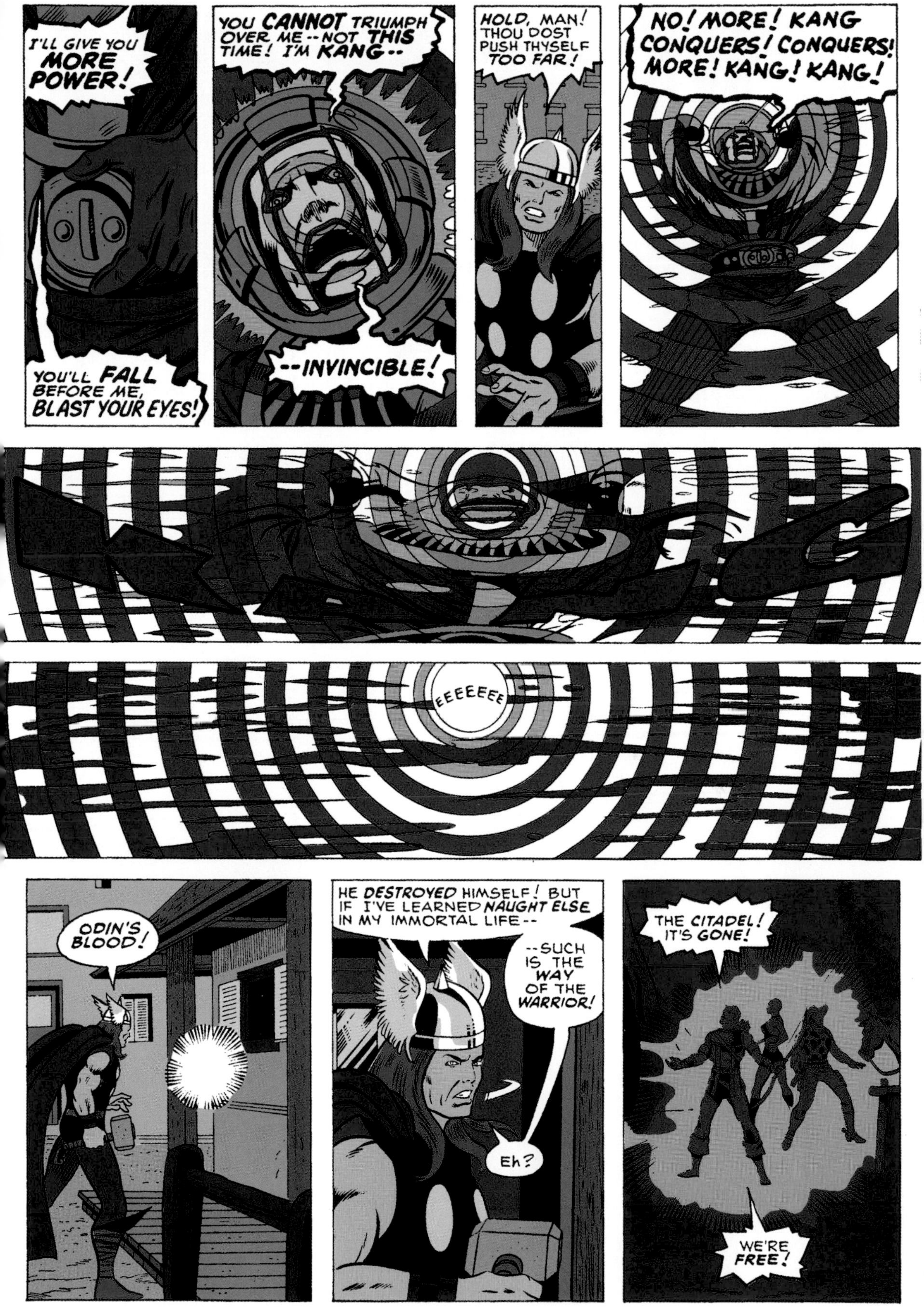
I'LL GIVE YOU MORE POWER!
YOU'LL FALL BEFORE ME, BLAST YOUR EYES!
YOU CANNOT TRIUMPH OVER ME -- NOT THIS TIME! I'M KANG --
-- INVINCIBLE!
HOLD, MAN! THOU DOST PUSH THYSELF TOO FAR!
NO! MORE! KANG CONQUERS! CONQUERS! MORE! KANG! KANG!
EEEEEEE
ODIN'S BLOOD!
HE DESTROYED HIMSELF! BUT IF I'VE LEARNED NAUGHT ELSE IN MY IMMORTAL LIFE --
-- SUCH IS THE WAY OF THE WARRIOR!
Eh?
THE CITADEL! IT'S GONE!
WE'RE FREE!

AND LOOK! AGAIN-- IN THE SKY!

IMMORTUS!

THIS, THEN, IS FATE!

KANG IS GONE-- HIS VERY ATOMS SPLIT AND SPREAD THROUGHOUT ALL TIME, NEVER AGAIN TO BE REJOINED...

...A FITTING END, AND ALL THE MORE SO, SINCE HE HIMSELF WAS ITS CAUSE!

BUT-- YOU ONCE TOLD THE AVENGERS THAT YOU WERE ANOTHER MANIFESTATION OF KANG --LIKE PHARAOH RAMA-TUT! *

IF HE IS DESTROYED--!

*G.S. AVENGERS #3.

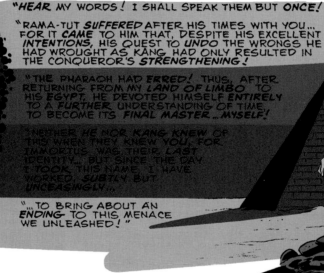

"HEAR MY WORDS! I SHALL SPEAK THEM BUT ONCE!

"RAMA-TUT SUFFERED AFTER HIS TIMES WITH YOU... FOR IT CAME TO HIM THAT, DESPITE HIS EXCELLENT INTENTIONS, HIS QUEST TO UNDO THE WRONGS HE HAD WROUGHT AS KANG HAD ONLY RESULTED IN THE CONQUEROR'S STRENGTHENING!

"THE PHARAOH HAD ERRED! THUS, AFTER RETURNING FROM MY LAND OF LIMBO TO HIS EGYPT, HE DEVOTED HIMSELF ENTIRELY TO A FURTHER UNDERSTANDING OF TIME TO BECOME ITS FINAL MASTER...MYSELF!

"NEITHER HE NOR KANG KNEW OF THIS WHEN THEY KNEW YOU, FOR IMMORTUS WAS THEIR LAST IDENTITY. BUT SINCE THE DAY I TOOK THIS NAME, I HAVE WORKED, SUBTLY BUT UNCEASINGLY...

"...TO BRING ABOUT AN ENDING TO THIS MENACE WE UNLEASHED!"

NOW, KANG NO LONGER EXISTS...

--AND RAMA-TUT SHALL NEVER COME INTO BEING!

THE CIRCLE IS BROKEN!

NEITHER, TOO, SHALL IMMORTUS HAVE BEEN!

WE ARE FREE!

TOMBSTONE, ARIZONA-- 1873. TODAY, AND FOREVER...

...THERE IS ONE LESS GOD.

NEXT: The CLAWS of the HELLCAT!

AVENGERS
MARVEL COMICS GROUP
APPROVED BY THE COMICS CODE AUTHORITY
25¢
144
FEB
02458
EARTH'S MIGHTIEST HEROES!
THE AVENGERS
AVENGERS ASSEMBLE-- TO MEET THE MOST FEARSOME NEW MEMBER OF ALL!
YOU WANTED HER--YOU'VE GOT HER!
THE HELLCAT COMETH!

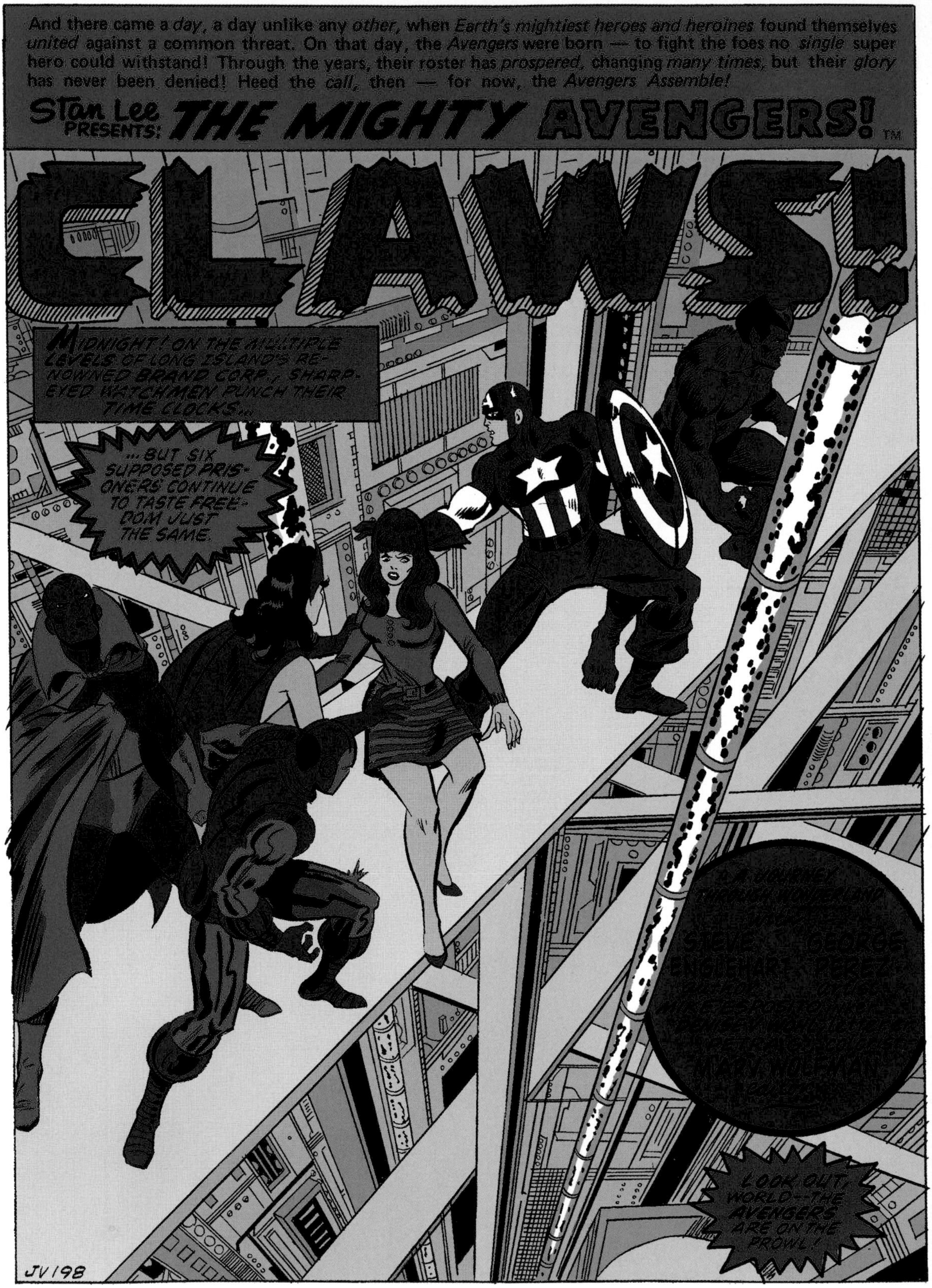
And there came a *day*, a day unlike any *other*, when *Earth's mightiest heroes and heroines* found themselves *united* against a common threat. On that day, the *Avengers* were born — to fight the foes no *single* super hero could withstand! Through the years, their roster has *prospered*, changing *many times*, but their *glory* has never been denied! Heed the *call*, then — for now, the *Avengers Assemble!*
Stan Lee PRESENTS: THE MIGHTY AVENGERS! TM
CLAWS!
MIDNIGHT! ON THE MULTIPLE LEVELS OF LONG ISLAND'S RE-NOWNED BRAND CORP., SHARP-EYED WATCHMEN PUNCH THEIR TIME CLOCKS...
...BUT SIX SUPPOSED PRIS-ONERS CONTINUE TO TASTE FREE-DOM JUST THE SAME.
STEVE ENGLEHART
GEORGE PEREZ
MARV WOLFMAN
LOOK OUT, WORLD--THE AVENGERS ARE ON THE PROWL!
JV198

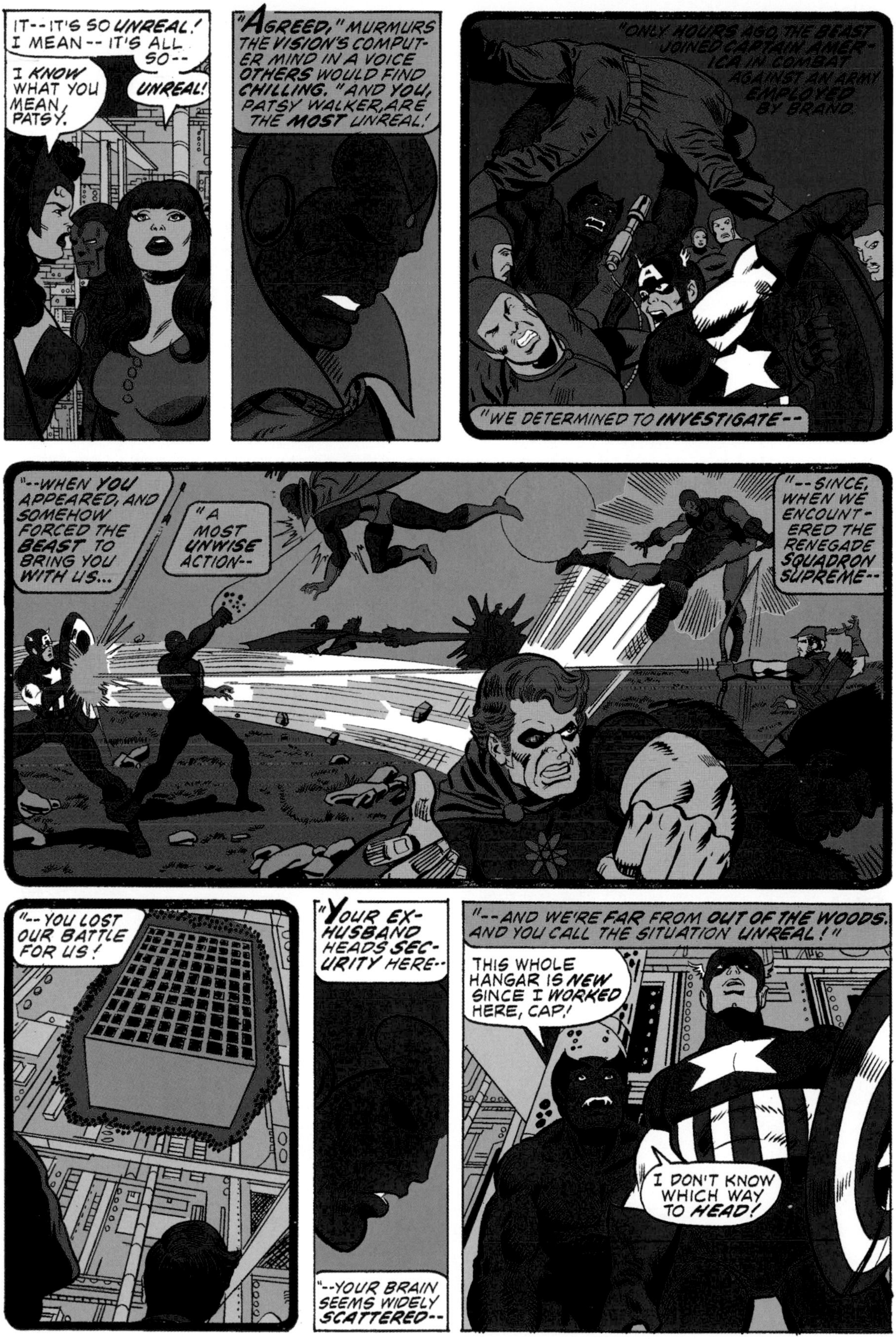
IT--IT'S SO UNREAL! I MEAN--IT'S ALL SO--
I KNOW WHAT YOU MEAN, PATSY.
UNREAL!
"AGREED," MURMURS THE VISION'S COMPUTER MIND IN A VOICE OTHERS WOULD FIND CHILLING. "AND YOU, PATSY WALKER, ARE THE MOST UNREAL!
"ONLY HOURS AGO, THE BEAST JOINED CAPTAIN AMERICA IN COMBAT AGAINST AN ARMY EMPLOYED BY BRAND.
"WE DETERMINED TO INVESTIGATE--
"--WHEN YOU APPEARED, AND SOMEHOW FORCED THE BEAST TO BRING YOU WITH US...
"A MOST UNWISE ACTION--
"--SINCE, WHEN WE ENCOUNTERED THE RENEGADE SQUADRON SUPREME--
"--YOU LOST OUR BATTLE FOR US!
"YOUR EX-HUSBAND HEADS SECURITY HERE--
"--YOUR BRAIN SEEMS WIDELY SCATTERED--
"--AND WE'RE FAR FROM OUT OF THE WOODS. AND YOU CALL THE SITUATION UNREAL!"
THIS WHOLE HANGAR IS NEW SINCE I WORKED HERE, CAP!
I DON'T KNOW WHICH WAY TO HEAD!

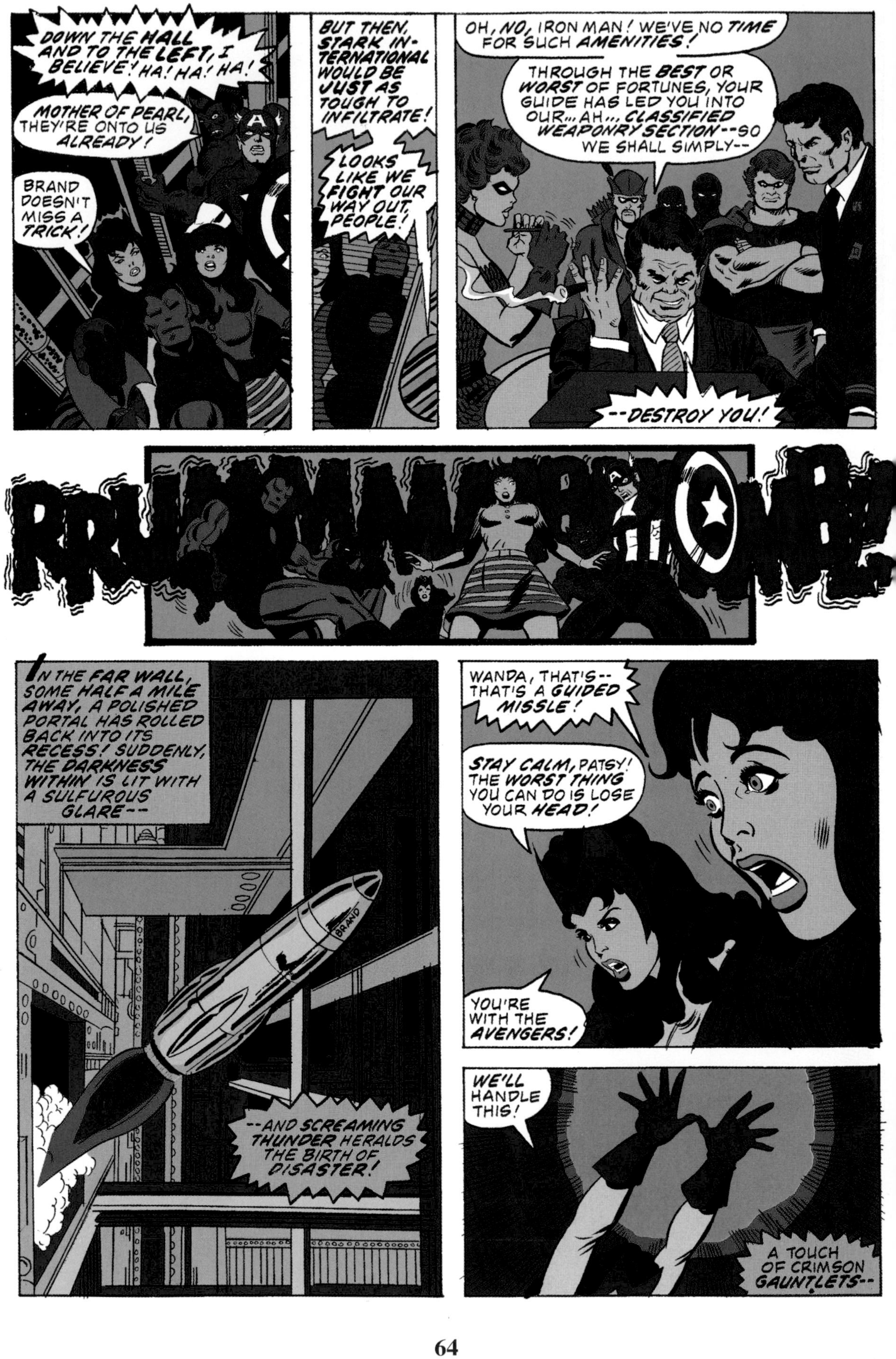
DOWN THE HALL AND TO THE LEFT, I BELIEVE! HA! HA! HA!
MOTHER OF PEARL, THEY'RE ONTO US ALREADY!
BRAND DOESN'T MISS A TRICK!
BUT THEN, STARK INTERNATIONAL WOULD BE JUST AS TOUGH TO INFILTRATE!
LOOKS LIKE WE FIGHT OUR WAY OUT, PEOPLE!
OH, NO, IRON MAN! WE'VE NO TIME FOR SUCH AMENITIES!
THROUGH THE BEST OR WORST OF FORTUNES, YOUR GUIDE HAS LED YOU INTO OUR... AH... CLASSIFIED WEAPONRY SECTION--SO WE SHALL SIMPLY--
--DESTROY YOU!
RRUMMMBBOOM!
IN THE FAR WALL, SOME HALF A MILE AWAY, A POLISHED PORTAL HAS ROLLED BACK INTO ITS RECESS! SUDDENLY, THE DARKNESS WITHIN IS LIT WITH A SULFUROUS GLARE--
BRAND
--AND SCREAMING THUNDER HERALDS THE BIRTH OF DISASTER!
WANDA, THAT'S-- THAT'S A GUIDED MISSLE!
STAY CALM, PATSY! THE WORST THING YOU CAN DO IS LOSE YOUR HEAD!
YOU'RE WITH THE AVENGERS!
WE'LL HANDLE THIS!
A TOUCH OF CRIMSON GAUNTLETS--

--A FURROW IN HER BROW-- AND THE SCARLET WITCH SHOWS WHY, MORE THAN EVER, SHE DESERVES HER OMINOUS NAME!

FORGED STEEL BENDS TO HER FORGED WILL--

--BUT--

--THERE'S ANOTHER BIRD ALREADY ON ITS WAY!

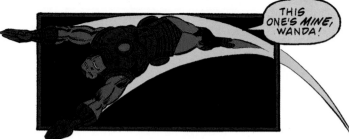

THIS ONE'S MINE, WANDA!

SET A MISSLE TO CATCH A MISSLE!

CLANG

SOMETIMES I GET TO FEELING THAT'S ALL I AM--

--BUT RIGHT ABOUT THEN, THE MAN INSIDE THE ARMOR ALWAYS WINDS UP BEING NEEDED!

AND I RE- MEMBER WHO TONY STARK IS:

THE GREATEST WEAPONS EXPERT ALIVE!

I DID IT! THE GUIDANCE SYSTEM'S SHOT!

MAYBE SO, BUT THE COST OF TRIUMPH RUNS HIGH TODAY!

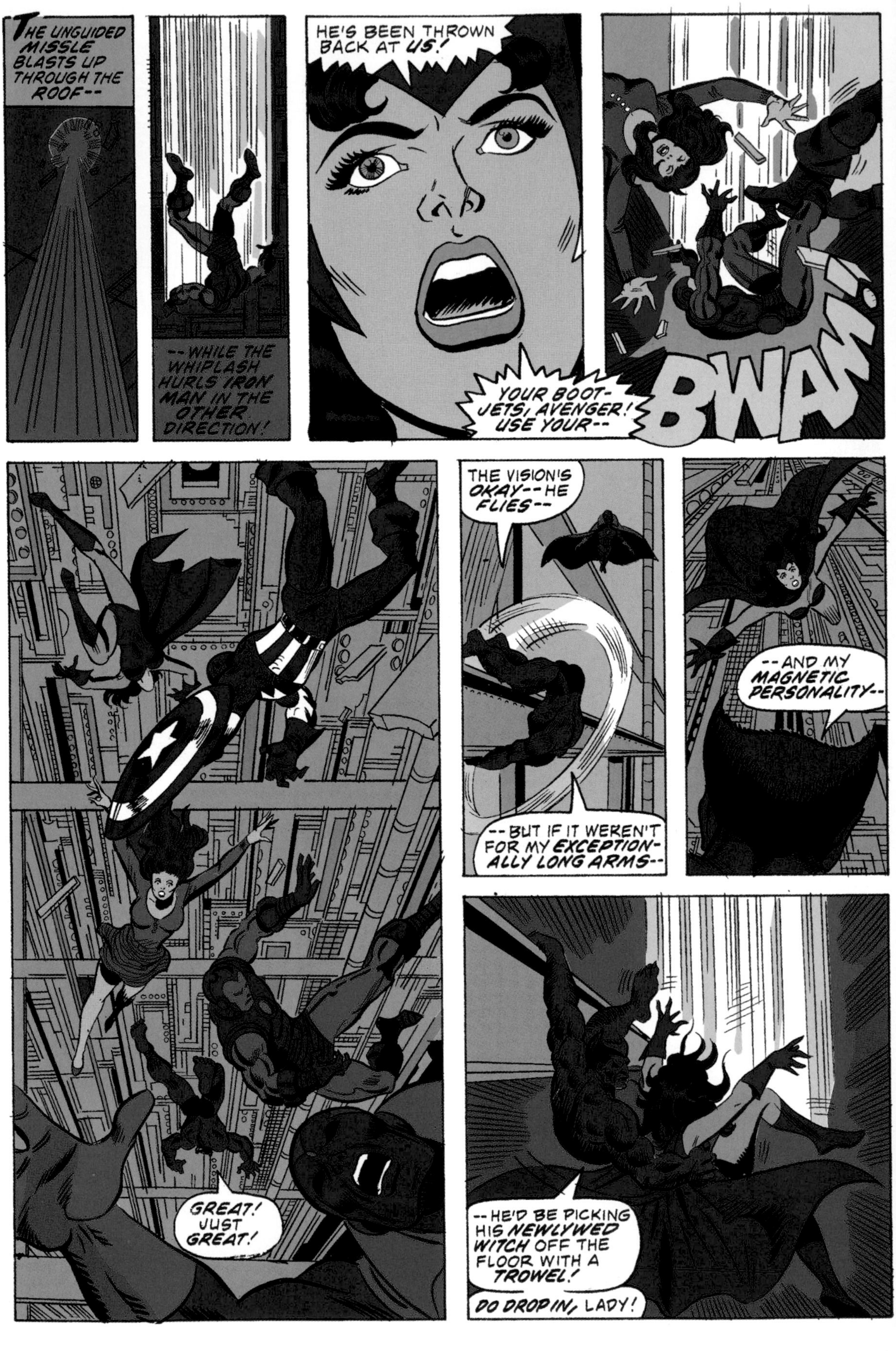
THE UNGUIDED MISSLE BLASTS UP THROUGH THE ROOF--
--WHILE THE WHIPLASH HURLS IRON MAN IN THE OTHER DIRECTION!
HE'S BEEN THROWN BACK AT US!
YOUR BOOT-JETS, AVENGER! USE YOUR--
BWAM
GREAT! JUST GREAT!
THE VISION'S OKAY--HE FLIES--
--BUT IF IT WEREN'T FOR MY EXCEPTION-ALLY LONG ARMS--
--AND MY MAGNETIC PERSONALITY--
--HE'D BE PICKING HIS NEWLYWED WITCH OFF THE FLOOR WITH A TROWEL!
DO DROP IN, LADY!

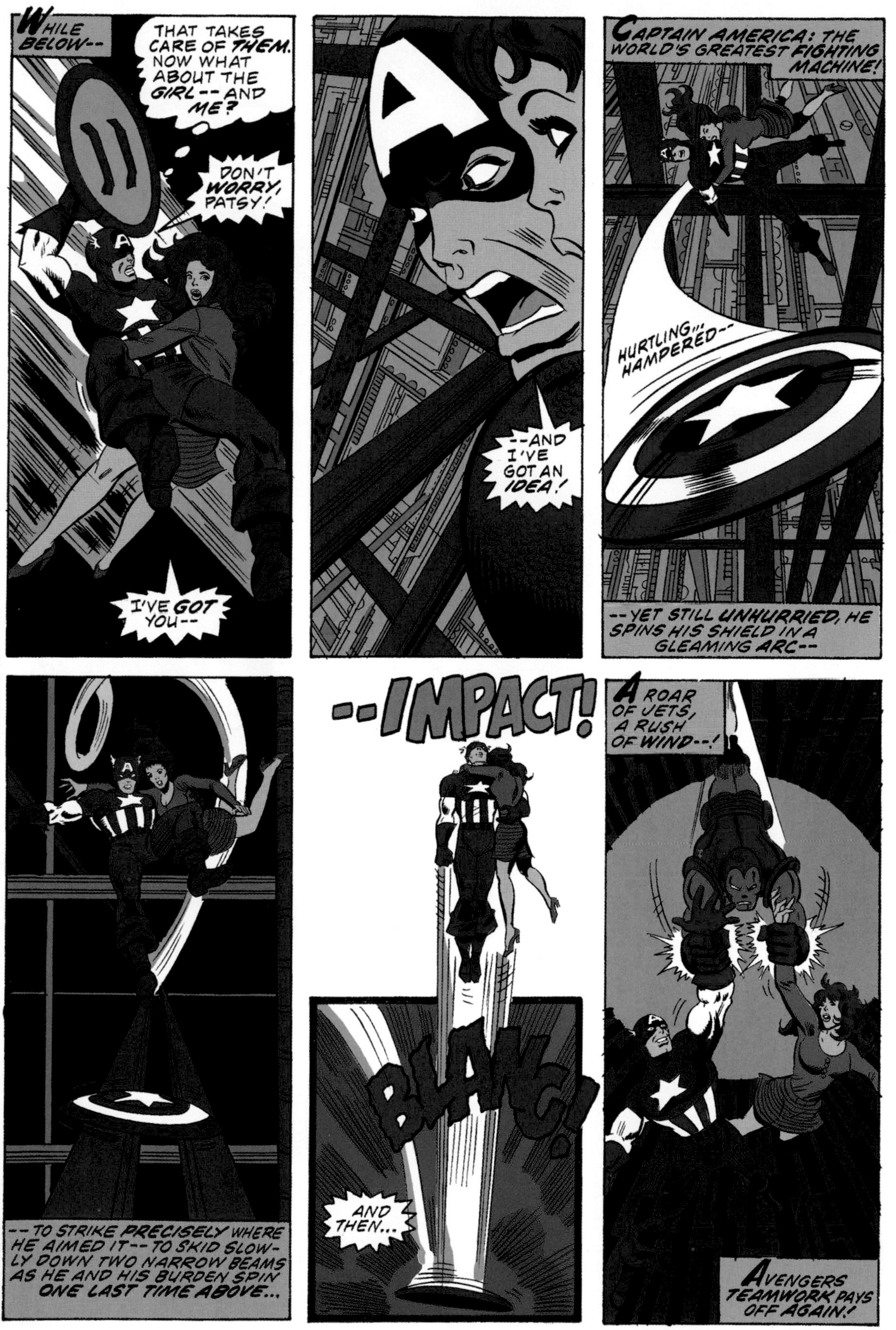

WHILE BELOW--
THAT TAKES CARE OF THEM. NOW WHAT ABOUT THE GIRL--AND ME?
DON'T WORRY, PATSY!
I'VE GOT YOU--
--AND I'VE GOT AN IDEA!
CAPTAIN AMERICA: THE WORLD'S GREATEST FIGHTING MACHINE!
HURTLING... HAMPERED--
--YET STILL UNHURRIED, HE SPINS HIS SHIELD IN A GLEAMING ARC--
--TO STRIKE PRECISELY WHERE HE AIMED IT--TO SKID SLOWLY DOWN TWO NARROW BEAMS AS HE AND HIS BURDEN SPIN ONE LAST TIME ABOVE...
--IMPACT!
BLANG!
AND THEN...
A ROAR OF JETS, A RUSH OF WIND--!
AVENGERS TEAMWORK PAYS OFF AGAIN!

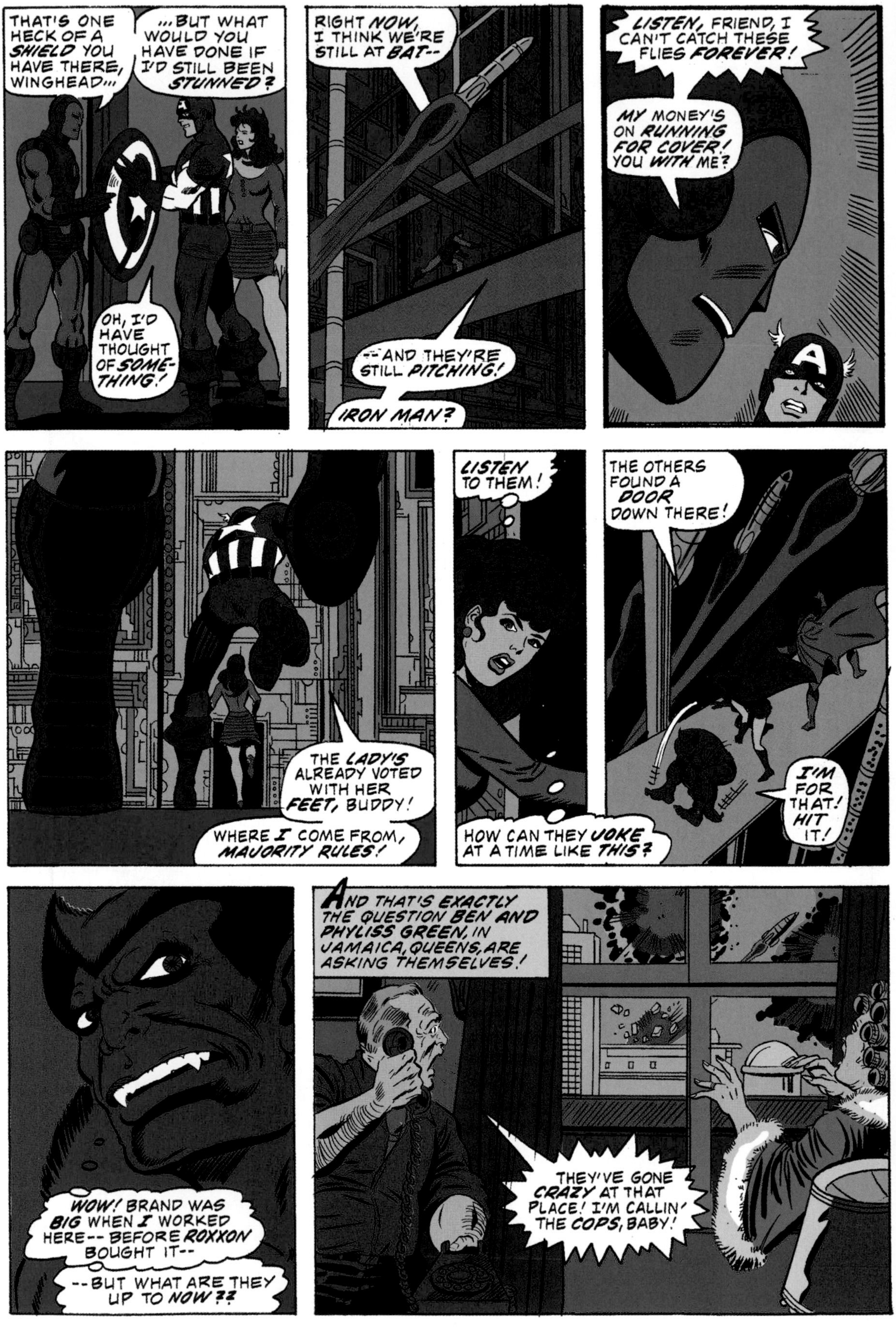
THAT'S ONE HECK OF A SHIELD YOU HAVE THERE, WINGHEAD...
...BUT WHAT WOULD YOU HAVE DONE IF I'D STILL BEEN STUNNED?
OH, I'D HAVE THOUGHT OF SOME-THING!
RIGHT NOW, I THINK WE'RE STILL AT BAT--
--AND THEY'RE STILL PITCHING!
IRON MAN?
LISTEN, FRIEND, I CAN'T CATCH THESE FLIES FOREVER!
MY MONEY'S ON RUNNING FOR COVER! YOU WITH ME?
THE LADY'S ALREADY VOTED WITH HER FEET, BUDDY!
WHERE I COME FROM, MAJORITY RULES!
LISTEN TO THEM!
HOW CAN THEY JOKE AT A TIME LIKE THIS?
THE OTHERS FOUND A DOOR DOWN THERE!
I'M FOR THAT! HIT IT!
WOW! BRAND WAS BIG WHEN I WORKED HERE-- BEFORE ROXXON BOUGHT IT--
--BUT WHAT ARE THEY UP TO NOW??
AND THAT'S EXACTLY THE QUESTION BEN AND PHYLISS GREEN, IN JAMAICA, QUEENS, ARE ASKING THEMSELVES!
THEY'VE GONE CRAZY AT THAT PLACE! I'M CALLIN' THE COPS, BABY!

THAT'S IT FOR BEN AND FOR PHYLISS THIS MONTH-- AND FOREVER-- BUT KEEP THAT FATEFUL PHONE CALL IN YOUR THOUGHTS--

--AS WE TURN BACK TO OUR STARS!

W-WHERE ARE WE?

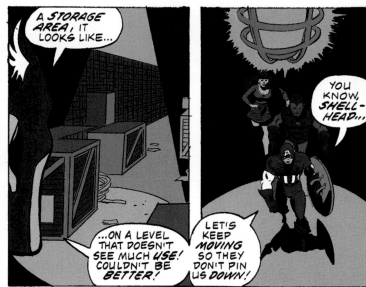

A STORAGE AREA, IT LOOKS LIKE...

...ON A LEVEL THAT DOESN'T SEE MUCH USE! COULDN'T BE BETTER!

YOU KNOW, SHELL-HEAD....

LET'S KEEP MOVING SO THEY DON'T PIN US DOWN!

...NOBODY'S CALLED ME "WINGHEAD" LIKE YOU JUST DID SINCE I LEFT THE AVENGERS LAST YEAR!

I MISS IT! I MISS THIS GROUP!

THINGS HAVE BEEN STRANGE FOR YOU, EH? ME, TOO!

HEY, YOU GUYS! DON'T GO SO FAST!

PATSY, YOU CATCH UP TO US, OR I'LL PERSONALLY---

WHAT IN THE WORLD!

I DON'T BELIEVE IT!

THAT COSTUME! IT'S --

--THE CAT!

IT SEEMS TO BE THE REAL GOODS! I GUESS IT WOULD BE, IF IT'S IN THIS ASYLUM!

BUT HOW DID IT GET HERE?

BRAND CORP

BRAND AND ROXXON PROB'BLY BOUGHT IT, LIKE THEY BUY EVERYTHING ELSE!

YOU--KNEW THE CAT?

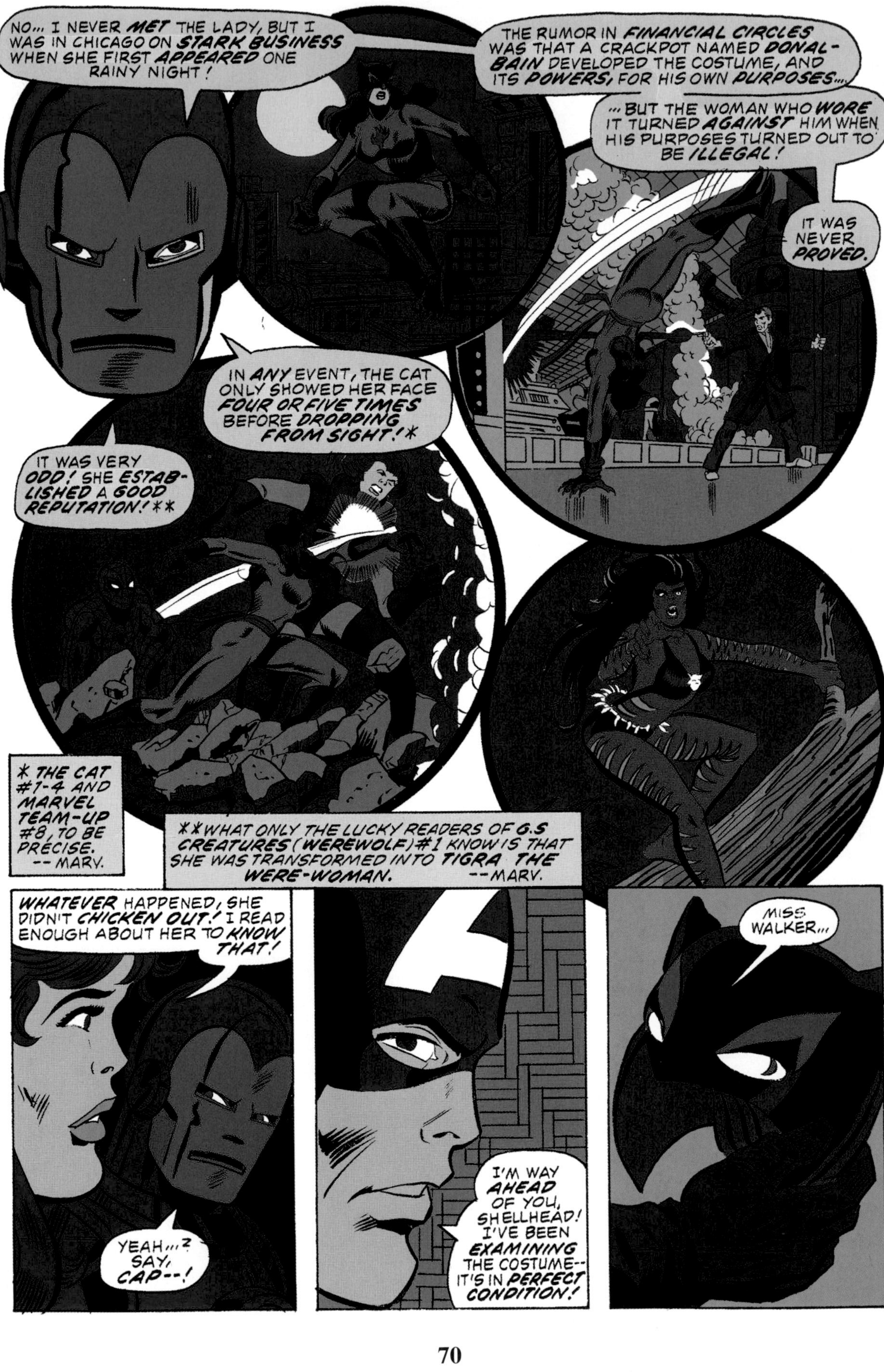
NO... I NEVER MET THE LADY, BUT I WAS IN CHICAGO ON STARK BUSINESS WHEN SHE FIRST APPEARED ONE RAINY NIGHT!
THE RUMOR IN FINANCIAL CIRCLES WAS THAT A CRACKPOT NAMED DONAL-BAIN DEVELOPED THE COSTUME, AND ITS POWERS, FOR HIS OWN PURPOSES...
...BUT THE WOMAN WHO WORE IT TURNED AGAINST HIM WHEN HIS PURPOSES TURNED OUT TO BE ILLEGAL!
IT WAS NEVER PROVED.
IN ANY EVENT, THE CAT ONLY SHOWED HER FACE FOUR OR FIVE TIMES BEFORE DROPPING FROM SIGHT!*
IT WAS VERY ODD! SHE ESTAB-LISHED A GOOD REPUTATION!**
* THE CAT #1-4 AND MARVEL TEAM-UP #8, TO BE PRECISE. --MARV.
**WHAT ONLY THE LUCKY READERS OF G.S CREATURES (WEREWOLF) #1 KNOW IS THAT SHE WAS TRANSFORMED INTO TIGRA THE WERE-WOMAN. --MARV.
WHATEVER HAPPENED, SHE DIDN'T CHICKEN OUT! I READ ENOUGH ABOUT HER TO KNOW THAT!
YEAH...? SAY, CAP--!
I'M WAY AHEAD OF YOU, SHELLHEAD! I'VE BEEN EXAMINING THE COSTUME-- IT'S IN PERFECT CONDITION!
MISS WALKER...

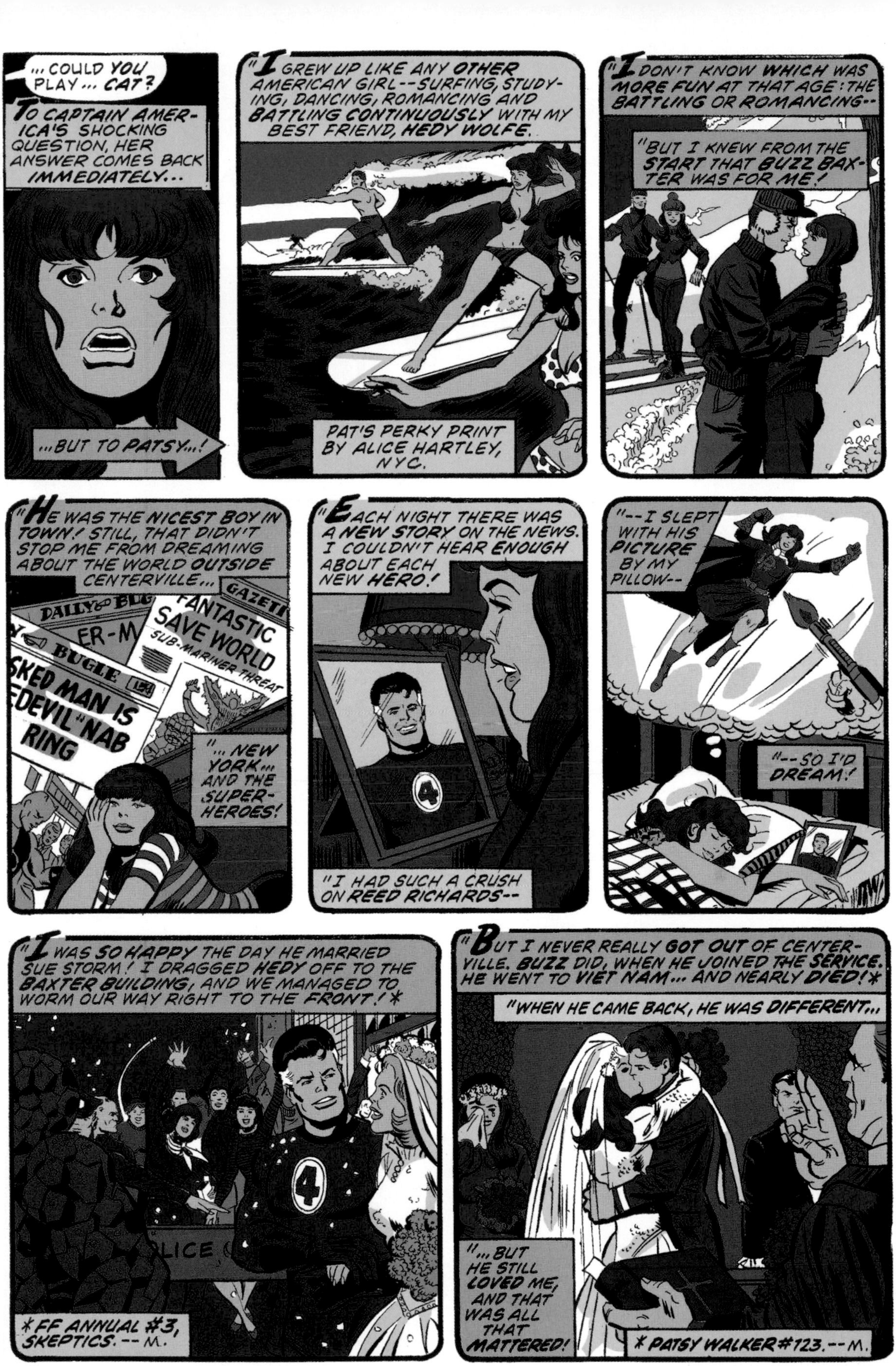
...COULD YOU PLAY... CAT?
TO CAPTAIN AMERICA'S SHOCKING QUESTION, HER ANSWER COMES BACK IMMEDIATELY...
...BUT TO PATSY...!
"I GREW UP LIKE ANY OTHER AMERICAN GIRL--SURFING, STUDYING, DANCING, ROMANCING AND BATTLING CONTINUOUSLY WITH MY BEST FRIEND, HEDY WOLFE.
PAT'S PERKY PRINT BY ALICE HARTLEY, NYC.
"I DON'T KNOW WHICH WAS MORE FUN AT THAT AGE: THE BATTLING OR ROMANCING--
"BUT I KNEW FROM THE START THAT BUZZ BAXTER WAS FOR ME!
"HE WAS THE NICEST BOY IN TOWN! STILL, THAT DIDN'T STOP ME FROM DREAMING ABOUT THE WORLD OUTSIDE CENTERVILLE...
FANTASTIC
SAVE WORLD
SUB-MARINER THREAT
BUGLE
"...NEW YORK... AND THE SUPER-HEROES!
"EACH NIGHT THERE WAS A NEW STORY ON THE NEWS. I COULDN'T HEAR ENOUGH ABOUT EACH NEW HERO!
"I HAD SUCH A CRUSH ON REED RICHARDS--
"--I SLEPT WITH HIS PICTURE BY MY PILLOW--
"--SO I'D DREAM!
"I WAS SO HAPPY THE DAY HE MARRIED SUE STORM! I DRAGGED HEDY OFF TO THE BAXTER BUILDING, AND WE MANAGED TO WORM OUR WAY RIGHT TO THE FRONT! *
*FF ANNUAL #3, SKEPTICS. --M.
"BUT I NEVER REALLY GOT OUT OF CENTERVILLE. BUZZ DID, WHEN HE JOINED THE SERVICE. HE WENT TO VIET NAM... AND NEARLY DIED! *
"WHEN HE CAME BACK, HE WAS DIFFERENT...
"...BUT HE STILL LOVED ME, AND THAT WAS ALL THAT MATTERED!
* PATSY WALKER #123. --M.

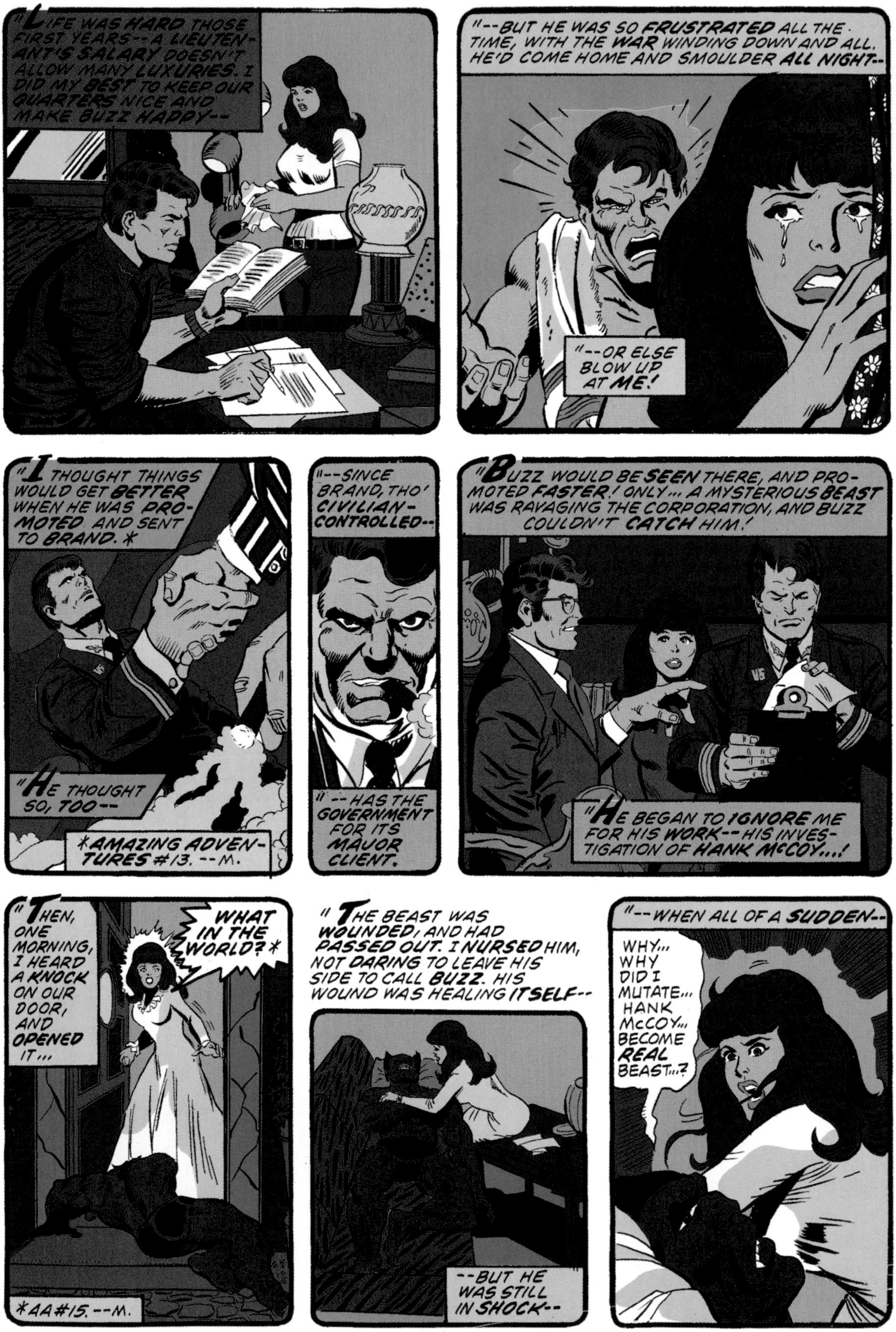
"LIFE WAS HARD THOSE FIRST YEARS-- A LIEUTENANT'S SALARY DOESN'T ALLOW MANY LUXURIES. I DID MY BEST TO KEEP OUR QUARTERS NICE AND MAKE BUZZ HAPPY--
"--BUT HE WAS SO FRUSTRATED ALL THE TIME, WITH THE WAR WINDING DOWN AND ALL. HE'D COME HOME AND SMOULDER ALL NIGHT--
"--OR ELSE BLOW UP AT ME!
"I THOUGHT THINGS WOULD GET BETTER WHEN HE WAS PROMOTED AND SENT TO BRAND.*
"HE THOUGHT SO, TOO--
*AMAZING ADVENTURES #13. --M.
"--SINCE BRAND, THO' CIVILIAN-CONTROLLED--
"--HAS THE GOVERNMENT FOR ITS MAJOR CLIENT.
"BUZZ WOULD BE SEEN THERE, AND PROMOTED FASTER! ONLY... A MYSTERIOUS BEAST WAS RAVAGING THE CORPORATION, AND BUZZ COULDN'T CATCH HIM!
"HE BEGAN TO IGNORE ME FOR HIS WORK-- HIS INVESTIGATION OF HANK McCOY...!
"THEN, ONE MORNING, I HEARD A KNOCK ON OUR DOOR, AND OPENED IT...
WHAT IN THE WORLD?*
*AA #15. --M.
"THE BEAST WAS WOUNDED, AND HAD PASSED OUT. I NURSED HIM, NOT DARING TO LEAVE HIS SIDE TO CALL BUZZ. HIS WOUND WAS HEALING ITSELF--
--BUT HE WAS STILL IN SHOCK--
"--WHEN ALL OF A SUDDEN--
WHY... WHY DID I MUTATE... HANK McCOY... BECOME REAL BEAST...?

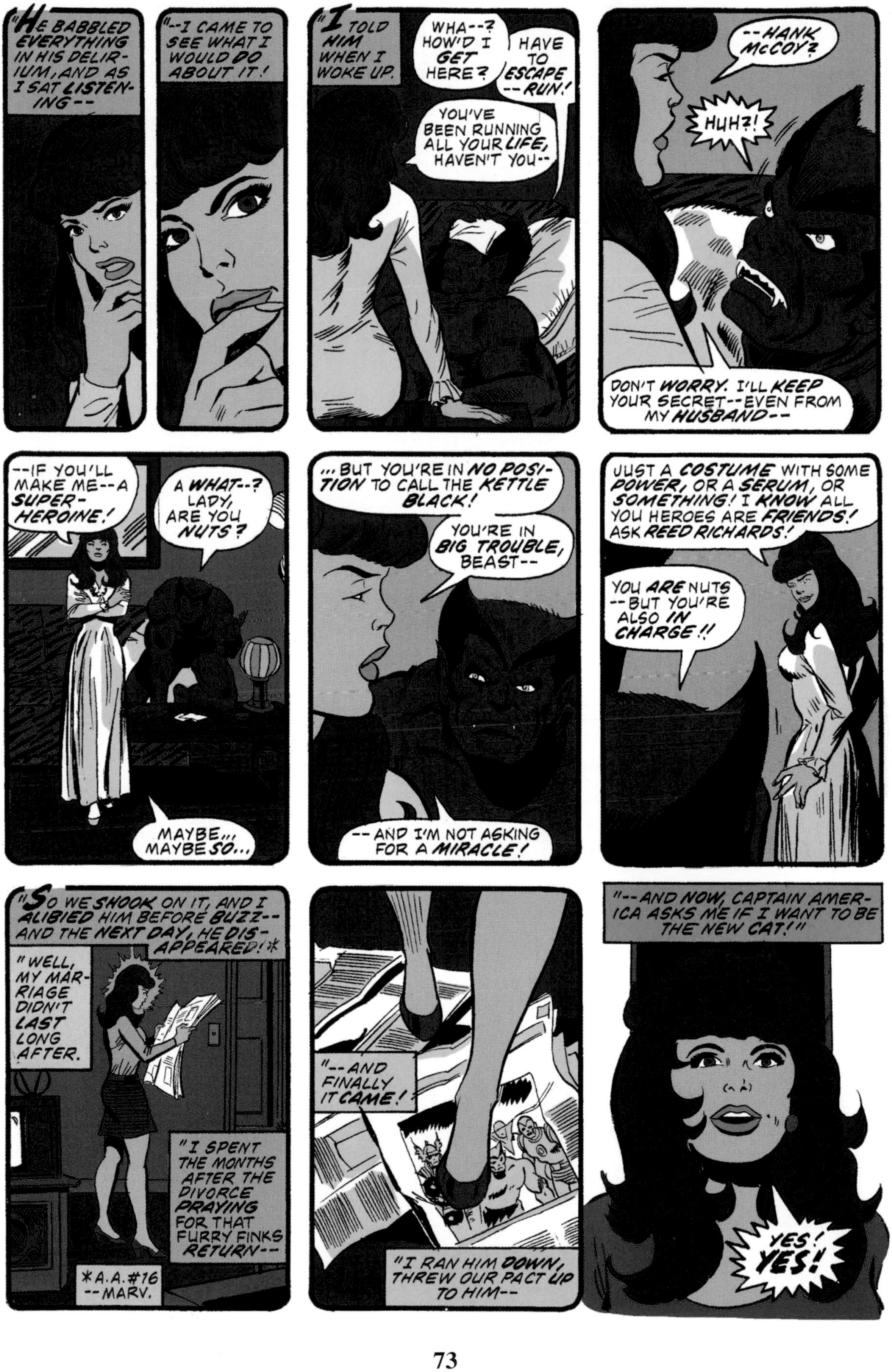
"HE BABBLED EVERYTHING IN HIS DELIRIUM, AND AS I SAT LISTENING--
"--I CAME TO SEE WHAT I WOULD DO ABOUT IT!
"I TOLD HIM WHEN I WOKE UP.
WHA--? HOW'D I GET HERE?
HAVE TO ESCAPE --RUN!
YOU'VE BEEN RUNNING ALL YOUR LIFE, HAVEN'T YOU--
--HANK McCOY?
HUH?!
DON'T WORRY. I'LL KEEP YOUR SECRET--EVEN FROM MY HUSBAND--
--IF YOU'LL MAKE ME--A SUPER-HEROINE!
A WHAT--? LADY, ARE YOU NUTS?
MAYBE... MAYBE SO...
...BUT YOU'RE IN NO POSITION TO CALL THE KETTLE BLACK!
YOU'RE IN BIG TROUBLE, BEAST--
--AND I'M NOT ASKING FOR A MIRACLE!
JUST A COSTUME WITH SOME POWER, OR A SERUM, OR SOMETHING! I KNOW ALL YOU HEROES ARE FRIENDS! ASK REED RICHARDS!
YOU ARE NUTS --BUT YOU'RE ALSO IN CHARGE!!
"SO WE SHOOK ON IT, AND I ALIBIED HIM BEFORE BUZZ--AND THE NEXT DAY, HE DISAPPEARED!*
"WELL, MY MARRIAGE DIDN'T LAST LONG AFTER.
"I SPENT THE MONTHS AFTER THE DIVORCE PRAYING FOR THAT FURRY FINKS RETURN--
*A.A. #16 --MARV.
"--AND FINALLY IT CAME!
"I RAN HIM DOWN, THREW OUR PACT UP TO HIM--
"--AND NOW, CAPTAIN AMERICA ASKS ME IF I WANT TO BE THE NEW CAT!"
YES! YES!

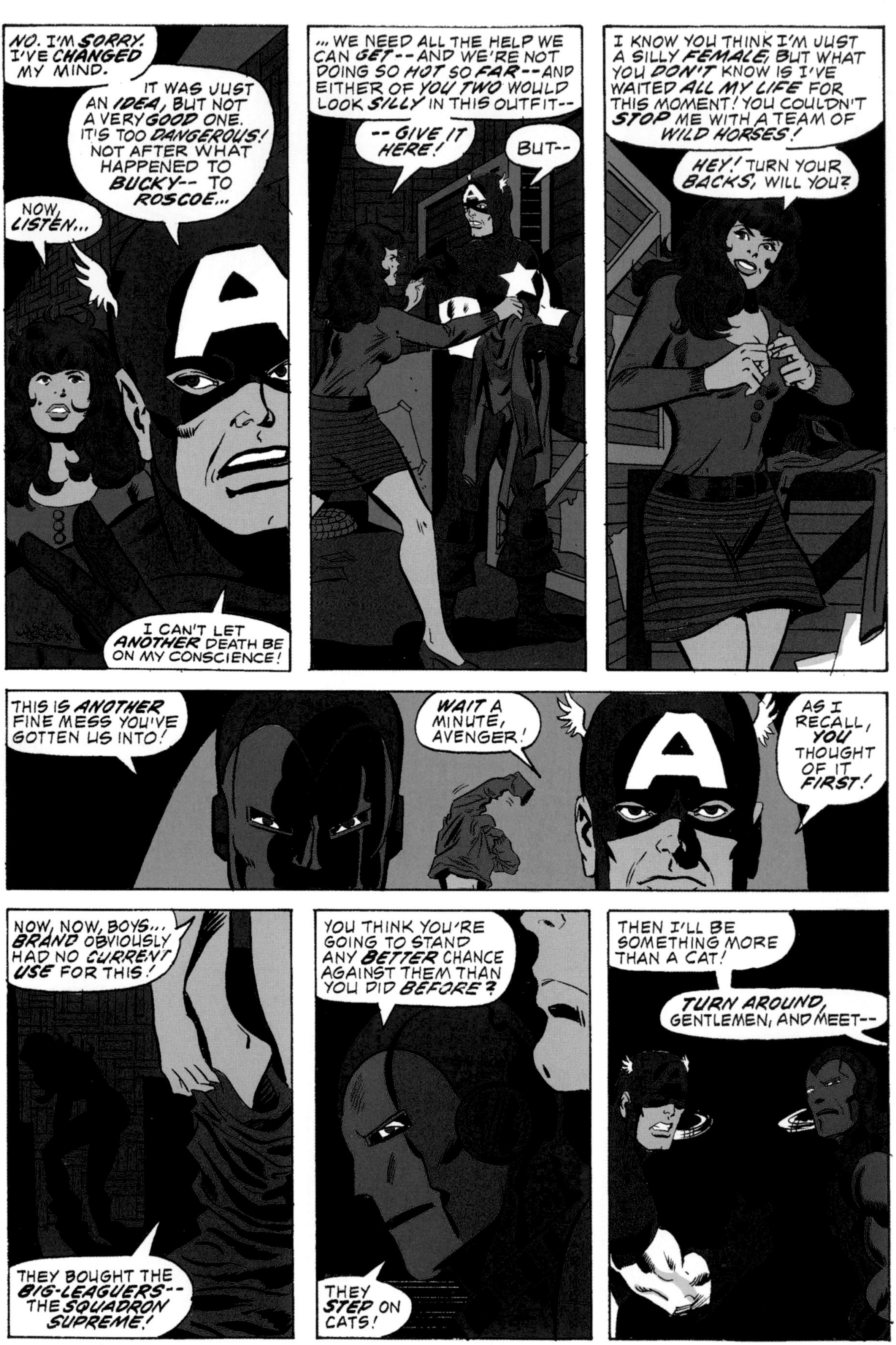
NO. I'M SORRY. I'VE CHANGED MY MIND.
IT WAS JUST AN IDEA, BUT NOT A VERY GOOD ONE. IT'S TOO DANGEROUS! NOT AFTER WHAT HAPPENED TO BUCKY-- TO ROSCOE...
NOW, LISTEN...
I CAN'T LET ANOTHER DEATH BE ON MY CONSCIENCE!
...WE NEED ALL THE HELP WE CAN GET--AND WE'RE NOT DOING SO HOT SO FAR--AND EITHER OF YOU TWO WOULD LOOK SILLY IN THIS OUTFIT--
--GIVE IT HERE!
BUT--
I KNOW YOU THINK I'M JUST A SILLY FEMALE, BUT WHAT YOU DON'T KNOW IS I'VE WAITED ALL MY LIFE FOR THIS MOMENT! YOU COULDN'T STOP ME WITH A TEAM OF WILD HORSES!
HEY! TURN YOUR BACKS, WILL YOU?
THIS IS ANOTHER FINE MESS YOU'VE GOTTEN US INTO!
WAIT A MINUTE, AVENGER!
AS I RECALL, YOU THOUGHT OF IT FIRST!
NOW, NOW, BOYS... BRAND OBVIOUSLY HAD NO CURRENT USE FOR THIS!
THEY BOUGHT THE BIG-LEAGUERS-- THE SQUADRON SUPREME!
YOU THINK YOU'RE GOING TO STAND ANY BETTER CHANCE AGAINST THEM THAN YOU DID BEFORE?
THEY STEP ON CATS!
THEN I'LL BE SOMETHING MORE THAN A CAT!
TURN AROUND, GENTLEMEN, AND MEET--

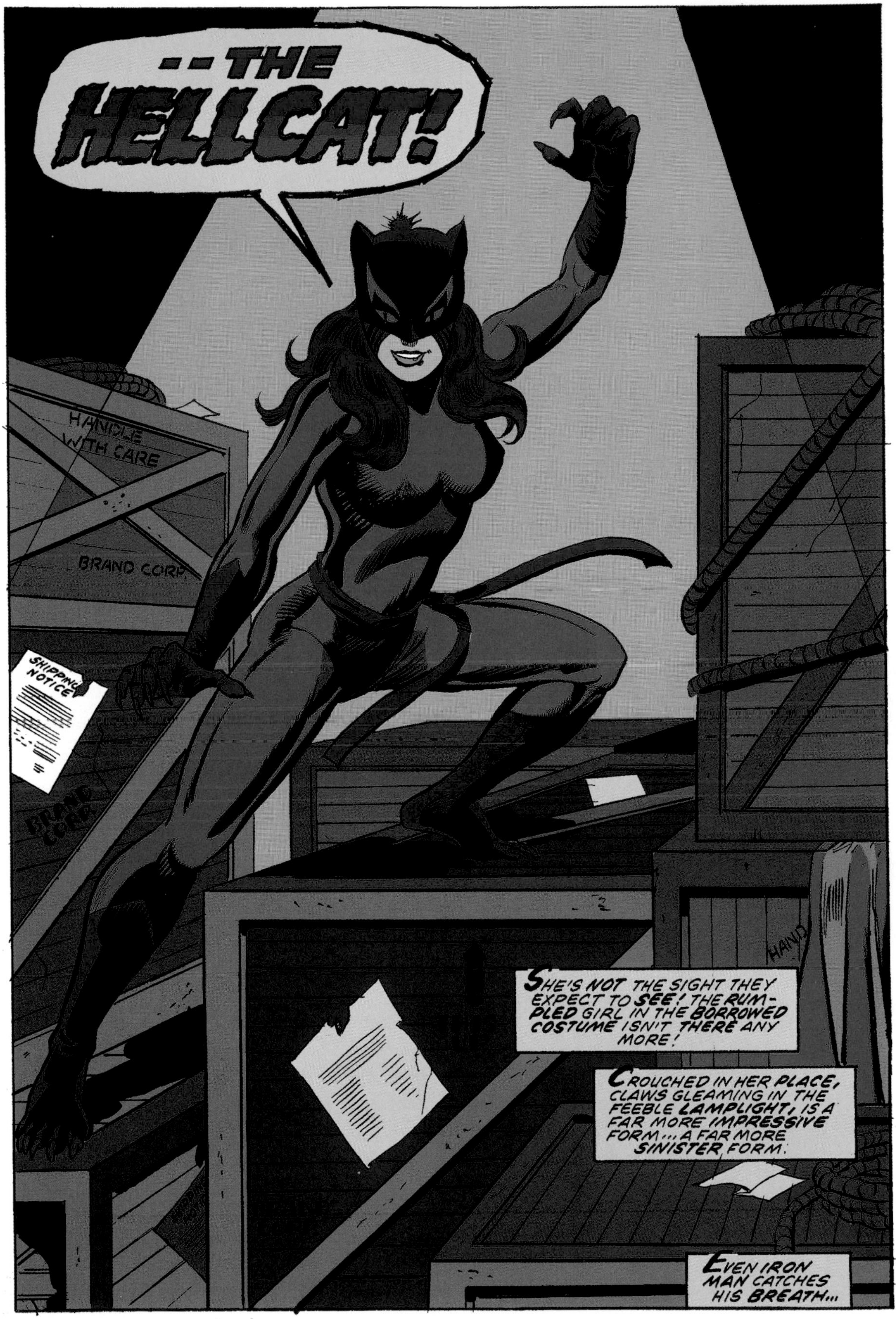
--THE HELLCAT!
HANDLE WITH CARE
BRAND CORP.
SHIPPING NOTICE
BRAND CORP.
SHE'S NOT THE SIGHT THEY EXPECT TO SEE! THE RUMPLED GIRL IN THE BORROWED COSTUME ISN'T THERE ANY MORE!
CROUCHED IN HER PLACE, CLAWS GLEAMING IN THE FEEBLE LAMPLIGHT, IS A FAR MORE IMPRESSIVE FORM... A FAR MORE SINISTER FORM.
EVEN IRON MAN CATCHES HIS BREATH...

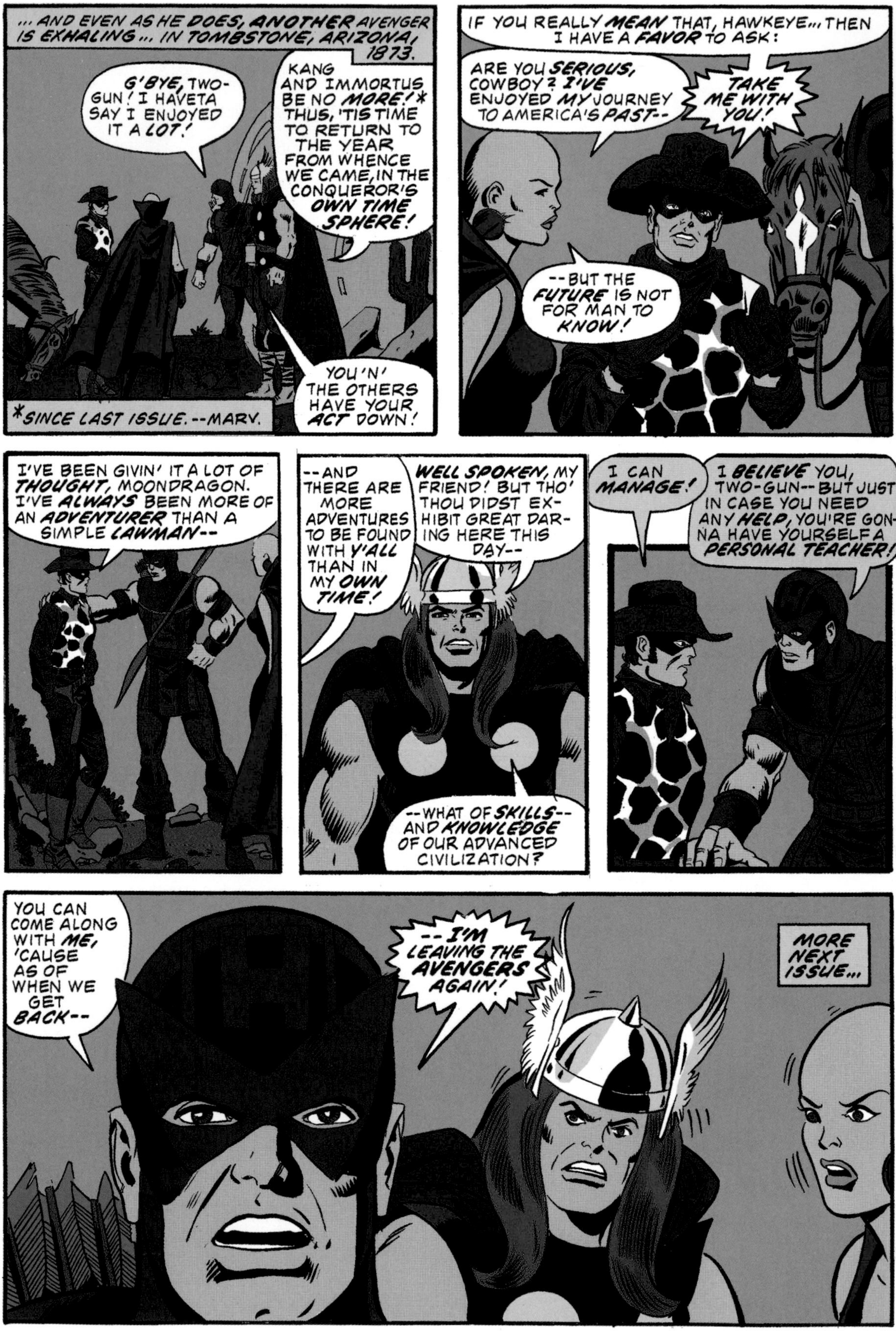

...AND EVEN AS HE DOES, ANOTHER AVENGER IS EXHALING... IN TOMBSTONE, ARIZONA, 1873.
G'BYE, TWO-GUN! I HAVETA SAY I ENJOYED IT A LOT!
KANG AND IMMORTUS BE NO MORE!* THUS, 'TIS TIME TO RETURN TO THE YEAR FROM WHENCE WE CAME, IN THE CONQUEROR'S OWN TIME SPHERE!
YOU 'N' THE OTHERS HAVE YOUR ACT DOWN!
*SINCE LAST ISSUE. --MARV.
IF YOU REALLY MEAN THAT, HAWKEYE... THEN I HAVE A FAVOR TO ASK:
ARE YOU SERIOUS, COWBOY? I'VE ENJOYED MY JOURNEY TO AMERICA'S PAST--
--BUT THE FUTURE IS NOT FOR MAN TO KNOW!
TAKE ME WITH YOU!
I'VE BEEN GIVIN' IT A LOT OF THOUGHT, MOONDRAGON. I'VE ALWAYS BEEN MORE OF AN ADVENTURER THAN A SIMPLE LAWMAN--
--AND THERE ARE MORE ADVENTURES TO BE FOUND WITH Y'ALL THAN IN MY OWN TIME!
WELL SPOKEN, MY FRIEND! BUT THO' THOU DIDST EXHIBIT GREAT DARING HERE THIS DAY--
--WHAT OF SKILLS--AND KNOWLEDGE OF OUR ADVANCED CIVILIZATION?
I CAN MANAGE!
I BELIEVE YOU, TWO-GUN--BUT JUST IN CASE YOU NEED ANY HELP, YOU'RE GONNA HAVE YOURSELF A PERSONAL TEACHER!
YOU CAN COME ALONG WITH ME, 'CAUSE AS OF WHEN WE GET BACK--
--I'M LEAVING THE AVENGERS AGAIN!
MORE NEXT ISSUE...

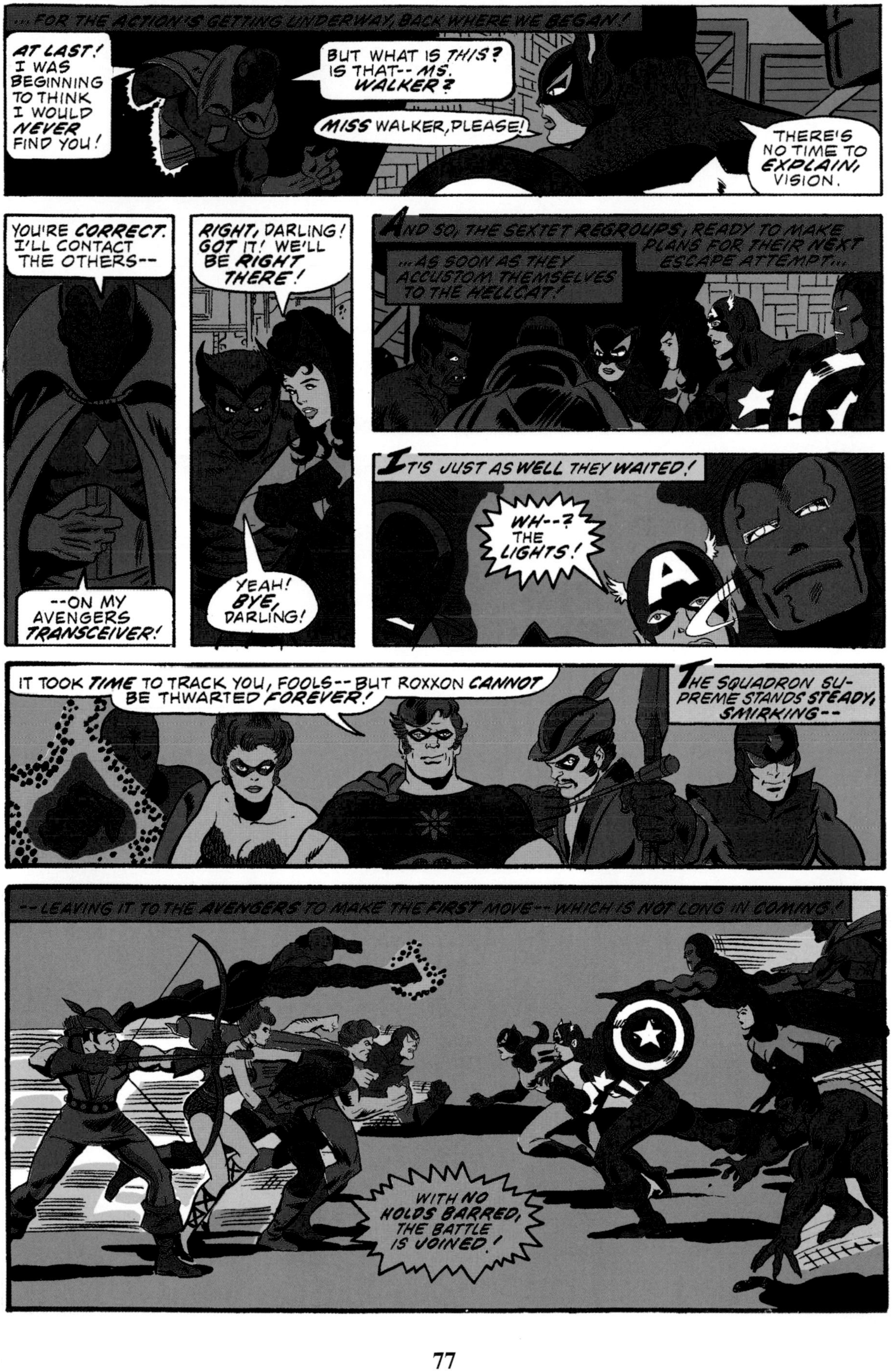
...FOR THE ACTION'S GETTING UNDERWAY, BACK WHERE WE BEGAN!
AT LAST! I WAS BEGINNING TO THINK I WOULD NEVER FIND YOU!
BUT WHAT IS THIS? IS THAT-- MS. WALKER?
MISS WALKER, PLEASE!
THERE'S NO TIME TO EXPLAIN, VISION.
YOU'RE CORRECT. I'LL CONTACT THE OTHERS--
--ON MY AVENGERS TRANSCEIVER!
RIGHT, DARLING! GOT IT! WE'LL BE RIGHT THERE!
YEAH! BYE, DARLING!
AND SO, THE SEXTET REGROUPS, READY TO MAKE PLANS FOR THEIR NEXT ESCAPE ATTEMPT...
...AS SOON AS THEY ACCUSTOM THEMSELVES TO THE HELLCAT!
IT'S JUST AS WELL THEY WAITED!
WH--? THE LIGHTS!
IT TOOK TIME TO TRACK YOU, FOOLS-- BUT ROXXON CANNOT BE THWARTED FOREVER!
THE SQUADRON SUPREME STANDS STEADY, SMIRKING--
--LEAVING IT TO THE AVENGERS TO MAKE THE FIRST MOVE-- WHICH IS NOT LONG IN COMING!
WITH NO HOLDS BARRED, THE BATTLE IS JOINED!

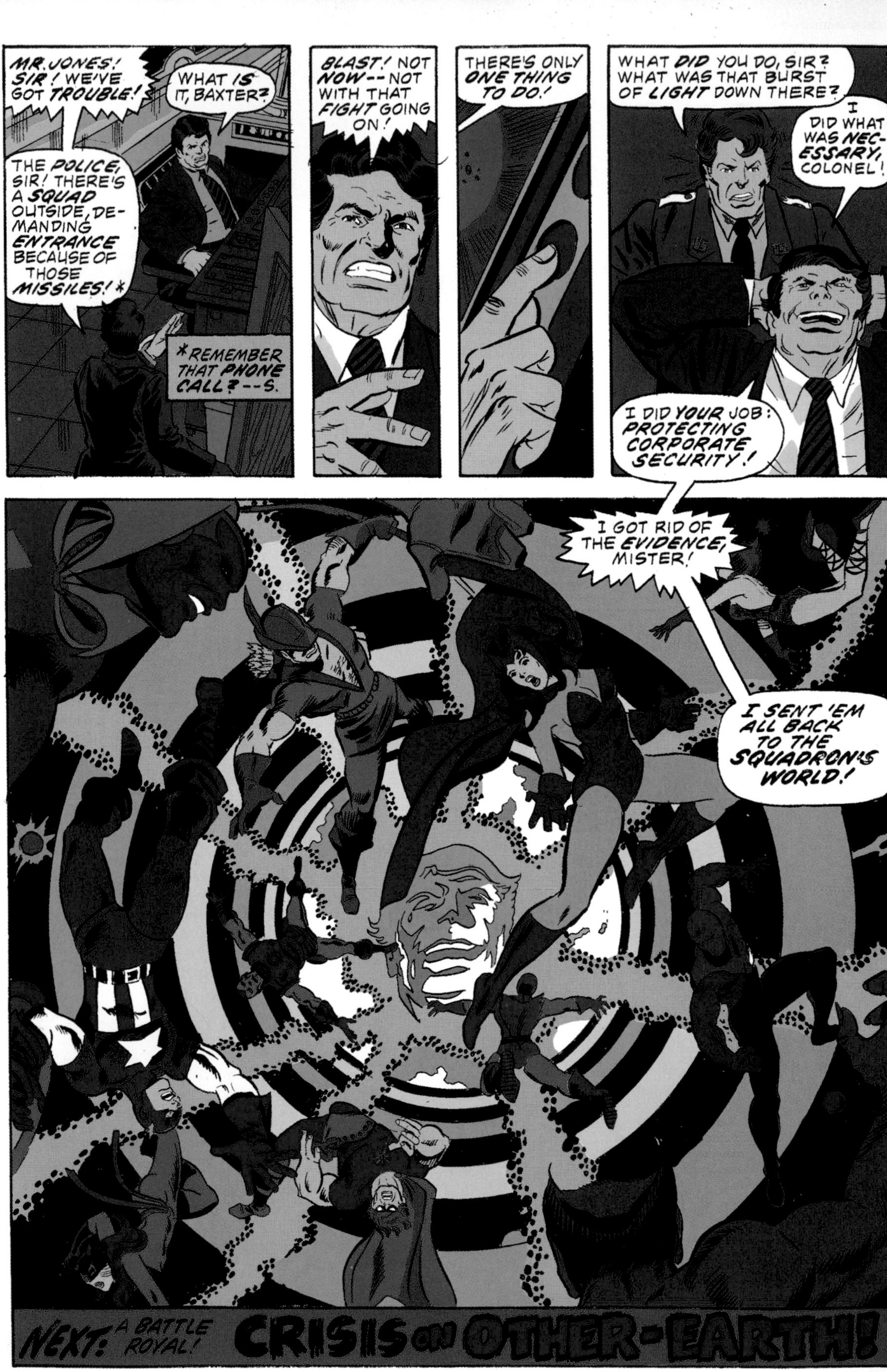
MR. JONES! SIR! WE'VE GOT TROUBLE!
WHAT IS IT, BAXTER?
THE POLICE, SIR! THERE'S A SQUAD OUTSIDE, DEMANDING ENTRANCE BECAUSE OF THOSE MISSILES! *
*REMEMBER THAT PHONE CALL? --S.
BLAST! NOT NOW -- NOT WITH THAT FIGHT GOING ON!
THERE'S ONLY ONE THING TO DO!
WHAT DID YOU DO, SIR? WHAT WAS THAT BURST OF LIGHT DOWN THERE?
I DID WHAT WAS NECESSARY, COLONEL!
I DID YOUR JOB: PROTECTING CORPORATE SECURITY!
I GOT RID OF THE EVIDENCE, MISTER!
I SENT 'EM ALL BACK TO THE SQUADRON'S WORLD!
NEXT: A BATTLE ROYAL! CRISIS ON OTHER-EARTH!

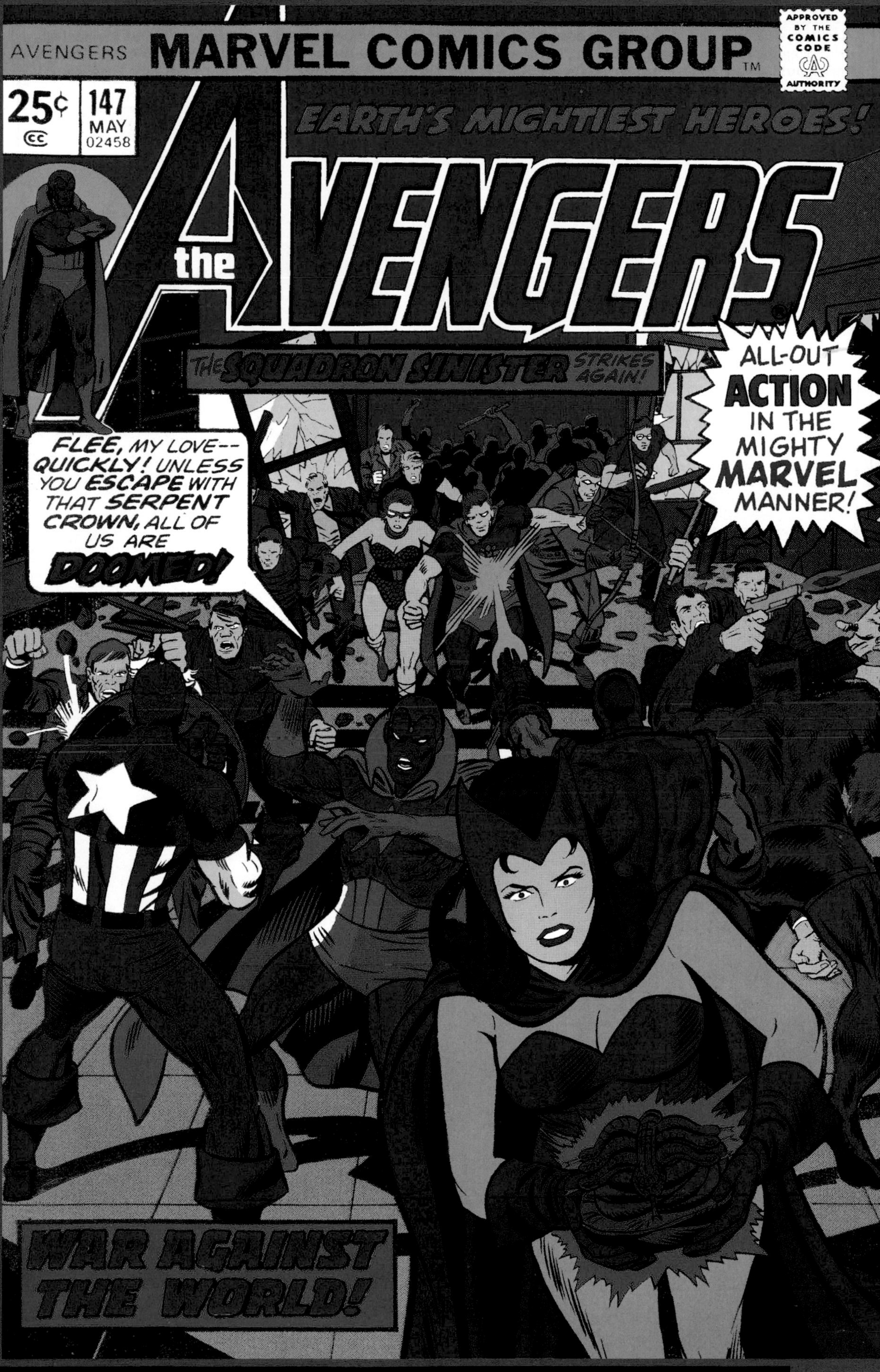

AVENGERS
MARVEL COMICS GROUP
APPROVED BY THE COMICS CODE AUTHORITY
25¢
147
MAY
02458
EARTH'S MIGHTIEST HEROES!
the AVENGERS
THE SQUADRON SINISTER STRIKES AGAIN!
ALL-OUT ACTION IN THE MIGHTY MARVEL MANNER!
FLEE, MY LOVE-- QUICKLY! UNLESS YOU ESCAPE WITH THAT SERPENT CROWN, ALL OF US ARE DOOMED!
WAR AGAINST THE WORLD!

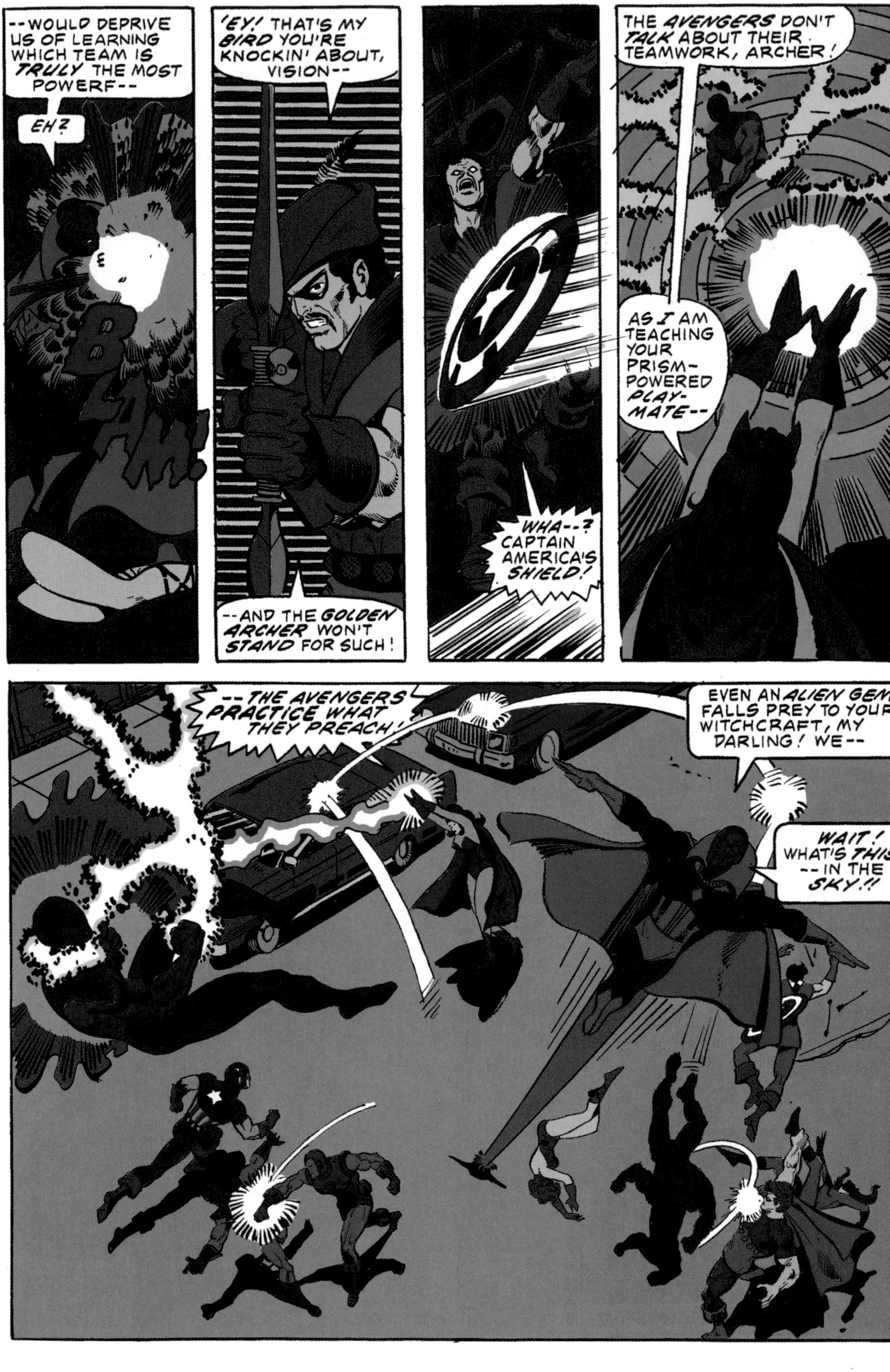
--WOULD DEPRIVE US OF LEARNING WHICH TEAM IS TRULY THE MOST POWERF--
EH?
B
LAM!
'EY! THAT'S MY BIRD YOU'RE KNOCKIN' ABOUT, VISION--
--AND THE GOLDEN ARCHER WON'T STAND FOR SUCH!
WHA--? CAPTAIN AMERICA'S SHIELD!
THE AVENGERS DON'T TALK ABOUT THEIR TEAMWORK, ARCHER!
AS I AM TEACHING YOUR PRISM-POWERED PLAY-MATE--
--THE AVENGERS PRACTICE WHAT THEY PREACH!
EVEN AN ALIEN GEM FALLS PREY TO YOUR WITCHCRAFT, MY DARLING! WE--
WAIT! WHAT'S THIS --IN THE SKY!!

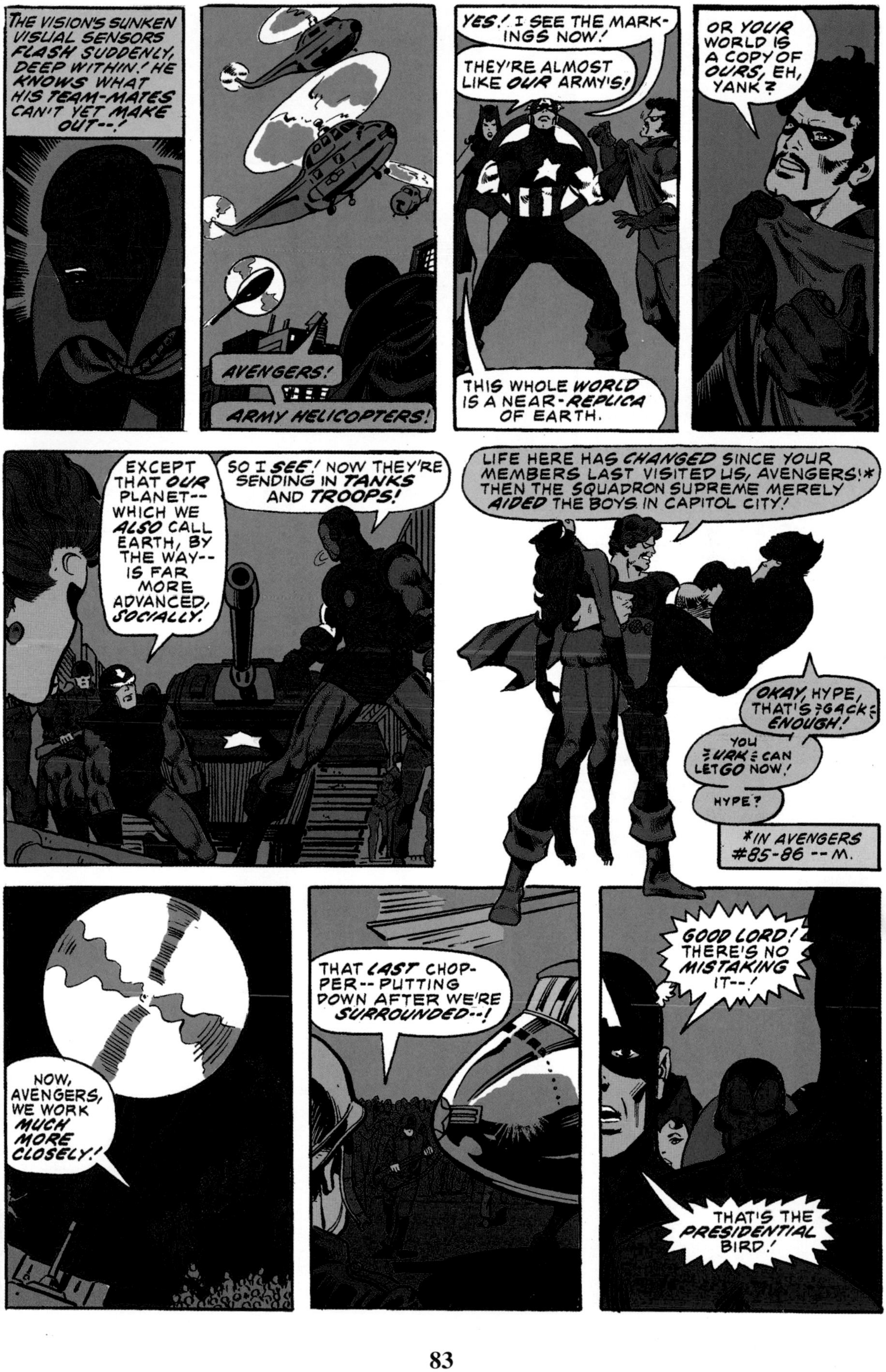
THE VISION'S SUNKEN VISUAL SENSORS FLASH SUDDENLY, DEEP WITHIN! HE KNOWS WHAT HIS TEAM-MATES CAN'T YET MAKE OUT--!
AVENGERS!
ARMY HELICOPTERS!
YES! I SEE THE MARKINGS NOW!
THEY'RE ALMOST LIKE OUR ARMY'S!
THIS WHOLE WORLD IS A NEAR-REPLICA OF EARTH.
OR YOUR WORLD IS A COPY OF OURS, EH, YANK?
EXCEPT THAT OUR PLANET--WHICH WE ALSO CALL EARTH, BY THE WAY--IS FAR MORE ADVANCED, SOCIALLY.
SO I SEE! NOW THEY'RE SENDING IN TANKS AND TROOPS!
LIFE HERE HAS CHANGED SINCE YOUR MEMBERS LAST VISITED US, AVENGERS!* THEN THE SQUADRON SUPREME MERELY AIDED THE BOYS IN CAPITOL CITY!
OKAY, HYPE, THAT'S =GACK= ENOUGH!
YOU =URK= CAN LET GO NOW!
HYPE?
*IN AVENGERS #85-86 --M.
NOW, AVENGERS, WE WORK MUCH MORE CLOSELY!
THAT LAST CHOPPER--PUTTING DOWN AFTER WE'RE SURROUNDED--!
GOOD LORD! THERE'S NO MISTAKING IT--!
THAT'S THE PRESIDENTIAL BIRD!

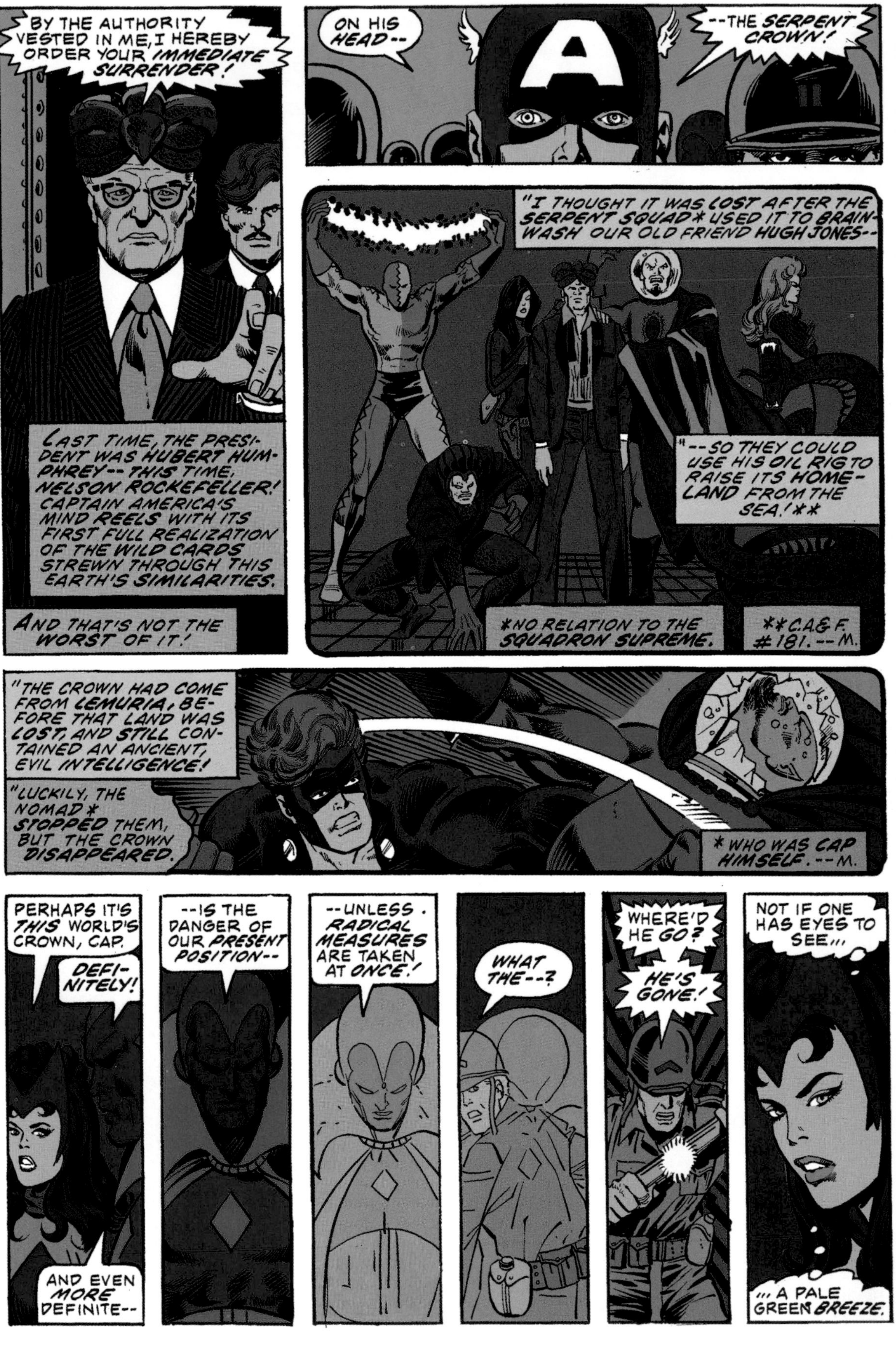
BY THE AUTHORITY VESTED IN ME, I HEREBY ORDER YOUR IMMEDIATE SURRENDER!
LAST TIME, THE PRESIDENT WAS HUBERT HUMPHREY -- THIS TIME, NELSON ROCKEFELLER! CAPTAIN AMERICA'S MIND REELS WITH ITS FIRST FULL REALIZATION OF THE WILD CARDS STREWN THROUGH THIS EARTH'S SIMILARITIES.
AND THAT'S NOT THE WORST OF IT!
ON HIS HEAD --
-- THE SERPENT CROWN!
"I THOUGHT IT WAS LOST AFTER THE SERPENT SQUAD* USED IT TO BRAINWASH OUR OLD FRIEND HUGH JONES --
"-- SO THEY COULD USE HIS OIL RIG TO RAISE ITS HOMELAND FROM THE SEA!**
*NO RELATION TO THE SQUADRON SUPREME.
**C.A.& F. #181. -- M.
"THE CROWN HAD COME FROM LEMURIA, BEFORE THAT LAND WAS LOST, AND STILL CONTAINED AN ANCIENT, EVIL INTELLIGENCE!
"LUCKILY, THE NOMAD* STOPPED THEM, BUT THE CROWN DISAPPEARED.
*WHO WAS CAP HIMSELF. -- M.
PERHAPS IT'S THIS WORLD'S CROWN, CAP.
DEFINITELY!
AND EVEN MORE DEFINITE --
-- IS THE DANGER OF OUR PRESENT POSITION --
-- UNLESS RADICAL MEASURES ARE TAKEN AT ONCE!
WHAT THE --?
WHERE'D HE GO?
HE'S GONE!
NOT IF ONE HAS EYES TO SEE...
... A PALE GREEN BREEZE.

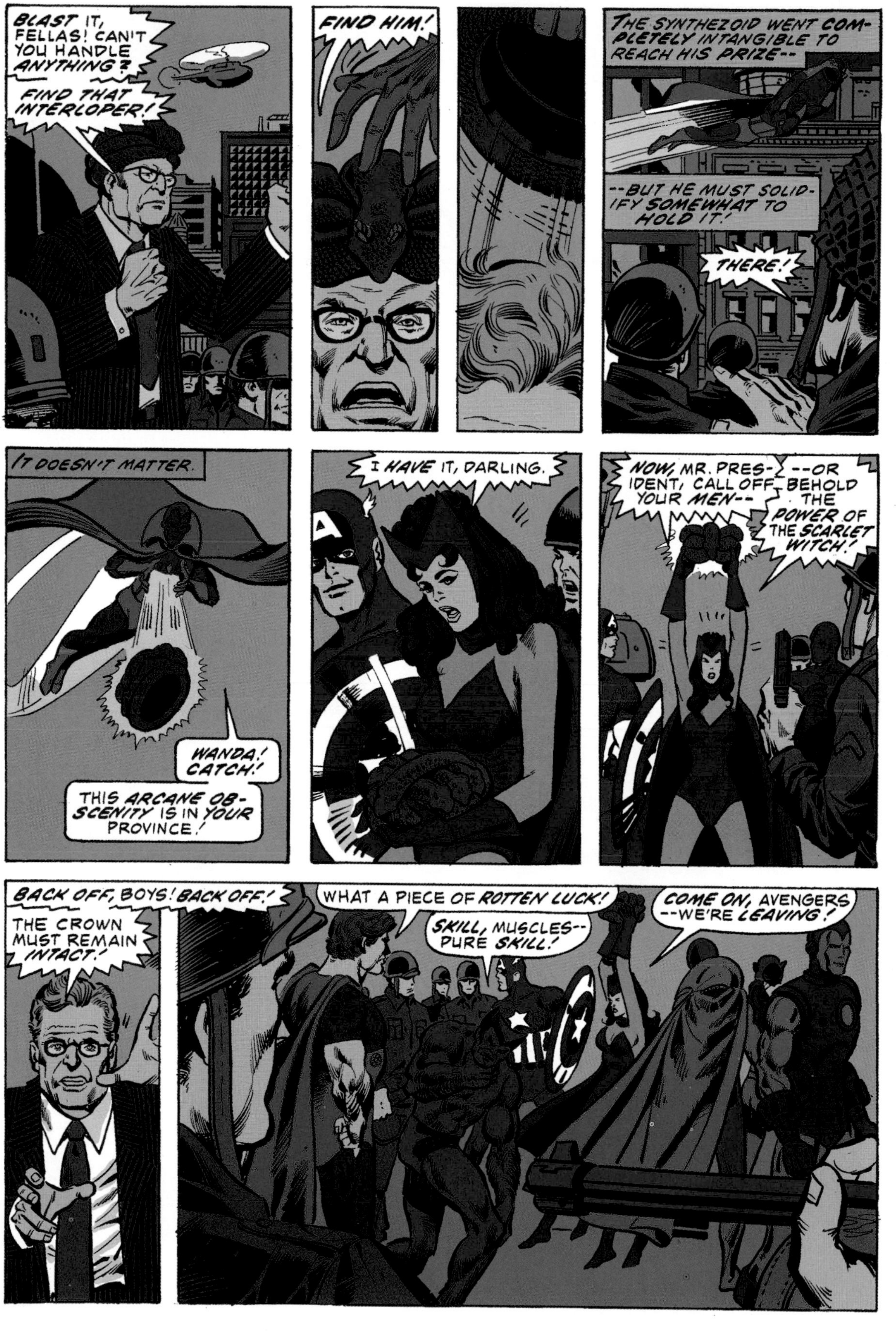
BLAST IT, FELLAS! CAN'T YOU HANDLE ANYTHING?
FIND THAT INTERLOPER!
FIND HIM!
THE SYNTHEZOID WENT COMPLETELY INTANGIBLE TO REACH HIS PRIZE--
--BUT HE MUST SOLIDIFY SOMEWHAT TO HOLD IT!
THERE!
IT DOESN'T MATTER.
WANDA! CATCH!
THIS ARCANE OBSCENITY IS IN YOUR PROVINCE!
I HAVE IT, DARLING.
NOW, MR. PRESIDENT, CALL OFF YOUR MEN--
--OR BEHOLD THE POWER OF THE SCARLET WITCH!
BACK OFF, BOYS! BACK OFF!
THE CROWN MUST REMAIN INTACT!
WHAT A PIECE OF ROTTEN LUCK!
SKILL, MUSCLES--PURE SKILL!
COME ON, AVENGERS--WE'RE LEAVING!

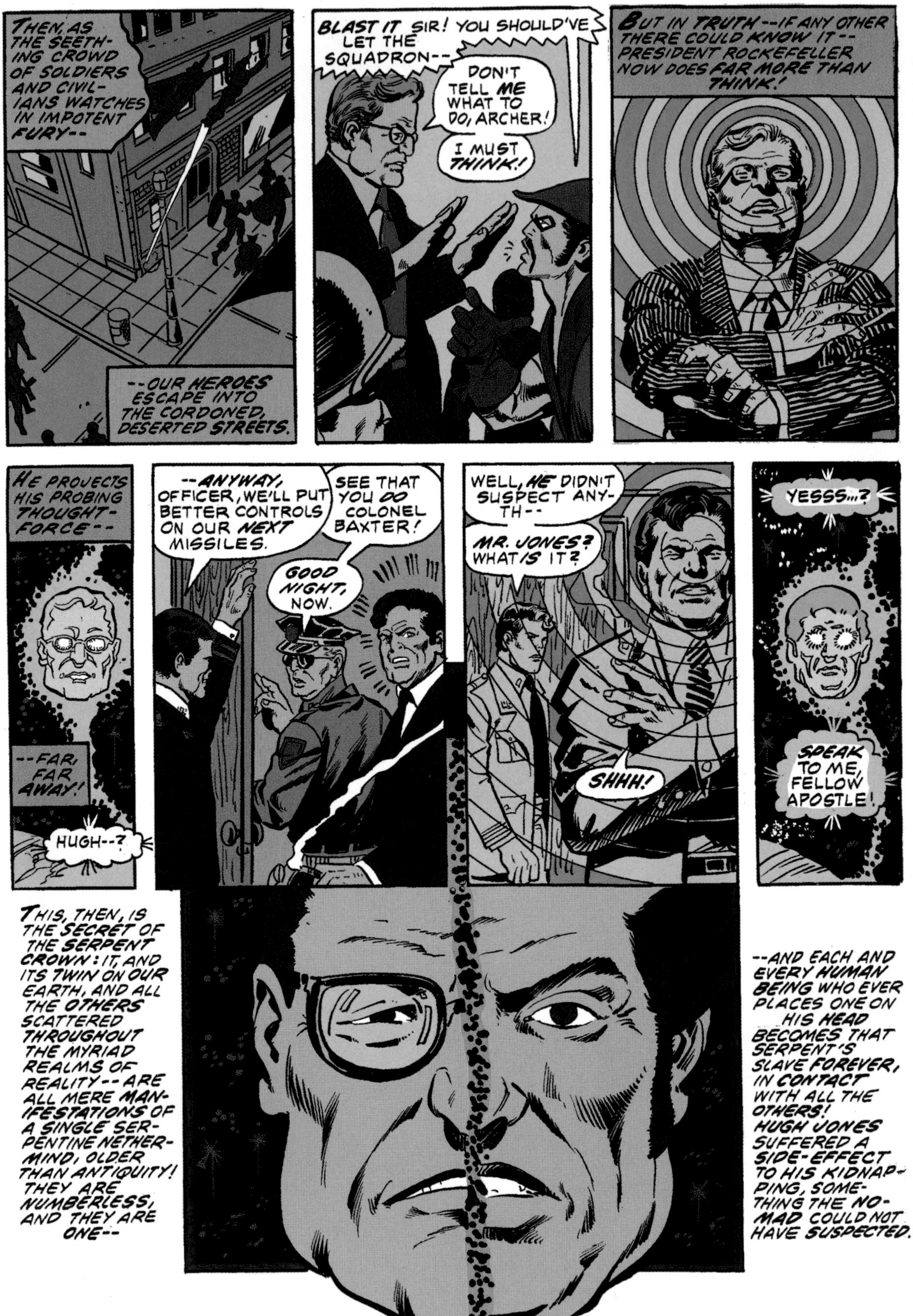

THEN, AS THE SEETHING CROWD OF SOLDIERS AND CIVILIANS WATCHES IN IMPOTENT FURY--
--OUR HEROES ESCAPE INTO THE CORDONED, DESERTED STREETS.
BLAST IT SIR! YOU SHOULD'VE LET THE SQUADRON--
DON'T TELL ME WHAT TO DO, ARCHER!
I MUST THINK!
BUT IN TRUTH--IF ANY OTHER THERE COULD KNOW IT--PRESIDENT ROCKEFELLER NOW DOES FAR MORE THAN THINK!
HE PROJECTS HIS PROBING THOUGHT-FORCE--
--FAR, FAR AWAY!
HUGH--?
--ANYWAY, OFFICER, WE'LL PUT BETTER CONTROLS ON OUR NEXT MISSILES.
SEE THAT YOU DO COLONEL BAXTER!
GOOD NIGHT, NOW.
WELL, HE DIDN'T SUSPECT ANYTH--
MR. JONES? WHAT IS IT?
SHHH!
YESSS...?
SPEAK TO ME, FELLOW APOSTLE!
THIS, THEN, IS THE SECRET OF THE SERPENT CROWN: IT, AND ITS TWIN ON OUR EARTH, AND ALL THE OTHERS SCATTERED THROUGHOUT THE MYRIAD REALMS OF REALITY--ARE ALL MERE MANIFESTATIONS OF A SINGLE SERPENTINE NETHER-MIND, OLDER THAN ANTIQUITY! THEY ARE NUMBERLESS, AND THEY ARE ONE--
--AND EACH AND EVERY HUMAN BEING WHO EVER PLACES ONE ON HIS HEAD BECOMES THAT SERPENT'S SLAVE FOREVER, IN CONTACT WITH ALL THE OTHERS! HUGH JONES SUFFERED A SIDE-EFFECT TO HIS KIDNAPPING, SOMETHING THE NOMAD COULD NOT HAVE SUSPECTED.

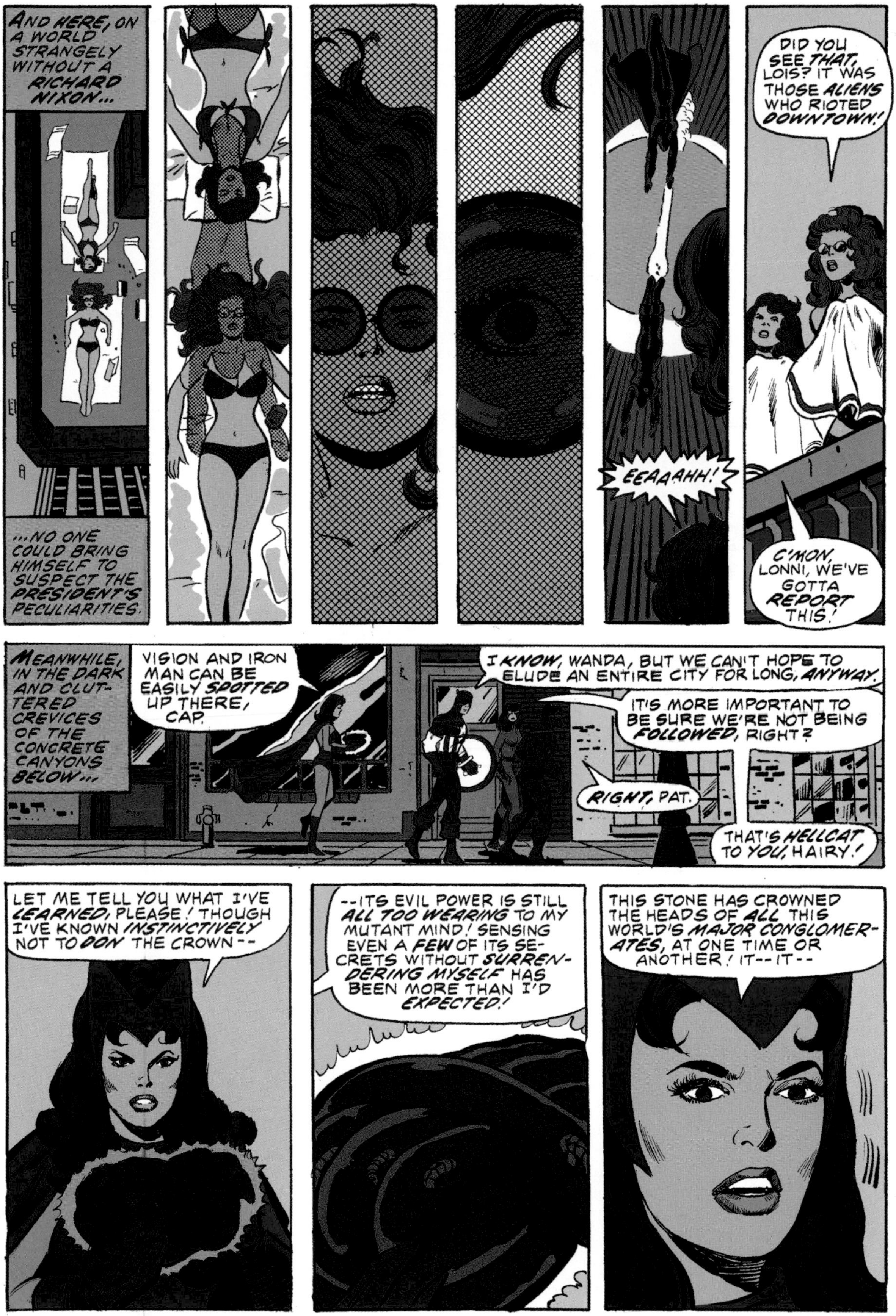
AND HERE, ON A WORLD STRANGELY WITHOUT A RICHARD NIXON...
...NO ONE COULD BRING HIMSELF TO SUSPECT THE PRESIDENT'S PECULIARITIES.
EEAAAHH!
DID YOU SEE THAT, LOIS? IT WAS THOSE ALIENS WHO RIOTED DOWNTOWN!
C'MON, LONNI, WE'VE GOTTA REPORT THIS!
MEANWHILE, IN THE DARK AND CLUTTERED CREVICES OF THE CONCRETE CANYONS BELOW...
VISION AND IRON MAN CAN BE EASILY SPOTTED UP THERE, CAP.
I KNOW, WANDA, BUT WE CAN'T HOPE TO ELUDE AN ENTIRE CITY FOR LONG, ANYWAY.
IT'S MORE IMPORTANT TO BE SURE WE'RE NOT BEING FOLLOWED, RIGHT?
RIGHT, PAT.
THAT'S HELLCAT TO YOU, HAIRY!
LET ME TELL YOU WHAT I'VE LEARNED, PLEASE! THOUGH I'VE KNOWN INSTINCTIVELY NOT TO DON THE CROWN--
--ITS EVIL POWER IS STILL ALL TOO WEARING TO MY MUTANT MIND! SENSING EVEN A FEW OF ITS SECRETS WITHOUT SURRENDERING MYSELF HAS BEEN MORE THAN I'D EXPECTED!
THIS STONE HAS CROWNED THE HEADS OF ALL THIS WORLD'S MAJOR CONGLOMERATES, AT ONE TIME OR ANOTHER! IT--IT--

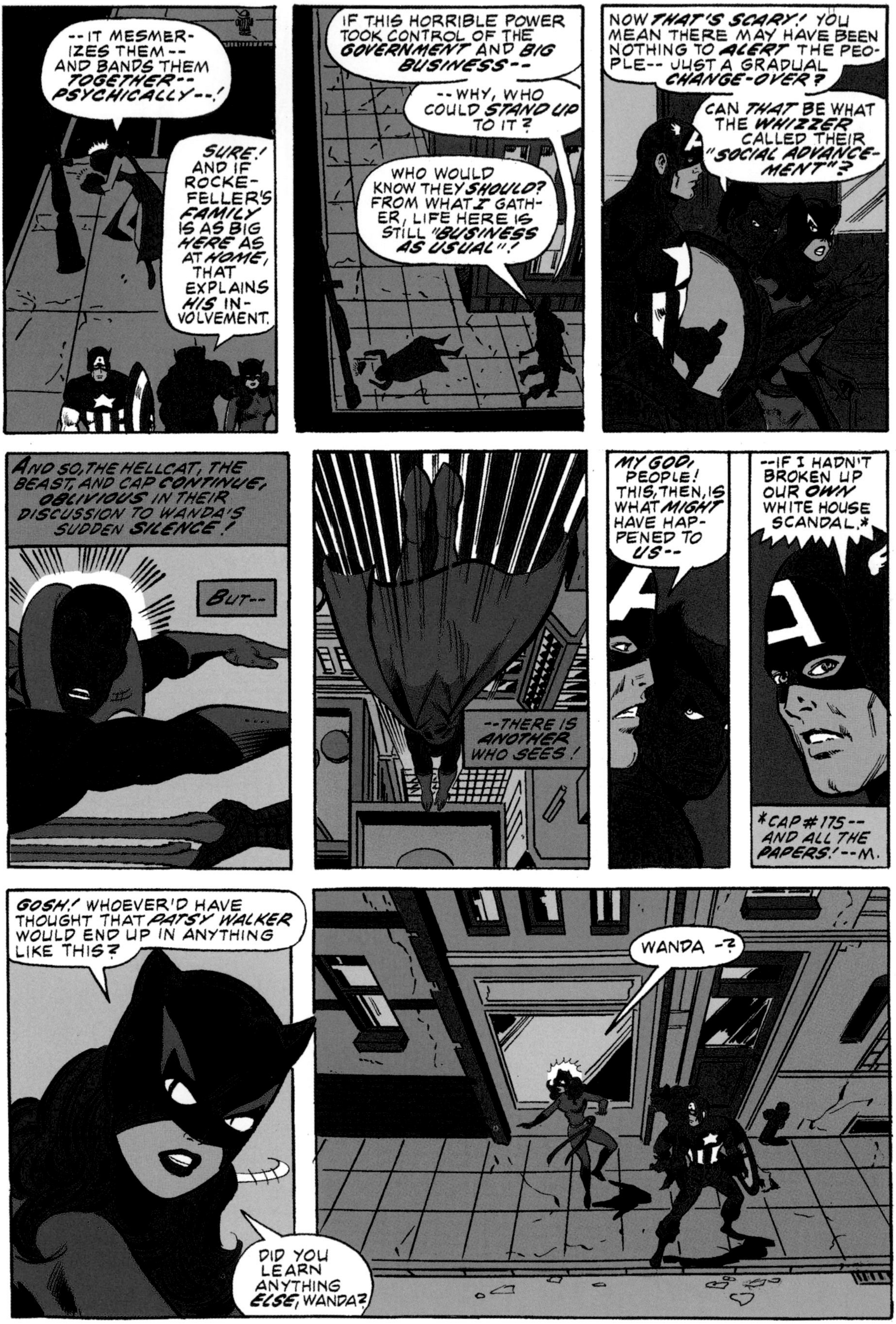
--IT MESMERIZES THEM--AND BANDS THEM TOGETHER--PSYCHICALLY--!
SURE! AND IF ROCKEFELLER'S FAMILY IS AS BIG HERE AS AT HOME, THAT EXPLAINS HIS INVOLVEMENT.
IF THIS HORRIBLE POWER TOOK CONTROL OF THE GOVERNMENT AND BIG BUSINESS--
--WHY, WHO COULD STAND UP TO IT?
WHO WOULD KNOW THEY SHOULD? FROM WHAT I GATHER, LIFE HERE IS STILL "BUSINESS AS USUAL"!
NOW THAT'S SCARY! YOU MEAN THERE MAY HAVE BEEN NOTHING TO ALERT THE PEOPLE-- JUST A GRADUAL CHANGE-OVER?
CAN THAT BE WHAT THE WHIZZER CALLED THEIR "SOCIAL ADVANCEMENT"?
AND SO, THE HELLCAT, THE BEAST, AND CAP CONTINUE, OBLIVIOUS IN THEIR DISCUSSION TO WANDA'S SUDDEN SILENCE!
BUT--
--THERE IS ANOTHER WHO SEES!
MY GOD, PEOPLE! THIS, THEN, IS WHAT MIGHT HAVE HAPPENED TO US--
--IF I HADN'T BROKEN UP OUR OWN WHITE HOUSE SCANDAL.*
*CAP #175--AND ALL THE PAPERS!--M.
GOSH! WHOEVER'D HAVE THOUGHT THAT PATSY WALKER WOULD END UP IN ANYTHING LIKE THIS?
DID YOU LEARN ANYTHING ELSE, WANDA?
WANDA-?

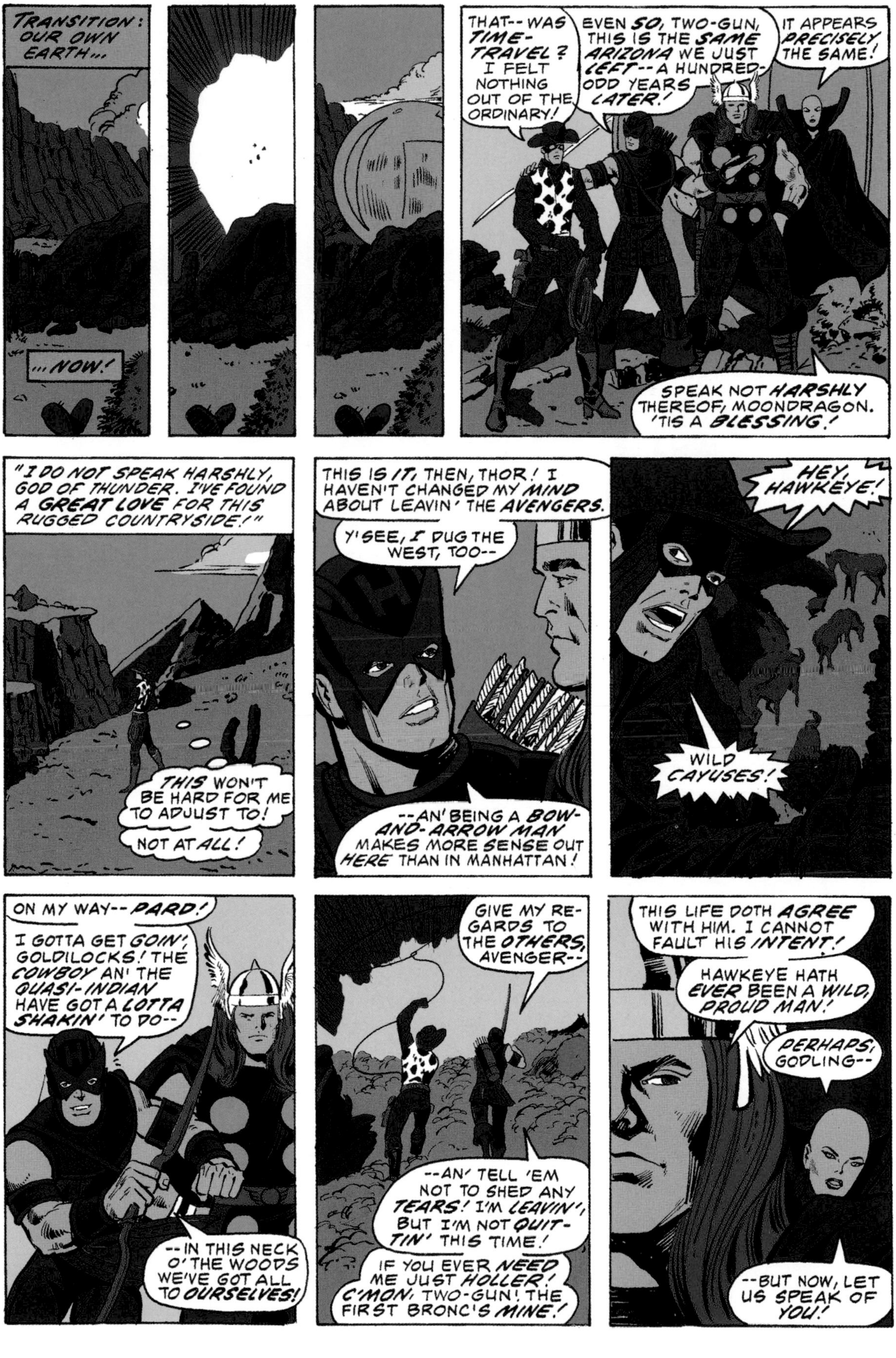
TRANSITION: OUR OWN EARTH...
...NOW!
THAT--WAS TIME-TRAVEL? I FELT NOTHING OUT OF THE ORDINARY!
EVEN SO, TWO-GUN, THIS IS THE SAME ARIZONA WE JUST LEFT--A HUNDRED-ODD YEARS LATER!
IT APPEARS PRECISELY THE SAME!
SPEAK NOT HARSHLY THEREOF, MOONDRAGON. 'TIS A BLESSING!
"I DO NOT SPEAK HARSHLY, GOD OF THUNDER. I'VE FOUND A GREAT LOVE FOR THIS RUGGED COUNTRYSIDE!"
THIS WON'T BE HARD FOR ME TO ADJUST TO!
NOT AT ALL!
THIS IS IT, THEN, THOR! I HAVEN'T CHANGED MY MIND ABOUT LEAVIN' THE AVENGERS.
Y'SEE, I DUG THE WEST, TOO--
--AN' BEING A BOW-AND-ARROW MAN MAKES MORE SENSE OUT HERE THAN IN MANHATTAN!
HEY, HAWKEYE!
WILD CAYUSES!
ON MY WAY--PARD!
I GOTTA GET GOIN', GOLDILOCKS! THE COWBOY AN' THE QUASI-INDIAN HAVE GOT A LOTTA SHAKIN' TO DO--
--IN THIS NECK O' THE WOODS WE'VE GOT ALL TO OURSELVES!
GIVE MY REGARDS TO THE OTHERS, AVENGER--
--AN' TELL 'EM NOT TO SHED ANY TEARS! I'M LEAVIN', BUT I'M NOT QUITTIN' THIS TIME!
IF YOU EVER NEED ME JUST HOLLER! C'MON, TWO-GUN! THE FIRST BRONC'S MINE!
THIS LIFE DOTH AGREE WITH HIM. I CANNOT FAULT HIS INTENT!
HAWKEYE HATH EVER BEEN A WILD, PROUD MAN!
PERHAPS, GODLING--
--BUT NOW, LET US SPEAK OF YOU!

WE'LL SEE MORE OF HAWK-EYE AND THE TWO-GUN KID IN A FUTURE *MARVEL SPOTLIGHT,* FOLKS*... BUT NOW...

WANDA, WHAT IS THE *MATTER?* WHY HAVE YOU *LAGGED BEHIND* THE *OTHERS?* COME-- WE MUST NOT BECOME *SEPARATED.*

NO...!

I SEE IT *ALL* NOW!

*GET ON THE STICK WITH IT, STEVE-- THE BULLPEN.

YOU'RE JUST A *COLD, UNFEELING COMPUTER!* YOU DON'T *CARE ABOUT ME.* YOU *NEVER CARED* ABOUT ME.

GOD *FORGIVE* ME FOR EVER *CHEAPENING* MYSELF WITH YOU!

NOT FOR AN *INSTANT* DOES THE ANDROID AVENGER *HESITATE* IN HIS *REPLY.*

THIS IS THE *SERPENT CROWN* SPEAKING THROUGH YOU, MY *DARLING--!*

APPARENTLY, THE MERE *POSSESSION* OF IT FOR ANY LENGTH OF TIME IS *DANGEROUS.* YOU HAD BEST ALLOW *ME* TO RUN THAT RISK FROM NOW ON.

YOU WANT TO TAKE MY *CROWN* FROM ME?

DON'T BE *ABSURD!*

FWAM!

I AM A *WITCH*-- A MU-TANT WITCH! I AM NOT SUBJECT TO *OTHER PEOPLE'S* DESIRES!

I DO WHAT I *WILL*-- GO WHERE I *WILL*--

--EVEN BACK TO THE *PRESIDENT!*

WANDA! DON'T *RUN* FROM ME!

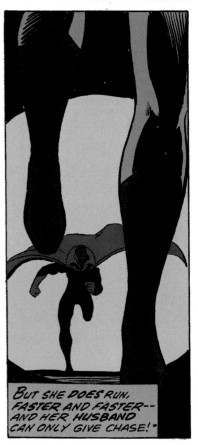

BUT SHE *DOES* RUN, *FASTER* AND *FASTER*-- AND HER HUSBAND CAN ONLY GIVE CHASE!*

MEANWHILE...

FINDING OUR FOES SHOULD NOT BE *DIFFICULT*, SQUAD MEMBERS. AFTER ALL, *WE* ARE A TEAM NOT VERY DIFFERENT FROM *THEMSELVES*.

THAT'S WHAT *YOU* SAY, HYPERION! TO ME, THEY SEEM SLIGHTLY *BARMY!*

I MAY HAVE BORROWED THE NAME *"GOLDEN ARCHER"* FROM ONE OF THEIR *ABSENT COMRADES*--

--BUT THAT'S WHERE ALL SIMILARITIES *END!*

TRUST YOU TO *OVER-DRAMATIZE!*

YOUR *BRASHNESS* I CAN *STAND* -- YOUR *COCKINESS* I LOVE--

--BUT YOUR *INTENSITY* WEARS A LITTLE THIN AFTER A TIME!

WHA-AT?

LISTEN, BIRD LADY, I DIDN'T HEAR ANY COMPLAINTS *LAST NIGHT*--OR THE *NIGHT BEFORE*--!

THAT'S *DIFFERENT!* JUST BECAUSE I *GO OUT* WITH YOU DOESN'T MEAN I THINK YOU'RE *PERFECT.*

YOU'RE AS MAD AS THE *AVENGERS*, WOMAN.

QUIET, YOU LOVEBIRDS! WE HAVE A *JOB* TO DO HERE!

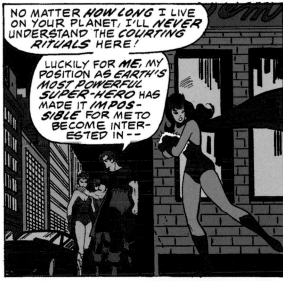

NO MATTER *HOW LONG* I LIVE ON YOUR PLANET, I'LL *NEVER* UNDERSTAND THE *COURTING RITUALS* HERE!

LUCKILY FOR *ME*, MY POSITION AS *EARTH'S MOST POWERFUL SUPER-HERO* HAS MADE IT *IMPOSSIBLE* FOR ME TO BECOME INTERESTED IN--

--WOMEN--

HELIUM AND ARGON! IT'S THE ONE WE SEEK--

--THE *SCARLET WITCH!*

YET THE SQUAD MEMBERS CANNOT LONG ENJOY THEIR GOOD FORTUNE-- FOR SUDDENLY, A *CHILL VOICE* KNIFES THRU THEIR SOULS!

UNHAND HER, HYPERION--*NOW!!*

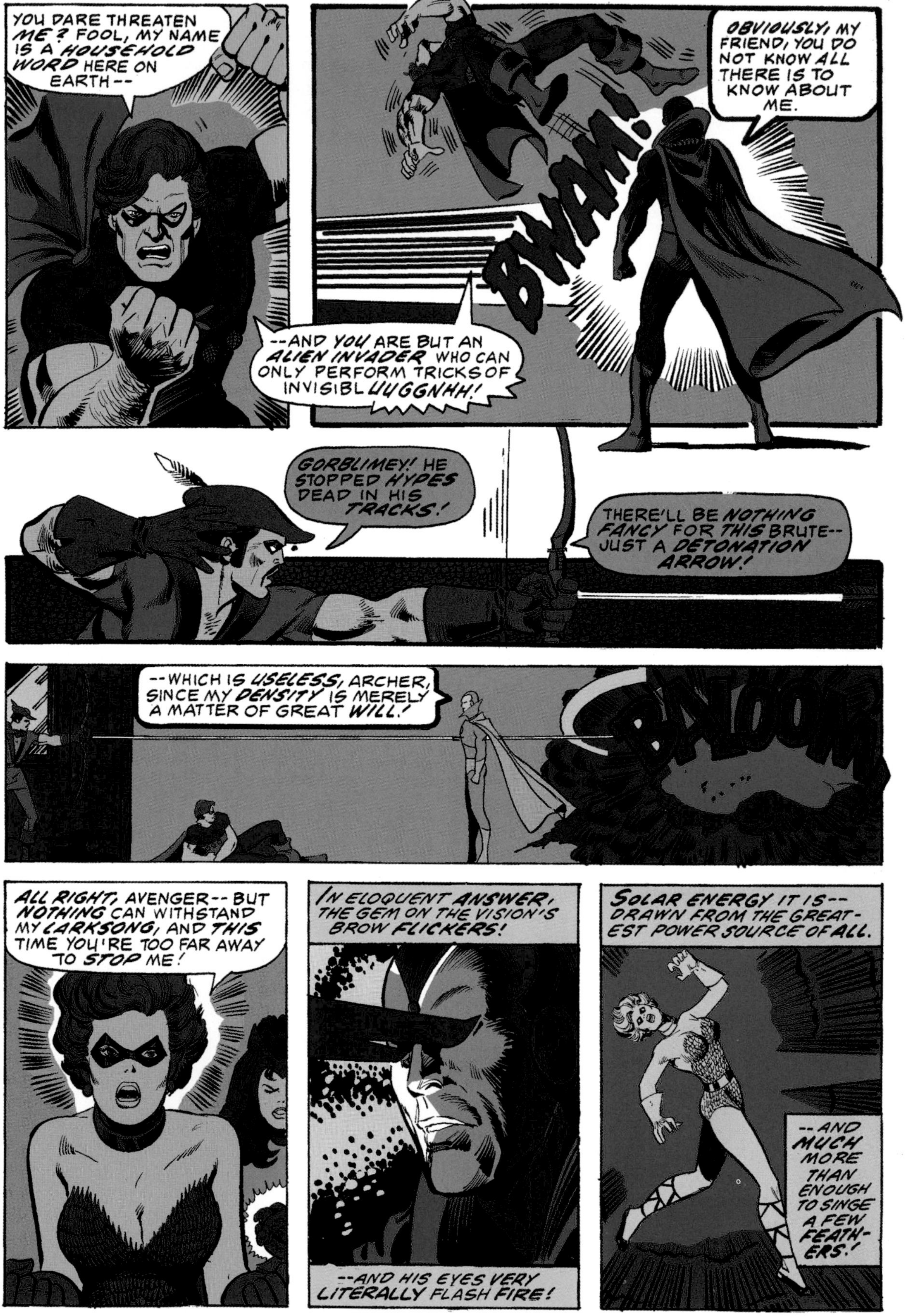
YOU DARE THREATEN ME? FOOL, MY NAME IS A HOUSEHOLD WORD HERE ON EARTH--
--AND YOU ARE BUT AN ALIEN INVADER WHO CAN ONLY PERFORM TRICKS OF INVISIBL UUGGNHH!
BWAM!
OBVIOUSLY, MY FRIEND, YOU DO NOT KNOW ALL THERE IS TO KNOW ABOUT ME.
GORBLIMEY! HE STOPPED HYPES DEAD IN HIS TRACKS!
THERE'LL BE NOTHING FANCY FOR THIS BRUTE-- JUST A DETONATION ARROW!
--WHICH IS USELESS, ARCHER, SINCE MY DENSITY IS MERELY A MATTER OF GREAT WILL!
BALOOM
ALL RIGHT, AVENGER-- BUT NOTHING CAN WITHSTAND MY LARKSONG, AND THIS TIME YOU'RE TOO FAR AWAY TO STOP ME!
IN ELOQUENT ANSWER, THE GEM ON THE VISION'S BROW FLICKERS!
--AND HIS EYES VERY LITERALLY FLASH FIRE!
SOLAR ENERGY IT IS-- DRAWN FROM THE GREATEST POWER SOURCE OF ALL.
--AND MUCH MORE THAN ENOUGH TO SINGE A FEW FEATHERS!

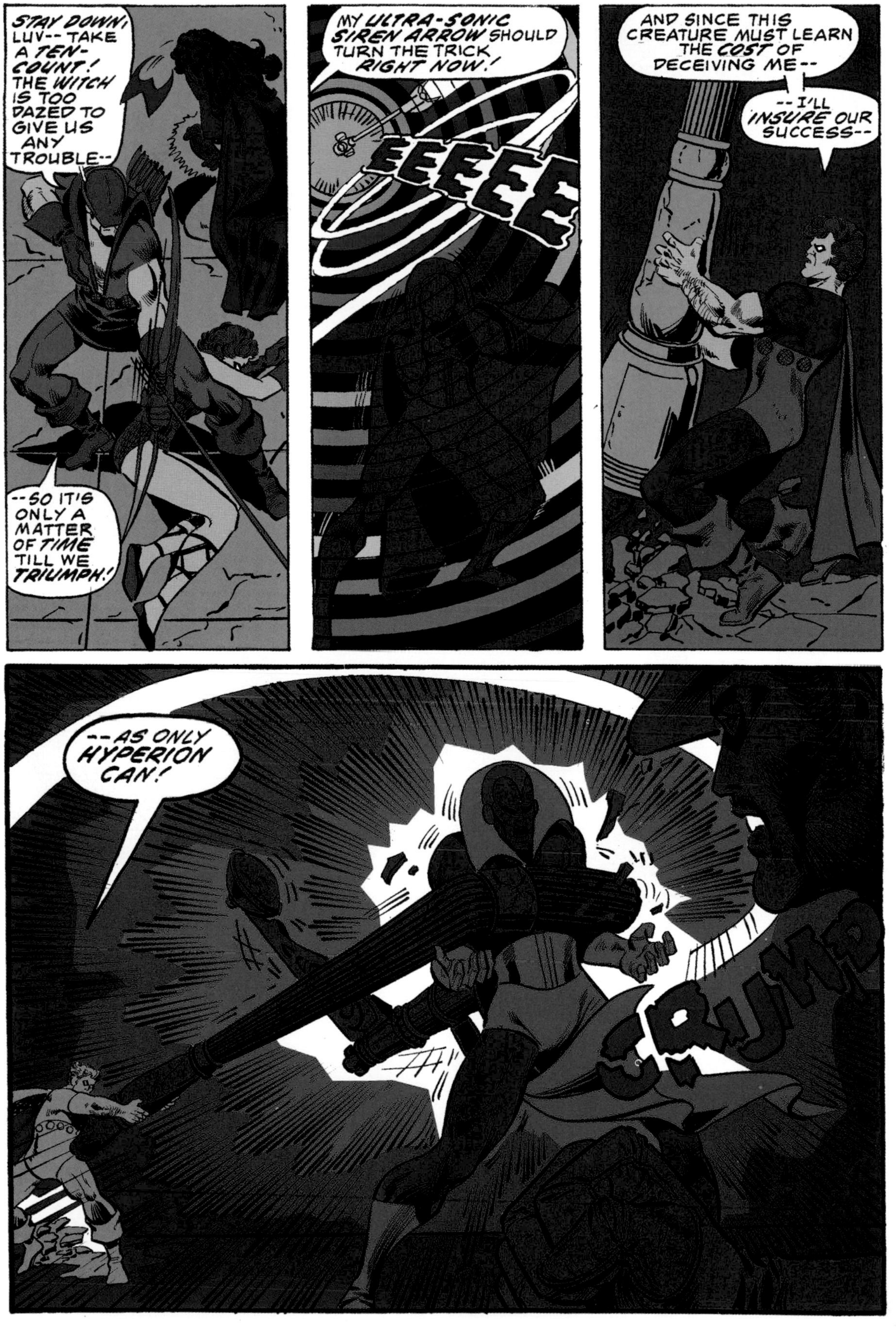
STAY DOWN, LUV-- TAKE A TEN-COUNT! THE WITCH IS TOO DAZED TO GIVE US ANY TROUBLE--
--SO IT'S ONLY A MATTER OF TIME TILL WE TRIUMPH!
MY ULTRA-SONIC SIREN ARROW SHOULD TURN THE TRICK RIGHT NOW!
EEEEE
AND SINCE THIS CREATURE MUST LEARN THE COST OF DECEIVING ME--
--I'LL INSURE OUR SUCCESS--
--AS ONLY HYPERION CAN!
CRUNCH

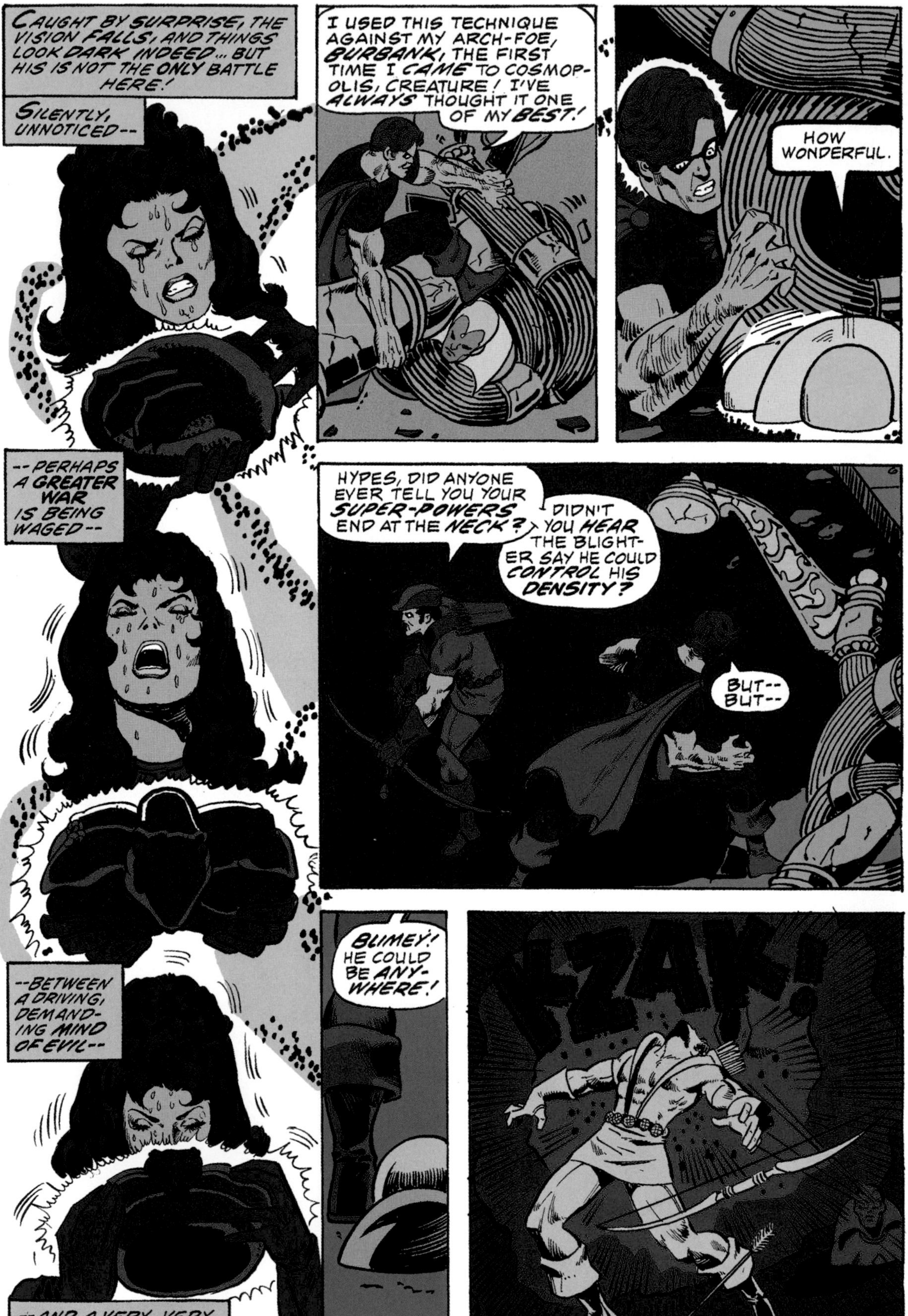
CAUGHT BY SURPRISE, THE VISION FALLS, AND THINGS LOOK DARK INDEED... BUT HIS IS NOT THE ONLY BATTLE HERE!
SILENTLY, UNNOTICED--
I USED THIS TECHNIQUE AGAINST MY ARCH-FOE, BURBANK, THE FIRST TIME I CAME TO COSMOPOLIS, CREATURE! I'VE ALWAYS THOUGHT IT ONE OF MY BEST!
HOW WONDERFUL.
--PERHAPS A GREATER WAR IS BEING WAGED--
HYPES, DID ANYONE EVER TELL YOU YOUR SUPER-POWERS END AT THE NECK?
DIDN'T YOU HEAR THE BLIGHTER SAY HE COULD CONTROL HIS DENSITY?
BUT-- BUT--
--BETWEEN A DRIVING, DEMANDING MIND OF EVIL--
BLIMEY! HE COULD BE ANYWHERE!
--AND A VERY, VERY NEW, YOUNG WITCH!

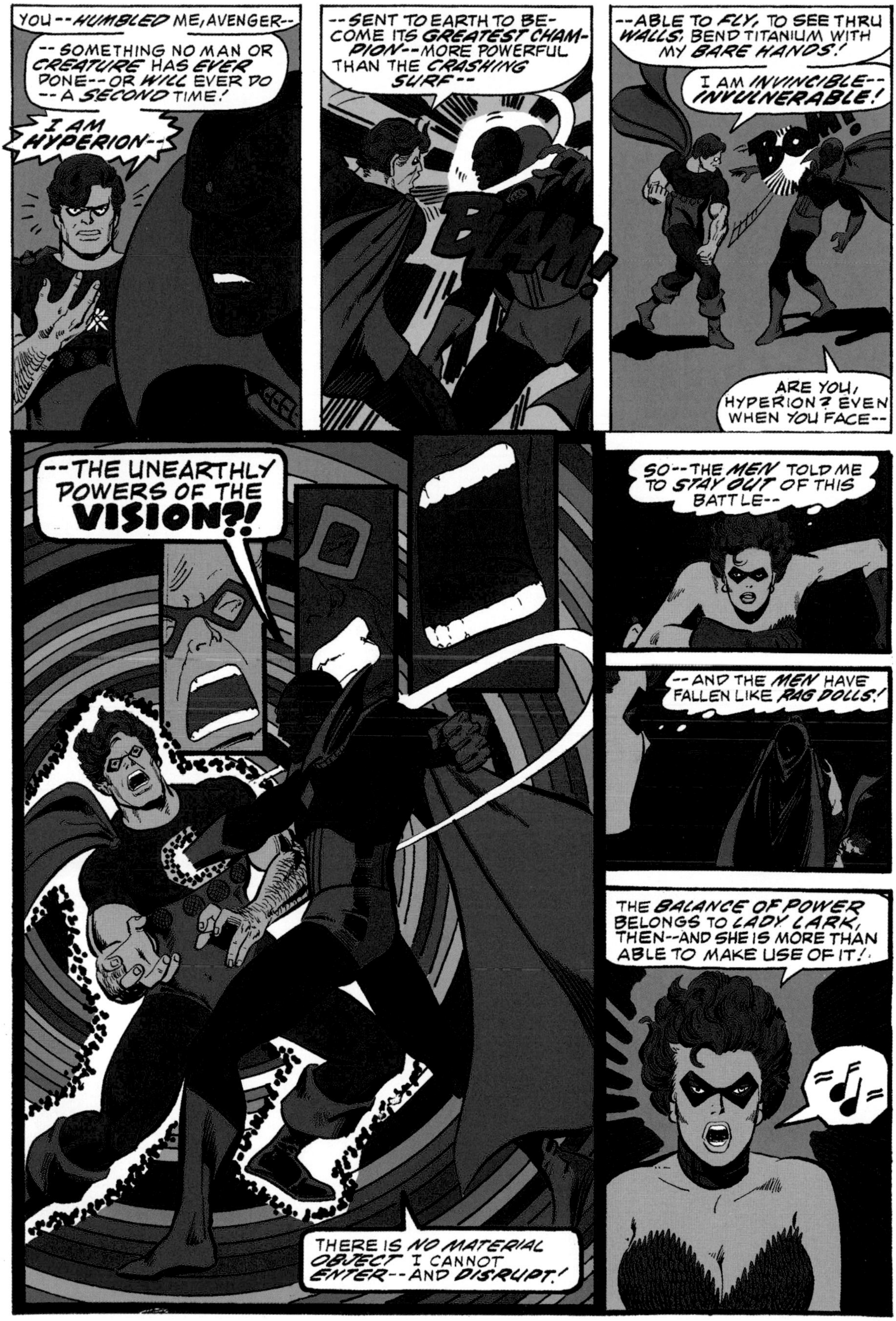
YOU--HUMBLED ME, AVENGER--
--SOMETHING NO MAN OR CREATURE HAS EVER DONE--OR WILL EVER DO--A SECOND TIME!
I AM HYPERION--
--SENT TO EARTH TO BECOME ITS GREATEST CHAMPION--MORE POWERFUL THAN THE CRASHING SURF--
BLAM!
--ABLE TO FLY, TO SEE THRU WALLS, BEND TITANIUM WITH MY BARE HANDS!
I AM INVINCIBLE--INVULNERABLE!
BOM!
ARE YOU, HYPERION? EVEN WHEN YOU FACE--
--THE UNEARTHLY POWERS OF THE VISION?!
THERE IS NO MATERIAL OBJECT I CANNOT ENTER--AND DISRUPT!
SO--THE MEN TOLD ME TO STAY OUT OF THIS BATTLE--
--AND THE MEN HAVE FALLEN LIKE RAG DOLLS!
THE BALANCE OF POWER BELONGS TO LADY LARK, THEN--AND SHE IS MORE THAN ABLE TO MAKE USE OF IT!

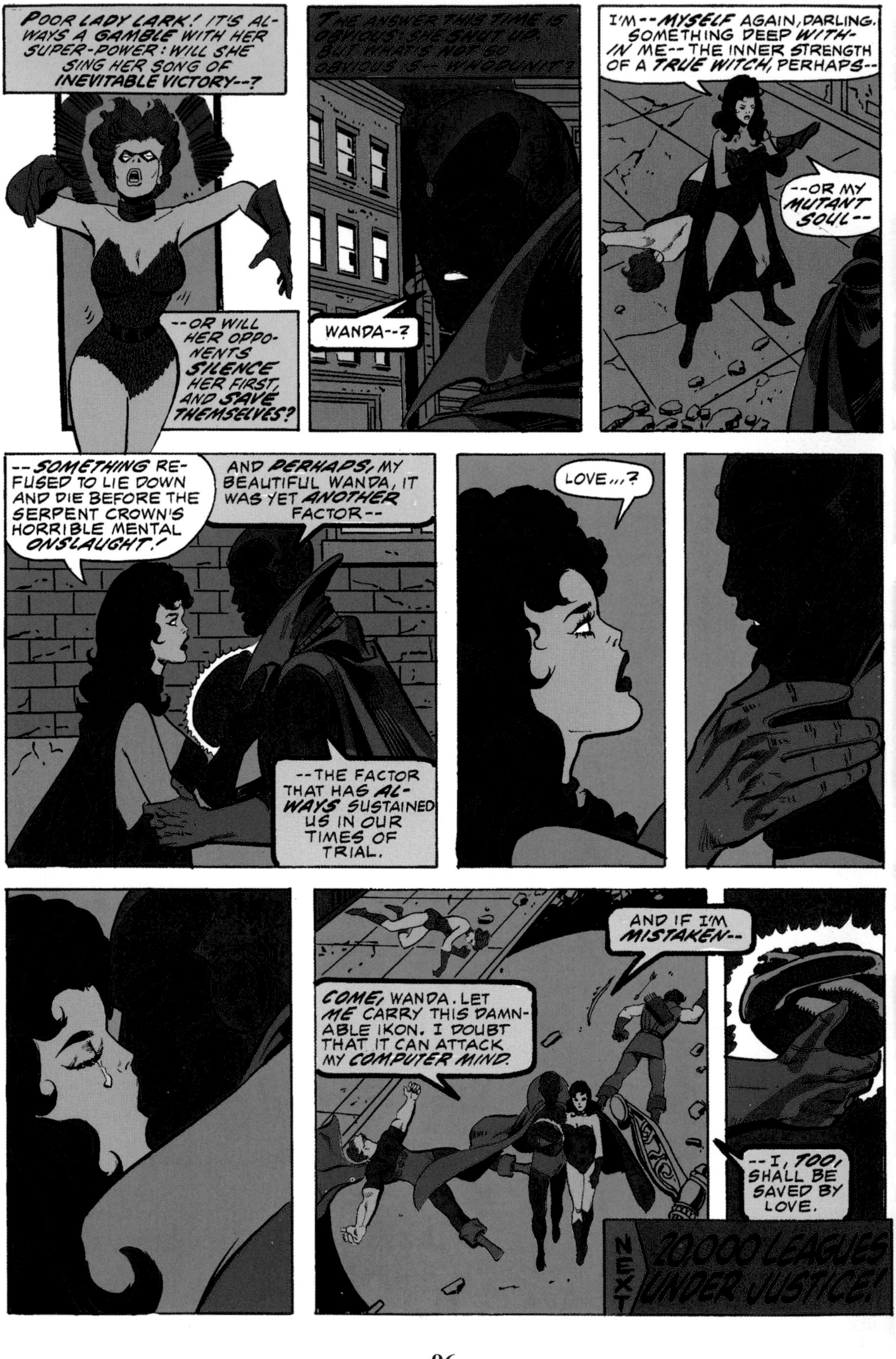
POOR LADY LARK! IT'S ALWAYS A GAMBLE WITH HER SUPER-POWER: WILL SHE SING HER SONG OF INEVITABLE VICTORY--?
--OR WILL HER OPPONENTS SILENCE HER FIRST, AND SAVE THEMSELVES?
THE ANSWER THIS TIME IS OBVIOUS: SHE SHUT UP. BUT WHAT'S NOT SO OBVIOUS IS-- WHODUNIT?
WANDA--?
I'M--MYSELF AGAIN, DARLING. SOMETHING DEEP WITHIN ME--THE INNER STRENGTH OF A TRUE WITCH, PERHAPS--
--OR MY MUTANT SOUL--
--SOMETHING REFUSED TO LIE DOWN AND DIE BEFORE THE SERPENT CROWN'S HORRIBLE MENTAL ONSLAUGHT!
AND PERHAPS, MY BEAUTIFUL WANDA, IT WAS YET ANOTHER FACTOR--
--THE FACTOR THAT HAS ALWAYS SUSTAINED US IN OUR TIMES OF TRIAL.
LOVE...?
COME, WANDA. LET ME CARRY THIS DAMNABLE IKON. I DOUBT THAT IT CAN ATTACK MY COMPUTER MIND.
AND IF I'M MISTAKEN--
--I, TOO, SHALL BE SAVED BY LOVE.
NEXT
20,000 LEAGUES UNDER JUSTICE!

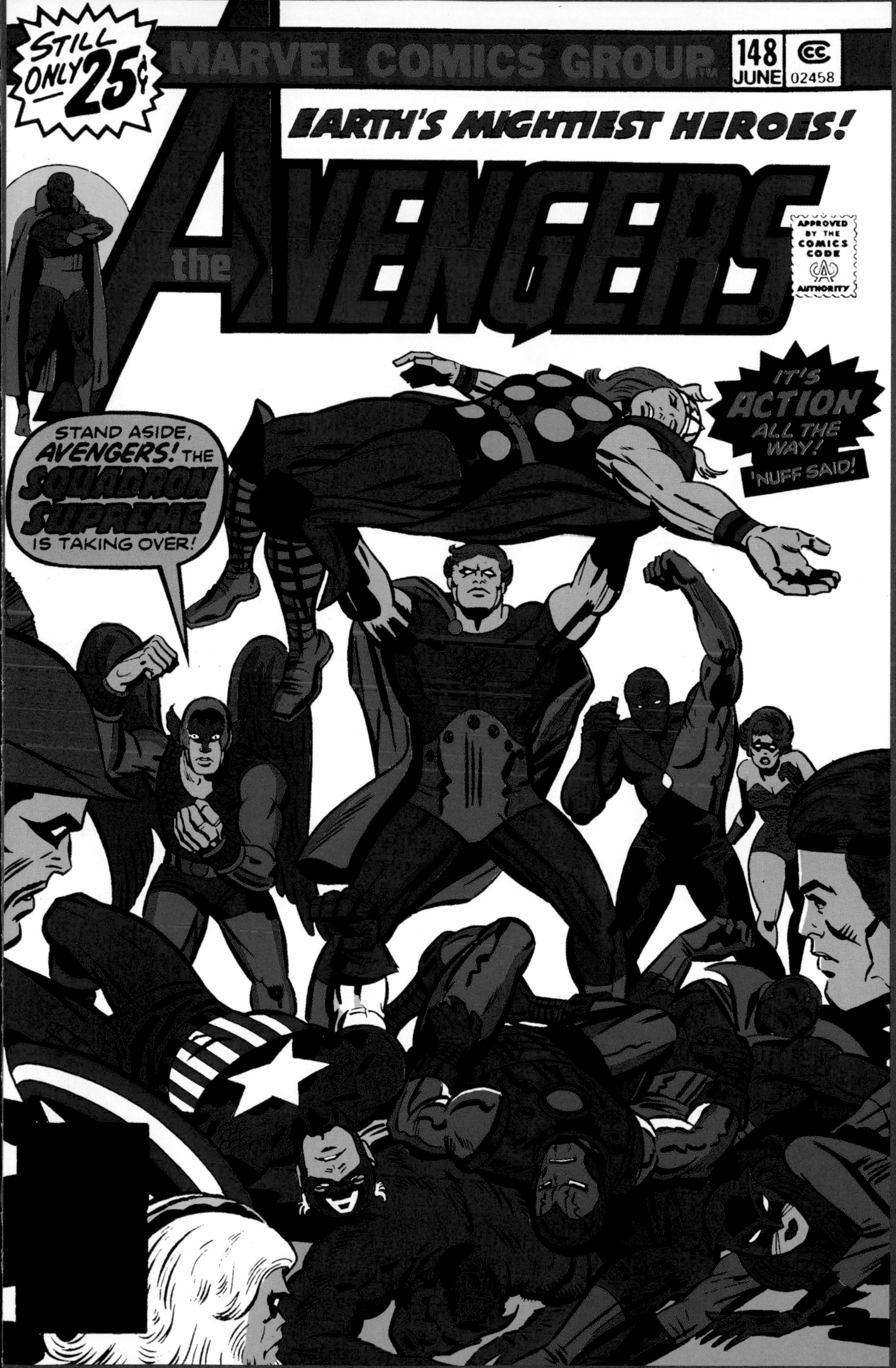
STILL ONLY 25¢
MARVEL COMICS GROUP
148 JUNE
CC 02458
EARTH'S MIGHTIEST HEROES!
the AVENGERS
APPROVED BY THE COMICS CODE AUTHORITY
STAND ASIDE, AVENGERS! THE SQUADRON SUPREME IS TAKING OVER!
IT'S ACTION ALL THE WAY! 'NUFF SAID!

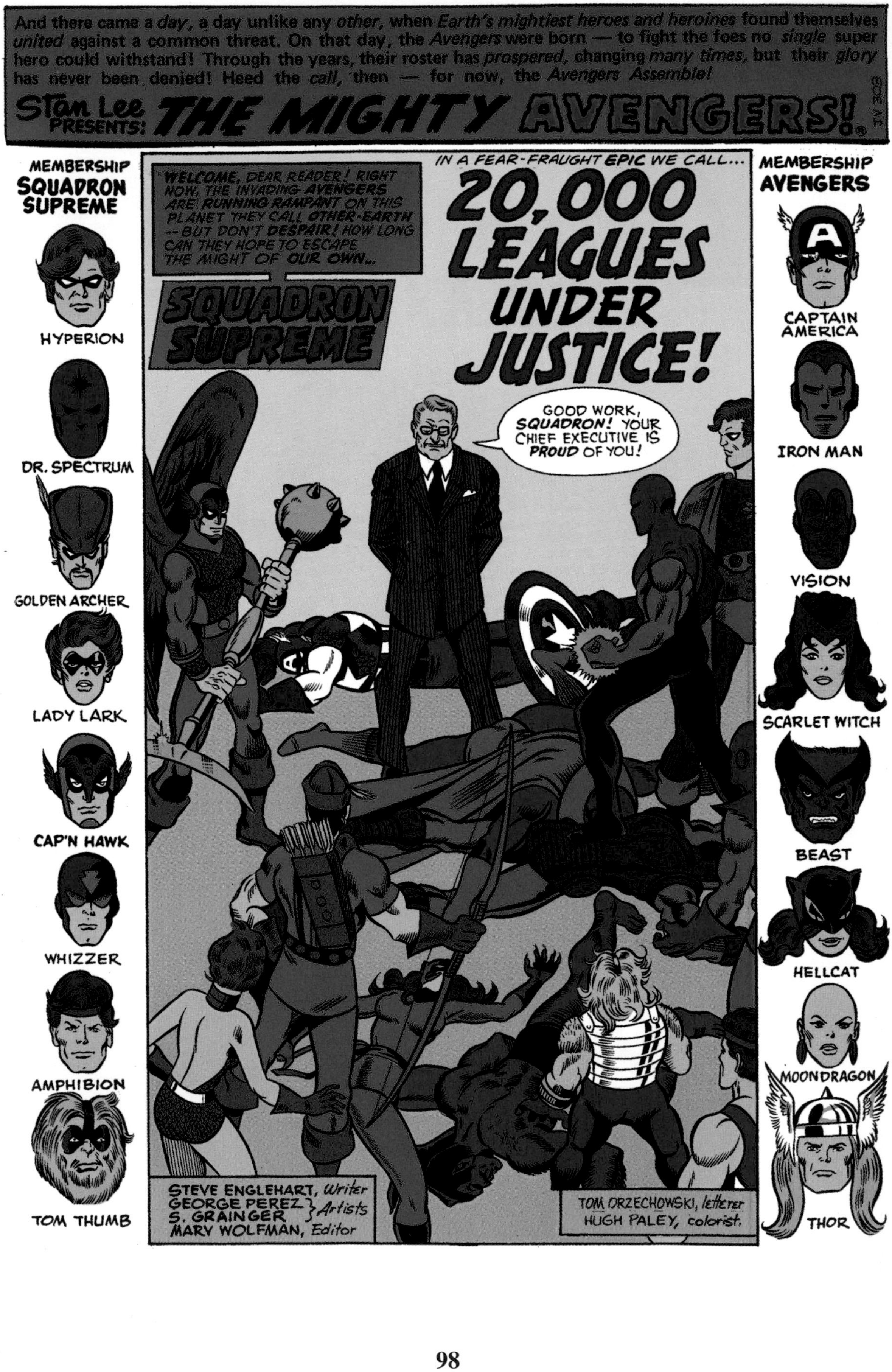
And there came a day, a day unlike any other, when Earth's mightiest heroes and heroines found themselves united against a common threat. On that day, the Avengers were born — to fight the foes no single super hero could withstand! Through the years, their roster has prospered, changing many times, but their glory has never been denied! Heed the call, then — for now, the Avengers Assemble!
Stan Lee PRESENTS: THE MIGHTY AVENGERS!
MEMBERSHIP SQUADRON SUPREME
HYPERION
DR. SPECTRUM
GOLDEN ARCHER
LADY LARK
CAP'N HAWK
WHIZZER
AMPHIBION
TOM THUMB
IN A FEAR-FRAUGHT EPIC WE CALL...
WELCOME, DEAR READER! RIGHT NOW, THE INVADING AVENGERS ARE RUNNING RAMPANT ON THIS PLANET THEY CALL OTHER-EARTH --BUT DON'T DESPAIR! HOW LONG CAN THEY HOPE TO ESCAPE THE MIGHT OF OUR OWN...
SQUADRON SUPREME
20,000 LEAGUES UNDER JUSTICE!
GOOD WORK, SQUADRON! YOUR CHIEF EXECUTIVE IS PROUD OF YOU!
STEVE ENGLEHART, Writer
GEORGE PEREZ, S. GRAINGER, Artists
MARY WOLFMAN, Editor
TOM ORZECHOWSKI, letterer
HUGH PALEY, colorist
MEMBERSHIP AVENGERS
CAPTAIN AMERICA
IRON MAN
VISION
SCARLET WITCH
BEAST
HELLCAT
MOONDRAGON
THOR

SCENE: THE **SQUADRON SUPREME'S** ROCKET CENTRAL--

-- HANGING STILL AND COLD, LIKE THE CRESCENT *QUARTER-MOON.*

WITHIN: AN ASSEMBLAGE OF THIS WORLD'S **GREATEST** SUPER-HEROES! READING LEFT TO RIGHT: --

AMPHIBION!

THE **WHIZZER!**

TOM THUMB!

DR. **SPECTRUM!**

CAP'N **HAWK!**

STILL NO **WORD!**

RELAX, TOMMY! HYPERION, LADY LARK, AND THE GOLDEN ARCHER ARE **SURE** TO CATCH --

DON'T **BET** ON IT, DOCTOR! I HAVE TO REPORT THAT WE **FAILED** IN OUR MISSION!

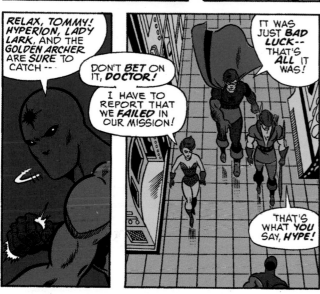

IT WAS JUST **BAD LUCK** -- THAT'S **ALL** IT WAS!

THAT'S WHAT **YOU** SAY, HYPE!

* BUT YOU SHOULD HAVE FLEXED YOUR **HYPER-MUSCLES** LESS AND USED YOUR **HYPER-BRAINS** MORE, AND FIGURED THAT EVEN YOU WEREN'T IMPERVIOUS TO THE VISION'S POWERS! *

*ALL THIS IN OUR LAST ISSUE. --Editor.

"OF COURSE, MY LADY AND I FELL, **TOO** -- BUT WE WERE BOTH VICTIMS OF **SURPRISE!** FRANKLY, I THOUGHT THE **SCARLET WITCH** WAS TOO **DAZED** TO FIGHT!"

LET IT **PASS,** ARCHER! THE **POINT** IS, THEY STILL HAVE PRESIDENT ROCKEFELLER'S **SERPENT CROWN!**

YEAH! I WONDER WHY THAT THING'S SO **VALUABLE,** THOUGH.

OURS IS NOT TO **QUESTION WHY,** HONEY.

NO, **OURS** IS TO GET THAT ANCIENT TALISMAN **BACK** --

--AND LOOK WHAT OUR **SPY-EYE** IN THE **SKY** HAS SPOTTED **NOW!**

99

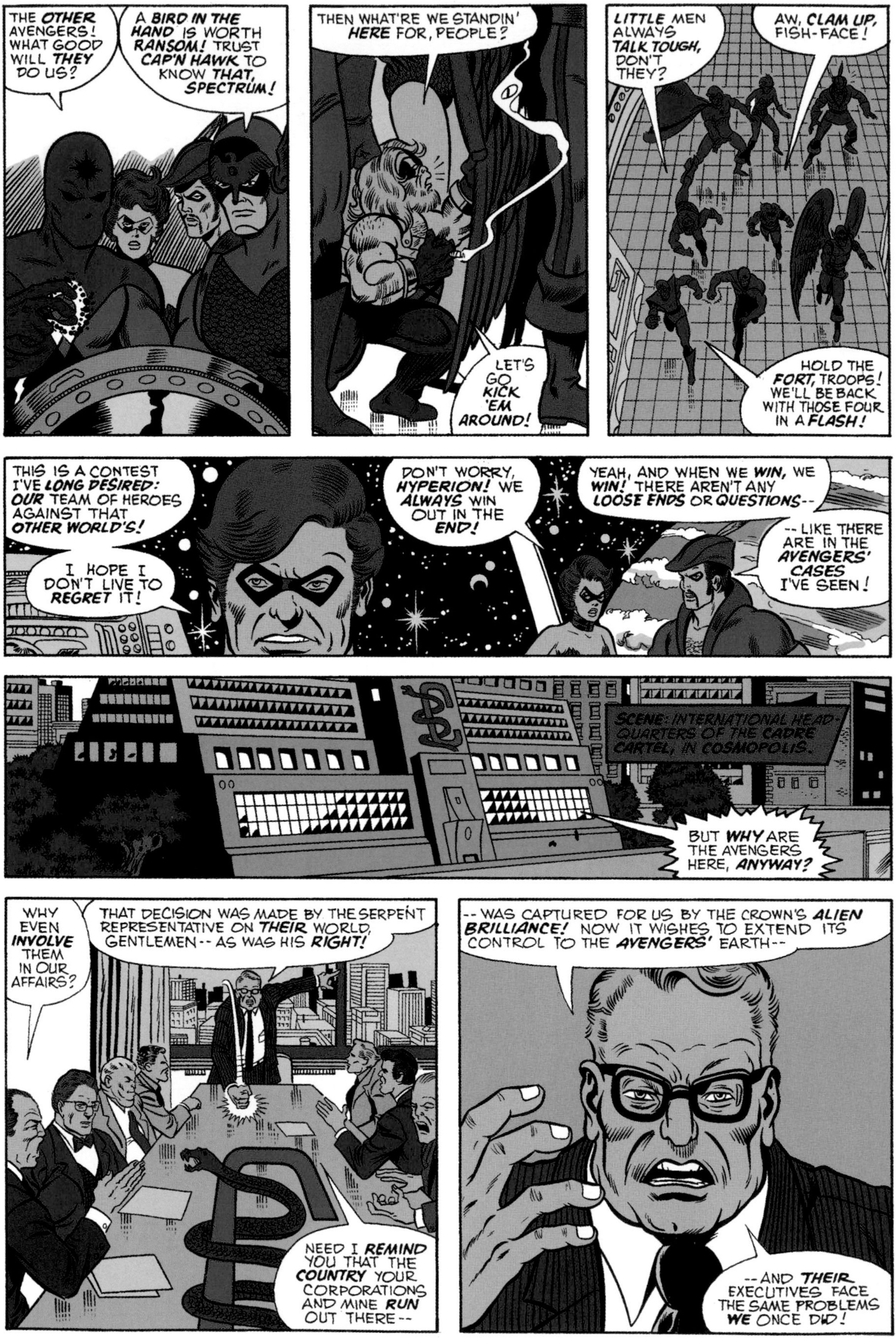
THE OTHER AVENGERS! WHAT GOOD WILL THEY DO US?
A BIRD IN THE HAND IS WORTH RANSOM! TRUST CAP'N HAWK TO KNOW THAT, SPECTRUM!
THEN WHAT'RE WE STANDIN' HERE FOR, PEOPLE?
LET'S GO KICK 'EM AROUND!
LITTLE MEN ALWAYS TALK TOUGH, DON'T THEY?
AW, CLAM UP, FISH-FACE!
HOLD THE FORT, TROOPS! WE'LL BE BACK WITH THOSE FOUR IN A FLASH!
THIS IS A CONTEST I'VE LONG DESIRED: OUR TEAM OF HEROES AGAINST THAT OTHER WORLD'S!
I HOPE I DON'T LIVE TO REGRET IT!
DON'T WORRY, HYPERION! WE ALWAYS WIN OUT IN THE END!
YEAH, AND WHEN WE WIN, WE WIN! THERE AREN'T ANY LOOSE ENDS OR QUESTIONS--
--LIKE THERE ARE IN THE AVENGERS' CASES I'VE SEEN!
SCENE: INTERNATIONAL HEAD-QUARTERS OF THE CADRE CARTEL, IN COSMOPOLIS.
BUT WHY ARE THE AVENGERS HERE, ANYWAY?
WHY EVEN INVOLVE THEM IN OUR AFFAIRS?
THAT DECISION WAS MADE BY THE SERPENT REPRESENTATIVE ON THEIR WORLD, GENTLEMEN-- AS WAS HIS RIGHT!
NEED I REMIND YOU THAT THE COUNTRY YOUR CORPORATIONS AND MINE RUN OUT THERE--
--WAS CAPTURED FOR US BY THE CROWN'S ALIEN BRILLIANCE! NOW IT WISHES TO EXTEND ITS CONTROL TO THE AVENGERS' EARTH--
--AND THEIR EXECUTIVES FACE THE SAME PROBLEMS WE ONCE DID!

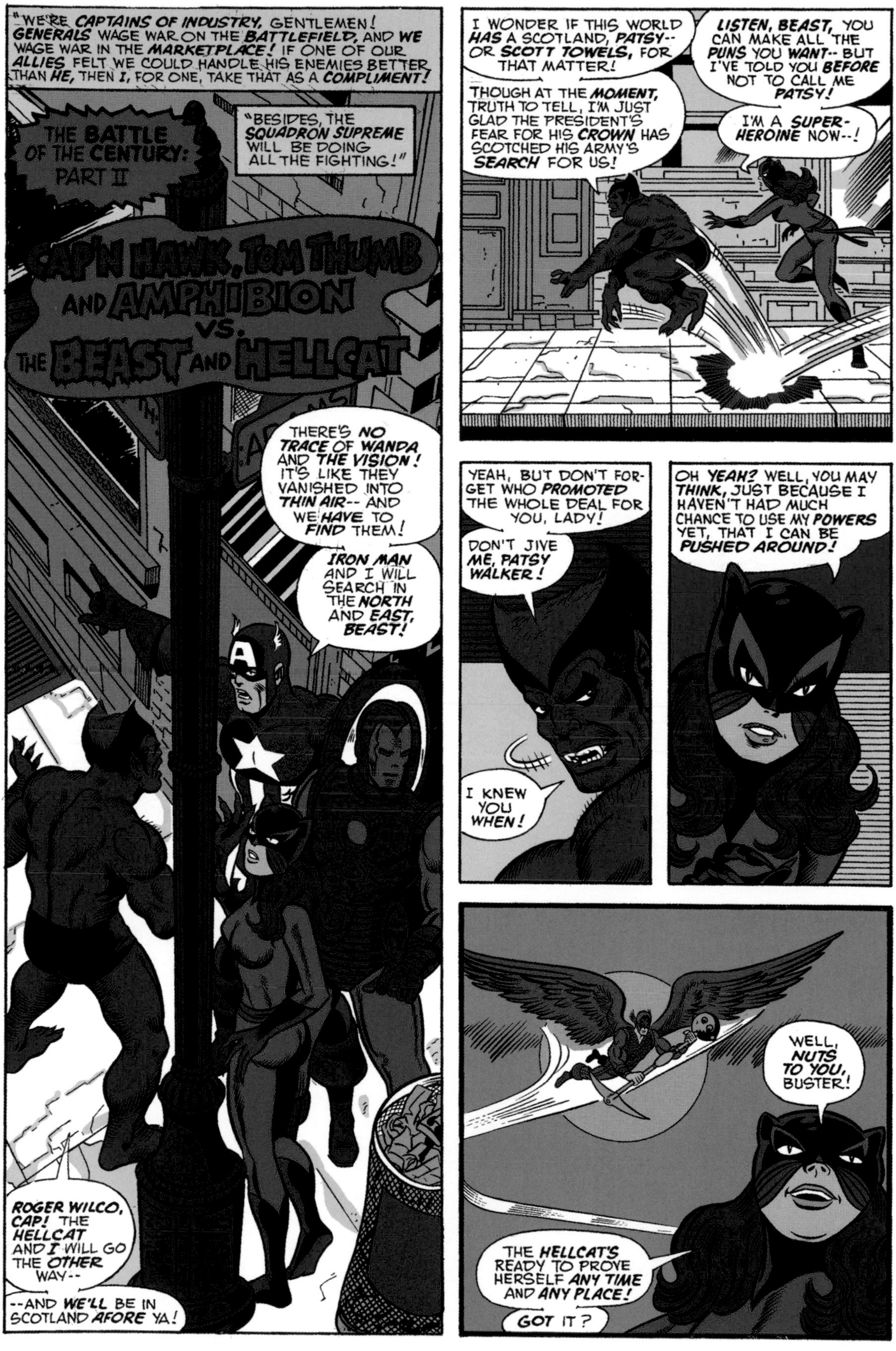

"WE'RE CAPTAINS OF INDUSTRY, GENTLEMEN! GENERALS WAGE WAR ON THE BATTLEFIELD, AND WE WAGE WAR IN THE MARKETPLACE! IF ONE OF OUR ALLIES FELT WE COULD HANDLE HIS ENEMIES BETTER THAN HE, THEN I, FOR ONE, TAKE THAT AS A COMPLIMENT!
THE BATTLE OF THE CENTURY: PART II
"BESIDES, THE SQUADRON SUPREME WILL BE DOING ALL THE FIGHTING!"
CAP'N HAWK, TOM THUMB AND AMPHIBION VS. THE BEAST AND HELLCAT
THERE'S NO TRACE OF WANDA AND THE VISION! IT'S LIKE THEY VANISHED INTO THIN AIR-- AND WE HAVE TO FIND THEM!
IRON MAN AND I WILL SEARCH IN THE NORTH AND EAST, BEAST!
ROGER WILCO, CAP! THE HELLCAT AND I WILL GO THE OTHER WAY--
--AND WE'LL BE IN SCOTLAND AFORE YA!
I WONDER IF THIS WORLD HAS A SCOTLAND, PATSY-- OR SCOTT TOWELS, FOR THAT MATTER!
THOUGH AT THE MOMENT, TRUTH TO TELL, I'M JUST GLAD THE PRESIDENT'S FEAR FOR HIS CROWN HAS SCOTCHED HIS ARMY'S SEARCH FOR US!
LISTEN, BEAST, YOU CAN MAKE ALL THE PUNS YOU WANT-- BUT I'VE TOLD YOU BEFORE NOT TO CALL ME PATSY!
I'M A SUPER-HEROINE NOW--!
YEAH, BUT DON'T FORGET WHO PROMOTED THE WHOLE DEAL FOR YOU, LADY!
DON'T JIVE ME, PATSY WALKER!
I KNEW YOU WHEN!
OH YEAH? WELL, YOU MAY THINK, JUST BECAUSE I HAVEN'T HAD MUCH CHANCE TO USE MY POWERS YET, THAT I CAN BE PUSHED AROUND!
WELL, NUTS TO YOU, BUSTER!
THE HELLCAT'S READY TO PROVE HERSELF ANY TIME AND ANY PLACE!
GOT IT?

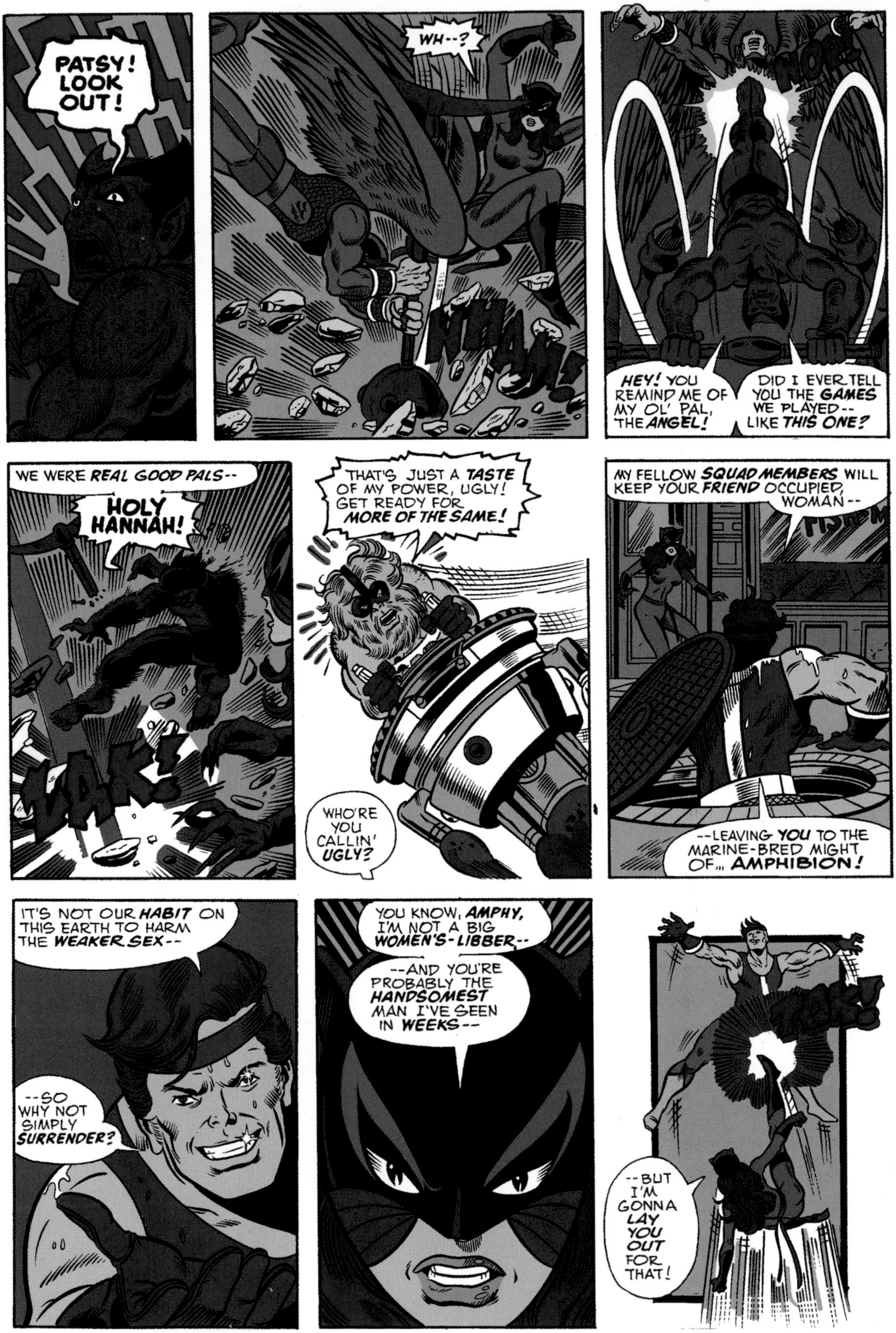

PATSY! LOOK OUT!
WH--?
HEY! YOU REMIND ME OF MY OL' PAL, THE ANGEL!
DID I EVER TELL YOU THE GAMES WE PLAYED-- LIKE THIS ONE?
WE WERE REAL GOOD PALS--
HOLY HANNAH!
THAT'S JUST A TASTE OF MY POWER, UGLY! GET READY FOR MORE OF THE SAME!
WHO'RE YOU CALLIN' UGLY?
MY FELLOW SQUAD MEMBERS WILL KEEP YOUR FRIEND OCCUPIED, WOMAN--
--LEAVING YOU TO THE MARINE-BRED MIGHT OF... AMPHIBION!
IT'S NOT OUR HABIT ON THIS EARTH TO HARM THE WEAKER SEX--
--SO WHY NOT SIMPLY SURRENDER?
YOU KNOW, AMPHY, I'M NOT A BIG WOMEN'S-LIBBER--
--AND YOU'RE PROBABLY THE HANDSOMEST MAN I'VE SEEN IN WEEKS--
--BUT I'M GONNA LAY YOU OUT FOR THAT!

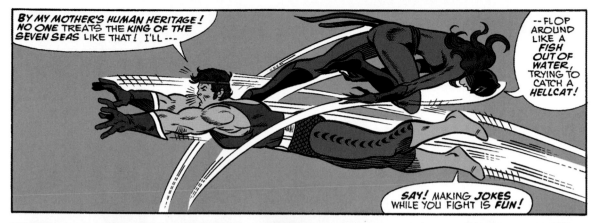

BY MY MOTHER'S HUMAN HERITAGE! NO ONE TREATS THE KING OF THE SEVEN SEAS LIKE THAT! I'LL ---

--FLOP AROUND LIKE A FISH OUT OF WATER, TRYING TO CATCH A HELLCAT!

SAY! MAKING JOKES WHILE YOU FIGHT IS FUN!

FISH MARKET

KRASH!

AND WINNING'S EVEN MORE FUN!

I SWEAR-- WITH THIS SUIT, I CAN'T LOSE!

OH MY STARS AND GARTERS!

PATSY! LOOK OUT AGAIN!

TOO LATE! SHE DIDN'T EVEN HEAR MY MICRO-MODULE COMING UP BEHIND --

--AND NOW, SHE'S COVERED WITH PASTE!

THERE'S NO END TO TOM THUMB'S TRICKS!

RIGHT, YOU HAIRY APE?

WHO'RE YOU CALLIN' HAIRY?

WHEN I GET MY HANDS ON YOU--

--IT'LL BE 1977, HAIRY! IN THE MEANTIME--

--WILL YOU SETTLE FOR MY CLAWS?

HA! A DESPERATE ACT FROM A DESPERATE FOE --

--BUT ALL I HAVE TO DO IS ADD MORE JET-POWER, AND I'LL RIP YOU LIMB FROM LIMB!

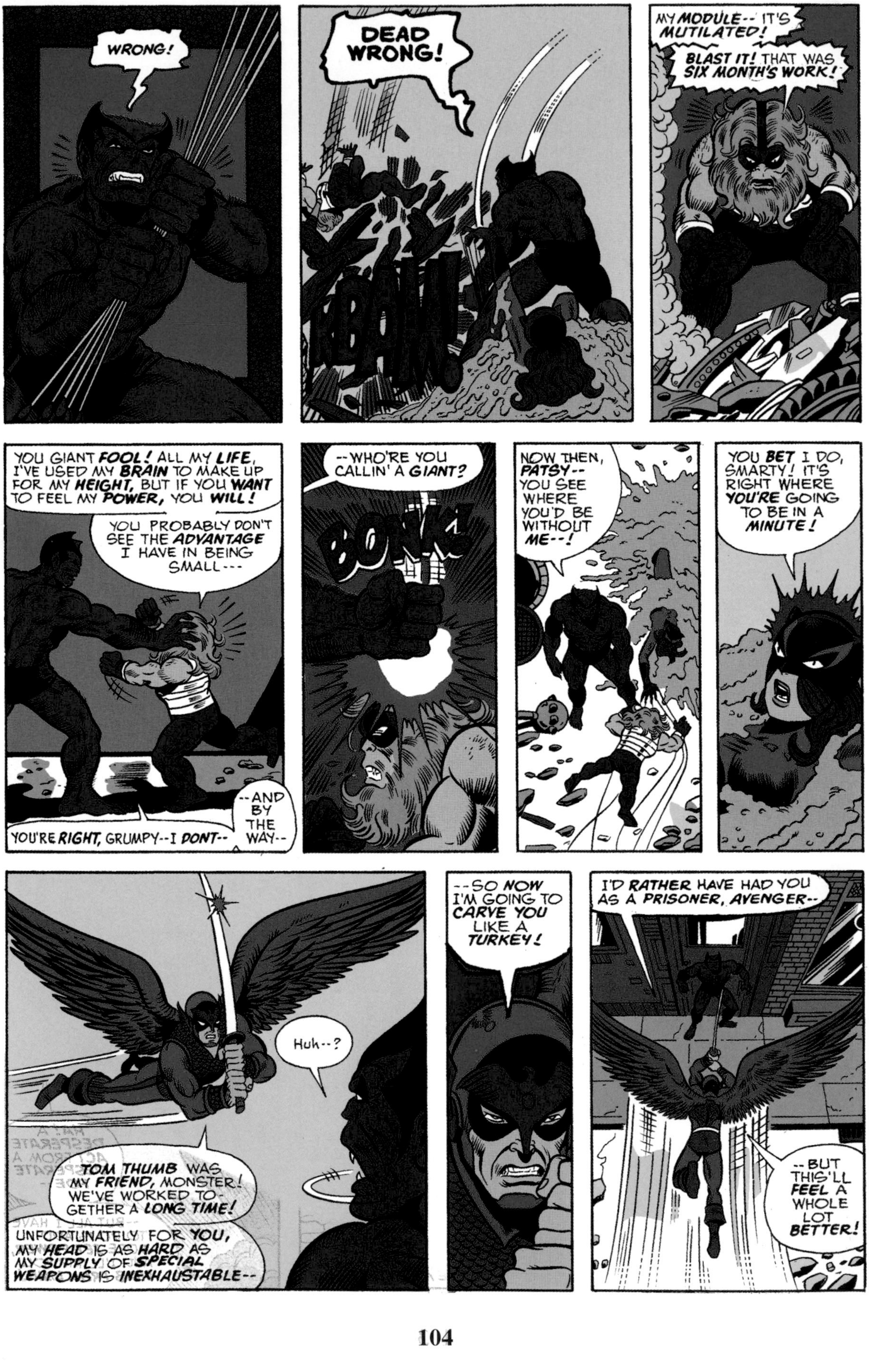
WRONG!
DEAD WRONG!
KBAM!
MY MODULE-- IT'S MUTILATED!
BLAST IT! THAT WAS SIX MONTH'S WORK!
YOU GIANT FOOL! ALL MY LIFE, I'VE USED MY BRAIN TO MAKE UP FOR MY HEIGHT, BUT IF YOU WANT TO FEEL MY POWER, YOU WILL!
YOU PROBABLY DON'T SEE THE ADVANTAGE I HAVE IN BEING SMALL---
YOU'RE RIGHT, GRUMPY--I DONT--
--AND BY THE WAY--
--WHO'RE YOU CALLIN' A GIANT?
BONK!
NOW THEN, PATSY-- YOU SEE WHERE YOU'D BE WITHOUT ME--!
YOU BET I DO, SMARTY! IT'S RIGHT WHERE YOU'RE GOING TO BE IN A MINUTE!
Huh--?
TOM THUMB WAS MY FRIEND, MONSTER! WE'VE WORKED TO-GETHER A LONG TIME!
UNFORTUNATELY FOR YOU, MY HEAD IS AS HARD AS MY SUPPLY OF SPECIAL WEAPONS IS INEXHAUSTABLE--
--SO NOW I'M GOING TO CARVE YOU LIKE A TURKEY!
I'D RATHER HAVE HAD YOU AS A PRISONER, AVENGER--
--BUT THIS'LL FEEL A WHOLE LOT BETTER!

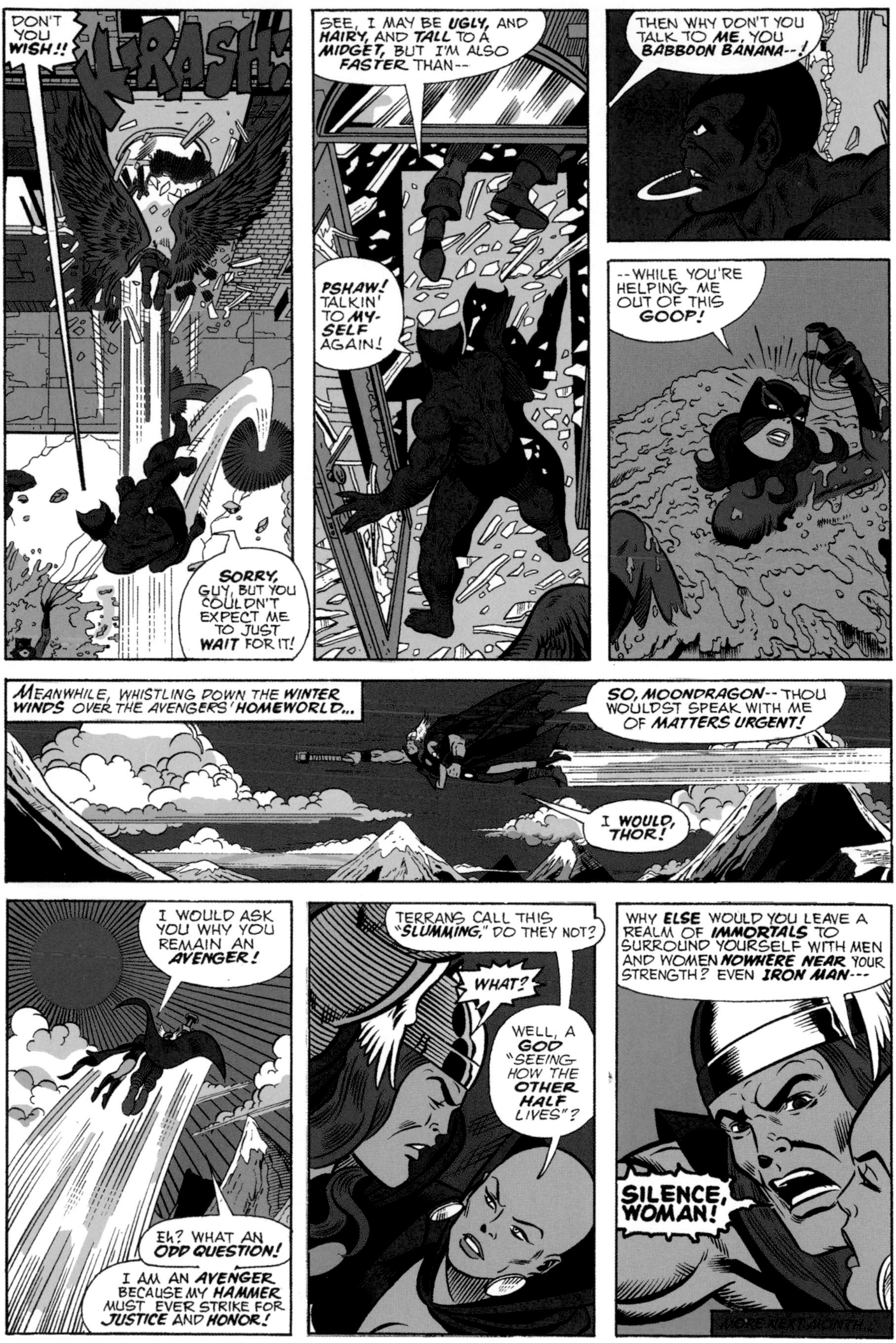
DON'T YOU WISH!!
K-RASH!
SORRY, GUY, BUT YOU COULDN'T EXPECT ME TO JUST WAIT FOR IT!
SEE, I MAY BE UGLY, AND HAIRY, AND TALL TO A MIDGET, BUT I'M ALSO FASTER THAN--
PSHAW! TALKIN' TO MY-SELF AGAIN!
THEN WHY DON'T YOU TALK TO ME, YOU BABBOON BANANA--!
--WHILE YOU'RE HELPING ME OUT OF THIS GOOP!
MEANWHILE, WHISTLING DOWN THE WINTER WINDS OVER THE AVENGERS' HOMEWORLD...
SO, MOONDRAGON-- THOU WOULDST SPEAK WITH ME OF MATTERS URGENT!
I WOULD, THOR!
I WOULD ASK YOU WHY YOU REMAIN AN AVENGER!
Eh? WHAT AN ODD QUESTION!
I AM AN AVENGER BECAUSE MY HAMMER MUST EVER STRIKE FOR JUSTICE AND HONOR!
TERRANS CALL THIS "SLUMMING," DO THEY NOT?
WHAT?
WELL, A GOD "SEEING HOW THE OTHER HALF LIVES"?
WHY ELSE WOULD YOU LEAVE A REALM OF IMMORTALS TO SURROUND YOURSELF WITH MEN AND WOMEN NOWHERE NEAR YOUR STRENGTH? EVEN IRON MAN---
SILENCE, WOMAN!
MORE NEXT MONTH...

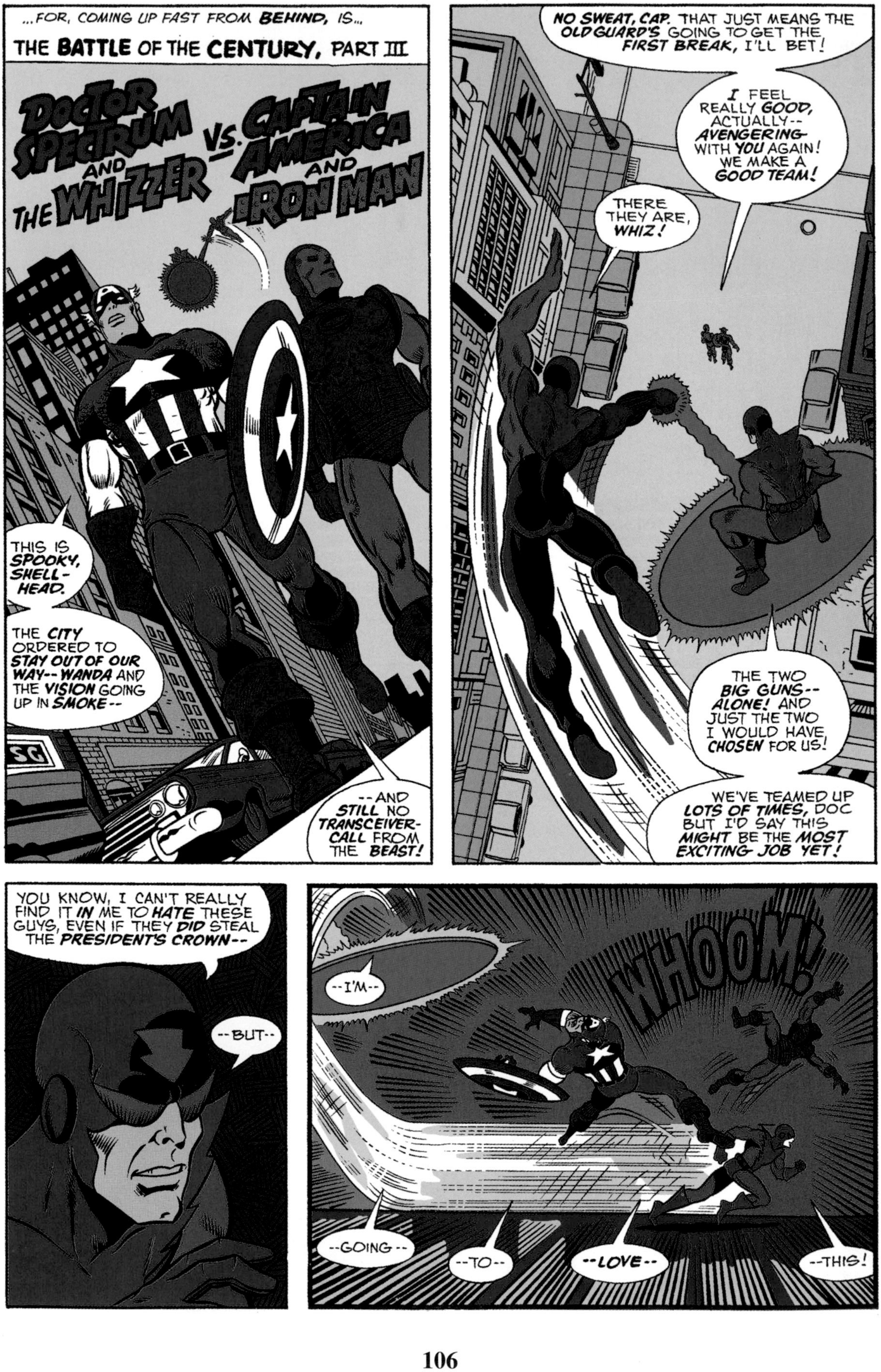
...FOR, COMING UP FAST FROM BEHIND, IS...
THE BATTLE OF THE CENTURY, PART III
DOCTOR SPECTRUM AND THE WHIZZER VS. CAPTAIN AMERICA AND IRON MAN
THIS IS SPOOKY, SHELL-HEAD.
THE CITY ORDERED TO STAY OUT OF OUR WAY-- WANDA AND THE VISION GOING UP IN SMOKE--
--AND STILL NO TRANSCEIVER-CALL FROM THE BEAST!
NO SWEAT, CAP. THAT JUST MEANS THE OLD GUARD'S GOING TO GET THE FIRST BREAK, I'LL BET!
I FEEL REALLY GOOD, ACTUALLY-- AVENGERING WITH YOU AGAIN! WE MAKE A GOOD TEAM!
THERE THEY ARE, WHIZ!
THE TWO BIG GUNS-- ALONE! AND JUST THE TWO I WOULD HAVE CHOSEN FOR US!
WE'VE TEAMED UP LOTS OF TIMES, DOC BUT I'D SAY THIS MIGHT BE THE MOST EXCITING JOB YET!
YOU KNOW, I CAN'T REALLY FIND IT IN ME TO HATE THESE GUYS, EVEN IF THEY DID STEAL THE PRESIDENT'S CROWN--
--BUT--
--I'M--
WHOOM!
--GOING--
--TO--
--LOVE--
--THIS!

THAT WAS THE FIRST BREAK, AVENGER! HE THINKS WE'RE BILLIARD BALLS!
THIS GUY'S GOING TO BE TROUBLE, WINGHEAD!
KLANG!
HE'S LIKE GREASED LIGHTNINNNNGHH
HERE I AM, CAPTAIN AMERICA!
DR. SPECTRUM!
--AND HIS MAGIC POWER PRISM!
--AND--
--HIS--
POW!
--FRIEND!
THEY DON'T KNOW WHETHER THEY'RE COMING OR GOING, WHIZZER!
WE'LL WRAP THIS ONE UP WITH-OUT EVEN BREATHING HARD!
ALL I HAVE TO DO IS LEND AN EXTRA HAND FOR THIS SO-CALLED IRON MAN--
--AND I'LL OPEN HIM UP LIKE A TUBE OF TOOTHPASTE!
CRUSHING ME--! HIS PRISM'S POWER-- LIMITLESS!
OKAY, DOC! I HAVE MY END OF IT WELL IN HAND, TOO!

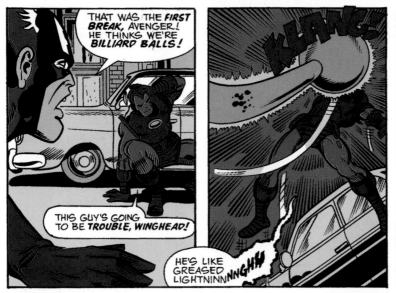

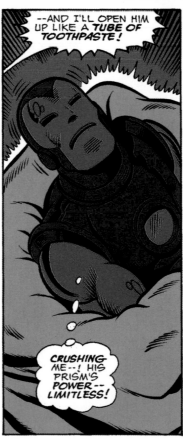

I COULD KEEP THAT TORNADO BLOWING *ALL DAY LONG*--

--BUT THAT'S TOO *EASY!*

CHUNK!

THAT *SINKS* IT, MISTER! YOU'VE JUST MADE ME *MAD!*

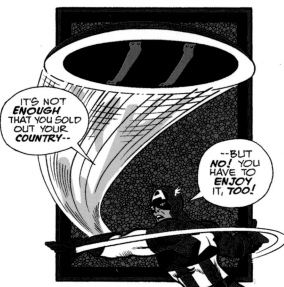

IT'S NOT *ENOUGH* THAT YOU SOLD OUT YOUR *COUNTRY*--

--BUT *NO!* YOU HAVE TO *ENJOY* IT, *TOO!*

THE COUNTRY *CHANGED*, AVENGER-- *THAT'S* ALL! AND THE *SQUADRON SUPREME* CHANGED *WITH* IT!

WHEN I TOLD *IRON MAN* WE'D *SOLD OUT**, ALL I *MEANT* WAS THAT WE'D STARTED DRAWING *PAYCHECKS* FROM THE *CORPORATE MEN!*

BUT THE *CARTEL RUNS* THE COUNTRY, SO WHAT DOES IT *MATTER?*

*IN #141.--M.

I'M THE SAME SUPER-SPEEDSTER I *ALWAYS* WAS-- STILL SERVING THE GOOD OLD *U.S. OF A.!*

SO DON'T GIVE ME ANY OF THAT "*HOLIER THAN THOU*" NONSENSE!

WE'RE *EVERY BIT* AS PATRIOTIC AS *YOU* ARE! NOW *GET UP*--

--AND LET ME *FINISH YOU OFF!*

FWAM!

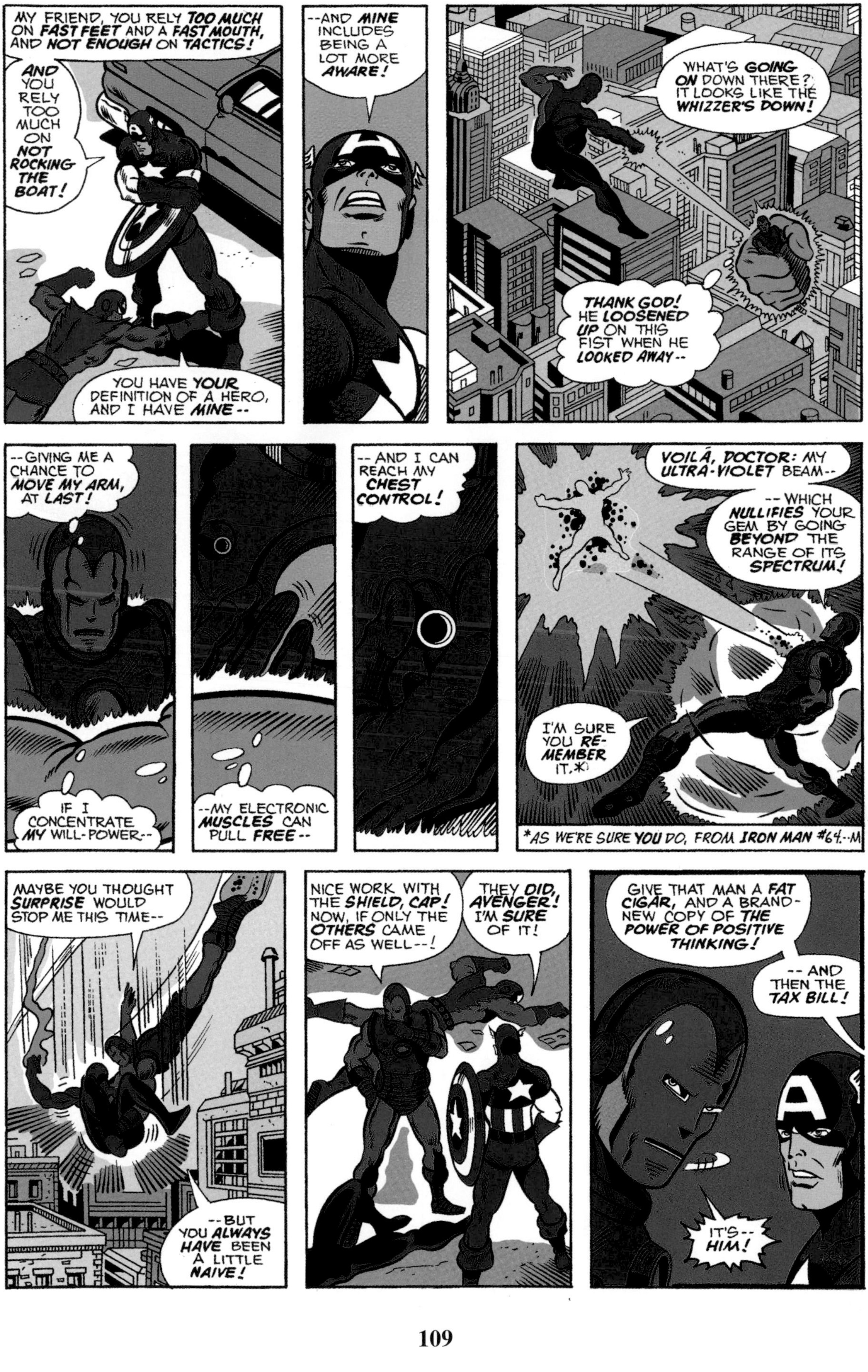
MY FRIEND, YOU RELY TOO MUCH ON FAST FEET AND A FAST MOUTH, AND NOT ENOUGH ON TACTICS!
AND YOU RELY TOO MUCH ON NOT ROCKING THE BOAT!
YOU HAVE YOUR DEFINITION OF A HERO, AND I HAVE MINE--
--AND MINE INCLUDES BEING A LOT MORE AWARE!
WHAT'S GOING ON DOWN THERE? IT LOOKS LIKE THE WHIZZER'S DOWN!
THANK GOD! HE LOOSENED UP ON THIS FIST WHEN HE LOOKED AWAY--
--GIVING ME A CHANCE TO MOVE MY ARM, AT LAST!
IF I CONCENTRATE MY WILL-POWER--
--MY ELECTRONIC MUSCLES CAN PULL FREE--
--AND I CAN REACH MY CHEST CONTROL!
VOILÁ, DOCTOR: MY ULTRA-VIOLET BEAM--
--WHICH NULLIFIES YOUR GEM BY GOING BEYOND THE RANGE OF ITS SPECTRUM!
I'M SURE YOU RE-MEMBER IT.*
*AS WE'RE SURE YOU DO, FROM IRON MAN #64.--M
MAYBE YOU THOUGHT SURPRISE WOULD STOP ME THIS TIME--
--BUT YOU ALWAYS HAVE BEEN A LITTLE NAIVE!
NICE WORK WITH THE SHIELD, CAP! NOW, IF ONLY THE OTHERS CAME OFF AS WELL--!
THEY DID, AVENGER! I'M SURE OF IT!
GIVE THAT MAN A FAT CIGAR, AND A BRAND-NEW COPY OF THE POWER OF POSITIVE THINKING!
--AND THEN THE TAX BILL!
IT'S--HIM!

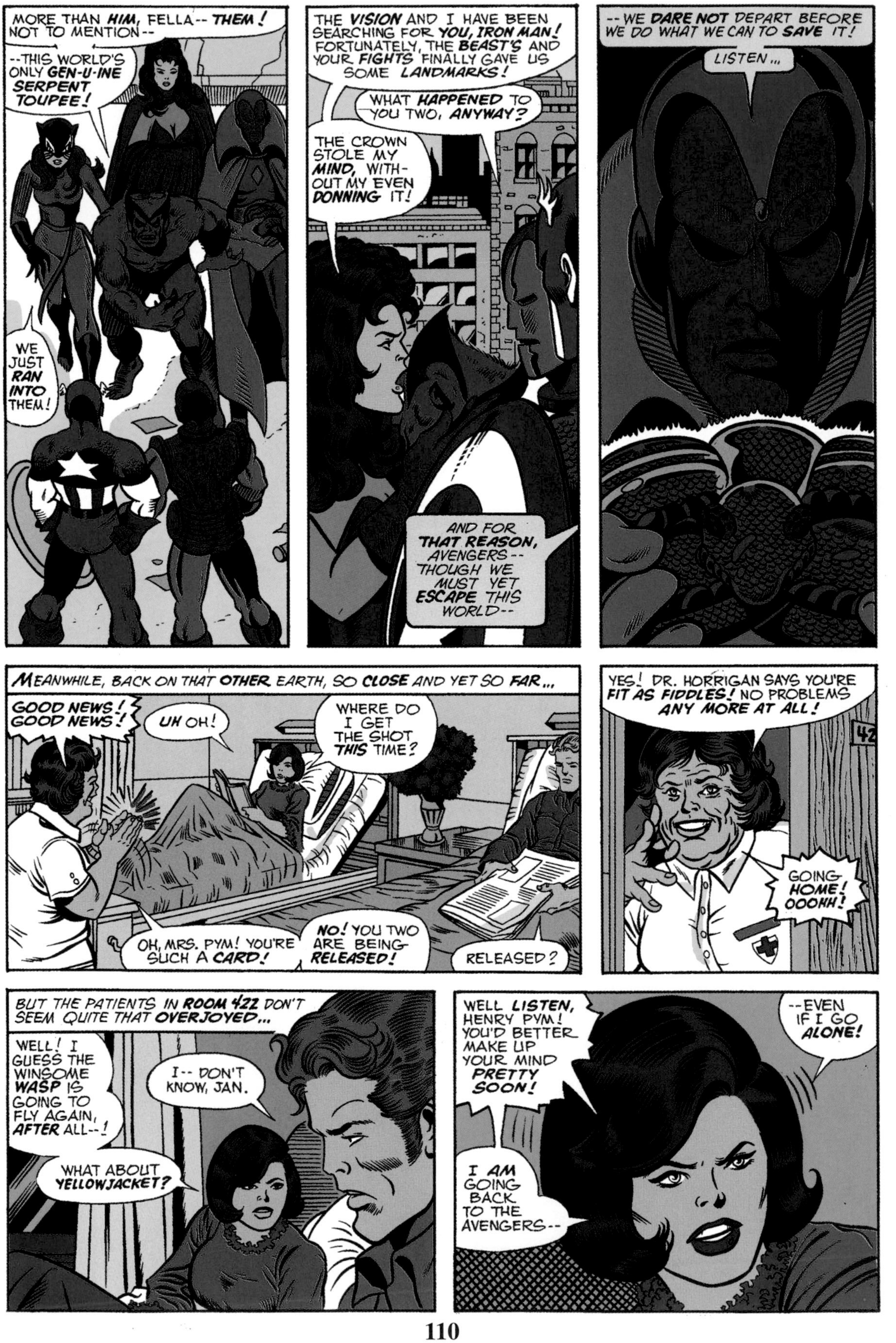
MORE THAN HIM, FELLA-- THEM! NOT TO MENTION--
--THIS WORLD'S ONLY GEN-U-INE SERPENT TOUPEE!
WE JUST RAN INTO THEM!
THE VISION AND I HAVE BEEN SEARCHING FOR YOU, IRON MAN! FORTUNATELY, THE BEAST'S AND YOUR FIGHTS FINALLY GAVE US SOME LANDMARKS!
WHAT HAPPENED TO YOU TWO, ANYWAY?
THE CROWN STOLE MY MIND, WITH-OUT MY EVEN DONNING IT!
AND FOR THAT REASON, AVENGERS-- THOUGH WE MUST YET ESCAPE THIS WORLD--
--WE DARE NOT DEPART BEFORE WE DO WHAT WE CAN TO SAVE IT!
LISTEN...
MEANWHILE, BACK ON THAT OTHER EARTH, SO CLOSE AND YET SO FAR...
GOOD NEWS! GOOD NEWS!
UH OH!
WHERE DO I GET THE SHOT THIS TIME?
OH, MRS. PYM! YOU'RE SUCH A CARD!
NO! YOU TWO ARE BEING RELEASED!
RELEASED?
YES! DR. HORRIGAN SAYS YOU'RE FIT AS FIDDLES! NO PROBLEMS ANY MORE AT ALL!
GOING HOME! OOOHH!
BUT THE PATIENTS IN ROOM 422 DON'T SEEM QUITE THAT OVERJOYED...
WELL! I GUESS THE WINSOME WASP IS GOING TO FLY AGAIN, AFTER ALL--!
I-- DON'T KNOW, JAN.
WHAT ABOUT YELLOWJACKET?
WELL LISTEN, HENRY PYM! YOU'D BETTER MAKE UP YOUR MIND PRETTY SOON!
I AM GOING BACK TO THE AVENGERS--
--EVEN IF I GO ALONE!

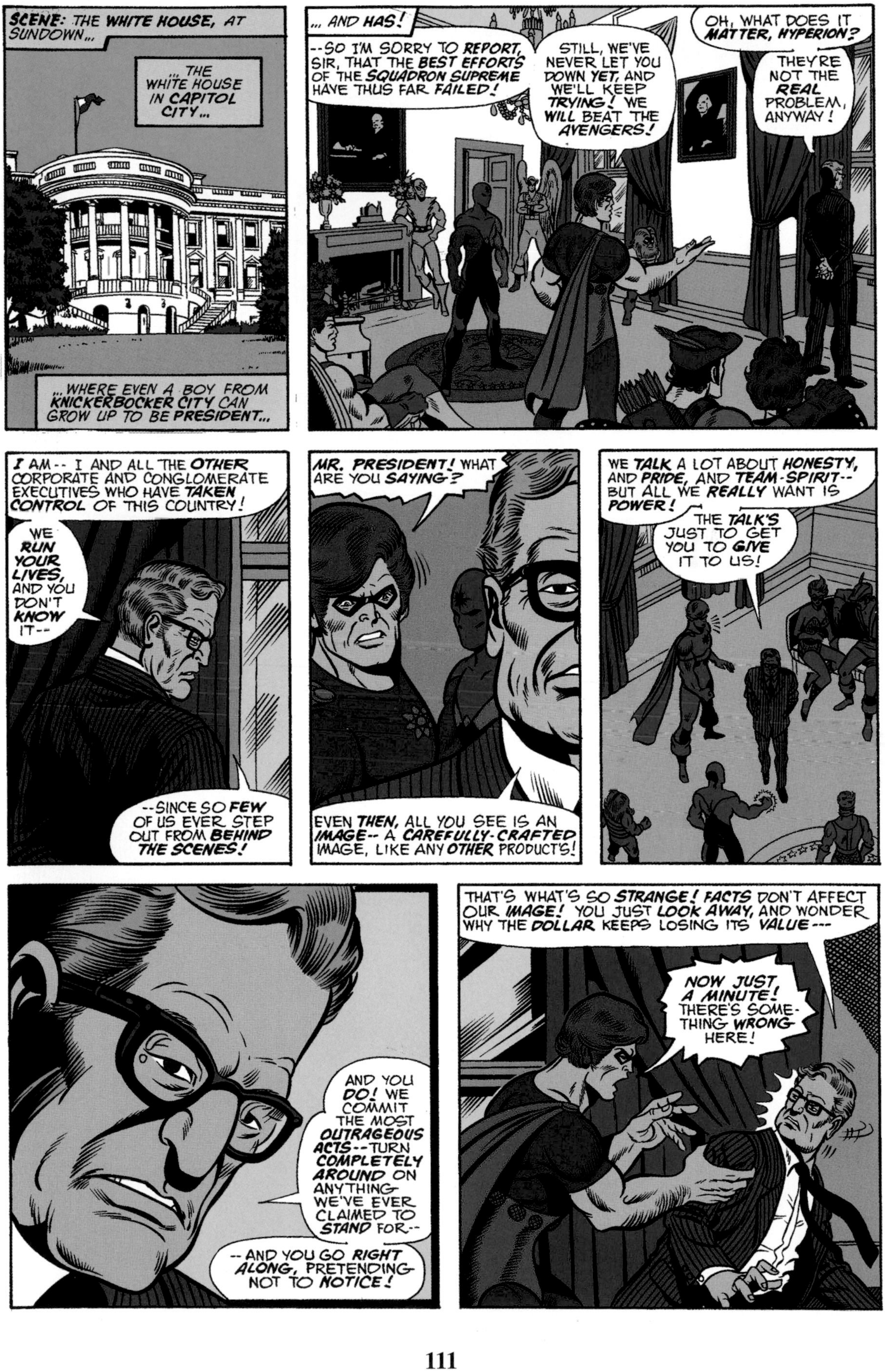
SCENE: THE WHITE HOUSE, AT SUNDOWN...
...THE WHITE HOUSE IN CAPITOL CITY...
...WHERE EVEN A BOY FROM KNICKERBOCKER CITY CAN GROW UP TO BE PRESIDENT...
...AND HAS!
--SO I'M SORRY TO REPORT, SIR, THAT THE BEST EFFORTS OF THE SQUADRON SUPREME HAVE THUS FAR FAILED!
STILL, WE'VE NEVER LET YOU DOWN YET, AND WE'LL KEEP TRYING! WE WILL BEAT THE AVENGERS!
OH, WHAT DOES IT MATTER, HYPERION?
THEY'RE NOT THE REAL PROBLEM, ANYWAY!
I AM-- I AND ALL THE OTHER CORPORATE AND CONGLOMERATE EXECUTIVES WHO HAVE TAKEN CONTROL OF THIS COUNTRY!
WE RUN YOUR LIVES, AND YOU DON'T KNOW IT--
--SINCE SO FEW OF US EVER STEP OUT FROM BEHIND THE SCENES!
MR. PRESIDENT! WHAT ARE YOU SAYING?
EVEN THEN, ALL YOU SEE IS AN IMAGE-- A CAREFULLY-CRAFTED IMAGE, LIKE ANY OTHER PRODUCT'S!
WE TALK A LOT ABOUT HONESTY, AND PRIDE, AND TEAM-SPIRIT-- BUT ALL WE REALLY WANT IS POWER!
THE TALK'S JUST TO GET YOU TO GIVE IT TO US!
AND YOU DO! WE COMMIT THE MOST OUTRAGEOUS ACTS--TURN COMPLETELY AROUND ON ANYTHING WE'VE EVER CLAIMED TO STAND FOR--
--AND YOU GO RIGHT ALONG, PRETENDING NOT TO NOTICE!
THAT'S WHAT'S SO STRANGE! FACTS DON'T AFFECT OUR IMAGE! YOU JUST LOOK AWAY, AND WONDER WHY THE DOLLAR KEEPS LOSING ITS VALUE---
NOW JUST A MINUTE! THERE'S SOME-THING WRONG HERE!

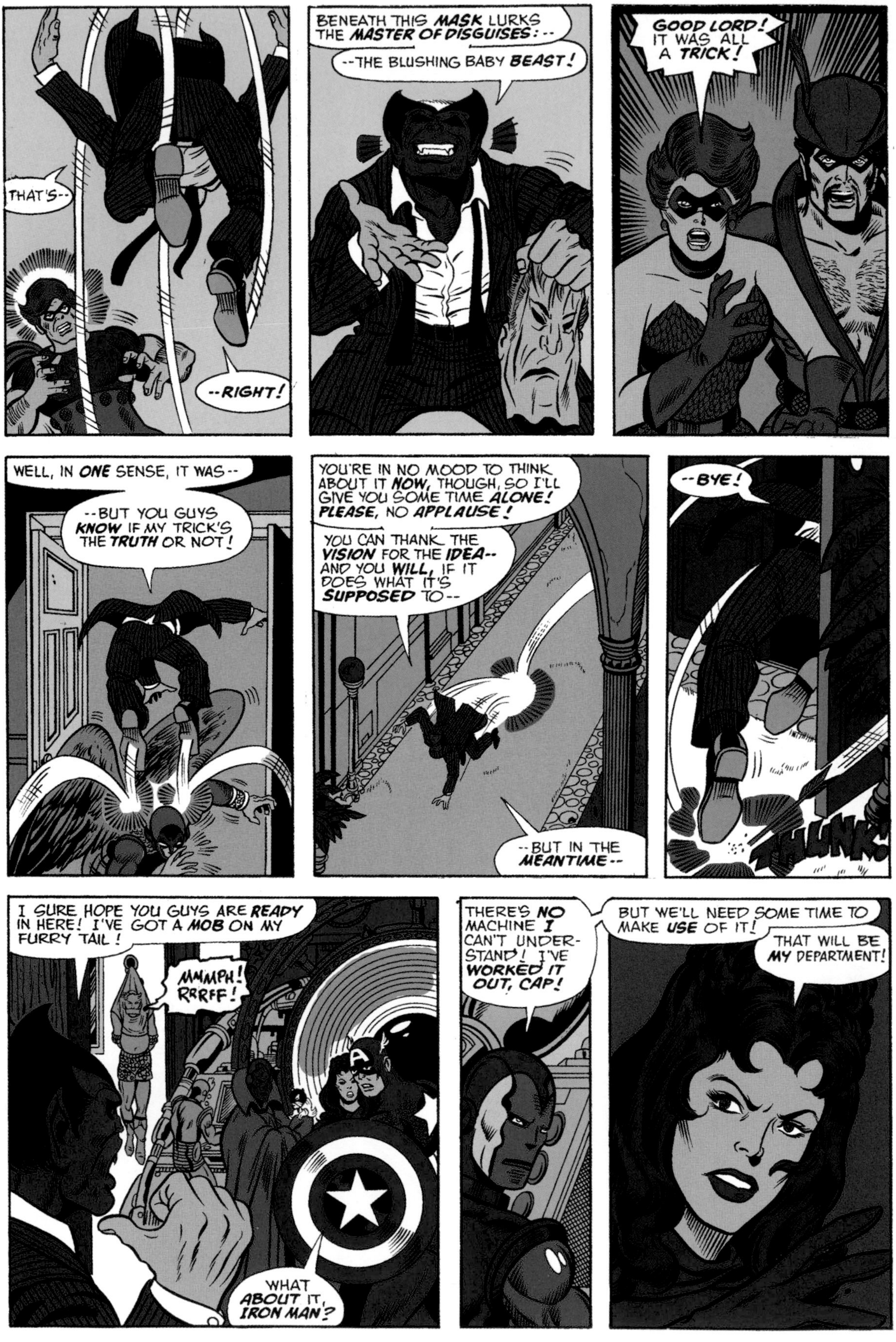
THAT'S--
--RIGHT!
BENEATH THIS MASK LURKS THE MASTER OF DISGUISES: --
--THE BLUSHING BABY BEAST!
GOOD LORD! IT WAS ALL A TRICK!
WELL, IN ONE SENSE, IT WAS--
--BUT YOU GUYS KNOW IF MY TRICK'S THE TRUTH OR NOT!
YOU'RE IN NO MOOD TO THINK ABOUT IT NOW, THOUGH, SO I'LL GIVE YOU SOME TIME ALONE! PLEASE, NO APPLAUSE!
YOU CAN THANK THE VISION FOR THE IDEA-- AND YOU WILL, IF IT DOES WHAT IT'S SUPPOSED TO--
--BUT IN THE MEANTIME--
--BYE!
THUNK!
I SURE HOPE YOU GUYS ARE READY IN HERE! I'VE GOT A MOB ON MY FURRY TAIL!
MMMPH! RRRFF!
WHAT ABOUT IT, IRON MAN?
THERE'S NO MACHINE I CAN'T UNDERSTAND! I'VE WORKED IT OUT, CAP!
BUT WE'LL NEED SOME TIME TO MAKE USE OF IT!
THAT WILL BE MY DEPARTMENT!

ON **ANY** EARTH, **ANYWHERE**-- NO MATTER IF THERE BE A **THOUSAND** OF THESE PARALLEL DIMENSIONS--

--THE POWERS OF **NATURE** BE EVER THE **SAME**--

--AND **THUS**, THE POWERS OF **WITCHCRAFT!** SO SPEAKS-- THE **SCARLET WITCH!**

INSTANTLY, THE **SPELL** CONTAINED IN HER SEEMINGLY INNOCUOUS WORDS **FUELED** BY HER INBRED **MUTANT MIGHT**, TAKES **HOLD!**

GREAT **XENON!** THE **PLANT**--!

FANTASTIC, **WANDA!** NOW HURRY UP AND FOLLOW THE **OTHERS!**

OUR EARTH IS RIGHT THRU **THERE!**

THERE **HAD TO BE** SOME **COUNTERPART** ON **THIS** PLANET TO THE MACHINE THAT SENT US HERE IN THE **FIRST PLACE**--

--AND CONSIDERING THE **SITUATION** HERE, WHAT **SAFER** PLACE FOR IT THAN THE **WHITE HOUSE?**

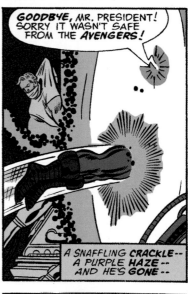

GOODBYE, MR. PRESIDENT! SORRY IT WASN'T SAFE FROM THE **AVENGERS!**

A SNAFFLING **CRACKLE**-- A PURPLE **HAZE**-- AND HE'S **GONE**--

--**SCANT SECONDS** BEFORE THE **CAVALRY** ARRIVES!

NO OVER- GROWN **FERN** CAN HOLD **HYPERION!**

THOSE **RESPONSIBLE** WILL **NOT** ESCAPE!

THE **SQUADRON SUPREME** WILL FOLLOW THEM--

NOT SO **FAST**, HYPE! THAT MAY **NOT** BE TRUE!

WHAT, **GOLDEN ARCHER?**

WHAT THE **BEAST** TOLD US, SQUAD- MEMBER-- I'VE BEEN **THINKING**--!

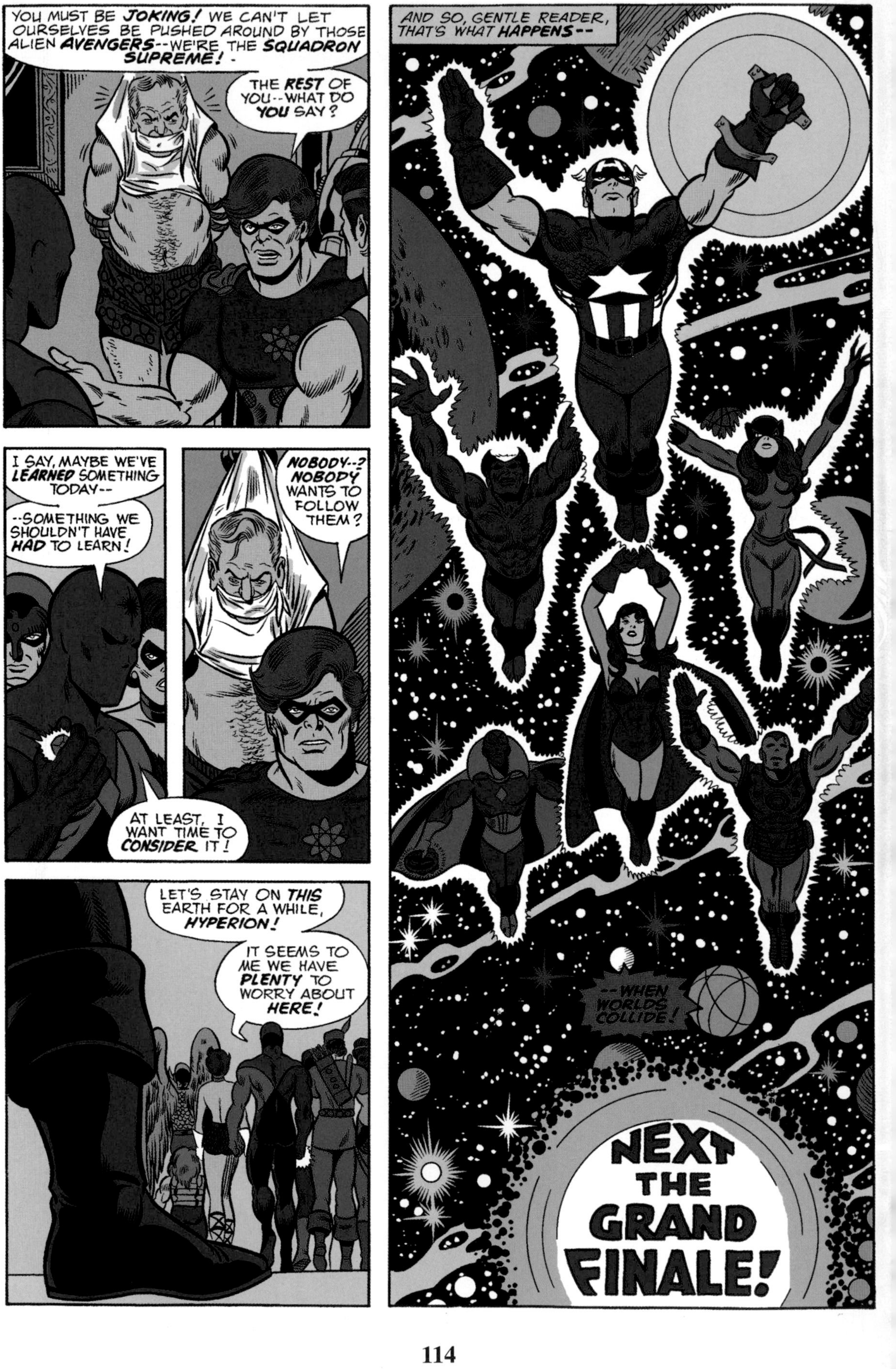
YOU MUST BE JOKING! WE CAN'T LET OURSELVES BE PUSHED AROUND BY THOSE ALIEN AVENGERS--WE'RE THE SQUADRON SUPREME! -
THE REST OF YOU--WHAT DO YOU SAY?
I SAY, MAYBE WE'VE LEARNED SOMETHING TODAY--
--SOMETHING WE SHOULDN'T HAVE HAD TO LEARN!
NOBODY--? NOBODY WANTS TO FOLLOW THEM?
AT LEAST, I WANT TIME TO CONSIDER IT!
LET'S STAY ON THIS EARTH FOR A WHILE, HYPERION!
IT SEEMS TO ME WE HAVE PLENTY TO WORRY ABOUT HERE!
AND SO, GENTLE READER, THAT'S WHAT HAPPENS--
--WHEN WORLDS COLLIDE!
NEXT THE GRAND FINALE!

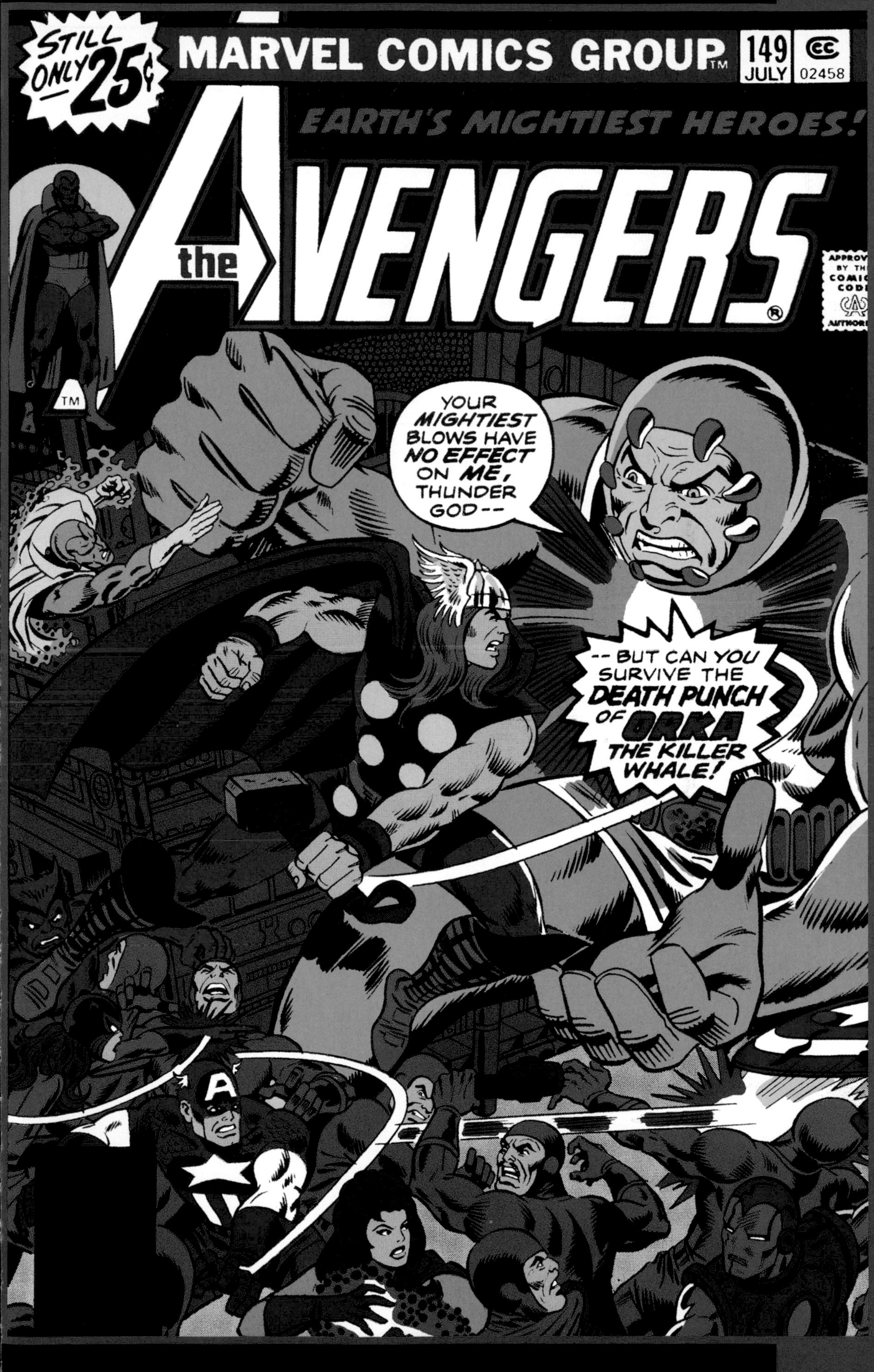
STILL ONLY 25¢
MARVEL COMICS GROUP
149 JULY
CC 02458
EARTH'S MIGHTIEST HEROES!
THE AVENGERS
YOUR MIGHTIEST BLOWS HAVE NO EFFECT ON ME, THUNDER GOD--
-- BUT CAN YOU SURVIVE THE DEATH PUNCH OF ORKA THE KILLER WHALE!

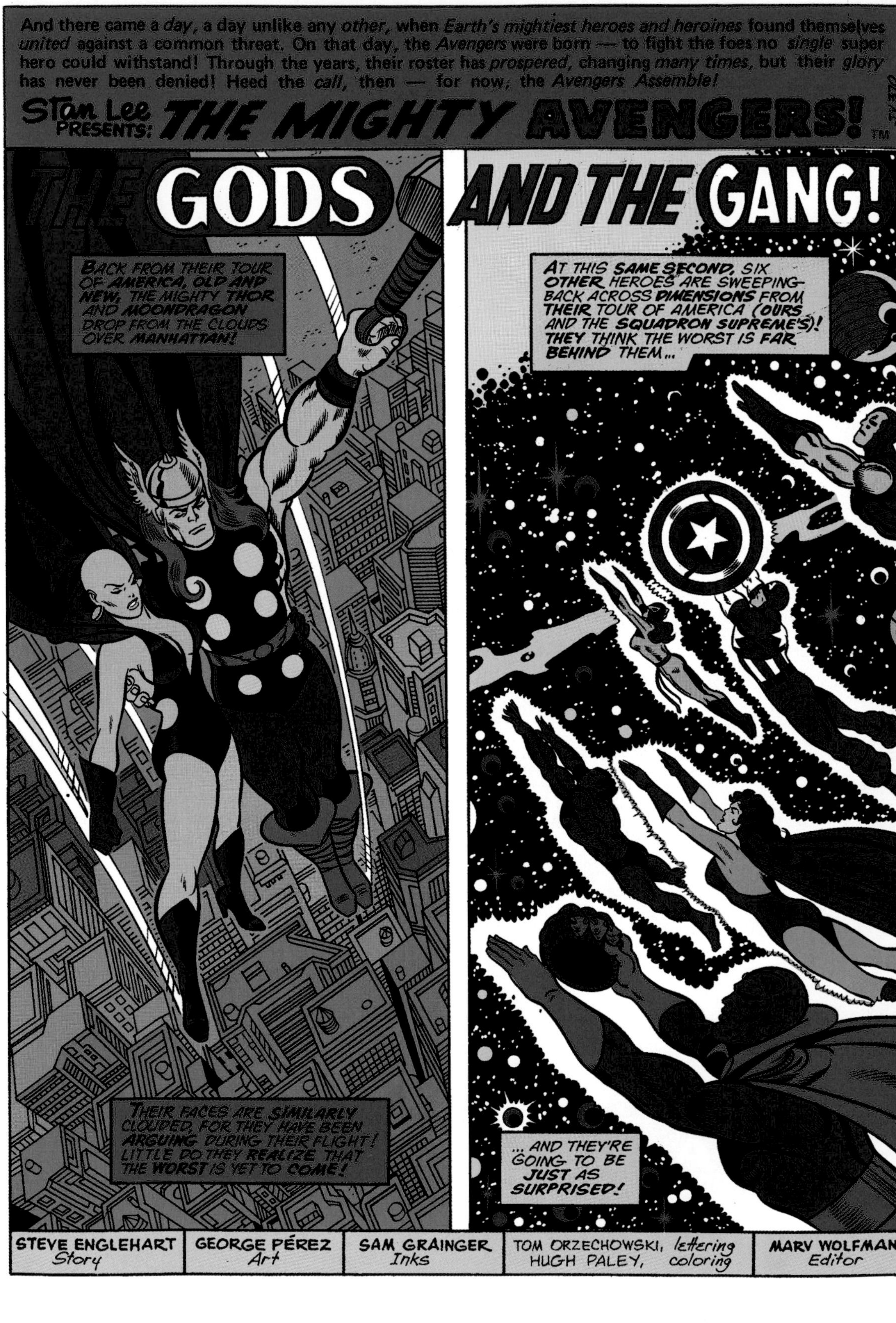
And there came a day, a day unlike any other, when Earth's mightiest heroes and heroines found themselves united against a common threat. On that day, the Avengers were born — to fight the foes no single super hero could withstand! Through the years, their roster has prospered, changing many times, but their glory has never been denied! Heed the call, then — for now, the Avengers Assemble!
Stan Lee PRESENTS: THE MIGHTY AVENGERS!
THE GODS AND THE GANG!
BACK FROM THEIR TOUR OF AMERICA, OLD AND NEW, THE MIGHTY THOR AND MOONDRAGON DROP FROM THE CLOUDS OVER MANHATTAN!
AT THIS SAME SECOND, SIX OTHER HEROES ARE SWEEPING BACK ACROSS DIMENSIONS FROM THEIR TOUR OF AMERICA (OURS AND THE SQUADRON SUPREME'S)! THEY THINK THE WORST IS FAR BEHIND THEM...
THEIR FACES ARE SIMILARLY CLOUDED, FOR THEY HAVE BEEN ARGUING DURING THEIR FLIGHT! LITTLE DO THEY REALIZE THAT THE WORST IS YET TO COME!
...AND THEY'RE GOING TO BE JUST AS SURPRISED!
STEVE ENGLEHART Story
GEORGE PÉREZ Art
SAM GRAINGER Inks
TOM ORZECHOWSKI, lettering
HUGH PALEY, coloring
MARV WOLFMAN Editor

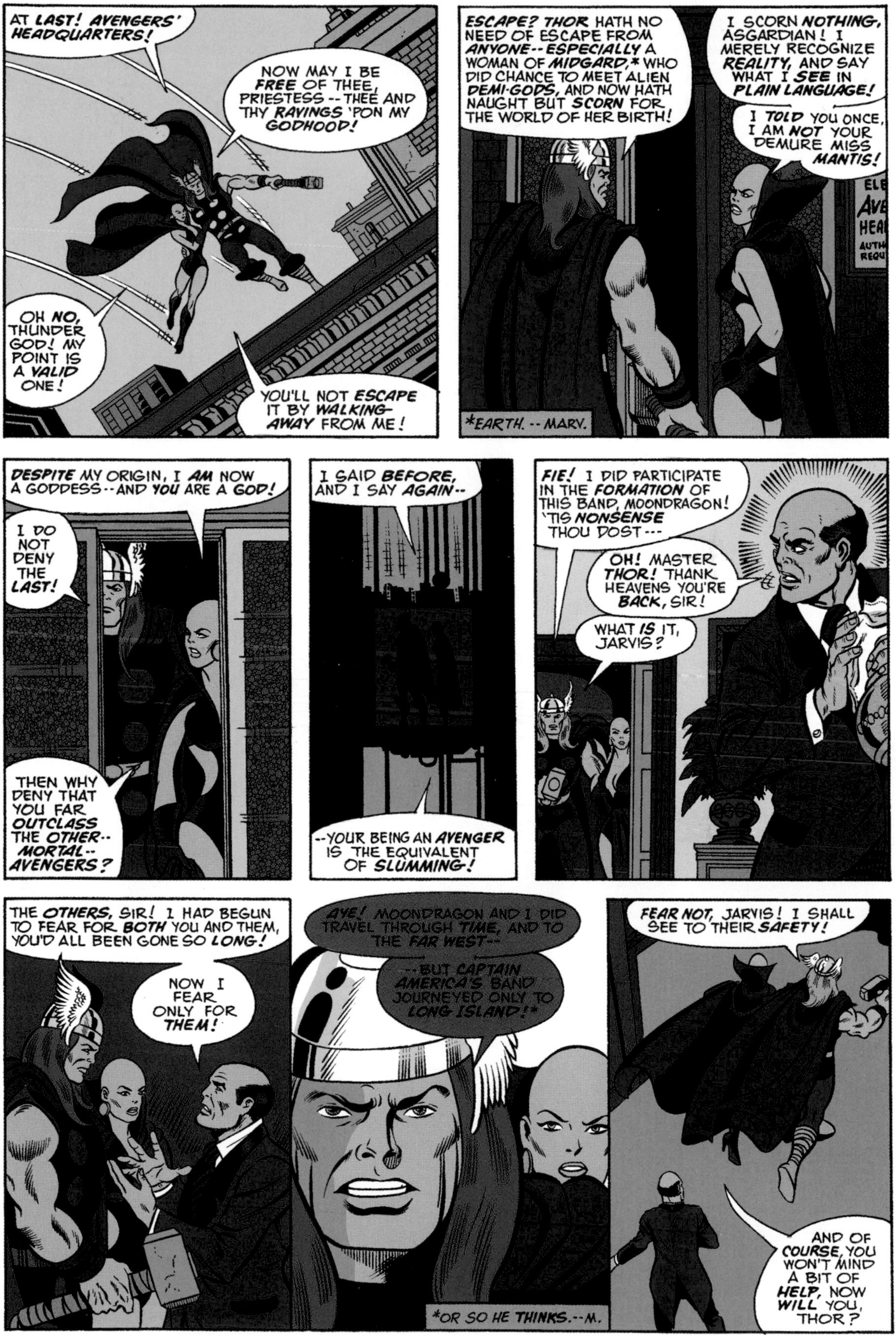
AT LAST! AVENGERS' HEADQUARTERS!
NOW MAY I BE FREE OF THEE, PRIESTESS -- THEE AND THY RAVINGS 'PON MY GODHOOD!
OH NO, THUNDER GOD! MY POINT IS A VALID ONE!
YOU'LL NOT ESCAPE IT BY WALKING-AWAY FROM ME!
ESCAPE? THOR HATH NO NEED OF ESCAPE FROM ANYONE-- ESPECIALLY A WOMAN OF MIDGARD,* WHO DID CHANCE TO MEET ALIEN DEMI-GODS, AND NOW HATH NAUGHT BUT SCORN FOR THE WORLD OF HER BIRTH!
I SCORN NOTHING, ASGARDIAN! I MERELY RECOGNIZE REALITY, AND SAY WHAT I SEE IN PLAIN LANGUAGE!
I TOLD YOU ONCE, I AM NOT YOUR DEMURE MISS MANTIS!
*EARTH. -- MARV.
DESPITE MY ORIGIN, I AM NOW A GODDESS -- AND YOU ARE A GOD!
I DO NOT DENY THE LAST!
THEN WHY DENY THAT YOU FAR OUTCLASS THE OTHER -- MORTAL -- AVENGERS?
I SAID BEFORE, AND I SAY AGAIN--
--YOUR BEING AN AVENGER IS THE EQUIVALENT OF SLUMMING!
FIE! I DID PARTICIPATE IN THE FORMATION OF THIS BAND, MOONDRAGON! 'TIS NONSENSE THOU DOST---
OH! MASTER THOR! THANK HEAVENS YOU'RE BACK, SIR!
WHAT IS IT, JARVIS?
THE OTHERS, SIR! I HAD BEGUN TO FEAR FOR BOTH YOU AND THEM, YOU'D ALL BEEN GONE SO LONG!
NOW I FEAR ONLY FOR THEM!
AYE! MOONDRAGON AND I DID TRAVEL THROUGH TIME, AND TO THE FAR WEST--
--BUT CAPTAIN AMERICA'S BAND JOURNEYED ONLY TO LONG ISLAND!*
*OR SO HE THINKS. -- M.
FEAR NOT, JARVIS! I SHALL SEE TO THEIR SAFETY!
AND OF COURSE, YOU WON'T MIND A BIT OF HELP, NOW WILL YOU, THOR?

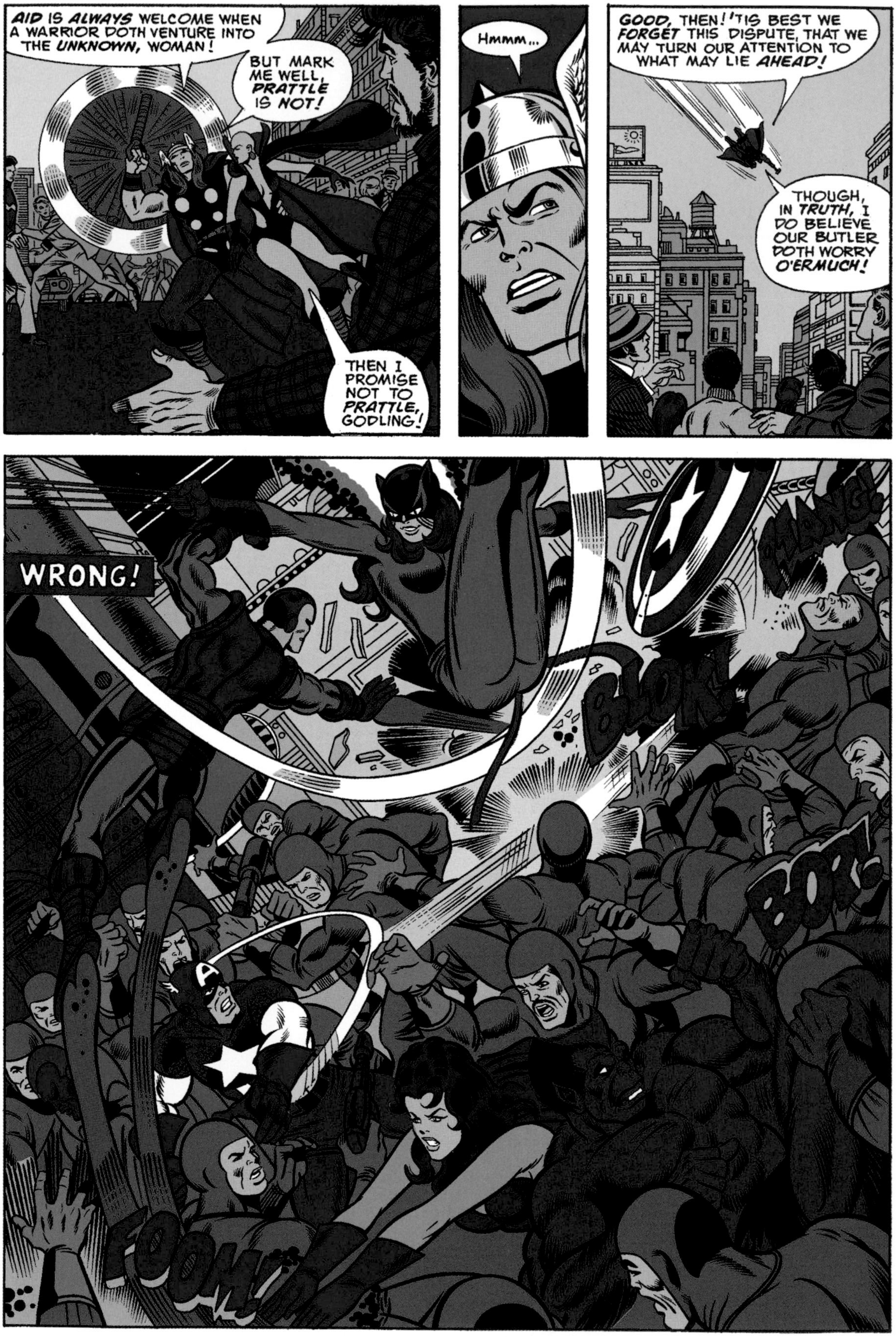
AID IS ALWAYS WELCOME WHEN A WARRIOR DOTH VENTURE INTO THE UNKNOWN, WOMAN!
BUT MARK ME WELL, PRATTLE IS NOT!
THEN I PROMISE NOT TO PRATTLE, GODLING!
Hmmm...
GOOD, THEN! 'TIS BEST WE FORGET THIS DISPUTE, THAT WE MAY TURN OUR ATTENTION TO WHAT MAY LIE AHEAD!
THOUGH, IN TRUTH, I DO BELIEVE OUR BUTLER DOTH WORRY O'ERMUCH!
WRONG!

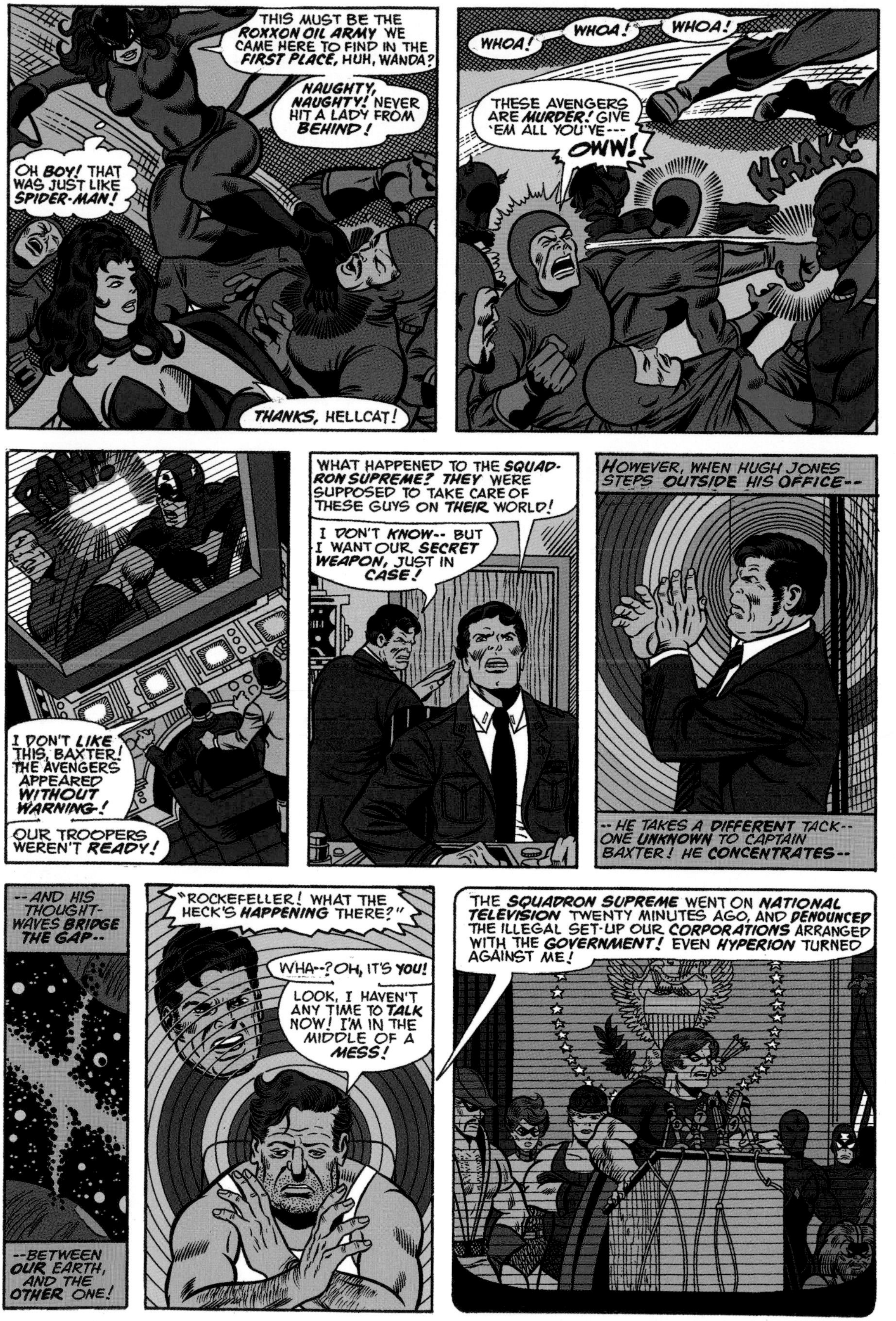
THIS MUST BE THE ROXXON OIL ARMY WE CAME HERE TO FIND IN THE FIRST PLACE, HUH, WANDA?
NAUGHTY, NAUGHTY! NEVER HIT A LADY FROM BEHIND!
OH BOY! THAT WAS JUST LIKE SPIDER-MAN!
THANKS, HELLCAT!
WHOA!
WHOA!
WHOA!
THESE AVENGERS ARE MURDER! GIVE 'EM ALL YOU'VE---
OWW!
KRAK!
I DON'T LIKE THIS, BAXTER! THE AVENGERS APPEARED WITHOUT WARNING-!
OUR TROOPERS WEREN'T READY!
WHAT HAPPENED TO THE SQUADRON SUPREME? THEY WERE SUPPOSED TO TAKE CARE OF THESE GUYS ON THEIR WORLD!
I DON'T KNOW-- BUT I WANT OUR SECRET WEAPON, JUST IN CASE!
HOWEVER, WHEN HUGH JONES STEPS OUTSIDE HIS OFFICE--
--HE TAKES A DIFFERENT TACK--ONE UNKNOWN TO CAPTAIN BAXTER! HE CONCENTRATES--
--AND HIS THOUGHT-WAVES BRIDGE THE GAP--
--BETWEEN OUR EARTH, AND THE OTHER ONE!
"ROCKEFELLER! WHAT THE HECK'S HAPPENING THERE?"
WHA--? OH, IT'S YOU!
LOOK, I HAVEN'T ANY TIME TO TALK NOW! I'M IN THE MIDDLE OF A MESS!
THE SQUADRON SUPREME WENT ON NATIONAL TELEVISION TWENTY MINUTES AGO, AND DENOUNCED THE ILLEGAL SET-UP OUR CORPORATIONS ARRANGED WITH THE GOVERNMENT! EVEN HYPERION TURNED AGAINST ME!

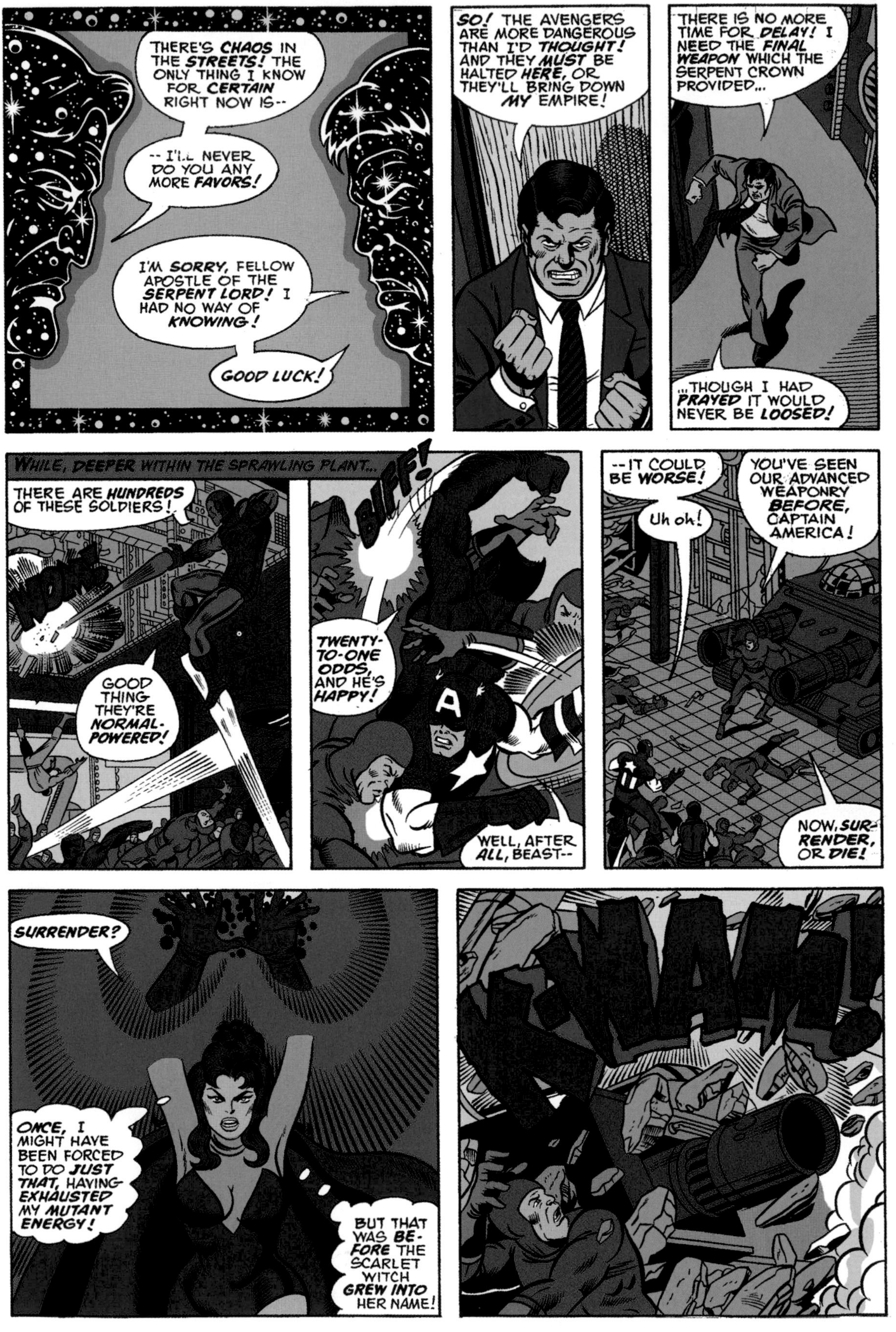
THERE'S CHAOS IN THE STREETS! THE ONLY THING I KNOW FOR CERTAIN RIGHT NOW IS--
-- I'LL NEVER DO YOU ANY MORE FAVORS!
I'M SORRY, FELLOW APOSTLE OF THE SERPENT LORD! I HAD NO WAY OF KNOWING!
GOOD LUCK!
SO! THE AVENGERS ARE MORE DANGEROUS THAN I'D THOUGHT! AND THEY MUST BE HALTED HERE, OR THEY'LL BRING DOWN MY EMPIRE!
THERE IS NO MORE TIME FOR DELAY! I NEED THE FINAL WEAPON WHICH THE SERPENT CROWN PROVIDED...
...THOUGH I HAD PRAYED IT WOULD NEVER BE LOOSED!
WHILE, DEEPER WITHIN THE SPRAWLING PLANT...
THERE ARE HUNDREDS OF THESE SOLDIERS!
GOOD THING THEY'RE NORMAL-POWERED!
BIFF!
TWENTY-TO-ONE ODDS, AND HE'S HAPPY!
WELL, AFTER ALL, BEAST--
--IT COULD BE WORSE!
Uh oh!
YOU'VE SEEN OUR ADVANCED WEAPONRY BEFORE, CAPTAIN AMERICA!
NOW, SURRENDER, OR DIE!
SURRENDER?
ONCE, I MIGHT HAVE BEEN FORCED TO DO JUST THAT, HAVING EXHAUSTED MY MUTANT ENERGY!
BUT THAT WAS BEFORE THE SCARLET WITCH GREW INTO HER NAME!
WAM!

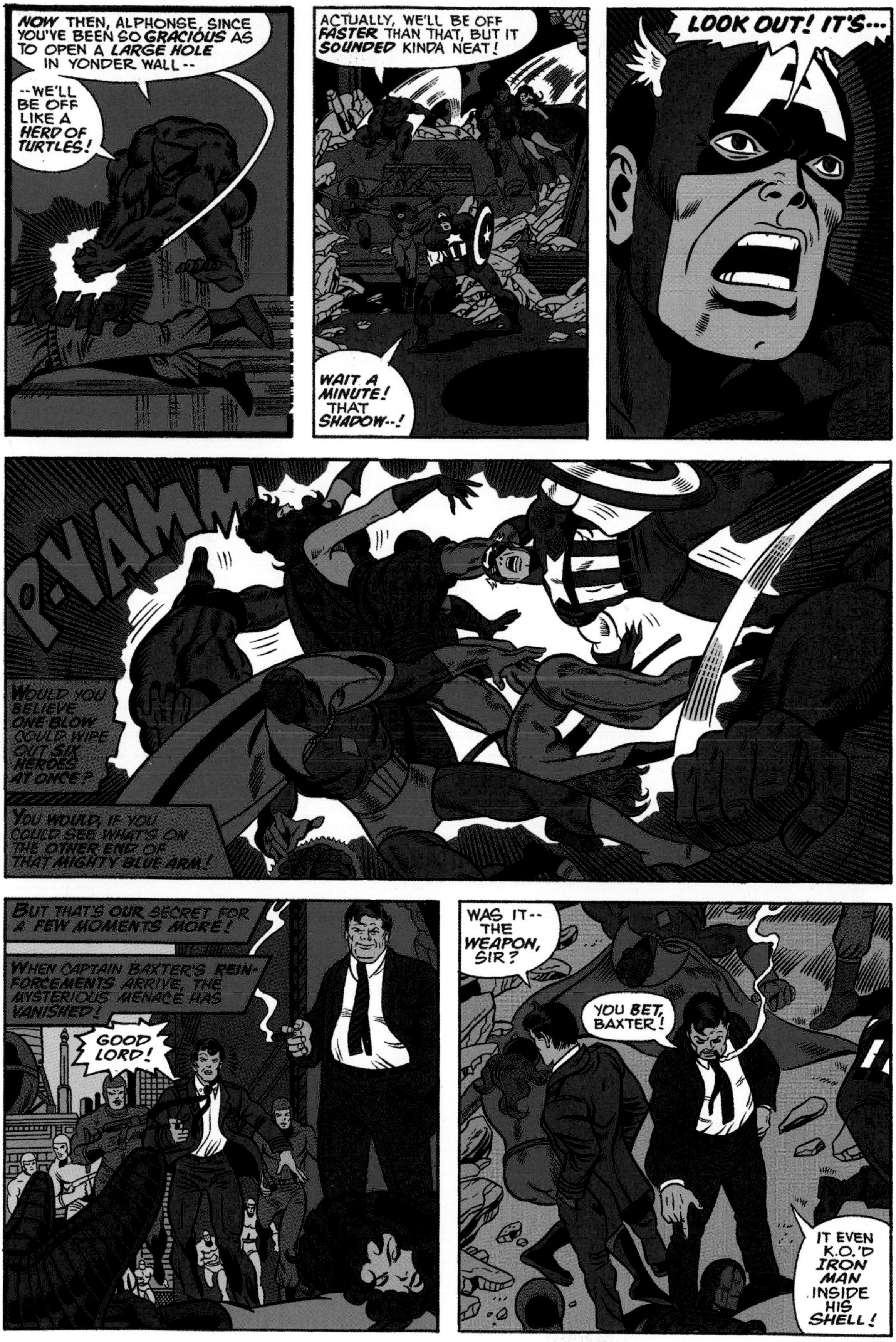

NOW THEN, ALPHONSE, SINCE YOU'VE BEEN SO GRACIOUS AS TO OPEN A LARGE HOLE IN YONDER WALL --
--WE'LL BE OFF LIKE A HERD OF TURTLES!
KLIP!
ACTUALLY, WE'LL BE OFF FASTER THAN THAT, BUT IT SOUNDED KINDA NEAT!
WAIT A MINUTE! THAT SHADOW--!
LOOK OUT! IT'S...
P-YAMM
WOULD YOU BELIEVE ONE BLOW COULD WIPE OUT SIX HEROES AT ONCE?
YOU WOULD, IF YOU COULD SEE WHAT'S ON THE OTHER END OF THAT MIGHTY BLUE ARM!
BUT THAT'S OUR SECRET FOR A FEW MOMENTS MORE!
WHEN CAPTAIN BAXTER'S REINFORCEMENTS ARRIVE, THE MYSTERIOUS MENACE HAS VANISHED!
GOOD LORD!
WAS IT-- THE WEAPON, SIR?
YOU BET, BAXTER!
IT EVEN K.O.'D IRON MAN INSIDE HIS SHELL!

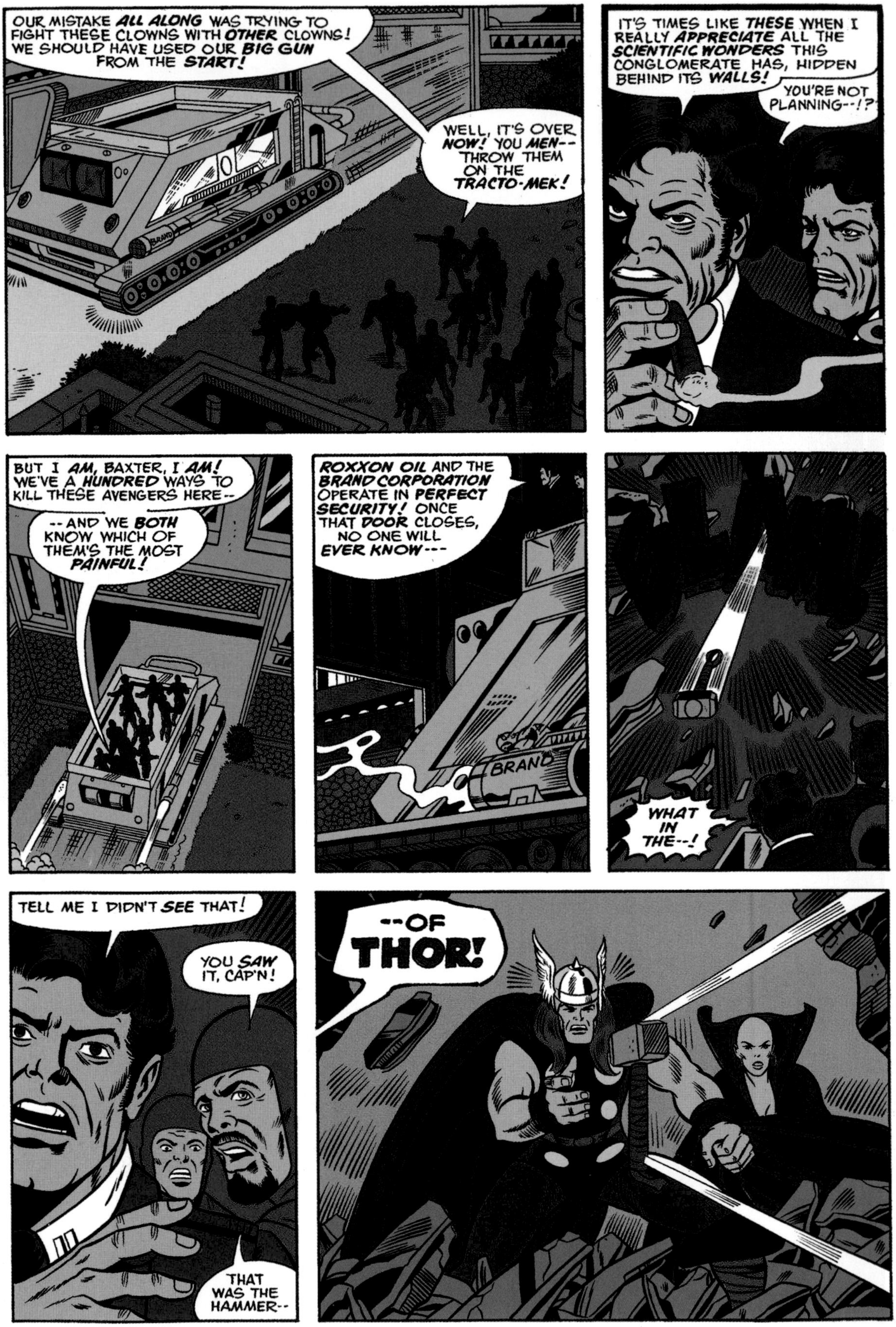
OUR MISTAKE ALL ALONG WAS TRYING TO FIGHT THESE CLOWNS WITH OTHER CLOWNS! WE SHOULD HAVE USED OUR BIG GUN FROM THE START!
WELL, IT'S OVER NOW! YOU MEN-- THROW THEM ON THE TRACTO-MEK!
BRAND
IT'S TIMES LIKE THESE WHEN I REALLY APPRECIATE ALL THE SCIENTIFIC WONDERS THIS CONGLOMERATE HAS, HIDDEN BEHIND ITS WALLS!
YOU'RE NOT PLANNING--!?
BUT I AM, BAXTER, I AM! WE'VE A HUNDRED WAYS TO KILL THESE AVENGERS HERE--
--AND WE BOTH KNOW WHICH OF THEM'S THE MOST PAINFUL!
ROXXON OIL AND THE BRAND CORPORATION OPERATE IN PERFECT SECURITY! ONCE THAT DOOR CLOSES, NO ONE WILL EVER KNOW---
BRAND
WHAT IN THE--!
TELL ME I DIDN'T SEE THAT!
YOU SAW IT, CAP'N!
THAT WAS THE HAMMER--
--OF THOR!

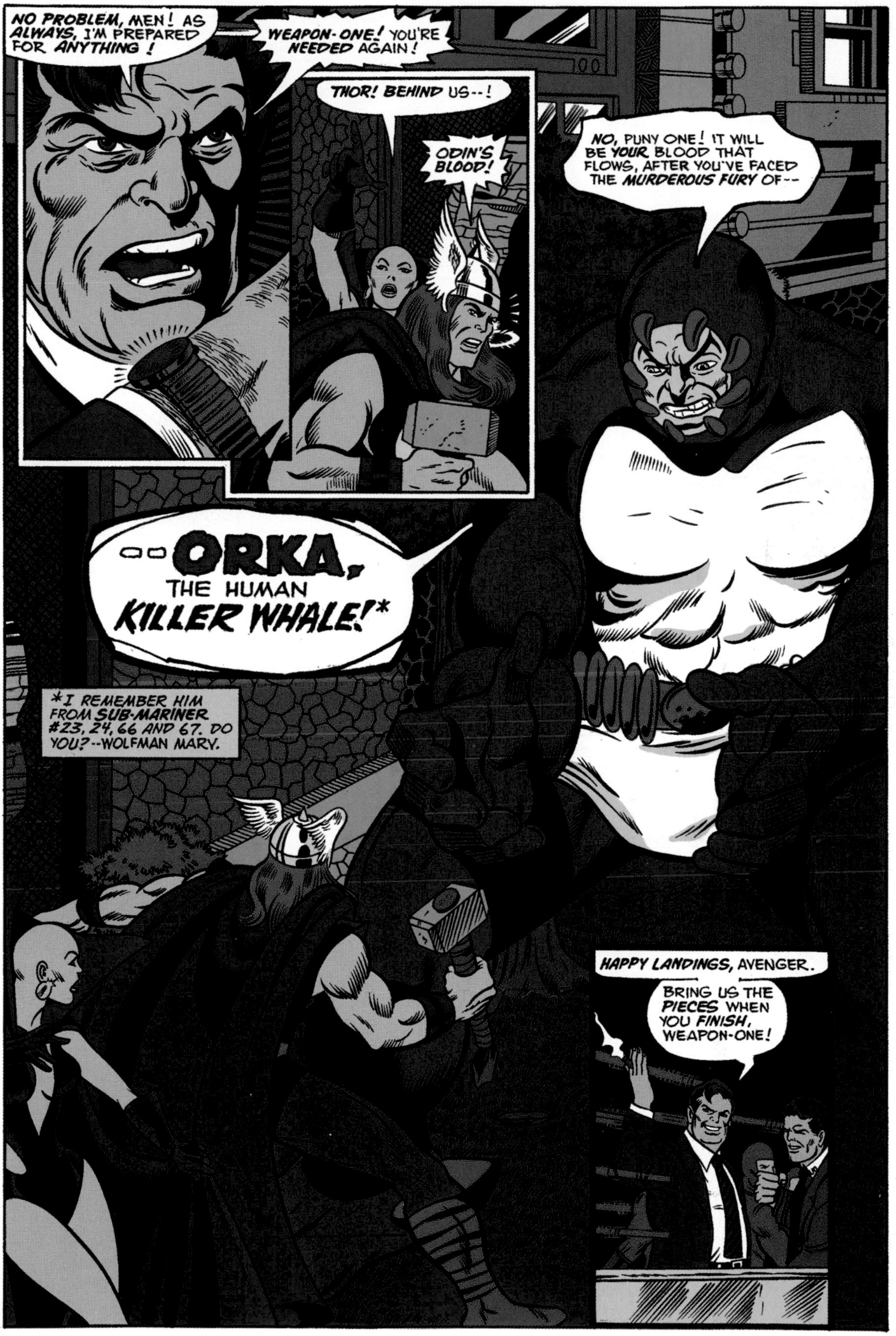
NO PROBLEM, MEN! AS ALWAYS, I'M PREPARED FOR ANYTHING!
WEAPON-ONE! YOU'RE NEEDED AGAIN!
THOR! BEHIND US--!
ODIN'S BLOOD!
NO, PUNY ONE! IT WILL BE YOUR BLOOD THAT FLOWS, AFTER YOU'VE FACED THE MURDEROUS FURY OF--
--ORKA, THE HUMAN KILLER WHALE!*
*I REMEMBER HIM FROM SUB-MARINER #23, 24, 66 AND 67. DO YOU?--WOLFMAN MARV.
HAPPY LANDINGS, AVENGER.
BRING US THE PIECES WHEN YOU FINISH, WEAPON-ONE!

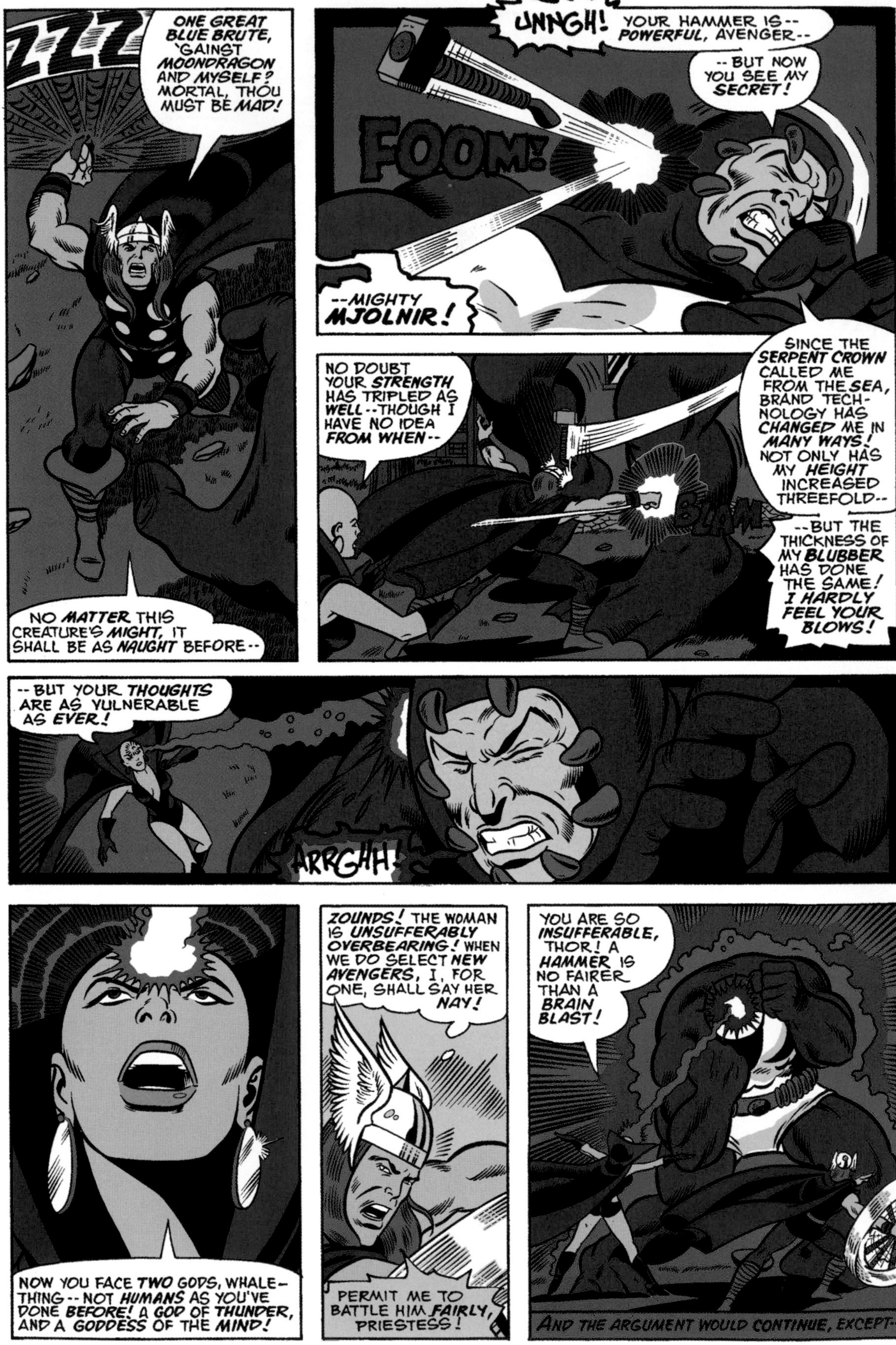
ZZZ
ONE GREAT BLUE BRUTE, 'GAINST MOONDRAGON AND MYSELF? MORTAL, THOU MUST BE MAD!
NO MATTER THIS CREATURE'S MIGHT, IT SHALL BE AS NAUGHT BEFORE--
UNNGH!
YOUR HAMMER IS--POWERFUL, AVENGER--
--BUT NOW YOU SEE MY SECRET!
FOOM!
--MIGHTY MJOLNIR!
NO DOUBT YOUR STRENGTH HAS TRIPLED AS WELL--THOUGH I HAVE NO IDEA FROM WHEN--
SINCE THE SERPENT CROWN CALLED ME FROM THE SEA, BRAND TECHNOLOGY HAS CHANGED ME IN MANY WAYS! NOT ONLY HAS MY HEIGHT INCREASED THREEFOLD--
BLAM!
--BUT THE THICKNESS OF MY BLUBBER HAS DONE THE SAME! I HARDLY FEEL YOUR BLOWS!
--BUT YOUR THOUGHTS ARE AS VULNERABLE AS EVER!
ARRGHH!
NOW YOU FACE TWO GODS, WHALE-THING--NOT HUMANS AS YOU'VE DONE BEFORE! A GOD OF THUNDER, AND A GODDESS OF THE MIND!
ZOUNDS! THE WOMAN IS UNSUFFERABLY OVERBEARING! WHEN WE DO SELECT NEW AVENGERS, I, FOR ONE, SHALL SAY HER NAY!
PERMIT ME TO BATTLE HIM FAIRLY, PRIESTESS!
YOU ARE SO INSUFFERABLE, THOR! A HAMMER IS NO FAIRER THAN A BRAIN BLAST!
AND THE ARGUMENT WOULD CONTINUE, EXCEPT--

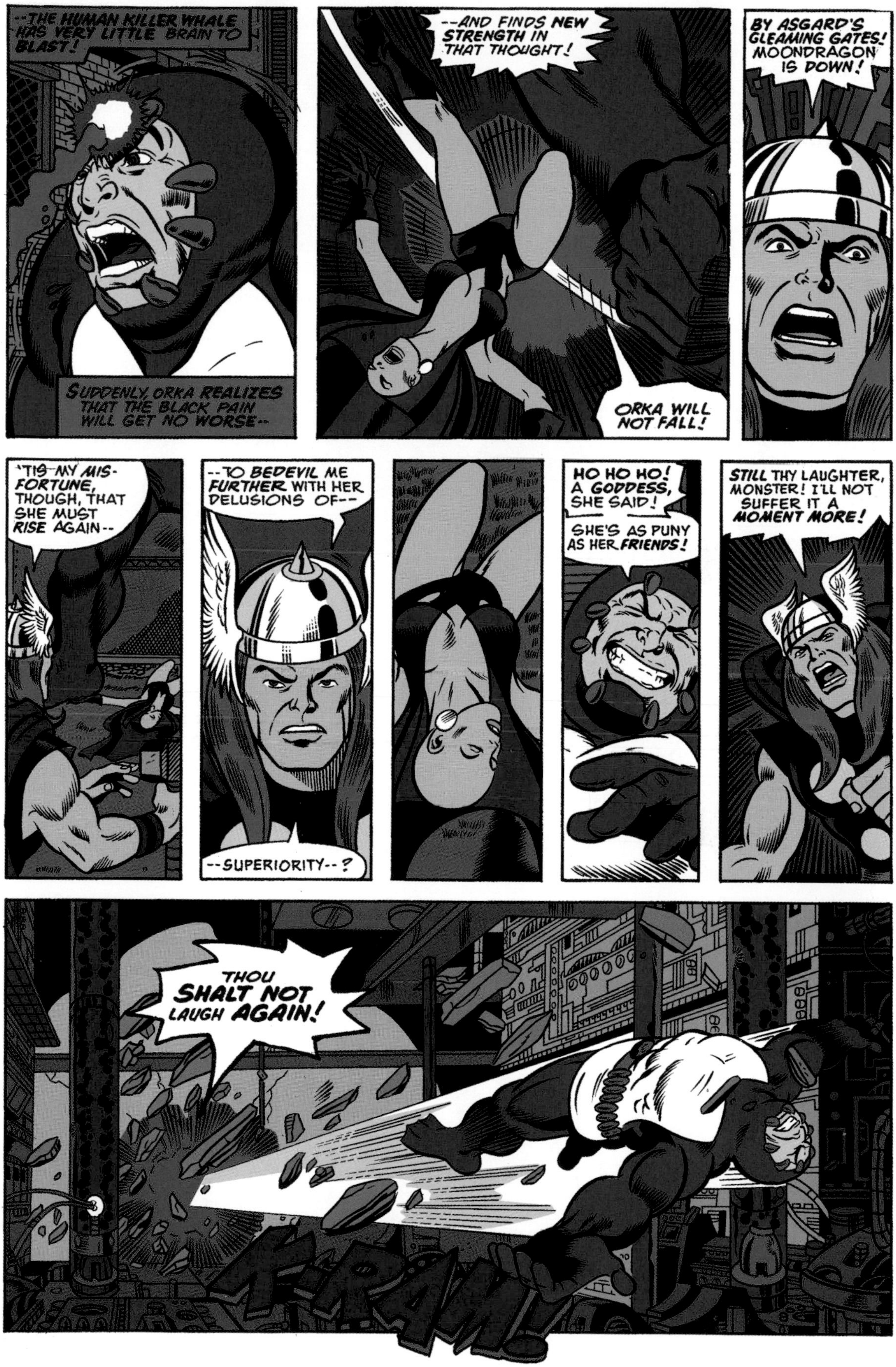
--THE HUMAN KILLER WHALE HAS VERY LITTLE BRAIN TO BLAST!
SUDDENLY, ORKA REALIZES THAT THE BLACK PAIN WILL GET NO WORSE--
--AND FINDS NEW STRENGTH IN THAT THOUGHT!
ORKA WILL NOT FALL!
BY ASGARD'S GLEAMING GATES! MOONDRAGON IS DOWN!
'TIS MY MIS-FORTUNE, THOUGH, THAT SHE MUST RISE AGAIN--
--TO BEDEVIL ME FURTHER WITH HER DELUSIONS OF--
--SUPERIORITY--?
HO HO HO! A GODDESS, SHE SAID!
SHE'S AS PUNY AS HER FRIENDS!
STILL THY LAUGHTER, MONSTER! I'LL NOT SUFFER IT A MOMENT MORE!
THOU SHALT NOT LAUGH AGAIN!
K-RAM!

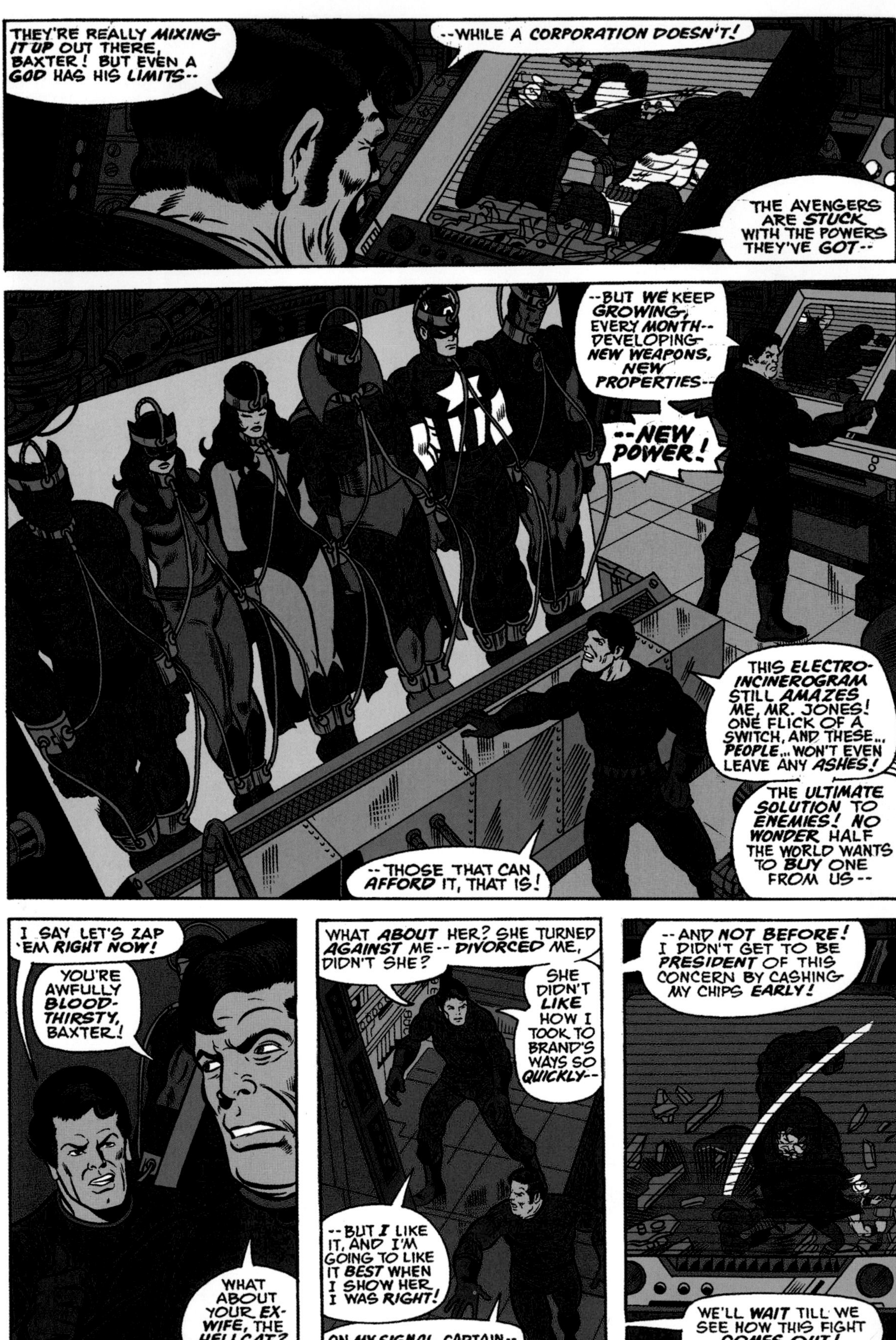
THEY'RE REALLY MIXING IT UP OUT THERE, BAXTER! BUT EVEN A GOD HAS HIS LIMITS--
--WHILE A CORPORATION DOESN'T!
THE AVENGERS ARE STUCK WITH THE POWERS THEY'VE GOT--
--BUT WE KEEP GROWING EVERY MONTH--DEVELOPING NEW WEAPONS, NEW PROPERTIES--
--NEW POWER!
THIS ELECTRO-INCINEROGRAM STILL AMAZES ME, MR. JONES! ONE FLICK OF A SWITCH, AND THESE... PEOPLE... WON'T EVEN LEAVE ANY ASHES!
THE ULTIMATE SOLUTION TO ENEMIES! NO WONDER HALF THE WORLD WANTS TO BUY ONE FROM US--
--THOSE THAT CAN AFFORD IT, THAT IS!
I SAY LET'S ZAP 'EM RIGHT NOW!
YOU'RE AWFULLY BLOOD-THIRSTY, BAXTER!
WHAT ABOUT YOUR EX-WIFE, THE HELLCAT?
WHAT ABOUT HER? SHE TURNED AGAINST ME--DIVORCED ME, DIDN'T SHE?
SHE DIDN'T LIKE HOW I TOOK TO BRAND'S WAYS SO QUICKLY--
--BUT I LIKE IT, AND I'M GOING TO LIKE IT BEST WHEN I SHOW HER I WAS RIGHT!
ON MY SIGNAL, CAPTAIN--
--AND NOT BEFORE! I DIDN'T GET TO BE PRESIDENT OF THIS CONCERN BY CASHING MY CHIPS EARLY!
WE'LL WAIT TILL WE SEE HOW THIS FIGHT COMES OUT!

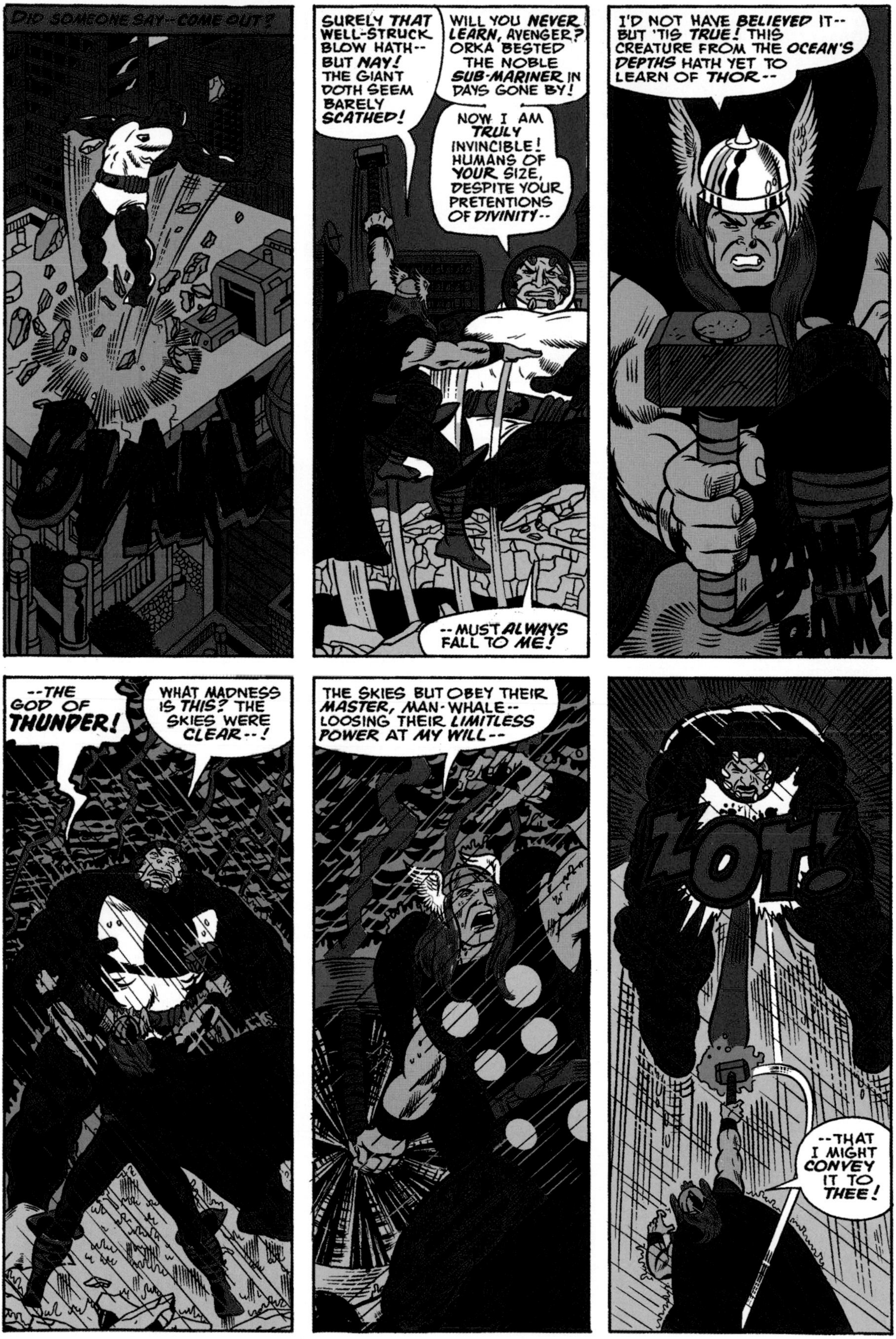
DID SOMEONE SAY--COME OUT?
BAM!
SURELY THAT WELL-STRUCK BLOW HATH-- BUT NAY! THE GIANT DOTH SEEM BARELY SCATHED!
WILL YOU NEVER LEARN, AVENGER? ORKA BESTED THE NOBLE SUB-MARINER IN DAYS GONE BY!
NOW I AM TRULY INVINCIBLE! HUMANS OF YOUR SIZE, DESPITE YOUR PRETENTIONS OF DIVINITY--
--MUST ALWAYS FALL TO ME!
I'D NOT HAVE BELIEVED IT-- BUT 'TIS TRUE! THIS CREATURE FROM THE OCEAN'S DEPTHS HATH YET TO LEARN OF THOR--
--THE GOD OF THUNDER!
WHAT MADNESS IS THIS? THE SKIES WERE CLEAR--!
THE SKIES BUT OBEY THEIR MASTER, MAN-WHALE-- LOOSING THEIR LIMITLESS POWER AT MY WILL--
ZOT!
--THAT I MIGHT CONVEY IT TO THEE!

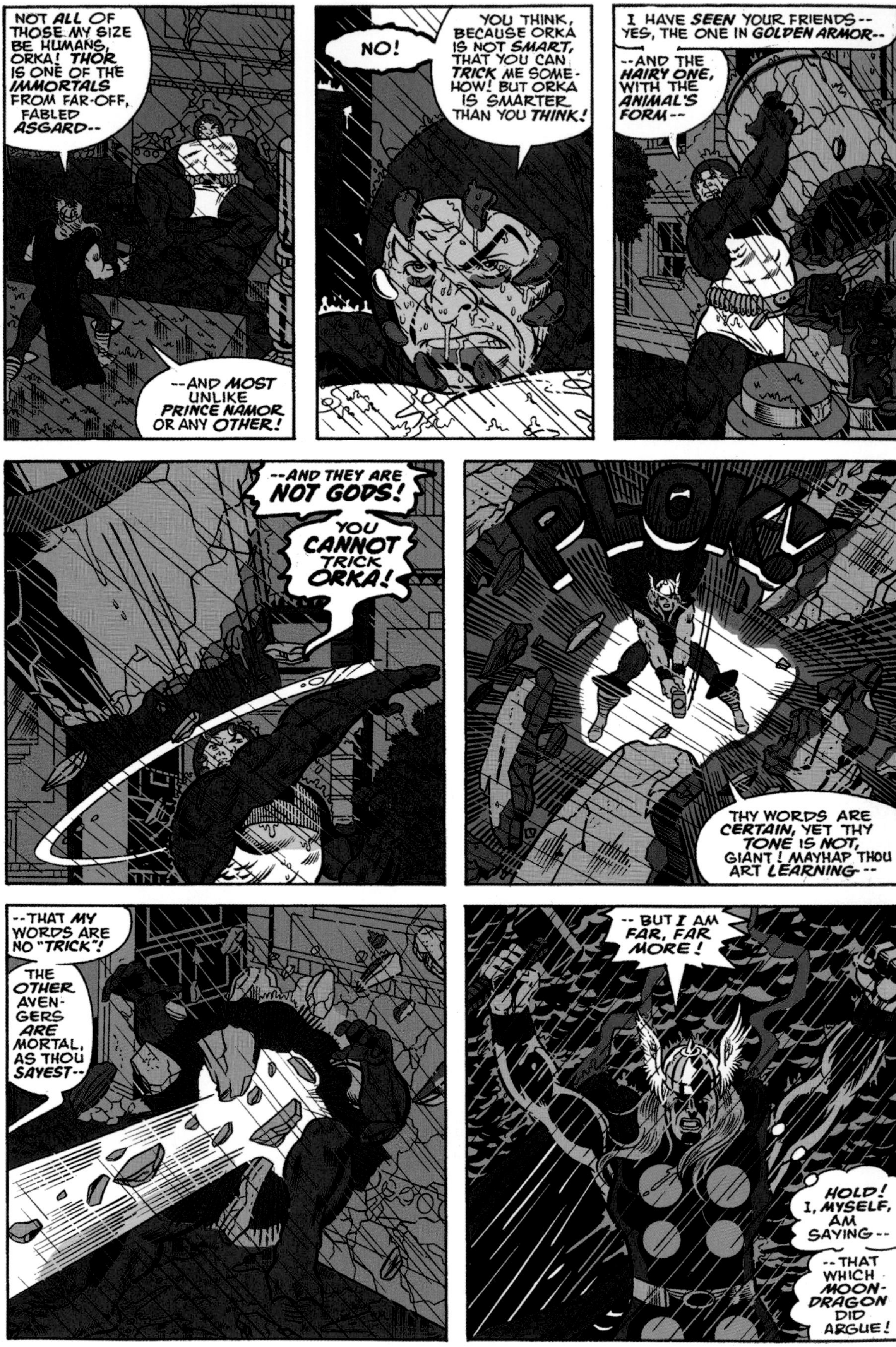
NOT ALL OF THOSE MY SIZE BE HUMANS, ORKA! THOR IS ONE OF THE IMMORTALS FROM FAR-OFF, FABLED ASGARD--
--AND MOST UNLIKE PRINCE NAMOR OR ANY OTHER!
NO!
YOU THINK, BECAUSE ORKA IS NOT SMART, THAT YOU CAN TRICK ME SOME-HOW! BUT ORKA IS SMARTER THAN YOU THINK!
I HAVE SEEN YOUR FRIENDS-- YES, THE ONE IN GOLDEN ARMOR--
--AND THE HAIRY ONE, WITH THE ANIMAL'S FORM--
--AND THEY ARE NOT GODS!
YOU CANNOT TRICK ORKA!
PLOK!
THY WORDS ARE CERTAIN, YET THY TONE IS NOT, GIANT! MAYHAP THOU ART LEARNING--
--THAT MY WORDS ARE NO "TRICK"!
THE OTHER AVEN-GERS ARE MORTAL, AS THOU SAYEST--
-- BUT I AM FAR, FAR MORE!
HOLD! I, MYSELF, AM SAYING--
--THAT WHICH MOON-DRAGON DID ARGUE!

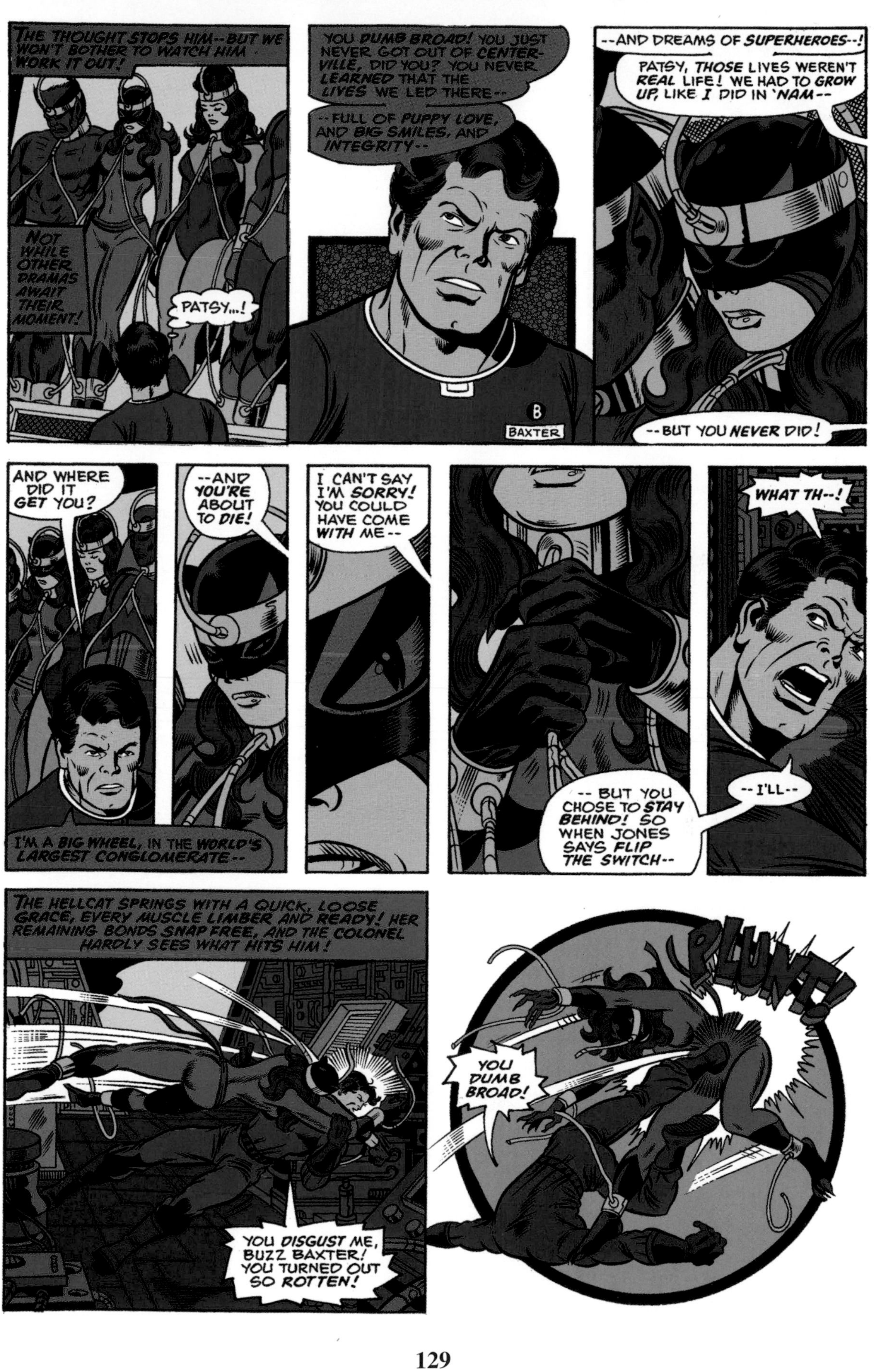
THE THOUGHT STOPS HIM--BUT WE WON'T BOTHER TO WATCH HIM WORK IT OUT!
NOT WHILE OTHER DRAMAS AWAIT THEIR MOMENT!
PATSY...!
YOU DUMB BROAD! YOU JUST NEVER GOT OUT OF CENTERVILLE, DID YOU? YOU NEVER LEARNED THAT THE LIVES WE LED THERE--
--FULL OF PUPPY LOVE, AND BIG SMILES, AND INTEGRITY--
B
BAXTER
--AND DREAMS OF SUPERHEROES--!
PATSY, THOSE LIVES WEREN'T REAL LIFE! WE HAD TO GROW UP, LIKE I DID IN 'NAM--
--BUT YOU NEVER DID!
AND WHERE DID IT GET YOU?
--AND YOU'RE ABOUT TO DIE!
I'M A BIG WHEEL, IN THE WORLD'S LARGEST CONGLOMERATE--
I CAN'T SAY I'M SORRY! YOU COULD HAVE COME WITH ME--
-- BUT YOU CHOSE TO STAY BEHIND! SO WHEN JONES SAYS FLIP THE SWITCH--
WHAT TH--!
--I'LL--
THE HELLCAT SPRINGS WITH A QUICK, LOOSE GRACE, EVERY MUSCLE LIMBER AND READY! HER REMAINING BONDS SNAP FREE, AND THE COLONEL HARDLY SEES WHAT HITS HIM!
YOU DISGUST ME, BUZZ BAXTER! YOU TURNED OUT SO ROTTEN!
PLUNT!
YOU DUMB BROAD!

YOU'VE GOT *GUTS*, PAT! THAT'S WHAT I ALWAYS *LIKED* ABOUT YOU! BUT YOU HAVEN'T GOT THE *SENSE* OF A *GOOSE!*

ORKA MAY HAVE *SLIPPED UP* ON YOU--

BANG

--BUT YOU SHOULDN'T HAVE GIVEN *ME* A CHANCE ---

TO DO *WHAT?* TO SINK ANY *LOWER* THAN YOU ALREADY *HAVE?*

I *LOVED* YOU, BUZZ!

YOU WERE THE ONLY BOY I EVER *WANTED!*

I *MARRIED* YOU! I *TOOK CARE* OF YOU!

ALL RIGHT! ALL RIGHT! PEDDLE IT TO *MARY HARTMAN!*

SO YOU'VE GOT A *BROKEN HEART* AND A *SUPER-SUIT!* SO WHAT?

SO FREE MY *FRIENDS,* LOVER-BOY--

--OR I'LL *SCRATCH YOUR EYES OUT!*

AT THAT MOMENT...

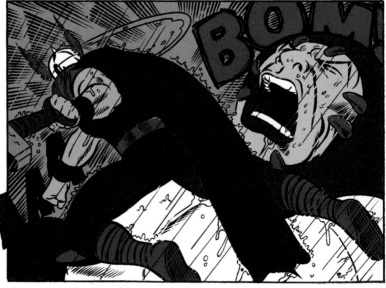

BOM

130

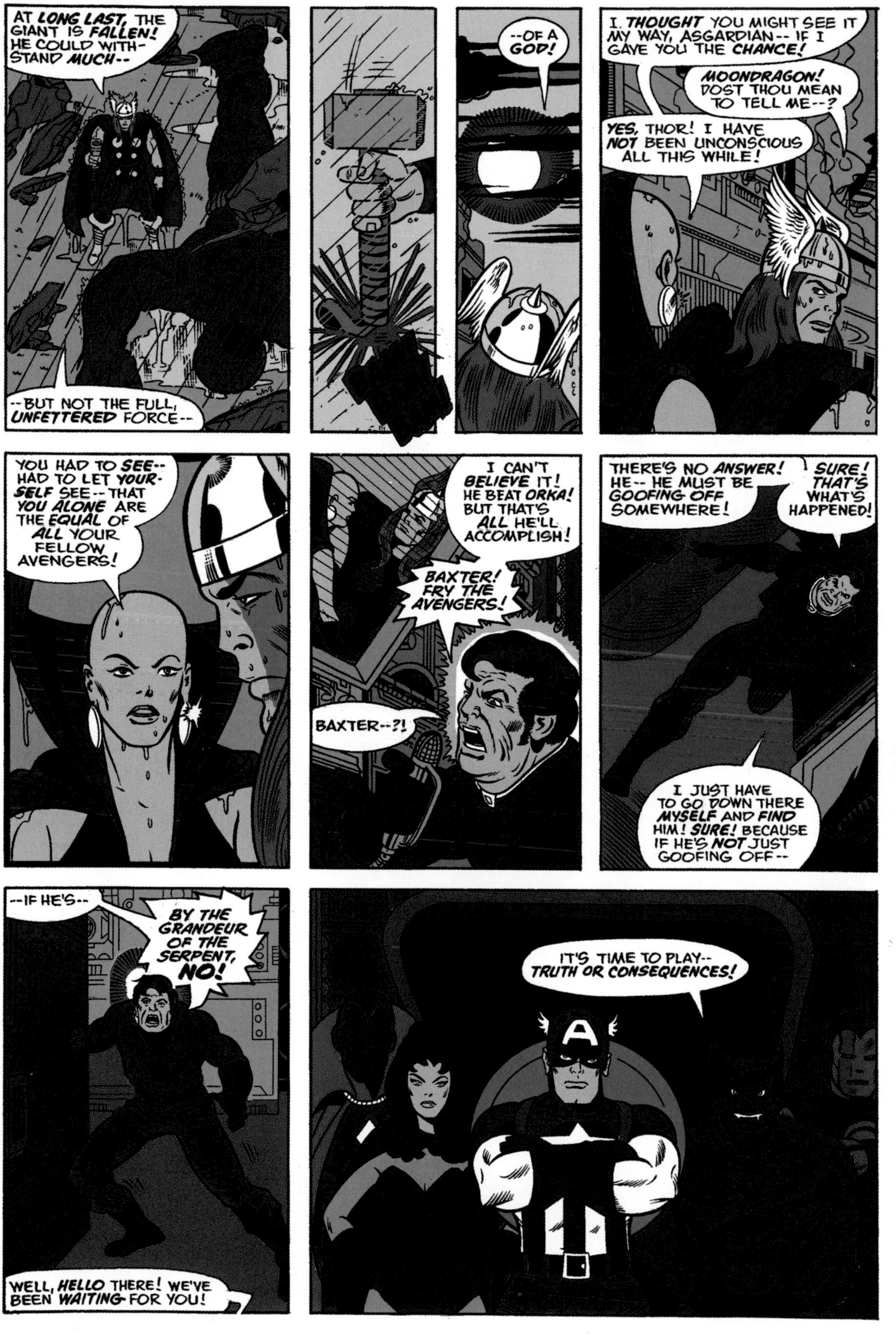
AT LONG LAST, THE GIANT IS FALLEN! HE COULD WITHSTAND MUCH--
--BUT NOT THE FULL, UNFETTERED FORCE--
--OF A GOD!
I THOUGHT YOU MIGHT SEE IT MY WAY, ASGARDIAN-- IF I GAVE YOU THE CHANCE!
MOONDRAGON! DOST THOU MEAN TO TELL ME--?
YES, THOR! I HAVE NOT BEEN UNCONSCIOUS ALL THIS WHILE!
YOU HAD TO SEE-- HAD TO LET YOURSELF SEE-- THAT YOU ALONE ARE THE EQUAL OF ALL YOUR FELLOW AVENGERS!
I CAN'T BELIEVE IT! HE BEAT ORKA! BUT THAT'S ALL HE'LL ACCOMPLISH!
BAXTER! FRY THE AVENGERS!
BAXTER--?!
THERE'S NO ANSWER! HE-- HE MUST BE GOOFING OFF SOMEWHERE!
SURE! THAT'S WHAT'S HAPPENED!
I JUST HAVE TO GO DOWN THERE MYSELF AND FIND HIM! SURE! BECAUSE IF HE'S NOT JUST GOOFING OFF--
--IF HE'S--
BY THE GRANDEUR OF THE SERPENT, NO!
WELL, HELLO THERE! WE'VE BEEN WAITING FOR YOU!
IT'S TIME TO PLAY-- TRUTH OR CONSEQUENCES!

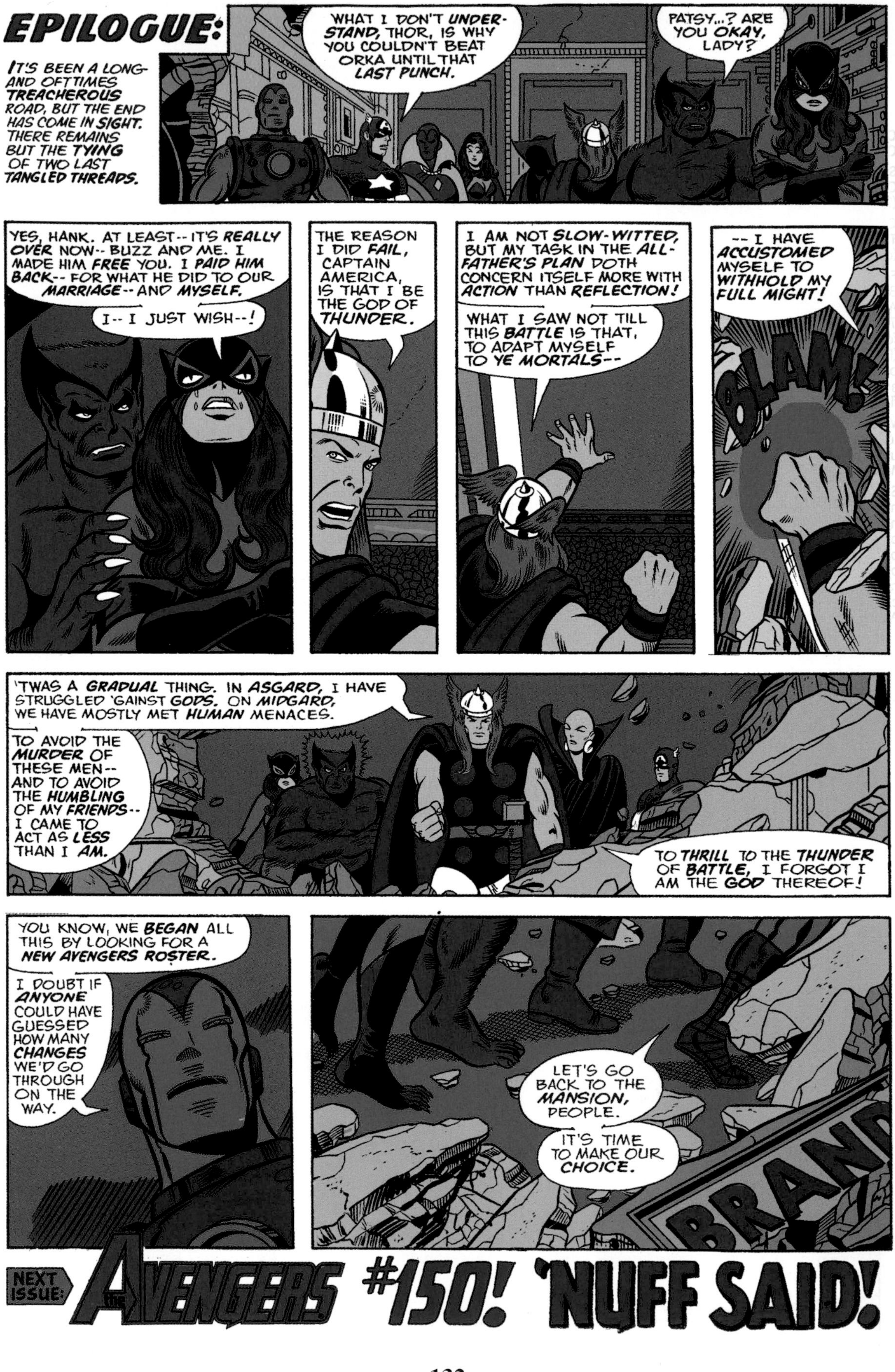
EPILOGUE:
IT'S BEEN A LONG- AND OFTTIMES TREACHEROUS ROAD, BUT THE END HAS COME IN SIGHT. THERE REMAINS BUT THE TYING OF TWO LAST TANGLED THREADS.
WHAT I DON'T UNDER-STAND, THOR, IS WHY YOU COULDN'T BEAT ORKA UNTIL THAT LAST PUNCH.
PATSY...? ARE YOU OKAY, LADY?
YES, HANK. AT LEAST-- IT'S REALLY OVER NOW-- BUZZ AND ME. I MADE HIM FREE YOU. I PAID HIM BACK-- FOR WHAT HE DID TO OUR MARRIAGE-- AND MYSELF.
I-- I JUST WISH--!
THE REASON I DID FAIL, CAPTAIN AMERICA, IS THAT I BE THE GOD OF THUNDER.
I AM NOT SLOW-WITTED, BUT MY TASK IN THE ALL-FATHER'S PLAN DOTH CONCERN ITSELF MORE WITH ACTION THAN REFLECTION!
WHAT I SAW NOT TILL THIS BATTLE IS THAT, TO ADAPT MYSELF TO YE MORTALS--
-- I HAVE ACCUSTOMED MYSELF TO WITHHOLD MY FULL MIGHT!
BLAM!
'TWAS A GRADUAL THING. IN ASGARD, I HAVE STRUGGLED 'GAINST GODS. ON MIDGARD, WE HAVE MOSTLY MET HUMAN MENACES.
TO AVOID THE MURDER OF THESE MEN-- AND TO AVOID THE HUMBLING OF MY FRIENDS-- I CAME TO ACT AS LESS THAN I AM.
TO THRILL TO THE THUNDER OF BATTLE, I FORGOT I AM THE GOD THEREOF!
YOU KNOW, WE BEGAN ALL THIS BY LOOKING FOR A NEW AVENGERS ROSTER.
I DOUBT IF ANYONE COULD HAVE GUESSED HOW MANY CHANGES WE'D GO THROUGH ON THE WAY.
LET'S GO BACK TO THE MANSION, PEOPLE.
IT'S TIME TO MAKE OUR CHOICE.
BRAND
NEXT ISSUE: THE AVENGERS #150! 'NUFF SAID!

AVENGERS #145
March 1976

Cover: **Gil Kane** (penciller; signed); **Dan Adkins** (inker; signed); **Dan Crespi** (letterer)

Story: "The Taking of the Avengers;" Ch. 1: "Billion-Dollar Death" (4 Pages); Ch. 2: "Target: Captain America" (7 Pages); Ch. 3: "The Small Hours" (7 Pages)

Credits: **Tony Isabella** (plotter, scripter); **Don Heck** (penciller); **John Tartaglione** (inker); **David Hunt** and **Denise Wohl** (letterers); **Don Warfield** (colorist); **Marv Wolfman** (editor)

Feature Characters: Thor (chairman), the Scarlet Witch, the Vision, the Beast (all last in issue #149), Iron Man (last in *Black Goliath* #4), Captain America (last in *Captain America Annual* #3; in flashback following *Strange Tales* Vol. 1 #161 and preceding flashback in issue #280; also in flashback following issue #29 and preceding *Tales of Suspense* #77/2), Hawkeye (last in *Marvel Tales* #100/2; in flashback following *Marvels* #2 and preceding flashback in issue #280; also in flashback following issue #29 and preceding flashback in *Tales of Suspense* #91/2; latter two also in flashbacks in between pages of issue #25)

Villains: The Assassin II (Maria; last name unrevealed; first appearance; not to be confused with the villain in *Daredevil* #81); her father (real name unrevealed; first appearance); the Maggia (in between *Amazing Spider-Man* #131 and #159; behind the scenes)

Synopsis: An agent acting on behalf of several of the Avengers' former foes hires a masked killer known only as the Assassin to eliminate the team of heroes for one billion dollars. The Assassin demands a full year to make preparations, then accepts the contract. One year later, Captain America's battle with a gang wearing duplicates of his own mask sets him up to be shot by the Assassin. Near death, Cap is hospitalized, and his fellow Avengers rally to guard him from further assaults. After Hawkeye skirmishes with two costumed intruders, he and the others are on the alert, unaware that the Assassin plots not merely Cap's demise, but their own, as well.

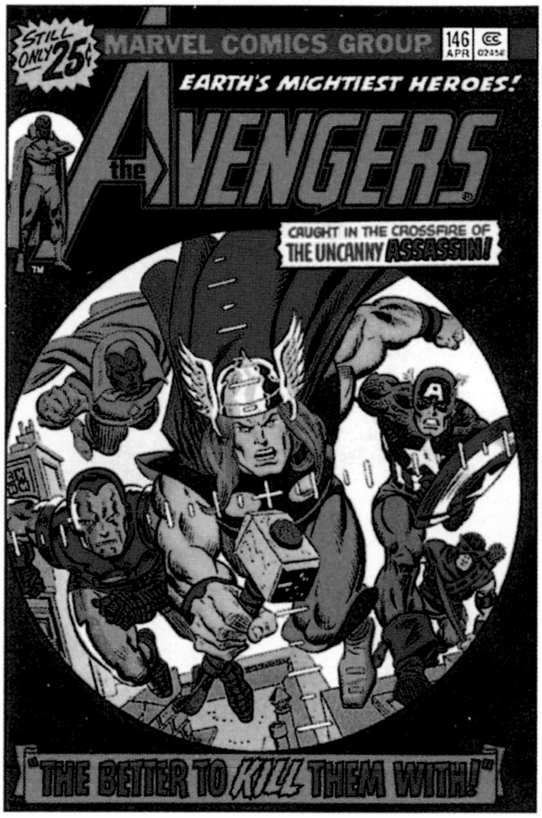
STILL ONLY 25¢
MARVEL COMICS GROUP
146 APR
EARTH'S MIGHTIEST HEROES!
the AVENGERS
CAUGHT IN THE CROSSFIRE OF THE UNCANNY ASSASSIN!
"THE BETTER TO KILL THEM WITH!"

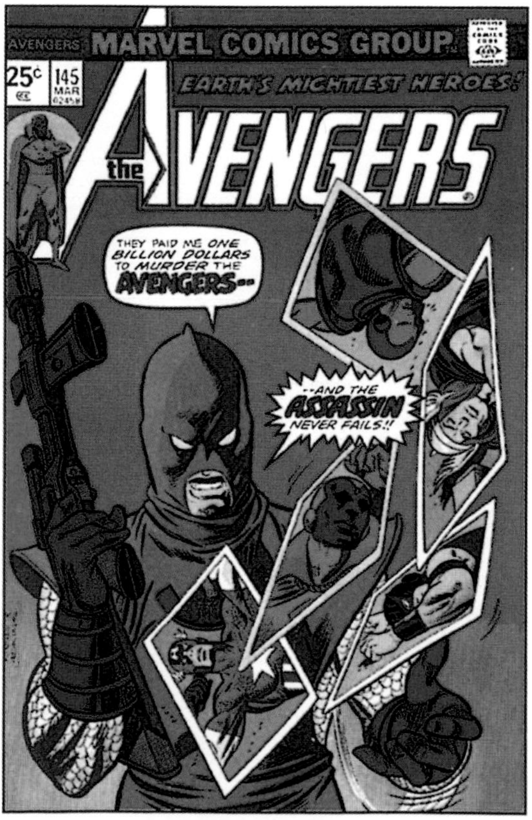
AVENGERS
MARVEL COMICS GROUP
25¢ 145 MAR
EARTH'S MIGHTIEST HEROES!
the AVENGERS
THEY PAID ME ONE BILLION DOLLARS TO MURDER THE AVENGERS--
--AND THE ASSASSIN NEVER FAILS!!

AVENGERS #146
April 1976

Cover: **Gil Kane** (penciller; signed); **Al Milgrom** (inker; signed); **Irving Watanabe** (letterer)

Story: "The Assassin Never Fails" (3 Pages); Ch. 2: "The Better to Kill Them With" (8 Pages); Ch. 3: "Nothing But Our Own Death" (7 Pages)

Credits: **Tony Isabella** (plotter, scripter); **Keith Pollard** and **Don Heck** (pencillers); **John Tartaglione** (inker); **David Hunt** (letterer); **Petra Goldberg** (colorist); **Marv Wolfman** (editor)

Feature Characters: Thor (chairman; next in *Thor* #237), Iron Man (also in flashback in between *Iron Man* #23-24; next in *Iron Man Annual* #3, pages 1-3), Captain America (next in *Marvel Treasury Special* Vol. 1 #1), Hawkeye (next in *Champions* #11), Yellowjacket, the Wasp (latter two next in *Captain America* #224, then Yellowjacket behind the scenes in *Incredible Hulk* Vol. 2 #200), the Scarlet Witch, the Vision (latter two next in *Captain America* #224, then Vision in *Iron Man Annual* #3, then both in *Marvel Team-Up* #41-44), the Beast (next in *Captain America* #224, then in *X-Men* Vol. 1 #94, then in *Iron Man* #90)

Guest Star: The Falcon (in between *Captain America* #191 and #193)

Villains: The Assassin II, her father (both die)

Guest Appearances: Mr. Fantastic (last in *Marvel Two-in-One* #9; behind the scenes; next in *Fantastic Four* #158); Bill Foster (last in *Black Goliath* #5; behind the scenes; next in *Marvel Two-in-One* #24); Jose Santini (last in *Iron Man* #19; in flashback)

Other Character: Angelo (last name unrevealed; first appearance; the Assassin's brother; dies)

Synopsis: Dr. Don Blake operates to save Captain America's life, while Iron Man patrols the hospital corridors alongside a Thor LMD. Suddenly, the Assassin's costumed agents attack. Hawkeye and Iron Man have been given drugged coffee and fall swiftly, as does the robotic copy of Thor. The Assassin attaches a device to the Vision's cloak and the android falls, frozen in his diamond-hard form. Discovering that "Thor" is merely a mechanical double, the killer deduces the Thunder God's secret and is about to shoot Dr. Blake, when Hawkeye, Iron Man, and the Vision suddenly appear. They have failed to succumb to the poisoned coffee, thanks to Hawkeye's sensitive stomach and Iron Man's artificial heart, and have freed the Vision. To their astonishment, the Assassin is unmasked as a woman. A gas grenade covers her escape, but when she orders her followers to fire on her pursuers, they fail to recognize her and open fire, killing her.

HELLSTROM, PATSY WALKER

Real Name: Patricia "Patsy" Walker Hellstrom
Occupation: Former housewife, former model, former adventurer, now supernatural investigator
Identity: Secret
Legal status: Citizen of the United States with no criminal record
Former aliases: None
Place of birth: Centerville, California
Marital status: Married
Known relatives: Joshua (father), Dorothy (mother, deceased), Bea (step-mother), Robert "Buzz" Baxter (ex-husband), Daimon Hellstrom (husband)
Group affiliation: Former provisional Avenger, former Defender
Base of operations: San Francisco, California
First appearance: (as Patsy Walker) FANTASTIC FOUR #3, (as Hellcat) AVENGERS #144
History: Patricia Walker was the only daughter of Joshua Walker, an aeronautical engineer, and Dorothy Walker, a comic book writer. While she was still a child her mother acted as her agent, helping her at modeling and commercial work. Dorothy Walker's greatest success was the creation of a comic book named after her young daughter, featuring romantic adventures of Patsy and her real-life friends as teenagers. The *Patsy Walker* comic book was very popular and continued for over a decade, as Patsy grew into and out of her teens. Patsy Walker felt very strange about her mother's fictionalized exploitation of her, and was relieved when the series ceased publication. Constantly exposed to comic books, Walker grew to idolize the heroes her mother's colleagues wrote about. However, she ceased daydreaming soon after high school and married her childhood friend, Robert Baxter (who had appeared in the *Patsy Walker* comic as her romantic interest). Baxter was in the officers training program of the Air Force, and Walker spent the next several years of her life on numerous Air Force bases.

While her husband was assigned to a security post at the heavily government-subsidized Brand Corporation in New Jersey, Patsy Walker met the Beast and learned his secret identity (see *Beast, Roxxon*). Walker had long idolized "super heroes," and she elicited the promise from him that in exchange for keeping his secret, he would help her become a "super heroine." Walker's marriage eventually came to a bitter end, and she sought out the Beast, who was now a member of the Avengers, to remind him of his promise (see *Avengers*). Tagging along with the Avengers to investigate criminal activities at the Brand Corporation, Walker discovered the costume worn by Greer Nelson in her identity as the Cat (see *Tigra*). (The man who financed the creation of the Cat, Mal Donalbain, was a former employee at Brand. His property, including the prototype Cat-suits, was later confiscated by the Brand Corporation.) Putting the costume on, Walker dubbed herself Hellcat and used her natural athletic abilties to help the Avengers. Walker believed that the costume had somehow enhanced her agility and speed, and by the power of suggestion more than anything else, it had.

Although she hoped to join the Avengers, Hellcat was persuaded by the Titanian priestess Moondragon to accompany her to Titan to undergo a period of training (see

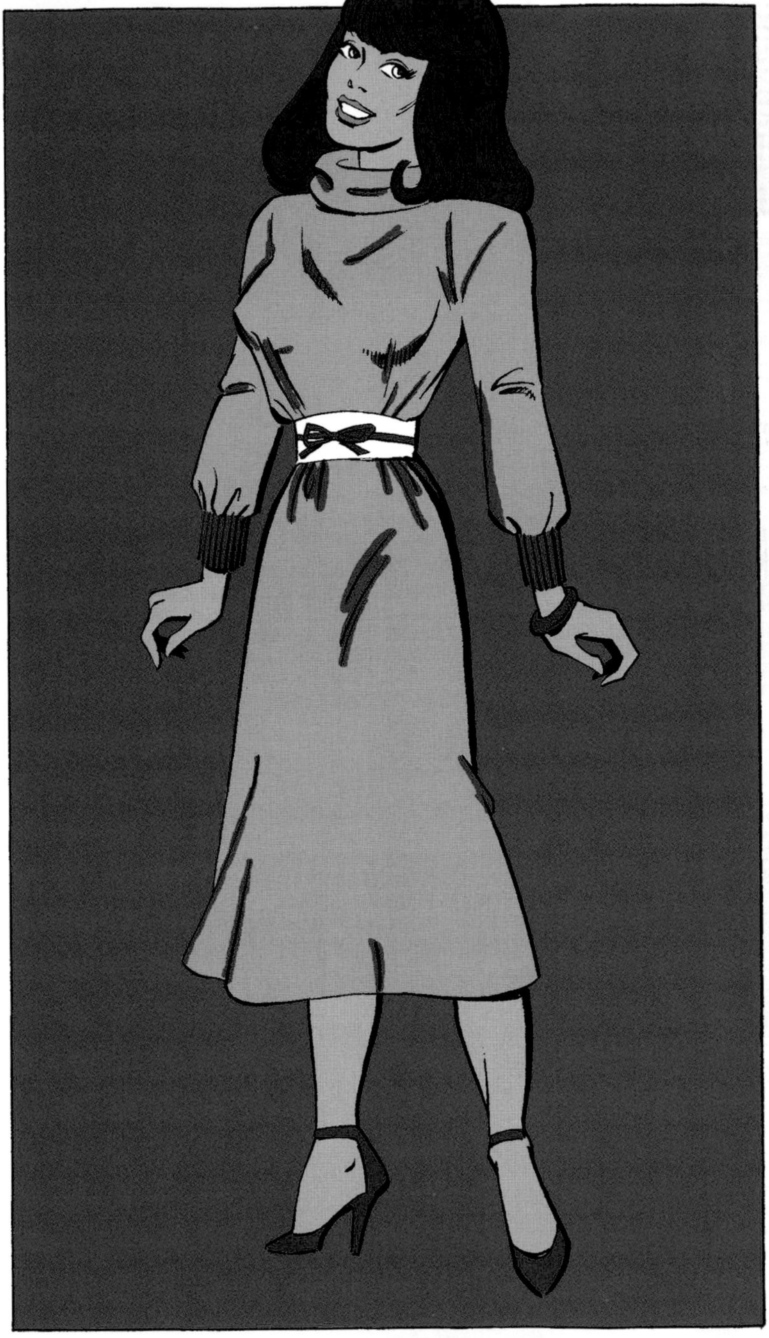

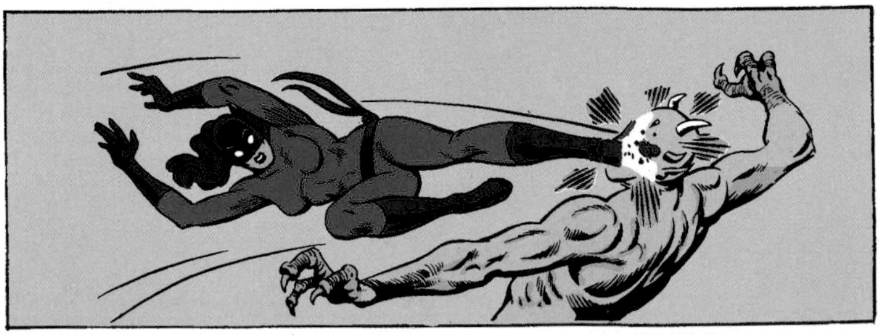

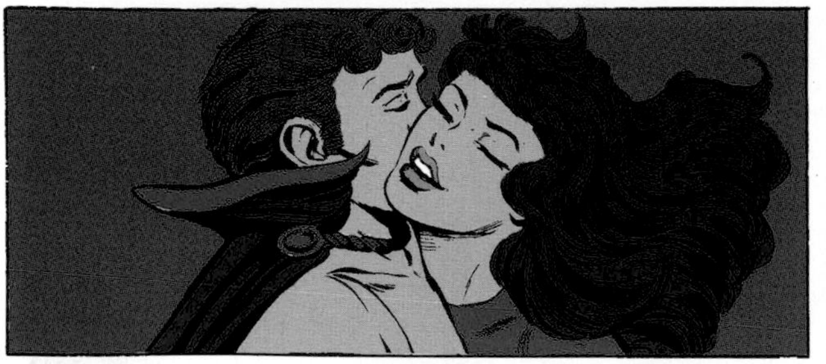

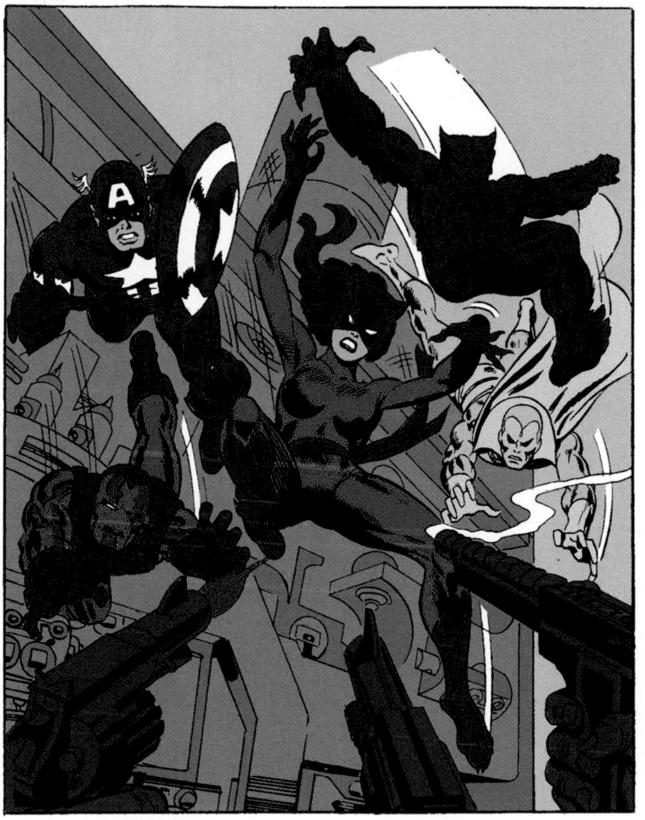

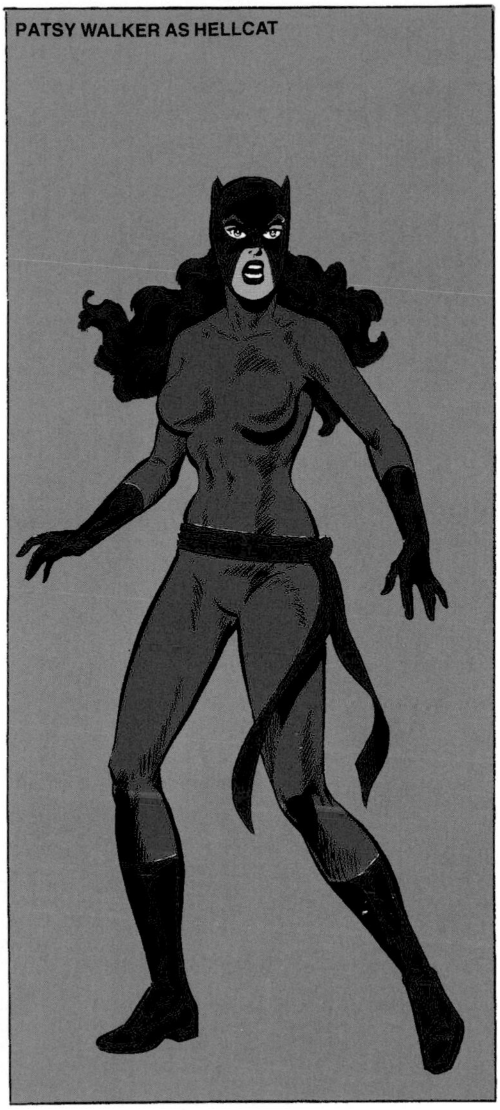
PATSY WALKER AS HELLCAT

Moondragon, Titan). During her stay on Titan, Hellcat's minor psionic potential was artificially enhanced by various electronic/organic devices (Moondragon used similar technology to give powers to Angar the Screamer and Ramrod) and was given extensive martial arts training. Upon her return to Earth, she met the Defenders and decided to accept their offer of membership rather than the Avengers' (see *Inactive: Defenders*). Hellcat remained a core member of the loosely-organized Defenders for several years, becoming particularly close to the Valkyrie and Nighthawk (see *Valkyrie, Deceased: Nighthawk*). Eventually she met Daimon Hellstrom, who in his costumed guise of the Son of Satan, joined the Defenders for a short time, and after he was cured of his demonic aspect found that she was in love with him (see *Hellstrom, Daimon*). Renouncing her costumed identity, Patsy Walker decided to marry Hellstrom. The couple was married in Greentown, Ohio, where her father currently resided. The wedding, attended by several of her Defenders colleagues, was interrupted by her ex-husband "Buzz" Baxter who had assumed the costumed guise of Mad Dog, and the Mutant Force (see *Mad Dog, Mutant Force*). The Defenders repulsed the attack and Hellstrom himself subdued Mad Dog. The Hellstroms then moved to San Francisco where they established themselves as occult investigators.

Height: 5′ 8″
Weight: 135 lbs.
Eyes: Blue
Hair: Red
Strength level: Patsy Walker Hellstrom possesses the normal human strength of a woman of her age, height, and build who engages in intensive regular exercise.
Known superhuman powers: Patsy Walker once possessed enhanced psionic abilities, due to the mental stimulation of Moondragon's Titanian technology. She could move small objects telekineticaly, resist mental control, and on one occasion was able to generate a psychokinetic force-blast. Moondragon has since used her own advanced psionic powers to undo the effects of her psychic augmenter. Since then, Walker's psychic abilities have returned but to a far lesser degree than at their peak. She no longer has any psychokinetic ability, but she is still sensitive to certain psychic phenomena.
Abilities: Patsy Walker Hellstrom is a natural athlete who was coached in field combat techniques by the Avengers and the martial arts by Moondragon.
Weapons: As Hellcat, Patsy Walker at first wore a costume outfitted with retractable, case-hardened, steel-alloy claws on both the gloves and boots, enabling her to rend brick or stone. She later replaced them with conventional gloves and boots. Hellcat occasionally employed her cable-claw, which straps to her wrist and uses a compressed-gas firing mechanism to propel a four-clawed grappling hook connected to a 30-foot length of steel-niobium alloy memory-cable (that coils itself back into its spool upon rewinding), which she used for swinging or tightrope walking.

Hellcat used a Shadow-Cloak confiscated from an Agent of Fortune for a brief period, employing it to move psychokinetically and to produce weapons from its interdimensional pocket (see *Appendix: Devil-Slayer*). Eventually deciding it was too dangerous to use, Hellcat folded it up into its own pocket dimension. ■

TWO-GUN KID

Real name: Matt Hawk
Occupation: Lawyer
Identity: Secret
Legal status: Citizen of the United States with no criminal record
Other aliases: None known
Place of birth: Boston, Massachusetts
Place of death: Unrevealed
Marital status: Single (during his recorded history)
Known relatives: None
Group affiliation: None
Base of operations: Tombstone, Texas in the 1870s
First appearance and origin: TWO-GUN KID #60
Final appearance: The Two-Gun Kid's death has not yet been depicted.
History: Matt Hawk was a young lawyer from Boston, Massachusetts who settled in Tombstone, Texas after the Civil War. Soon after arriving, Hawk was roughed up by a gang of rowdies led by Clem Carter until Carter's stepsister, Nancy Carter, a young schoolteacher, stopped them. Nancy Carter befriended Hawk, welcoming him to town.

Later, Hawk saw members of Carter's gang harassing an elderly man named Ben Dancer, who was formerly a leading gunfighter. Hawk went to try to help Dancer, who finally drew his gun on his tormentors and drove them away. Impressed with the young lawyer's courage in trying to help him, Dancer undertook teaching Hawk how to use a gun. Over the following months, under Dancer's tutelage, Hawk not only became Dancer's superior as a gunfighter, but also learned lassoing from him and became a superb horseback rider. Moreover, Hawk trained himself athletically until he was in excellent physical condition.

Dancer warned Hawk that if people knew how fast Hawk had become in drawing a gun, gunslingers would go after him to make their reputations by beating him in shootouts. Therefore, Hawk adopted a masked identity, calling himself the Two-Gun Kid after Clay Harder, a fictional gunslinger about whom he had read. (Harder's fictional exploits were presented in issues of TWO-GUN KID before #60.) Hence, if Hawk ever needed to use his guns against an opponent, he could do so in the guise of the Two-Gun Kid without his true identity being suspected. Dancer gave him a strong, fast horse named Thunder.

Dancer decided to return East to live, and boarded a stagecoach leaving Tombstone. But Clem Carter and his gang sought vengeance on Dancer, overturned the stagecoach, and were about to kill Dancer when Hawk intervened as the Two-Gun Kid. Together, the Two-Gun Kid and Ben Dancer succeeded in overcoming the gang.

From then on Matt Hawk continued to fight against criminals as the Two-Gun Kid. Among his more unusual opponents were such criminals as Hurricane and the Rattler (see *Appendix: Hurricane, Rattler I-II*). Hawk had a long-running romantic relationship with Nancy Carter. His best friend was "Boom-Boom" Brown, a former boxer whom Hawk trusted with the knowledge of his double identity.

At times the Two-Gun Kid allied himself with other legendary gunfighters of his time, including Kid Colt, the Rawhide Kid, and the second Phantom Rider (see *Phantom Rider, Deceased: Kid Colt, Rawhide Kid*). In 1873 the Two-Gun Kid, Kid Colt, the Rawhide Kid, the Ringo Kid, and the Phantom Rider all joined forces with three members of the Avengers — Hawkeye, Mondragon, and Thor — who had traveled back in time to battle Kang the Conqueror (see *Avengers, Hawkeye, Kang, Moondragon, Thor, Appendix: Ringo Kid*). The Two-Gun Kid and Hawkeye became good friends, and the Two-Gun Kid journeyed to Hawkeye's own time with him. Preferring his own time period, the Two-Gun Kid returned via a time machine to 1874. In 1876 the Two-Gun Kid encountered Hawkeye again, who had gone back in time along with his wife Mockingbird and other members of the West Coast Avengers (see *Mockingbird*). The Two-Gun Kid and the Rawhide Kid then fought the second Phantom Rider, who had abducted Mockingbird. She, Hawkeye, and the other West Coast Avengers safely returned to their own time.

Before Hawkeye left, though, the Two-Gun Kid told him that someday he might want to return to Hawkeye's time period himself. It is as yet unknown whether or not the Two-Gun Kid ever did so. It is not known how or when the Two-Gun Kid died, but it is quite possible that the Two-Gun Kid did not die in the past, but journeyed through time into the Twentieth Century, and hence will actually die sometime in the as yet unrecorded future.
Height: 5' 9"
Weight: 160 lbs.
Eyes: Blue
Hair: Brown
Strength level: The Two-Gun Kid possessed the normal human strength of a man of his age, height, and build who engaged in intensive regular exercise.
Known superhuman powers: None
Other abilities: The Two-Gun Kid was one of the fastest and best gunfighters of his time, rivaled only by such people as Kid Colt and the Rawhide Kid. The Two-Gun Kid was also an excellent hand-to-hand combatant, a superb horseback rider, and a master of the lasso. ∎